DOCTOR WHO EPISODE GUIDE
THE
WILLIAM HARTNELL YEARS
BY
BENEDICT JACKSON

DID YOU KNOW THAT?

The Tardis was supposed to blend in with its surroundings?

The Tardis has a translator which helps The Doctor and his companions understand languages they do not speak, but this was not revealed until the Tom Baker years in 1976?

The Daleks nearly never appeared at all because the cast and crew thought they were 'ludicrous'?

The First Doctor and Susan were telepathically linked?

The First Doctor was engaged to be married to an Aztec?

The First Doctor once had an argument with King Henry VIII after his Tardis was parked in the Tower of London?

The First Doctor had a stand-in double, an idea which found no great favour with him?

Discussions took place about terminating Dr Who in 1964?

Fifteen different outside locations were used in 'The Dalek Invasion of Earth'?

William Russell refused to appear in a shot where ants crawled up his arm and a double was required?

READ ON!

This and much more will be revealed in this dazzling new book by Benedict Jackson as the lid is lifted to reveal everything about the very first series of Doctor Who- the William Hartnell Years.

Benedict Jackson is an Honours Graduate in English and Film. Benedict has watched Doctor Who since he was seven years old and has become fascinated by and immersed in the series ever since. He is also a collector of memorabilia and his website www.doctorwhoreviewer.com is a very popular destination for Dr Who fans like himself.

The questions asked above and many more are addressed by Benedict in this book, the most detailed, comprehensive and illuminating analysis of the first series of Dr Who to date. The author brings his extensive knowledge of the technical and practical aspects of film making to explain, in an accessible and entertaining way, just why Dr Who has been such an iconic sci-fi TV series since its first broadcast in 1963. He lives with his family in rural Angus, Scotland.

I wish to dedicate this book several ways. Firstly to my supporting and ever-loving parents who have been with me through countless journeys to get this book into your hands. Secondly, to all of the talented production and cast personnel, both one-timers and regular contributors, who breathed life into *Doctor Who* when no one else could. Lastly to the one and only **William Hartnell,** the first and the greatest man behind the time travelling legend, without whom who would have put the who in Doctor Who?

Benedict Jackson

THE DR WHO EPISODE GUIDE: THE WILLIAM HARTNELL YEARS (1963-66)

<7> Publishing   Amazon Kindle edition

Copyright © Benedict Jackson (2021)

The right of Benedict Jackson to be identified as author of this work has been asserted by the author in accordance with section 77 and 78 of the Copyright, Designs and Patents Act, 1988.

All rights reserved, no part of this publication may be reproduced, stored in a retrieval system or transmitted in any form or by any means, electronic, mechanical, photocopying, recording or otherwise, without the prior permission of the author.

The images used in the guide are used in conjunction with the Copyright Designs and Patent Act 1988. All images are used with the sole purpose to review and critique. The author of this book does not own any of the characters mentioned or displayed in this guide, and are the intellectual property of the prospective creator(s). Doctor Who is a copyrighted trademark to the BBC.

Please contact benedictjackson1997@outlook.com for clarification of the above as **'7' publishing** welcomes the use of limited quotations from its books and will respond promptly to any enquiries. Any feedback on our books or enquiries about publishing would be welcomed. If wishing to contact Benedict directly please use the **'7' publishing** e-mail benedictjackson1997@outlook.com.

I know that free movement time and space is a scientific dream I don't expect to find solved in a junkyard.

    Ian Chesterton, **An Unearthly Child** "An Unearthly Child"

If you could touch the alien sand and hear the cries of strange birds and watch them wheel in another sky, would that satisfy you?

    The Doctor, **An Unearthly Child** "The Cave of Skulls"

Table of Contents

GUIDE TO THE EPISODE GUIDE 1

   1) **AN UNEARTHLY CHILD** 3
   2) **THE DALEKS** 9
   3) **THE EDGE OF DESTRUCTION** 15
   4) **MARCO POLO** 18
   5) **THE KEYS OF MARINUS** 22
   6) **THE AZTECS** 28
   7) **THE SENSORITES** 32
   8) **THE REIGN OF TERROR** 36
   9) **PLANET OF GIANTS** 41
  10) **THE DALEK INVASION OF EARTH** 45
  11) **THE RESCUE** 52
  12) **THE ROMANS** 56
  13) **THE WEB PLANET** 61
  14) **THE CRUSADE** 66
  15) **THE SPACE MUSEUM** 70
  16) **THE CHASE** 74
  17) **THE TIME MEDDLER** 82
  18) **GALAXY 4** 87
  19) **MISSION TO THE UNKNOWN** 93
  20) **THE MYTH MAKERS** 96
  21) **THE DALEKS' MASTER PLAN** 100
  22) **THE MASSACRE OF ST BARTHOLOMEW'S EVE** 108
  23) **THE ARK** 113
  24) **THE CELESTIAL TOYMAKER** 119
  25) **THE GUNFIGHTERS** 124
  27) **THE WAR MACHINES** 133
  28) **THE SMUGGLERS** 140
  29) **THE TENTH PLANET** 144

FIRST DOCTOR: OTHER MEDIA 151
   AUDIO 152
   BOOKS 156
   COMICS 159

    SHORT STORIES 164

    VIDEO GAMES 168

DOCTOR WHO CONTRIBUTORS 1963-66 169

TARDIS DATA LOGS: 1963-66 183

THE COST OF DOCTOR WHO: 1963-66 186

THE MISSING EPISODES: 1963-66 187

THE UNMADE EPISODES: 1963-66 188

BIBLIOGRAPHY 192

GUIDE TO THE EPISODE GUIDE

Plot: A brief summary of the main storyline of the serial. Any spoilers will not be mentioned to allow those who have not seen the serial to enjoy it in its entirety.

Cast: A complete list of the cast members who appear in the serial. All cast members (both credited and uncredited) have been included. Other cast members included in the listings include body doubles, stunt doubles and hand doubles. The cast listing is laid out with the character name to the left and the appropriate actor(s) and/or actress(es) to the right.

Credits: A listing of the crew members who worked on the serial. Unlike the cast listing, uncredited production personnel will not be included. Many of the credit listings in this volume will vary from serial to serial. This is because sometimes a particular member of the production personnel e.g lighting and sound weren't always credited. The crew listing is laid out with the production member title on the left and the crew member's name to the right.

Actor Biographies: A little biography or biographies of at least one or more actors who appear in a particular serial. Actor's name will appear in **bold** and TV and/or Films they appeared in will be in *italics*. This will be followed by the year they appeared in a particular TV series or film in brackets. Sometimes the case may be that an actor's name, usually someone playing a companion, will not be included in their introductory serial. For example **Jacqueline Hill** and **Carole Ann Ford**'s biographies appear in *The Edge of Destruction* and not *An Unearthly Child*, due to the fact that only the series regulars appear in the serial, and no one else. All actors' biographies are correct up to the publication date of this volume.

Behind the Scenes: A list of important events during the pre-production, production and post-production stages of a particular serial. This section does not have a set limit due to the fact that every serial varies in length. Details may or may not include the writing stage, the casting of the serial, the filming and editing process, any historical and/or scientific research carried out for episodes, the recruitment of production personnel, the change and handover of production personnel – e.g, producer and script editing duties, and the change of episode titles during production. The number of production days it took to record a serial will also be displayed.

Broadcast: Details of the original broadcast. A table laid out with six columns provides essential information regarding the original broadcast. The tables are laid out as follows – 1) episode: the episode number of a serial, 2) date: the date of the original broadcast of the episode, 3) time: the time that the episode aired on BBC1, 4) viewing figure: the number of people who watched the episode when aired. The viewing figure has been displayed to the nearest million, and not expressed as an exact number, 5) chart position: the position an episode finished based on the weekly viewing of all television programmes, 6) appreciation index: a whole single number between 0-100, usually based on the critical response of an episode shortly after broadcast. The appreciation index is basically a score out of 100, the higher the number the more positive reviews an episode received, the lower the number, the less liked the episode was.

Cliffhangers: SPOILER SECTION! A list of cliffhangers for every episode within a serial. These will undoubtedly contain spoilers – the death of a character, a plot twist etc. I strongly advise that if you have not seen a particular serial, do not read the cliffhangers, as these will undoubtedly spoil the story for you.

Commercial Releases: A list of commercial releases related to the serial. Releases may include DVD, NOVELISATION, SCRIPT, VIDEO etc, and will be displayed in alphabetical order. A particular media release will be followed by the date in which it was made available to the public. Media forms will be displayed in **bold**. Any reissues or releases of certain media will also be displayed; no foreign editions or releases will be displayed. In terms of novelisations not every edition may be displayed, as there is not enough information to give a detail explanation of the publication, and what differed it from the original release.

Continuity Notes: A list of continuity notes about a particular serial. Continuity notes are general observations rather than critical analysis. Observations may be made about recurring themes and styles seen in *Doctor Who* over the years, any linking material across all media forms – AUDIO, PROSE, COMIC, a recurring monster, character or alien planet etc, and any recurring gags. This section has no limit to it, and will vary from serial to serial.

Critical Response: A study about how well an episode has been received over the years. This section has various parts to it. The first is the **review range**. This will be followed by the overwhelming consensus of a particular serial e.g. negative, mixed, positive, negative-mixed, mixed-positive, so on and so forth. The second is the *Doctor Who Magazine 2014 Poll* listing which was marked out of 241. The position in which the serial finished will be displayed like a fraction e.g. 45th/241st or 175th/241st etc. The third will be a list of brief summarised reviews, both original and contemporary/modern made by newspaper critics, production personnel, and other *Doctor Who* critics over the years. Details about audience research reviews and internal BBC meetings will also be included when appropriate.

Deaths: Any deaths which occur in a particular episode will be displayed in a table separated in four columns. The first of which is titled **Number:** this is the death count so to speak with the number corresponding to a particular character(s). All deaths which occur before The Doctor arrives, occur off-screen, or represented in a flashback – see *Galaxy 4* - will be included as well as deaths of robots. The second column is **Character:** this is where the name of the character(s) killed off will be displayed. The third column is **Time of Death:** this is the time a particular death occurs within a serial, the best effort has been made to ensure that all times are accurate. Sometimes this will be guesswork and approximated since massive deaths scenes – battle sequences etc. are hard to keep track of for 100% reliable results. The fourth column is **Cause of Death**: details about how a particular character dies will be displayed here.

Filming Locations: A complete list of all filming locations, both studio and location used during the filming and recording process. The filming locations will be presented in alphabetical order rather than the order they were used in.

Influences: This section is the most arbitrary in the volume. Any 'influence' which may or may not have had any bearing on the episode will be displayed. This section will be displayed in alphabetical order. The influences will be displayed as follows, the source material – BOOK, FILM, TV etc will be displayed in **bold**, the title will be given in *italics*, the year in which the source material was published and/or released and the writers, creators etc of the source material will be displayed in brackets. If a particular fictional character had any bearing on a *Doctor Who* character, then the characters' creator will be listed and not the actor or actress who played said character. Again this section is not necessarily 100% accurate. Most influences may bear similarities to an episode's narrative, and therefore have been listed under the influences section.

Production Blunders: A listing of production errors and/or mistakes made during the production and editing process of a serial. Blunders might include fluffed lines, inconsistencies in the stories, accidental disturbance of set pieces, production personnel being heard in the studio, referential errors made about previous serials etc. This section is not meant to be taken that seriously and is purely here for fun. Just because a serial may have 10 or so production errors does not necessarily mean it is entirely bad. . However there will be a few discrepancies here, where a production blunder is so big it heavily impacts the review of the episode will need to be taken into account.

Publicity: A list of publicity notes in which a serial received some media attention before airing on the television. These might include radio times listing, trailers compiled for an upcoming adventure, public appearances to promote the series, interviews for newspapers, photographs and or stills taken during the recording process.

Working Titles: A list of working titles for a particular serial used during the pre-production process. Sometimes a serial may not have had a working title. In this case the 'working title' ended up being used for the broadcast. Sometimes a serial may have several working titles, where the title was continually changed until one was arrived that for the original broadcast. In the case of the First Doctor era, the first 25 serials all had individual titles for all episodes. If an individual episode had a working title, then these titles will be displayed as well.

Verdict: DISCLAIMER ONE: All reviews included in this volume are of the writer's personal opinion and do not represent that of the fandom. Reviews are simply a guidance and not be taken as gospel. If a particular reader likes a serial reviewed negatively within this volume, that's fine. Vice versa is also fine. DISCLAIMER TWO: As someone who has studied filmmaking both at a practical and theoretical level, I fully understand just how hard it is for someone to break into the world of television. Everyone who has ever worked on *Doctor Who* undoubtedly worked hard throughout their career. Rating are displayed using a star system, with ***** being the highest rating and * being the lowest.

1) AN UNEARTHLY CHILD

Plot: Susan Foreman is an extremely intelligent student at Coal Hill School, but her teachers Ian Chesterton and Barbara Wright are a little bit suspicious as to how she has acquired her vast knowledge of Science and History. When they follow her home one night they stumble upon a strange Police Box in a junkyard and soon find themselves travelling through time, and becoming prisoners of a Stone Age Tribe in 100,000 BC.

CAST

Dr Who	William Hartnell
Ian Chesterton	William Russell
Barbara Wright	Jacqueline Hill
Susan Foreman	Carole Ann Ford
Kal	Jeremy Young
Za	Derek Newark
Hur	Alethea Charlton
Old Mother	Eileen Way
Horg	Howard Lang
Policeman	Reg Cranfield
Schoolgirls	Carole Clarke, Mavis Ranson, Francesca Bertorelli, Heather Lyons
Schoolboys	Cedric Schoeman, Richard Wilson, Brian Thomas
Tribesmen	Frank Wheatley, Al Davis, Roy Denton, Bill Nichols, Billie Davis, Leslie Bates, Bob Haddow
Tribeswomen	Jean Denyer, Brenda Proctor, Elizabeth Body, Veronica Dyson, Diane Gray, Doreen Ubells, Lyn Turner
Tribeschildren	Antonia Moss, David Rosen, Julie Moss, Trevor Thomas, Elizabeth White, Janet Fairhead, Timothy Palmer
Pursuing Tribespeople	8 unknown extras
Double for Kal's Shadow	Leslie Bates
Stunt Double for Kal	Derek Ware
Stunt Double for Za	Billy Cornelius

CREDITS

Written by Anthony Coburn [and CE Webber]
Special Effects by the Visual Effects Department of the BBC
Fight Arranger: Derek Ware
Title Music by Ron Grainger with the BBC Radiophonic Workshop
Incidental music by Norman Kay
Story Editor: David Whitaker
Designer: Peter Brachacki, Barry Newbery
Associate Producer: Mervyn Pinfield
Producer: Verity Lambert
Directed by Waris Hussein

ACTOR BIOGRAPHIES: **William Hartnell** is best known for playing CSM Percy Bullimore in *The Army Game* (1957-60) and appeared in many films notably; *Sabotage at Sea* (1942), *Brighton Rock* (1948), *The Pickwick Papers* (1952), *Double Cross* (1956) and *Carry on Sergeant* (1958); **William Russell** was a popular face on TV at the time landing lead roles in *St Ives* (1955), *The Adventures of Sir Lancelot* (1956-57), *Nicholas Nickleby* (1957) and regular roles in *Harriet's Back in Town* (1972-73) and *Coronation Street* (1992) after leaving *Doctor Who*. Russell has also appeared in *Superman* (1978); **Howard Lang** played Captain Baines in *The Onedin Line* (1971-80); **Derek Newark** played Det. Insp. Eddie Tucker in *Barlow* (1974-75) and appeared in 3 separate episodes of *The Bill* (1989/93/96); **Eileen Way** can be seen in *The Newcomers* (1966) as Cora Brassett and *The Doctors* (1970) as Alice Platt.

BEHIND-THE-SCENES

- **Number of Production Days:** 12
- The creation of *Doctor Who* cannot be wholly credited to just one person, but rather several. With many minds putting forth ideas during the conception process, it could have ended in disaster. It was originally envisioned that the show would appeal to older children, but the show would be something which the whole family could watch together.

- Throughout late 1962 and early 1963 various ideas were being put forward for the new show *Doctor Who* and it was quickly decided that the hero of the series should travel in a time machine as a means of exploring periods of history and other alien worlds. The idea came about when newly appointed Head of Drama **Sydney Newman** kept **H.G.Wells**' famous sci-fi novel *The War of the Worlds* at the back of his mind. Over time Sydney Newman decided that the main character should be several hundred years old, senile, bewildered, but overall brilliant. The 'old man' in question would come from a distant planet which had been invaded by aliens, but the old man escaped in a time machine. Overtime the old man attempted to return home, but did not know how to successfully pilot the time machine in question.
- During May 1963, an early meeting document written by **C.E. Webber** outlined that the ship should disguise itself as something which was 'humdrum', but what exactly, was the main question. **Sydney Newman** a short while later rejected the idea of an invisible spaceship since there would be effectively no visuals for audiences to look at. The idea of a Police Box being the time machine was arrived at by writer **Anthony Coburn** outlined in a document on 15 May 1963. Apparently Coburn arrived at the idea after seeing a Police Box sitting at a street corner near his office. It was also decided that the Time Machine should remain as a Police Box since building a new spaceship every week, (keeping in mind that the ship could disguise itself to blend in with its surroundings), would prove to be too expensive.
- When The Doctor's ship was originally named as the Tardis – the acronym originally was going to be Time and Relative Dimension in Space before it became Dimensions in Space. Apparently this idea was also the brainchild of writer **Anthony Coburn**.
- Whilst developing the characters, Susan was originally going to be an older girl who travelled about with The Doctor; however **Anthony Coburn** was worried about this idea. The writer felt that the relationship between The Doctor and Susan would be seen as sexual, but this idea was later dropped from consideration. It was *also* apparently Coburn's idea that the relationship should be grandfather and granddaughter.
- Whilst casting the role of The Doctor, **Rex Tucker**, who was the original producer of the show, envisioned that The Doctor would be played by a young actor made up to look older. **Verity Lambert** however sought out an old actor to add to the character's authenticity.
- Doctor Who was originally going to open with a serial entitled 'The Giants'. The serial would have focused on the show's four main characters being shrunk down in size in Cliff's (Ian Chesterton's original name) laboratory. However, late into the writing process, the serial was deemed unusable and was scrapped.
- During the development process, **Donald Wilson** came up with various ideas for future serials which included episodes on Britain under Caesar's rule, and adventures set on Mars and Venus.
- When **William Hartnell** was approached to play the part of Doctor Who, the actor was originally sceptical and unconvinced with the idea. He was apparently taken in by the concept after meeting **Verity Lambert**, and became hooked after hearing more about the idea for the show.
- According to **Carole Ann Ford** the plants and animal skins used in the serial were infested with insects and fleas which caused some discomfort to the cast. During recording for the serial Carole Ann Ford also discovered a small lizard which had been brought into the studio in amongst the plants and foliage required for the episodes. She later took the lizard home as a pet; but not before keeping the animal alive by placing it in a sink full of water in her dressing room.
- The first day of recording for *Doctor Who* was on Thursday 19 September 1963 which included scenes where extra **Leslie Bates** doubled for Kal's shadow across the sandy landscape giving him the distinction of being the very first villain to appear in the show despite being off-camera.
- The first recorded version of "An Unearthly Child" was not well received. **Sydney Newman** informed **Verity Lambert** and **Waris Hussein** that the episode was to be re-recorded. During this time set designer **Peter Brachacki** was taken ill and **Barry Newbery** was hired in his place. Before the re-recording of the episodes Newbery discovered that junkyard and school sets had been destroyed in spite of Lambert's request to hold onto them. The sets had to be rebuilt from Brachacki's plans and drawings.
- The casting and involvement of the tribespeople was not an easy one; the actors who auditioned for the Cavemen were asked to show off their chests to see if they were hairy enough. Many of the auditioning actors believed this was a joke; whilst one of the female extras hired to play a tribeswoman, **Margot Maxine** was hired but never used. The actress refused to have her teeth blackened and stormed out of the studio before recording "The Cave of Skulls", no other actress was hired to replace her.
- The bones seen in the Cave of Skulls were in fact real. **Barry Newbery** obtained them from a abattoir, the bones gave off an unpleasant odor under the studio lights, and were extremely unpleasant to be around.

- The fight sequence in "The Firemaker" was directed by Production Assistant, **Douglas Camfield**. Director **Waris Hussein** had a limited knowledge of film whereas the young PA had worked on numerous BBC projects. **Derek Ware** also had a say in the final cut of the fight scene.
- **Waris Hussein** was mindful that *Doctor Who* was envisioned as a family show and kept the violence at a minimum, preferring violent scenes to take place off-screen such as the death of Old Mother. **Jacqueline Hill** raised concerns about a scene when Barbara falls into the remains of a dead animal.
- Stunt double **Derek Ware**, who doubled for Kal during the fight seen in "The Firemaker", made his first commitment on the show and went on to have a close relationship with the show for the next nine years.
- To stimulate the thrilling chase sequence towards the end of part four, the actors were shot mostly in close-ups whilst running on the spot to give the impression that they were in fact running.

BROADCAST

EPISODE	DATE	TIME	VIEWING FIGURE	CHART POSITION	APPRECIATION INDEX
1: *An Unearthly Child*	23/11/1963	5:15-5:40pm	4.4M	114th	63
2: *The Cave of Skulls*	30/11/1963	5:30-5:55pm	5.9M	85th	59
3: *The Forest of Fear*	7/12/1963	5:15-5:40pm	6.9M	61st	56
4: *The Firemaker*	14/12/1963	5:15-5:40pm	6.4M	70th	55

CLIFFHANGERS

1. The Tardis arrives in a sandy landscape. Inside the Tardis, Ian and Barbara have been knocked out cold, whilst a shadow of an unknown character (Kal) looms over the Tardis.
2. The Doctor and his companion are thrown into the Cave of Skulls. Whilst pondering what is to become of them, The Doctor notices that the skulls which surround them have been split open.
3. The Doctor and his companions successfully escape the Tribe of Gum, however when they approach the Tardis, various members of the tribe, who have been lying in wait emerge.
4. The Time Travellers successfully take off in the Tardis. They are in what appears to be a jungle, but as they emerge outside, the Tardis' radiation detector points to 'danger'.

COMMERCIAL RELEASES

- **DVD:** 30 January 2006
- **ELECTRONIC MUSIC/SOUND EFFECTS**
    - **5 July 1993:** *Doctor Who: 30 Years at the BBC Radiophonic Workshop*
    - **2000:** *Doctor Who at the BBC Radiophonic Workshop Volume 1: The Early Years 1963–1969*
- **NOVELISATION:** [Hardback/Paperback] - 15 October 1981; [Reissues] – 1982; 15 February 1990
    - *Target Doctor Who Library Number*: **68**
- **SCRIPT:** January 1988; [Reissue] - August 1992
- **SOUNDTRACK**
    - **9 December 2013 – 25 February 2016:** *Doctor Who: The 50th Anniversary Collection*
- **VIDEO:** 5 February 1990; [Rereleases] – 3 June 1991; 1 May 2000; 4 September 2000

CONTINUITY NOTES

- **Reg Cranfield** has the honour of being the very first person to appear in *Doctor Who* while **Jacqueline Hill** speaks the very first lines (if you exclude the lines spoken by the extras playing the school pupils).
- At the beginning of "The Cave of Skulls", The Doctor and Susan notice that The Tardis has not changed its appearance to blend in with its surroundings, thus setting off the popular trend where The Tardis will forever remain a Police Box. The Sixth Doctor does eventually try and fix the Tardis' chameleon circuit in *Attack of the Cybermen* with disastrous results much to the amusement of companion Peri Brown.

- Old Mother has the unfortunate distinction of being the very first speaking character to be killed in the show, whilst the Guard guarding the Cave of Skulls is the first extra character to die on the show.
- The fact that the Tribe of Gum speaks perfect modern-day English is never questioned by the Time Travellers. It is not until ***The Masque of Mandragora*** where The Fourth Doctor explains that the Tardis can translate languages for all those who have travelled in the ship. Until then the reason why EVERYONE, EVERYWHERE speaks English will remain a mystery.
- The death of Kal is the first graphic death to feature in the series. Other graphic deaths include; the shooting of Condo in ***The Brain of Morbius***, Harrison Chase being pulled into a shredder in ***The Seeds of Doom***, the strangulation of Kerril in ***The Robots of Death*** (although his death occurs off-screen), the Mortuary Attendants dying in a pool of acid in ***Vengeance on Varos***, and the melting of Kane in ***Dragonfire***.
- The Doctor's pockets are later revealed to be bigger on the inside than out (just like the Tardis), and during the serial he pulls out a pen light. Other odd and seemingly bizarre objects The Doctor keeps in his pockets include: conkers in ***The Highlanders***, marbles in ***The Space Pirates***, a pilot's license for a Mars-Venus Rocket Run in ***Robot***, a cricket ball in ***The Ark in Space*** and ***Doomsday***, a stuffed mouse in ***The Talons of Weng-Chiang***, a hammer in ***The Power of Kroll***, alien coins in ***Planet of Fire***, and ***Battlefield***, conjuring flowers in ***Trail of a Time Lord: Terror of the Vervoids***, and Christmas decorations in ***The Runaway Bride***.
- The Doctor later revisits 76 Totter's Lane many times during his later incarnations. Subsequent visits occur in **AUDIO:** *The Perpetual Bond*, **COMIC:** *Hunters of the Burning Stone*, **NOVEL:** *The Algebra of Ice*, **PROSE:** *Those Left Behind*, ***Attack of the Cybermen*** and ***Remembrance of the Daleks***.
- The history book which Barbara lends Susan focuses on The French Revolution. The time travellers later arrive during the final days of the French Revolution in ***The Reign of Terror***. The book in question is later picked up by Ace in ***Remembrance of the Daleks***.
- The second episode of ***An Unearthly Child*** "The Cave of Skulls" is the first and last time The Doctor smokes, after losing his pipe and matches to The Tribe of Gum. However various other characters will be seen smoking throughout the show's history including Johnny Ringo in ***The Gunfighters***, Maxtible in ***The Evil of the Daleks***, Luigi Rossini in ***Terror of the Autons***, The Master in ***The Mind of Evil***, Amelia Ducat in ***The Seeds of Doom***, Henry Gordon Jago in ***The Talons of Weng-Chiang***, de Vries in ***The Stones of Blood***, and an Elderly Man in ***Resurrection of the Daleks***.
- Despite being called The Tribe of Gum the tribe's name is never uttered on-screen by any of the characters.
- The First Doctor lands the Tardis in I. M. Foreman's junkyard, the first company who The Doctor has semi-dealings with. The Doctor will have a bad reputation of getting involved in deadly affairs with various companies across his incarnations which include: Chameleon Tours in ***The Faceless Ones***, Eurogas in ***Fury from the Deep***, Interplanetary Mining Company in ***Colony in Space***, and The Company in ***The Sun Makers***.
- The Tribe of Gum themselves later appear in **COMIC:** *Hunters of the Burning Stone*. It is revealed that the tribe had been given immortality by a race of aliens called the Prometheans after the story's events.
- Za is the first character in the show's history who utters the title of an individual episode title during one of his lines. During 'The Caves of Skulls' he says, 'I will take them to the Cave of Skulls'.
- Although not revealed until much later on in the show's run, The Doctor stole the Tardis before exploring the Universe. This is arguably his first criminal act. The Doctor will gain quite an amplitude of committing various thefts across his incarnations which include: The Meddling Monk's directional unit in ***The Time Meddler***, clothing in ***Spearhead from Space*** and ***Doctor Who: TV Movie***, Dr Beavis' car in ***Spearhead from Space***, The Master's dematerialisation unit in ***Terror of the Autons***, an aircar in ***The Pirate Planet***, Romana II's sonic screwdriver in ***The Horns of Nimon***, and The Master's temporal comparator in ***Planet of Fire***.

CRITICAL RESPONSE

- **Review Range:** Mixed to Positive.
- *Doctor Who Magazine 2014 Poll*: 78th/241st
- **Michael Gower** of the *Daily Mail* praised the first episode of the serial as did a writer for the *Daily Worker*.
- **Mary Crozier** of *The Guardian* was highly critical of the overall serial after the first episode, and was unimpressed with the second episode, commenting that the serial was on a downwards spiral.
- **Marjorie Norris** of *Television Today* commented that the series will eventually capture a wider audience if the show keeps up the standards of the first episodes.
- *Variety* was critical of certain aspects of the story, but held the camerawork in high regard.

- ➤ A review in 1982 praised the script, acting, and direction but was critical of the sets and scenery.
- ➤ **Patrick Mulkern** of the *Radio Times* wrote a positive review in 2008 praising the casting of **William Hartnell,** and the 'race back to The Tardis' scene.
- ➤ **Christopher Bahn** of *The A.V. Club* highlighted *An Unearthly Child* as an essential watch for background information on the show. He praised the characters of Ian, Barbara, and The Doctor, but commented that there was room for improvement with regards to Susan.
- ➤ **John Kenneth Muir** writing in *A Critical History of Doctor Who,* praised the writing, the cinematography and the production techniques.

DEATHS

DEATH	CHARACTER	TIME OF DEATH	CAUSE OF DEATH
1	Old Mother	[01:09:10]	Killed by Kal
2	Tribesman [Guard]	[01:22:39]	Killed by Kal
3	Kal	[01:25:05]	Killed by Za

FILMING LOCATIONS

- ➤ Ealing Film Studios
- ➤ Ealing Film Studios: Stage 3A
- ➤ Lime Grove: Studio D
- ➤ Television Centre: Studio 5

INFLUENCES

- ➤ **BOOK:** *20,000 Leagues Under the Sea* (1870, Jules Verne)
- ➤ **BOOK:** *The Chronicles of Narnia: The Lion, The Witch and the Wardrobe* (1950, C. S. Lewis)
- ➤ **BOOK:** *The Inheritors* (1955, William Golding)
- ➤ **BOOK:** *The Time Machine* (1895, H. G. Wells)
- ➤ **FILM:** *One Million BC* (1940, Hal Roach, Hal Roach Jr.)
- ➤ **TV:** *Dixon of Dock Green* (1955 -76, Ted Willis)
- ➤ **TV:** *Steptoe and Son* (1962 – 74, Ray Galton, Alan Simpson)
- ➤ **TV:** *Target Luna* and its sequels (1960 – 61, Malcolm Hulke, Eric Paice)

PRODUCTION BLUNDERS

1. Both **William Hartnell** and **Jacqueline Hill** fumble on some of their lines throughout the serial.
2. During "An Unearthly Child" a boom microphone enters the frame when Ian and Barbara enter the Tardis.
3. Whilst The Doctor explains to Ian and Barbara that he and Susan are cut-off from their own people, the Tardis wall behind him is evidently a painted canvas rather than a constructed set piece.
4. During the Tardis scenes in "An Unearthly Child" a crew member can be heard calling for Ian to fall to the floor before Ian is 'zapped' by the Tardis console.
5. The great stone is clearly made of polystyrene because the stone wobbles when a character touches it and squeaks when Za attempts to move it.
6. During one of the Tardis scene, a stagehand can be seen through a gap where two corners of the Tardis console room set meet.
7. The Caveman's shadow (Kal) is evidently too stretch out across the mountain landscape in the background.
8. At one point **William Hartnell** and **William Russell** interrupt each other whilst delivering their lines.

PUBLICITY

- ➤ **Stuart Hood** promoted the series at a BBC Press Conference in Blackpool on Thursday 12 September whilst *The Times* and *Television Mail* carried small insets about the show the following the day.
- ➤ *Radio Times* featured a specially-posed photograph of Ian and Barbara looking at their pupil, Susan Foreman in its *Next Week* section. The photograph appeared on Thursday 14 November.

- On Saturday 16 November, a short trailer was shown at 5:41pm to promote the series.
- *Radio Times* included another couple of photographs to promote the series on Thursday 21 November, the first of which was of The Doctor and the junkyard set. Further information about the series consisted of outlines of the show's main characters, and the upcoming adventures that viewers could look forward to. The second photograph was of **William Hartnell** and **Carole Ann Ford** posing for a publicity photo.
- Thursday 21 November 1964 saw the cast and crew meet the press in Room 222 at BBC's Langham Press.
- Further publicity for the series was slightly affected on Friday 22 November because of news coverage of the assassination of American President, **John F. Kennedy**. However **David Hunn's** *Show Piece* column in *Tit-Bits* commented on the upcoming family science-fiction show, declaring that TV was about to change.
- A further photograph, this time of **Verity Lambert** and **Carole Ann Ford**, appeared on the cover of *Television Today* on Thursday 28 November.
- **William Hartnell** recorded a sound trailer which was broadcast on BBC Radio to promote the first episode.

WORKING TITLES

- The Firemakers
- 100,000BC
- Episodes 2-4: The Tribe of Gum
- Episodes 2-4: Doctor Who and the Tribe of Gum
- Episodes 2-4: Doctor Who in 100,000BC
- Episode 4: The Dawn of Knowledge

VERDICT: The beginning of the legend starts here. The first episode is a captivating piece of television throwing both the audience and Ian and Barbara into a world where everything is about to be turned upside down. The Doctor and the Tardis are both introduced in a negative light; The Doctor comes across as someone whom everyone should run away from, with his seemingly sinister motivations and Edwardian attire. There is some clever writing at the helm here, Ian dismissing the possibilities of time travel one moment, and finding himself unwillingly taken back in time the next. The take-off sequence is almost cinematic in its execution, not only transporting Ian and Barbara through time, but also the audience. The rest of the production is top-notch. It's interesting that the very first antagonists to feature are not your typical BEMs (bug-eyed monsters) but rather a tribe of cave dwelling humans who are desperate to make fire to survive the approaching cold. The writing says a lot about human nature where Kal, a sole survivor of another tribe, wants to take control of The Tribe of Gum simply because he has a dislike for Za. There's little motivation behind Za's bloodthirsty acts, but the simplicity of the plot makes this excusable, and his ultimate failure is uncomfortably satisfying. Things get a little brutal throughout, a risky move considering Doctor Who would be a family show, rather than late night entertainment. There is also a light heartedness to the narrative. The Doctor, and his 'unwanted' companions are brought together as prisoners, but end up as allies as things progress. They're given time to appreciate one and other, where the only hope for escaping is by banding together. It's a smart move since the audience, whether they like them or not, would be stuck with the characters for weeks on end. The overall production values are superb; no-one would believe at the time that the skulls in the caves were actually real! *An Unearthly Child* has the honour of establishing the show's format, where more thrilling adventures are just around the bend. *****

2) THE DALEKS

Plot: The Tardis lands in a petrified jungle on the planet Skaro, home to the Daleks. The time travellers soon find themselves stranded and their only hope of escape lies with the pacifist Thals.

CAST

Dr Who	William Hartnell
Ian Chesterton	William Russell
Barbara Wright	Jacqueline Hill
Susan Foreman	Carole Ann Ford
Temmosus	Alan Wheatley
Alydon	John Lee
Ganatus	Philip Bond
Dalek Voices	Peter Hawkins, David Graham
Daleks	Robert Jewell, Kevin Manser
	Michael Summerton, Gerald Taylor, Peter Murphy
Dyoni	Virginia Wetherell
Elyon	Gerald Curtis
Kristas	Jonathan Crane
Antodus	Marcus Hammond
Thals	Chris Browning, Katie Cashfield
	Vez Delahunt, Kevin Glenny, Ruth Harrison
	Lesley Hill, Steve Pokol, Jeanette Rossini
	Eric Smith
Stunt Double for Antodus	Peter Diamond

CREW

Written by Terry Nation
Title Music by Ron Grainger with the BBC Radiophonic Workshop
Incidental music by Tristram Cary
Story Editor: David Whitaker
Costumes Supervisor: Daphne Dare
Make-Up Supervisor: Elizabeth Blattner
Designer: Raymond Cusick, Jeremy Davies
Associate Producer: Mervyn Pinfield
Producer: Verity Lambert
Directed by Christopher Barry, Richard Martin

ACTOR BIOGRAPHIES: David Graham is a prolific voice actor who has provided voices for *Supercar* (1961-62), *Fireball XL5* (1962-63), *Stingray* (1964-65), *Thunderbirds* (1965-66) and recently *Peppa Pig* (2014-19); **John Lee** played Lieutenant Commander Kiley in *Warship* (1973-77); **Alan Wheatley** played The Sheriff of Nottingham in *The Adventures of Robin Hood* (1955-60); **Marcus Hammond** briefly appeared in *Z Cars* (1964-65) playing PC Taylor; **Virginia Wetherell** landed a small role in *A Clockwork Orange* (1971); **Philip Bond** played Albert Frazer in *The Onedin Line* (1971-72).

BEHIND-THE-SCENES

- **Number of Production of Days:** 15
- This serial replaced a couple of proposed serials called 'The Hidden Planet' and 'The Masters of Luxor' which were never commissioned to feature in the season. **Anthony Coburn** was also developing another serial outline entitled 'Doctor Who and the Robots' which was eventually scrapped.
- The production of the serial was met with various interruptions, one of which concerned the coverage of the assassination of American President John F. Kennedy.
- For a time it seemed as though **Terry Nation** would not write for the series. The writer was formally invited to write for the show by **David Whitaker**. However Nation declined the offer since he was working in Nottingham on a stage play for comedian **Tony Hancock**, who reportedly told Terry Nation that the BBC had no right to ask a writer with high calibre to write for a children's television series. However the stage play fell through, and whilst on a train journey back to London. The writer remembered about the invitation, phoned his agent to ask if she had already declined the writing assignment. When he discovered she hadn't, he accepted the job and got straight to work.
- Terry Nation wrote a 26-page outline for the serial and drew inspiration from his childhood during World War II and the threat of racial extermination by the Nazis.
- The original designer for the serial was going to be **Ridley Scott** but he dropped out of the project and went on to have a successful directorial career helming such projects as *Alien* (1979), *Blade Runner* (1982), *Black Rain* (1989), *Gladiator* (2000), *Robin Hood* (2010), *Exodus: Gods and King* (2014) and *The Martian* (2015).
- The designer assigned to the serial was **Raymond Cusick** who would have the privilege and honour of designing The Daleks. The designer was originally confused by **Terry Nation**'s description of The Daleks in his script, and phoned the writer for

- further input. Both writer and designer had coincidentally seen a play in London by the Georgia State Dancers. The Dancers wore long dresses which created the illusion that they were gliding across the stage and this is how Nation envisioned how The Daleks would move.
- **Sydney Newman** was very reluctant to use the script for *The Daleks* because he believed they went against his vision for the series. When no other scripts were available he had no choice but to let the project run its full course. **Donald Wilson** was also very unhappy with the scripts stating that they were one of the worst things he had ever read and disliked The Daleks for their seemingly B-Movie quality. He had to accept and commission the serial because the production team had no other alternative. Both **Carole Ann Ford** and **William Russell** were equally unimpressed with The Daleks when they were presented on Friday 22 November 1963. Carole Ann Ford thought they looked funny whilst William Russell called them ludicrous.
- **Terry Nation** originally came up with the idea that The Dalek's power would come from the floors of their city, but **Mervyn Pinfield** later suggested that static electricity should be the power source of The Daleks.
- In the original scripts Terry Nation included a third race of aliens who were going to appear at the end of "The Rescue" who were omitted during the writing process. The aliens in question were going to be revealed as the ones who fired the neutron bombs on Skaro which devastated the planet. The aliens' presence in the story would have concluded with them reconciling with The Daleks and The Thals.
- **Terry Nation** envisioned that all the Thal characters were going to be male. He was asked to change one of them to a female. Dyoni became the only dominant female Thal character in the serial.
- Just like "An Unearthly Child", "The Dead Planet" was entirely reshot because production assistants' voices could be heard on the soundtrack. This was due to talk-back from their headphones.
- Assistant Floor Manager **Michael Ferguson** played The Thal who taps Susan on the shoulder and also played the first Dalek to be seen on-screen (the Dalek which advances towards Barbara at the end of episode one)
- The designer of The Daleks **Ray Cusick** originally wanted six Dalek props to be made, however the budget was not big enough and would only stretch to accommodate four Daleks.
- The Magnedon prop was expensive to produce and **Verity Lambert** later kept it in her production office.
- Many of the Thals' names underwent a few rewrites: Temmosus was originally called Stohl, Alydon was called Vahn, Ganatus was Kurt, Kristas was Jahl, Antodus was originally Ven, Dyoni was Daren, and Zhor became Elyon. These rewrites occurred on Wednesday 13 November 1963.
- The draft script for "The Rescue" originally contained a scene where The Daleks sent out a neutron bomb from the city which came to rest near The Tardis. The Doctor later defused the bomb.

BROADCAST

EPISODE	DATE	TIME	VIEWING FIGURE	CHART POSITION	APPRECIATION INDEX
1: *The Dead Planet*	21/12/1963	5:15-5:40pm	6.9M	67th	59
2: *The Survivors*	28/12/1963	5:15-5:40pm	6.4M	78th	58
3: *The Escape*	4/1/1964	5:15-5:40pm	8.9M	45th	62
4: *The Ambush*	11/1/1964	5:15-5:40pm	9.9M	29th	63
5: *The Expedition*	18/1/1964	5:15-5:40pm	9.9M	27th	63
6: *The Ordeal*	25/1/1964	5:15-5:40pm	10.4M	29th	63
7: *The Rescue*	1/2/1964	5:15-5:40pm	10.4M	25th	65

CLIFFHANGERS

1. Whilst exploring the Dalek City, Barbara is cornered against a wall as a Dalek [which remains off-screen] advances on her.
2. Susan retrieves some anti-radiation drugs from the Tardis, and prepares to head back to the Dalek City through the terrifying petrified jungle.
3. The Doctor and Ian remove a Dalek creature from its casing and leave it wrapped in a Thal cloak. Unbeknownst to both of them, the creature begins to push its way out from underneath the cloak.

4. The Time Travellers successfully escape the Daleks, but Ian realises that they cannot leave, because The Dalek still have the Tardis fluid link, a vital component to the ship, in their possession.
5. Whilst navigating through a swamp to get to the Dalek City, one Thal, Elyon, goes to a nearby lake to fetch water. Whilst Elyon fetches the water, something rises out of the water, and Elyon screams.
6. Navigating their way through a cave system, which leads into the Dalek City, one Thal, Antodus, falls into a crevasse. Ian, who is holding the other end of the rope, begins to be pulled towards the cliff edge.
7. The Tardis takes off from Skaro. Whilst inflight The Doctor works the console controls when the Time Travellers are all thrown to the floor.

COMMERCIAL RELEASES

- **AUDIOBOOK:** 7 March 2005
- **DVD:** 30 January 2006
- **ELECTRONIC MUSIC/SOUND EFFECTS**
  - **2000:** *Doctor Who at the BBC Radiophonic Workshop Volume 1: The Early Years 1963-1969*
- **NOVELISATION: [Hardback]** – 12 November 1964; **[Paperback]** – May 1973; **[Reissues]** – January 1992; July 2011
  - *Target Doctor Who Library Number*: **16**
- **SCRIPTS:** 12 December 1989; **[Reissue]** - 1992
- **SOUNDTRACK**
  - **1 September 2003:** *Doctor Who: Devils' Planets – The Music of Tristram Cary*
  - **9 December 2013 – 29 September 2014:** *Doctor Who: The 50th Anniversary Collection*
  - **15 September 2017:** *Doctor Who: The Daleks*
- **VIDEO:** 5 June 1989; **[Rerelease]** - 26 February 2001

CONTINUITY NOTES

- The exact date of the serial is unknown, but future events place it roughly in the twenty-first century; the creation of the Daleks in *Genesis of the Daleks* takes place roughly in the 15th century.
- The serial marks the first and last time The Doctor deliberately 'sabotages' the Tardis to explore an alien planet. The fluid link itself plays an important part in many future televised serials. In *The Web Planet*, the fluid link is accidentally realigned by Vicki restoring power to The Tardis, in *The Wheel in Space*, the link is broken causing deadly mercury fumes to fill The Tardis, whilst in *The Mind Robber* the link overheats causing The Doctor to take The Tardis out of reality itself, and into a realm populated by fictional characters.
- Both Skaro and The Thals do not appear again for quite some time, Skaro does not feature until *The Evil of the Daleks* whilst The Thals' next appearance occurs in *Planet of the Daleks*.
- The events of this story are later recalled by Ian in **PROSE:** *Byzantium!* and are also briefly mentioned by the Thal expedition team in *Planet of the Daleks*.
- The Magnedon which appears in "The Dead Planet", although dead, is technically the very first monster to appear in the show. Magnedons later appear in **GAME:** *Dalek Attack* and **COMIC:** *The Only Good Dalek*
- Skaro has the special attribute of being the very first alien planet seen in *Doctor Who*. The planet make many appearances through the show's history. Other appearances include **AUDIO:** *The Mutant Phase*, **AUDIO:** *Davros*, **AUDIO:** *The Light of Skaro*, **PROSE:** *War of the Daleks*, **GAME:** *City of the Daleks*, **SHORT STORY:** *Break-through!*, and **GRAPHIC NOVEL:** *The Only Good Dalek*, plus many, many more.
- The Magnedon is the first creature (apart from the Daleks) to originate on Skaro, and feature in the show. Other notable creatures who are natives to Skaro include the Varga Plants in *Mission to the Unknown*, the Slyther in *The Daleks Invasion of Earth*, giant clams, and an unidentifiable creature in *Genesis of the Daleks* and the Hand Mimes introduces in *The Magician's Apprentice*.
- Skaro (as mentioned before) is the first alien planet to feature in the show. Other notable alien planets visited by The Doctor include; Telos in *The Tomb of the Cybermen*, Dulkis in *The Dominators*, Uxarieus in *Colony in Space*, Peladon in *The Curse of Peladon, The Monster of Peladon* and **AUDIO:** *The Bride of Peladon*, Draconia in *Frontier in Space*, Zeta Minor in *Planet of Evil*, Kastria in *The Hand of Fear*, Pluto in *The Sun Makers*, Tara in *The Androids of Tara*, Chloris in *The Creature from the Pit*, Androzani Minor in *The Caves of Androzani*, Varos in *Vengeance on Varos*, Segonax in *The Greatest Show in the Galaxy*, Krop Tor in *The Impossible Planet/The Satan Pit*, Midnight in *Midnight*, Alpha Metraxis in *The Time of Angels/Flesh and Stones*, plus countless others across all forms of media.

- ➢ The Lake of Mutations also features in **COMIC:** *Impasse*, **COMIC:** *The Menace of the Monstrons*, **COMIC:** *The Terrorkon Harvest*, **AUDIO:** *Return to Skaro* and **AUDIO:** *Corruption*.
- ➢ The seventh episode of the serial "The Rescue" is the first time that an individual episode title shares the same name of an overall serial – *The Rescue*.
- ➢ Some of the music scores heard in this serial were later reused many times for *The Rescue, The Dalek's Master Plan, The Ark* and *The Power of the Daleks*.
- ➢ Despite believing otherwise The Daleks iconic cry of 'exterminate' is never utter during the serial. Their famous battle cry will later be used in future Dalek narratives.
- ➢ The use of medicine features for the first time with the use of anti-radiation drugs which are later used by The Fourth Doctor and Romana II in *Destiny of the Daleks*. Other uses of medicine feature in *Planet of the Daleks* with the anti-fungal preparations, aspirin in *The Web Planet*, the cure for the Silurian Plague in *Doctor Who and the Silurians*, and anaesthetic in *Doctor Who: TV Movie*.
- ➢ The serial marks the first time where a little bit more of the Tardis is revealed (not much though) other than the console room. Other fascinating areas of the Tardis which later crop up include: sleeping quarters in *The Edge of Destruction* and *The Web Planet*, a wardrobe room in *The Space Museum, The Twin Dilemma* and *Time and the Rani*, an unidentified black draped room in *The Stones of Blood*, the zero room in *Castrovalva*, and various bedroom throughout The Doctor's Fifth incarnation.

CRITICAL RESPONSE

- ➢ **Review Range:** Generally Positive
- ➢ *Doctor Who Magazine 2014 Poll*: 46th/241st
- ➢ **Richard Sear** of the *Daily Mirror* wrote a positive review after the broadcast of "The Expedition".
- ➢ **Christopher Bahn** of *The A.V. Club* was also positive towards the serial, but commented that the narrative and flow begin to slow down around the fifth episode. Bahn wrote that the swamp and cave system scenes moved the story on very slowly.
- ➢ **Patrick Mulkern** of the *Radio Times* praised Nation's scripts, the first three cliff-hangers, but felt that the finalé was slightly disappointing, and the claustrophobic atmospheres became less effective towards the end.
- ➢ **David J. Howe, Mark Stammers,** and **Stephen James Walker** awarded the serial a 9/10. When their book was first published, they commented that the serial was still one of the best Dalek stories of all time. They called the scripts excellent, and praised the direction and performances from the entire cast. They noted that the Daleks were ingenious creations, and commented that they were the reason *Doctor Who* became a cultural success with British audiences.

DEATHS

DEATH	CHARACTER	TIME OF DEATH	CAUSE OF DEATH
1	Dalek	[01:24:51]	Crushed in a lift(?) - *unconfirmed*
2	Temmosus	[01:30:37]	Exterminated
3	Tacanda	[01:33:21]	Exterminated
4-(?)	Daleks	[01:46:00]	Die due to power losses
5	Elyon	[01:58:54]	Pulled into the Lake of Mutations
6	Antodus	[02:31:30]	Falls into a chasm
7	Thal	[02:42:05]	Exterminated
8	Thal	[02:44:19]	Exterminated
9	Dalek	[02:44:28]	*unknown cause*
10	Dalek	[02:44:50]	Caught in an explosion
11	Dalek	[02:45:36]	Dies due to power losses

FILMING LOCATIONS

- ➤ Ealing Film Studios
- ➤ Ealing Film Studios: Stage 2
- ➤ Ealing Film Studios: Stage 3
- ➤ Lime Grove: Studio D

INFLUENCES

- ➤ **BOOK:** *The Time Machine* (1895, H. G. Wells)
- ➤ **BOOK:** *The War of the Worlds* (1898, H. G. Wells)
- ➤ **BOOKS:** *Lord of the Rings* (1954-55, J. R. R. Tolkien)
- ➤ **COMIC:** *Dan Dare* (1950-1967, Frank Hampson)
- ➤ **FILM:** *The Cabinet of Dr. Caligari* (1920, Robert Wiene)
- ➤ **FILM:** *The Time Machine* (1960, George Pal)
- ➤ **RADIO:** *Journey into Space* (1953-58, Charles Chilton)
- ➤ **SHORT STORY:** *The Machine Stops* (1909, E. M. Forster)
- ➤ **TV:** *Pathfinders to Venus* (1961, Malcolm Hulke, Eric Paice)

PRODUCTION ERRORS

1. During "The Dead Planet" the Tardis console moves when Susan checks the fault indicator.
2. During "The Survivors" and "The Escape" shadows of boom mics enter the frame.
3. During "The Survivors", one of the Daleks has faulty lights and its eye fails to turn on.
4. Whilst one of The Daleks succumbs to the effect of The Thals' drug, the Daleks positioned in the background are evidently cut out props rather than actual Dalek casings.
5. During "The Ordeal" and "The Rescue" both Barbara and Ian end with polystyrene in their hands after touching and grabbing hold of rocks.
6. As the Lake Monster raises out of the Lake of Mutations the rubber ring which supports the prop is visible.
7. Voices can be heard in the studio during certain scenes in "The Survivors".
8. During "The Ordeal" Ian throws a pebble down a down the chasm to see how far it is. The sound of the pebble hitting the studio floor is heard before the sound effect of the pebble hitting the bottom of the chasm.
9. One of the Daleks clearly rattles about during "The Ordeal".

PUBLICITY

- ➤ A photo-call on Friday 29 November was carried out after the camera rehearsals for "The Escape". The photo-call centred on the Thals as well as several shots of **William Hartnell**.
- ➤ On Monday 23 December 1963 two Daleks props appeared at Shepherd's Bush Market to promote the characters. This event was especially arranged by **Verity Lambert** and her team.
- ➤ On Friday 3 January 1964 schoolboy fan **Steven Qualtrough** took part in a photo-call with **William Hartnell** during the recording of "The Ordeal".
- ➤ Wednesday 8 January 1964 saw **William Hartnell** take part on *Junior Points of View* where he talked about the Daleks. The special programme was broadcast the next day.
- ➤ After the broadcast of "The Rescue" **Terry Nation** was interviewed on *Good Morning Wales*.

WORKING TITLES

- ➤ Beyond the Sun
- ➤ Episode 6: The Cave of Terror
- ➤ Episode 7: The Execution

VERDICT: *The Daleks* is a first-class science-fiction adventure which introduces the show's most memorable and beloved pepper-pot menaces, The Daleks. As a story, it's pretty straightforward, packed full of enduring chase scenes, audacious escapes, excellent production designs, heart pounding cliff-hangers, an excellent score by **Tristram Cary** (it's no surprise it was later reused many times), alien landscapes from a far off alien world, and a few secondary monsters to please the kiddies.

Terry Nation delivers seven scripts with plenty of imagery, but some risky messages for young children. The Thals who are seen as 'beautiful' are the good results after centuries of nuclear radiation, whilst The Daleks are worse off, evolving into mutant creatures that must be destroyed. It's a little risky to say that anything 'ugly' must be destroyed, and anything 'beautiful' must survive. That being said, the issues are explored in depth, with no easy answer to resolve both sides of the argument. Contrary to ugly vs. beauty imagery, The Daleks, on the whole, are the 'bad guys'. Terry Nation provides a solid platform where The Thals are given just cause to take up arms and fight for their survival. Besides this the scripts are incredibly strong, with various drawn-out scenes to up the tension, and plenty of frights to tighten the fear factor. Perhaps there are a bit too many convenient moments although *The Daleks* is not the worst offender for doing this, not by a long shot.

The direction is superb, **Christopher Barry** is the better of the two, but **Richard Martin** still shines. The direction is also ahead of its time, and often delves into the realm of voyeurism, where the viewers are positioned as the ones who are doing the menacing. The moment when Barbara is backed up against a wall, where a Dalek s-l-o-w-l-y advances towards her puts the viewers into an unnerving position the likes of which will never be seen again. *The Daleks* is a true delight and is a positive indicator for what is to come. ****

3) THE EDGE OF DESTRUCTION

Plot: During mid-flight, an explosion occurs in the Tardis which leads to a series of mysterious circumstances and events. When The Doctor and his companions begin to turn on each other they must find who or what is too blame.

CAST

Dr Who..............................William Hartnell
Ian Chesterton......................William Russell
Barbara Wright.....................Jacqueline Hill
Susan Foreman....................Carole Ann Ford

CREDITS

Written by David Whitaker
Title Music by Ron Grainger, BBC Radiophonic Workshop
Designer: Raymond Cusick
Associate Producer: Mervyn Pinfield
Producer: Verity Lambert
Directed by Richard Martin, Frank Cox

ACTOR BIOGRAPHIES: Jacqueline Hill made regular appearances in *Joyous Errand* (1957), *The Man From Room 13* (1961), *The Six Pound Walkers* (1962) and *Paradise Postponed* (1986). **Carole Ann Ford** can be seen in one-off roles in *Probation Office* (1959), *Emergency-Ward 10* (1960), *Dixon of Dock Green* (1961), *Z Cars* (1962), *Moonstrike* (1963), *Suspense* (1963) and *Public Eye* (1965) and the film *The Day of the Triffids* (1963).

BEHIND-THE-SCENES

- **Number of Production Days:** 2
- **Paddy Russell** was the first choice to direct the serial but had to pull out due to conflicting duties. She later directed *The Massacre, Invasion of the Dinosaurs, Pyramids of Mars* and *Horror of Fang Rock*
- The serial was designated as a budget saving episode costing just £2,986, making it the cheapest produced *Doctor Who* serial to date. Both instalments of the serial "The Edge of Destruction" and "The Brink of Disaster" came well under the £2,500 budget restriction placed on each individual episode at the time
- Because of the budget saving measures placed on the serial, it was decided that stock music would be used instead of hiring a composer to create a soundtrack. One musician's work that was selected for the serial was British-American jazz violinist **Eric Siday**.
- The scripts were met with a mixed reception from the cast: **William Hartnell** was not pleased with the long monologues he had to learn, **Jacqueline Hill** and **William Russell** liked the idea that the serial would allow a chance to explore the main characters in more detail whilst **Carole Ann Ford** did not the like the idea that the characters' strange behaviour was to go unexplained but looked forward to do some 'real acting'
- **William Hartnell** apparently messed up some of his lines to amuse **Carole Ann Ford**. One famous example of this occurred when **Hartnell** told Susan to turn on the "fornicator" instead of "fault locator".
- **David Whitaker** who was the script editor on the show at the time, was also the writer of the serial. The Writer's Guild at that time looked negatively upon script editors commissioning stories from themselves. To avoid potential problems Whitaker agreed that he would receive a sole credit as the writer.
- The serial sparked a bit of controversy, particularly the scene when Susan threatened Ian with a pair of scissors, **Verity Lambert** formerly apologised for the scene.

BROADCAST

EPISODE	DATE	TIME	VIEWING FIGURE	CHART POSITION	APPRECIATION INDEX
1: *The Edge of Destruction*	8/2/1964	5:15-5:40pm	10.4M	21st	61
2: *The Brink of Disaster*	15/2/1964	5:15-5:40pm	9.9M	31st	60

CLIFFHANGERS

1. Returning to the Tardis control room, The Doctor inspects the console controls when he is joined by somebody, who is about to strangle him.
2. Having resolved the problem with The Tardis, the ship lands in a new location. The Time Travellers leave the Tardis to explore their surroundings when Susan and Barbara discover a large footprint in the snow.

COMMERCIAL RELEASES

- **AUDIOBOOK:** 31 January 2010
- **CASSETTE:** September 1987
- **DVD:** 30 January 2006
- **ELECTRONIC MUSIC/SOUND EFFECTS**
  - **2000**: *Doctor Who at the BBC Radiophonic Workshop Volume 1: The Early Years 1963-1969*
- **NOVELISATION: [Hardback]** - 19 May 1988; **[Paperback]** 20 October 1988
  - *Target Doctor Who Library Number:* **132**
- **VIDEO:** June 1991; **[Rerelease]** - May 2000

CONTINUITY NOTES

- The serial has the smallest cast ensemble of all of the televised classic serials of *Doctor Who*. However, **Heaven Sent** in the revived series, has the smallest overall cast size of both the classical and revived series
- The serial is the first of very few stories where no character dies, there are another seven other examples of this; **The Savages, Fury from the Deep, The Mind Robber, The Empty Child/The Doctor Dances, Hide, Journey to the Centre of the Tardis** and **Listen**.
- This is the first time where viewers get to see a little bit more of the Tardis other than the console room which appeared in the previous two stories. Other serials which featured a little bit more of The Tardis include; **The Masque of Mandragora, The Invasion of Time, Castrovalva** and **Journey to the Centre of the Tardis**.
- The Doctor mentions that Susan and he are linked telepathically. This is later revisited many times including **The Three Doctors, The Five Doctors**, and **Dalek,** where The Ninth Doctor tells Rose that he would know if there were any other Time Lords in the universe, i.e. by pointing to his head.
- The planet which appears on The Tardis scanner is called Quinnis. The planet is brought up on numerous occasions including, **SHORT STORY:** *64 Carlyle Street*, **COMIC:** *A Religious Experience*, **AUDIO:** *Quinnis*, **AUDIO:** *Relative Dimensions* and **PROSE:** *The Devil Goblins from Neptune*.
- The is the first and only serial where is no antagonist to speak of (unless you discount The Doctor and Susan and their strange behaviour), and the possibility that an unknown identity go onboard the Tardis.
- The use of narcotics first features within the serial where The Doctor hands out sleeping draughts. Other examples of narcotics to feature in the show include the use of knockout drugs in **The Aztecs, The Brain of Morbius,** and **The Androids of Tara**, chloroform in **The Caves of Androzani** and **Ghost Light,** opium in **The Talons of Weng-Chiang**, and Vraxoin (a made-up drug) in **Nightmare of Eden**, plus others.
- This is the only serial where all of the action takes place within The Tardis without ever going outside and into another location.
- The first time in the show's history, the Tardis is shown to have living quarters for its occupants. The use of bedrooms will later be a regular factor throughout the Fifth Doctor era, predominately Adric's bedroom in **Earthshock** and **Terminus**, and Tegan and Nyssa's bedroom in **The Visitation** and **Snakedance**.

CRITICAL RESPONSE

- **Review Range:** Mixed to Positive
- *Doctor Who Magazine 2014 Poll*: 183rd/241st
- After the serial's first broadcast, **Stuart Hood**, the controller of Television Programmes at the time responded negatively towards the scenes where Susan threatened Ian with a pair of scissors at a Programme Review Board Meeting. **Verity Lambert** apologised about the scene.
- Subsequent reviews praised the dialogue, atmosphere, and characterization of the main characters, but have criticised the plot, and the resolution.

- Another review named *The Edge of Destruction* as the weakest of the first three serials whilst another review named "The Brink of Disaster" as the better of the two parts
- One review responded well to the serial describing it as a must watch for new viewers of the show.

FILMING LOCATION
- Lime Grove Studio D

INFLUENCES
- **BOOK:** *The Time Machine* (1895, H. G. Wells)
- **FOLKLORE:** *Ghost and Haunted House Stories*
- **TV:** *The Outer Limits* (1963-65, Leslie Stevens)

PRODUCTION ERRORS
1. A shadow can be seen on a wall when Barbara wakes Ian, which doesn't belong to any of the time travellers.
2. During the scenes in the white void in 'The Edge of Destruction', the studio floor is clearly visible
3. There is some confusion about where Quinnis is located in the Universe. In the serial, The Doctor mentions the planet is in the Fourth Universe, however this statement is later challenged in **NOVELISATION:** *The Edge of Destruction*, where The Doctor says it's in the Fourth Galaxy, whilst in **PROSE:** *The Devil Goblins*.
from Neptune The Third Doctor says the planet is located in Galaxy Four. Which is it Doctor? Which?
4. The shadows of two floor assistants can be seen during "The Edge of Destruction".
5. The words 'Fast Return' are clearly written on the Tardis in felt tip. Is this a translation for the audience, and Barbara and Ian? If so why is it written on the console in such a haphazard way?
6. Whilst The Doctor explains the birth of a New Solar System, a cough can be heard off-screen.
7. Susan gains and loses ankle-socks between scenes.

PUBLICITY
- The *Radio Times* ran a short preview of the serial with a photograph of the time travellers in The Tardis. The item included details of the plot, including the strange presence which has got on board the ship.

WORKING TITLES
- Inside the Spaceship

VERDICT: A lack of action and change of setting make for a decent serial which lacks an overall antagonist and a direct narrative. For a two-parter, the story holds itself together for the most part, and there is clearly an effort to bring new ideas to science fiction television drama. The lighting design and quiet moments here and there bring a new direction to the show and plunge the Tardis, often seen as a safe haven for The Doctor, into mortal danger. But then, the irrationality happens.

There is an interesting idea here concerning the possibility that a strange unknown identity has penetrated the safety of the Tardis, and has possessed one of the series regulars, the only question is, who? We get a frightening image of Susan threatening Ian with a pair of scissors – is it her? The Doctor's behaviour becomes excessively strange – is it him? The Tardis doors close when Ian approaches them, as if by some invisible command – is it him? Is it Barbara? Think of all of the possibilities to mislead the audiences, the dead ends, the red herrings, and finally the big reveal, and the exposure of the party responsible. 'Deep sigh'. Alas, no. The Doctor deduces that every strange occurrence is the result of a broken circuit. Really? It would seem that **David Whitaker** wasn't really sure where he wanted the story to go whilst writing it, so opted for a cheap get out of jail free card, with no regard for the silliness of the resolution. The Doctor seems very sceptical himself, in believing the illogicalness that is unravelling before him, and in turn so do the audience. The more one thinks about it, the less credible it becomes. The regulars are also a mixed bag, but **Carole Ann Ford** shines, and **William Hartnell** continues portraying The Doctor, as a heart-warming grandfatherly figure (Get used to Susan calling, "Oh Grandfather, Grandfather"). This claustrophobic tale makes great use of The Tardis sets and leaves viewers wanting to know more about the mysterious old ship. ***

4) MARCO POLO

Plot: In 1289 the Tardis crew join Marco Polo on his journey to meet Kublai Khan.

CAST

Dr Who	William Hartnell
Ian Chesterton	William Russell
Barbara Wright	Jacqueline Hill
Susan Foreman	Carole Ann Ford
Marco Polo	Mark Eden
Tegana	Derren Nesbitt
Ping-Cho	Zienia Merton
Man at Lop	Leslie Bates
Chenchu	Jimmy Gardner
Malik	Charles Wade
Acomat	Philip Voss
Mongol Bandit	Michael Guest
Ling-Tau	Paul Carson
Wang-Lo	Gabor Baraker
Kuiju	Tutte Lemkow
Vizier	Peter Lawrence
Kublai Khan	Martin Miller
Office Foreman	Basil Tang
Empress	Claire Davenport
Mongolian Warriors	John Lee, Roy Vincente, Ronald Chee, Carlton Ngui, Clem Choy, Bill Brandon, O Ikeda Yeng, Arnold Lee
Attendant on Ping-Cho	Zohra Segal
Chinese Lady of Quality	Violet Leon
Chinese Woman Attendant	Suk Hee S'Hng
Chinese Villagers (at Tun-Huang)	Clem Choy, Irene Ho, Peggy Sirr
Mongol Caravan Porters	Eton Fing-On, Aman Tokyo
Mongol Bandits	Gordon Bremworth, Leslie Bates, Roy Vincente, Santos Wong
Caravan Bearers	Henry Loy, Maung Hlashwe, LL Lim, Boon Wan Lee
Servant at Way Inn	Ying Win
Sentry	Valentino Musetti
Mongol Bandits (in forest)	Leslie Bates, Philip Lee, David Brewster, Valentino Musetti, Gordon Bremworth, Stanley Chen
Attendant's at Wang-Lo's Inn	Clem Choy, LL Lim, Aman Tokyo
Travelling Merchants	Gordon Bremworth, Stanley Chen
Noblewoman	Kay Fong
Caravan Warrior	David Anderson
Attendant at 2nd Way Inn	O Ikeda
Little Bearers	John Lee, Clem Choy
Travelling Gentlemen	Robert Chow, Lloyd Lim
Travelling Ladies	Peggy Sirr, Violet Leon
Noblemen at Court	Aman Tokyo, O Ikeda, Ying Wiu, Maung Hlashwe, Robert Chow, Lloyd Lam
Palace Guards	John Lee, Clem Choy, Philip Lee, Santos Wong, Ronald Chee, Gordon Bremworth, Carlton Ngui
Court Ladies	Peggy Sirr, Violet Leon, Kay Fong, Iris Loy, Suk Hee S'Hng
Male Courtiers	Roy Vincente, Henry Loy, WA Scully, Eton F'Ong, Basil Tang
Spittoon Bearer to the Khan	Harry Dillon
Soldiers	Clem Choy, David Anderson
Attendants to the Empress	Doreen Tang, Suchin
Double for Marco Polo's Hand	John Woodcock
Double for Man at Lop	[unknown]

CREDITS

Written by John Lucarotti
Sword Fight arranged by Derek Ware
Title Music by Ron Grainger with the BBC Radiophonic Workshop
Incidental Music by Tristram Cary
Costumes Supervised by Daphne Dare
Make-up Supervised by Ann Ferriggi
Story Editor: David Whitaker
Designer: Barry Newbery
Associate Producer: Mervyn Pinfield
Producer: Verity Lambert
Directed by Waris Hussein, John Crockett

ACTOR BIOGRAPHIES: Mark Eden appeared in many movies including *The Password is Courage* (1962), *Séance of a Wet Afternoon* (1964) and *Doctor Zhivago* (165) and appeared in *Coronation Street* (1986-89) as Alan Bradley; **Derren Nesbitt** played Detective Chief Inspector Jordan in *Special Branch* (1969-70); **Zienia Merton** is best known as Sandra Benes in *Space: 1999* (1975-77); **Jimmy Gardner** can be seen in *Harry Potter and the Prisoner of Azkaban* (2004) as Ernie the Bus Driver; **Tutte Lemkow** can be seen in *Raiders of the Lost Ark* (1981); **Philip Voss** landed a small role in *Frankenstein and the Monster from Hell* (1974); **Paul Carson** landed small roles in *You Only Live Twice* (1967) and *The 6th Day* (2000); **Peter Lawrence** appeared regularly in *Crossroads: Kings Oak* (1965) and *Weavers Green* (1966); **Martin Miller** landed movie roles in *Exodus* (1960), *The Pink Panther* (1963), and *Children of the Damned* (1964); uncredited **John Woodcock** landed a small role in *Skullduggery* (1970).

BEHIND-THE-SCENES

- **Number of Production Days:** 12
- For the first time in the show's history, live animals were used during the recording process which included the use of a spider-monkey. The spider-monkey was not trained and bit anyone who came near it. The serial also required the use of an exotic bird for "Assassin at Peking".
- **Barry Newbery** used many books during his research whilst designing the set including *Chinese Houses and Gardens* by Henry Inn, and *Chinese and Indian Architecture* by Nelson I. Wu
- It seemed that early in pre-production that **Verity Lambert** would be leaving the show to helm *Swizzlewick*, developed and launched by **Donald Wilson**. Lambert also considered transferring to produce *Play School*, a new pre-school programme made for BBC2.
- Director **John Crockett**, who handled "The Wall of Lies", submitted an encouraging memo to **David Whitaker** suggesting other possible historical-based *Doctor Who* serials. Among his suggestions were Sir Francis Drake and the Armada, Vikings, Boadicea, the Globe Theatre, Bonnie Prince Charlie, Roman Britain, Richard I and the Crusades, and Sir Walter Raleigh.
- For a time it seemed that **Richard Martin**, who directed episodes for *The Daleks*, would helm "The Wall of Lies", and "Mighty Kublai Khan" but on Thursday 9 January 1965, **Waris Hussein** was contracted to direct all seven episodes however he would not helm "The Wall of Lies" which was directed by **John Crockett**. Waris regarded the scripts for *Marco Polo* with high regard. He felt they were much better in quality compared to *An Unearthly Child*, and felt he now had a better understanding of the show.
- **Leslie Bates**, who was hired to play Man at Lop for "The Roof of the World", became the first actor, apart from the series regulars to appear in two *Doctor Who* serials, and play two different characters in the same season, having previously appeared as an uncredited tribesman in *An Unearthly Child*.
- To keep in line with **Sydney Newman's** vision that the show should 'educate the kids at home', during the writing process, **John Lucarotti** filled his scripts with historical and scientific information. Lucarotti was inspired by *The Boy's Own Paper*, a story paper which was produced between 1879 and 1967.
- *Marco Polo* was originally going to be the third adventure in the series. However when the scripts arrived slightly late *The Edge of Destruction* was added to the schedule and the ending of the newly devised serial was written to link to the beginning of *Marco Polo*.
- It was originally intended that The Doctor would have a short voice-over narration at the start of "The Singing Sand". Ian and Barbara would also provide small narrations at the start of preceding episodes. The speeches were eventually rewritten for Marco Polo.
- During production of the story, the show received its very first cover on the *Radio Times*. However, the cover which comprised a shot of **William Hartnell, Mark Eden,** and **Derren Nesbitt**, did not sit well with the series regulars. **William Russell** was unhappy about the cover and his agent contacted **Donald Wilson** about the actor's unhappiness. **Donald Wilson** was also unhappy with the cover, and did not understand why a photograph of the four regulars was rejected.
- **Zienia Merton** who played Ping-Cho was coached and trained by the uncredited actress **Zorah Segal** who was trained in dance and mime for her long recital of the legend of Aladdin in "Five Hundred Eyes".
- During recording for "Mighty Kublai Khan", **Derren Nesbitt** accidentally slashed **Mark Eden's** hand whilst holding a dagger. Recording for "Assassin at Peking" was interrupted when studio firemen raised concerns about equipment left on studio gangways.

BROADCAST

EPISODE	DATE	TIME	VIEWING FIGURE	CHART POSITION	APPRECIATION INDEX
1: *The Roof of the World*	22/2/1964	5:15-5:40pm	9.4M	33rd	63
2: *The Singing Sands*	29/2/1964	5:15-5:40pm	9.4M	33rd	62
3: *Five Hundred Eyes*	7/3/1964	5:15-5:40pm	9.4M	34th	62
4: *The Wall of Lies*	14/3/1964	5:15-5:40pm	9.9M	31st	60
5: *Rider from Shang-Tu*	21/3/1964	5:15-5:40pm	9.4M	37th	59
6: *Mighty Kublai Khan*	28/3/1964	5:30-5:55pm	8.4M	49th	59
7: *Assassin at Peking*	4/4/1964	5:30-5:55pm	10.4M	22nd	59

CLIFFHANGERS

1. Tegana obtains a phial of poison which he plans to use to murder Marco Polo and his party. When everyone is dead, he 'announces' his plans to steal The Tardis, believing it will bring Kublai Khan to his knees.
2. Tegana approaches a desert oasis and pours water into the sand. Tegana says "Here's water Marco Polo. Come for it!"
3. The Doctor, Susan, and Ping-Cho enter the Cave of Five Hundred Eyes to look for Barbara. During their search Susan screams and points to one of the carved faces because its eyes moved!
4. Having successfully escaped from the tent which he has been imprisoned in, Ian approaches a Guard who falls to the ground when Ian touches him. The Guard has a knife sticking out of his torso.
5. Susan approaches The Tardis when Tegana appears out of nowhere and grabs her around the neck.
6. Ian, who holds Kuiju at knife-point, is informed by the bandit that he is working with Tegana, and he was the one who ordered him to steal Ping-Cho's money. At the moment Tegana appears brandishing his sword.
7. Marco Polo ponders where the mysterious time travellers are now. An image of The Tardis appears on-screen superimposed against a landscape.

COMMERCIAL RELEASES

- **AUDIOBOOK:** 6 December 2018
- **DVD:** 30 January 2006 – a 30-minute reconstruction on the DVD release of *The Edge of Destruction*
- **LP (soundtrack):** September 2020
- **NOVELISATION: [Hardback]** 13 December 1984; **[Paperback]** – 11 April 1985; **[Rerelease]** – 1985
  - *Target Doctor Who Library Number:* **94**
- **SOUNDTRACK**
  - **3 November 2003:** *BBC Audio*
  - **5 August 2010:** *The Lost TV Episodes – Collection One*

CONTINUITY NOTES

- *Marco Polo* marks the first historical-based story in *Doctor Who*, a creative trend envisioned by **Sydney Newman**. Other examples of history-based narrative are, **The Reign of Terror, The Romans, The Crusade, The Time Meddler, The Myth Makers, The Massacre** and **The Highlanders**.
- It is revealed that The Doctor and Susan have seen the metal seas of Venus during their travels. Venus itself will become a popular destination for The Doctor, landing on the planet in **AUDIO:** *Voyage to Venus*, **PROSE:** *Venusian Lullaby* plus others. Venus also briefly appears in *Enlightenment* and *Partners in Crime*.
- Marco Polo is the very first historical figure to appear in the show. Many more historical-figures would go on to appear in the show including Agatha Christie, Charles Dickens, H.G. Wells, Nero, Richard the Lionheart, William Shakespeare and Winston Churchill.
- The serial marks the first time when the Tardis lands in Asia in a televised serial. The Doctor later revisits other areas of Asia in *The Crusade* and *The Abominable Snowmen*.

- The Second Doctor recalls his time in China in ***The Power of the Daleks***, the Fourth Doctor mentions that he hasn't visited China for 400 years in ***The Talons of Weng-Chiang***, and The Sixth Doctor recalls his time in China in **AUDIO:** *1963: The Space Race*.
- The First Doctor later revisits China in **PROSE:** *The Eleventh Tiger*, and had visited China with Susan previously in **AUDIO:** *The Flames of Cadiz*.

CRITICAL RESPONSE
- **Review Range:** Positive
- *Doctor Who Magazine 2014 Poll*: 84th/241st
- The BBC Programme Review Board had positive notes after the broadcast of "The Roof of the World".
- A review in *The Sunday Telegraph* written by **Philip Purser** praised **Mark Eden**'s portrayal of Marco Polo but felt that the main characters were not as strong, particularly Barbara.
- A letter from an 11-year-old fan highlighted that he liked serial set sometime in the past, but he did on the whole prefer narratives which take place in the future.
- The serial was fortunate enough that The Walt Disney Company approached the BBC in July 1964 to turn the serial into a feature length film, but no development was made.
- Writing in *Doctor Who: The Complete History – Volume 2*, editor **John Ainsworth** praised the simple plot, and exploration dedicating to the characters and described the serial as exotic and arresting.

FILMING LOCATIONS
- Ealing Film Studios Stage 3B
- Lime Grove Studio D

INFLUENCES
- Marco Polo and his travels

PRODUCTION BLUNDERS
1. During "Assassin at Peking" Kublai Khan incorrectly refers to backgammon as a game of cards.
2. Marco Polo's father and uncle, Niccolo Polo and Maffeo Polo, are strangely missing from the serial. Historical evidence reveals that both men accompanied Marco Polo on his travels and voyages.
3. The caption slide at the end of episode two reads Next Episode: The Cave of Five Hundred Eyes. The third episode of the serial is simply titled "Five Hundred Eyes".
4. The Doctor claims that he has never meet Genghis Khan despite **PROSE:** *Time and Relative*, and **AUDIO:** *An Earthly Child* claiming otherwise.

PUBLICITY
- "The Roof of the World" was covered in the BBC in-house magazine *Ariel* in the February 1964 edition
- On Thursday 20 February, *Doctor Who* received its first cover on the *Radio Times* with a picture of The Doctor, his companions, Marco Polo, Tegana, and Ping-Cho on a set for the first episode.
- Saturday 22 February saw a picture of **Carole Ann Ford** and her daughter appear in the *Daily Mirror* and comic writer **Sydney Jordan** commented on the Daleks' popularity.

WORKING TITLES
- Doctor Who: Journey to Cathy
- Doctor Who and Kublai Khan
- Episode 3: The Cave of Five Hundred Eyes

5) THE KEYS OF MARINUS

Plot: Arriving on the planet Marinus the Tardis travellers are unwittingly recruited to find the keys to the Conscience of Marinus, which have been scattered across the planet, to prevent the Voord, Yartek from taking over the planet

CAST

Dr Who	William Hartnell
Ian Chesterton	William Russell
Barbara Wright	Jacquline Hill
Susan Foreman	Carole Ann Ford
Arbitan	George Coulouris
Vasor	Francis de Wolff
Eyesen	Donald Pickering
Tarron	Henley Thomas
Altos	Robin Phillips
Sabetha	Katherine Schofield
Voords	Martin Cort, Peter Stenson, Gordon Wales
Voice of Morpho	Heron Carvic
Warrior	Martin Cort
Darrius	Edmund Warwick
Ice Soldiers	Michael Allaby, Alan James, Peter Stenson, Anthony Verner
Larn	Michael Allaby
Senior Judge	Raf de la Torre
First Judge	Alan James
Second Judge	Peter Stenson
Kala	Fiona Walker
Aydan	Martin Cort
Guard	Alan James
Yartek	Stephen Dartnell
Ladies in Waiting	Faith Hines, Daphne Thomas, Veronica Thornton, Sharon Young, Lynda Taylor
Idol	Bob Haddow
Eprin	Dougie Dean
Citizens of Millenius	Veronica Thornton, Valerie Stanton, David Kramer, Adrian Drotskie, Leslie Shannon, Patricia Anne, Billy Dean, Tony Lampton, Brian Bates, Monique Lewis, Heidi Laine, Rosina Stewart, Cecilia Johnson, Jill Howard, Yvonne Howard, Tony Hennessey, Johnny Crawford, Leslie Wilkinson, Desmond Cullum Jones, Perrin Lewis
Double for Arbitan	John Beerbohm

CREDITS

Written by Terry Nation
Title Music by Ron Grainger
 with the BBC Radiophonic Workshop
Incidental music composed by Norman Kay
Costumes Supervised by Daphne Dare
Make-up Supervised by Jill Summers
Story Editor: David Whitaker
Designer: Raymond P Cusick
Associate Producer: Mervyn Pinfield
Producer: Verity Lambert
Directed by John Gorrie

ACTOR BIOGRAPHIES: George Coulouris had a successful film career appearing in *Citizen Kane* (1941), *Between Two Worlds* (1944), *Hotel Berlin* (1945), *Joan of Arc* (1948), *Appointment with Venus* (1951), *Kill Me Tomorrow* (1957), *The Boy Who Stole a Million* (1960) and *Tower of Evil* (1972); **Francis de Wolff** was a well-known film actor appearing in *Treasure Island* (1950), *Scrooge* (1951), *Moby Dick* (1956), *The Hounds of the Baskervilles* (1959), *From Russia with Love* (1963), *Carry on Cleo* (1964) and *The Three Musketeers* (1973) and had an uncredited role in *The Curse of the Werewolf* (1961); **Donald Pickering** is best known as Dolly Langstaffe in *The Pallisters* (1973) and Doctor Watson in *Sherlock Holmes and Doctor Watson* (1979-80); **Katherine Schofield** landed a small role in *Lifeforce* (1985); **Robin Phillips** appeared briefly in *The Forsyte Saga* (1967); **Alan James** landed a small role in *Howards End* (1992); **Anthony Verner** played Sydney Huxley in 278 episodes of *The Newcomers* (1966-69).

BEHIND-THE-SCENES

- **Number of Production Days:** 7
- Before writing the scripts for **The Keys of Marinus**, **Terry Nation** claimed that he had forgotten all about the show until the broadcast of "The Dead Planet" in mid-December. Between production of **The Daleks** and **The Keys of Marinus**, Nation, was supposed to be working on a second serial entitled *The Red Fort*, however he was concentrating on another project at the time, and as such never delivered any scripts.
- The idea for **The Keys of Marinus** arose during a meeting between **Terry Nation**, script editor **David Whitaker**, producer **Verity Lambert**, and associate-producer **Mervyn Pinfield** on Tuesday 21 January 1964. Nation was invited to write a 'futuristic story', and the idea of having four mini-adventures occurring within the narrative was arrived at.

- The director for the serial **John Gorrie** was not very happy with the scripts, nor was he comfortable handling a science-fiction project. The director was encouraged by **Verity Lambert** to see the production through.
- Drawing inspiration from Latin words and Greek mythology whilst writing his scripts. Marinus derived from the Latin word 'marinus' which means 'of the sea', Morphoton comes from Morpheus, the Greek god of Dreams, whilst Arbitan was inspired by the Latin name 'Arbiter' meaning judge.
- The character of Altos was not originally going to join The Doctor to look for the Keys of Marinus, instead he was to stay behind and help with the reconstruction with the city of Morphoton.
- During rehearsals for "The Velvet Web" designer **Raymond Cusick** had the idea of placing stuffed rats around the 'reality' sets but was overruled by **John Gorrie**.
- Whilst writing the script for "The Snows of Terror", the Ice Soldiers were originally frozen in ice. Each of the Ice Soldiers sat on a chair, and carried a different weapon – a sword, an axe, a lance, and mace. "The Snows of Terror" also had the Ice Soldiers looking for icicles to form a new bridge when they became trapped on the other side of the chasm, and Vasor originally held a knife to Susan's throat during the final scenes.
- **Meryn Pinfield** was apparently very fond of the Voords whilst **David Whitaker** was disappointed.
- Uncredited stand-in actor **John Beerbohm** stood in for the role of Arbitan during certain scenes in "The Sea of Death" including the fight between Arbitan and a Voord where **Beerbohm**'s face was obscured by the hood of the cloak Arbitan wears to disguise this fact.
- During recording for "The Velvet Web" it became apparent to **Jacqueline Hill** that the scene when Barbara smashed the glass domes which housed the Morpho brains would only be recorded once. Hill later re-called that she kept hitting the glass domes until they broke which proved to be very difficult.
- When "The Snows of Terror" entered rehearsals on Monday 6 April **Peter Stenson**, who played a Voord in "The Sea of Death", was also hired to play an Ice Soldier. **Martin Cort** (who also played a Voord) was originally cast in the part, the actor was released by **John Gorrie** when the actor was offered work elsewhere.
- Set designer **Raymond Cusick** was very unhappy with the finished ice caves sets. To conceal the sets' misgivings, Cusick suggested lighting the sets darker and advised the crew to use tight shots.
- During "The Keys of Marinus" **Martin Cort** had trouble seeing out of his Voord mask. The actor tripped over the scenery and almost crashed into it at one point.

BROADCAST

EPISODE	DATE	TIME	VIEWING FIGURE	CHART POSITION	APPRECIATION INDEX
1: *The Sea of Death*	11/4/1964	5:30-5:55pm	9.9M	22nd	62
2: *The Velvet Web*	18/4/1964	5:30-5:55pm	9.4M	25th	60
3: *The Screaming Jungle*	25/4/1964	5:30-5:55pm	9.9M	22nd	61
4: *The Snows of Terror*	2/5/1964	5:30-5:55pm	10.4M	20th	60
5: *Sentence of Death*	9/5/1964	5:15-5:40pm	7.9M	29th	61
6: *The Keys of Marinus*	16/5/1964	5:15-5:40pm	6.9M	43rd	63

CLIFFHANGERS

1. The Doctor, Ian, and Susan arrive at the location where the first Key to the Conscience of Marinus is hidden. Upon arriving, Barbara is nowhere to be seen, and her travel dial is covered in blood!
2. Having found the first key, Susan moves onto the second location, alone. She finds herself in the middle of jungle filled with screaming. She covers her ears and cries out 'Go Away'.
3. Ian and Barbara arrive in a snowy, barren landscape. As Barbara succumbs to the freezing temperatures Ian stresses that they must move on or they won't stand a chance.
4. Ian arrives in what appears to be a room inside a museum. Ian finds the body of a dead man on the floor, and discovers the final key locked in a glass case. An unknown person enters the room, and knocks Ian out cold. The person places Ian's hand on a mace before retrieving the key, causing an alarm to sound.

5. Whilst investigating a way to clear Ian's name, Barbara gets a telephone call from Susan. Susan tells Barbara that she has been kidnapped and, if The Doctor reveals the location of the final key, she will be killed.
6. With Yartek defeated The Doctor and his companions depart in The Tardis.

COMMERCIAL RELEASES

- **AUDIOBOOK:** September 2022
- **DVD:** September 2009
- **ELECTORNIC MUSIC/SOUND EFFECTS**
  - **2000**: *Doctor Who at the BBC Radiophonic Workshop Volume 1: The Early Years* 1963-1969
- **NOVELISATION:** [Hardback/Paperback] – August 1980
  - *Target Doctor Who Library Number*: **38**
- **SOUNDTRACK**
  - **9 December 2013 – 19 September 2014**: *Doctor Who: The 50th Anniversary Collection*
- **VIDEO:** March 1999

CONTINUITY NOTES

- At the beginning of the serial, Ian is still wearing his costume from the previous serial, ***Marco Polo***.
- The exact date of the serial is never stated; however, **COMIC:** *The World Shapers* would appear to place the events of the serial at around 5000000BC or elsewhere during an unknown period.
- The Doctor will later go on other quests to achieve certain goals throughout his later incarnations: the Fourth Doctor joins a crew of Minyans to discover a lost spaceship in ***Underworld***; the Fourth Doctor is later sent by the White Guardian to find the segment of the Key to Time; the Seventh Doctor goes to Svartos to find a legendary crystal hidden somewhere on the planet Svartos in ***Dragonfire***; and the Tenth Doctor and Martha go on a quest to discover a crashed spaceship, the Infinite, in the animated special *The Infinite Quest*.
- Barbara and Ian later recall their time on Marinus in **COMIC:** *Hunters of the Burning Stone*.
- "The Screaming Jungle" is the first episode of *Doctor Who* where The Doctor does not appear at all. Other episodes where The First Doctor does not make an appearance are "The Snows of Terror", "The Dead of Tomorrow" and ***Mission to the Unknown***. The First Doctor also doesn't appear in "The Hall of Dolls" and "The Dancing Floor" although his voice is still heard, and he is absent from episode 3 of ***The Tenth Planet***.
- The Voords can also be seen in **AUDIO:** *Domain of the Voord,* **AUDIO:** *Beachhead,* **COMIC:** *Land of the Bill,* **SHORT STORY:** *The Fishmen of Kandalinga,* and **SHORT STORY:** *Doctor Who and The Daleks*
- Arbitan, although on the good side, is arguably the first 'mad' scientist to feature in the show since his actions are both questionable and almost lead to disastrous results. Other mad scientists who appear in Dr Who include; Lesterton in ***The Power of the Daleks***, Professor Zaroff in ***The Underwater Menace***, Dr Charles Lawrence in ***Doctor Who and the Silurians***, Professor Whitaker in ***Invasion of the Dinosaurs***, Sorenson in ***Planet of Evil***, Solon in ***The Brain of Morbius***, Magnus Greel in ***The Talons of Weng Chiang***, Crozier in ***Trial of a Time Lord: Mindwarp***, and Professor Richard Lazarus in ***The Lazarus Experiment***.
- Yartek is later mentioned in **PROSE:** *No Future* and **PROSE:** *The Taking of Planet of Five*. Whilst in **AUDIO:** *Doman of the Voord*, Tarlak describes Yartek as his 'brother'.
- Towards the end of "The Snows of Terror" Ian is bashed on the head with a large object. He will suffer this misfortune twice more, both times being mere accidents; the first time at the hands of Barbara in ***The Romans***, and the second time at the hands of Vicki during ***The Chase***.
- Morpho are the first *Doctor Who* monsters who are killed by a companion. Other companions who meet their end at the hands of companions include an Ice Warrior killed when Victoria's screams cause an avalanche, and the Weed Creature in ***Fury from the Deep*** defeated by a recording of her screams. Nyssa and Ace destroy various Cybermen in ***Earthshock*** and ***Silver Nemesis*** respectively.
- Ian is still wearing the clothes Marco Polo gave him at the start of "The Sea of Death".
- It seems possible that the Voord are actually an early version of the Cybermen, before the Cybermen were introduced on *Doctor Who*. **COMIC:** *The World Shapers* features some Voord who have been partially upgraded into Cybermen although The Twelfth Doctor believes that both the Mondasian Cybermen and the Marinus Cybermen evolved separately on two different planets in *The Doctors Falls*.

CRITICAL RESPONSE

- **Review Range:** Negative to Mixed
- *Doctor Who Magazine 2014 Poll*: 192nd/241st
- **Kenneth Adam,** Director of Television at the time, discussed 'concerns' that his three-year-old-granddaughter had about the show. She remarked that the time travellers were always getting separated, and always landed themselves in trouble. The 'concern' were later discussed with **Donald Wilson, Verity Lambert,** and **Sydney Newman** – [no resolution obviously came to pass]
- In a 'negative' outlook, the BBC's board of manager expressed concern that the show, was at times, a little too creepy for their liking.
- **Bob Lesson** of the *Daily Worker* wrote that "Sentence of Death" was the show's lowest point and felt that the trial scenes suggested a rushed script.
- **Arnold T. Blumberg** described the plot as clichéd, the production values as poor and frowned upon the jumping about between various locations.
- Another review wrote that The Doctor's absence in certain episodes and an overall antagonist attributed to the serial's misgivings.
- Audiences seemed to enjoy the serial since all six episode achieved an appreciation index score of 60+, similar results to what *Marco Polo* received.
- **Mark Campbell** gave the serial a disappointing rating of 3/10. He described the serial as the show's first turkey, and wrote that the scripts were bad. He did not appreciate the production values either, and felt that there were some, but not many effective moments.
- Later reviews did praise the story and the structure but still felt that the trial episodes do not work well.

DEATHS

DEATH	CHARACTER	TIME OF DEATH	CAUSE OF DEATH
1	Voord	00:07:30	Victim of the sea of acid
2	Voord	00:09:07	*death unconfirmed*
3	Voord	00:11:36	Stabbed in the back
4	Voord	00:14:00	Falls into sea of acid
5	Arbitan	00:22:06	Stabbed by a Voord
6	Morpho	00:44:23-00:44:31	Destroyed by Barbara
7	Darrius	01:05:56	Dies of old age
8	Ice Soldier	01:34:16	Falls down a chasm
9	Vasor	01:35:19	Stabbed by an Ice Soldier
10	Eprin	01:35:37	Murdered by Aydan
11	Aydan	01:57:02	Killed by Kala
12	Yartek	02:24:52	Killed in an explosion
13	Voord	02:24:52	Killed in an explosion

FILMING LOCATIONS

- Ealing Film Studios
- Lime Grove Studio D

INFLUENCES

- **MYTHOLOGY:** *Celtic Myths*
- **MYTHOLOGY:** *The Labourers of Hercules*
- **TV:** *Courtroom Dramas, 30s serials*

- **TV:** *Fireball XL5*: "Hypnotic Sphere" (1963: Alan Pattillo)

PRODUCTION ERRORS

1. Three crew members can be seen throughout "The Sea of Death": when one of the Voords disappears behind a revolving wall, another crew member's leg can be seen after The Doctor enters the pyramid, yet another crew member can be seen in the background when Ian enters the pyramid.
2. The Voord who falls into the sea of acid in The Sea of Death is clearly a cut-out model rather than an actor performing a stunt fall. This becomes evident when the model turns sideways.
3. There appears to be some timing issues between the cliffhanger to "The Sea of Death" and the opening scenes of "The Velvet Web". At the end of the first episode Barbara teleports to the city of Morphoton a few seconds before the others. However, the opening of the second episode makes it look like Barbara has been in the city for a short period of time with no explanation to resolve this problem.
4. During "The Velvet Web" a boom microphone enters the shot when the characters prepare to go to sleep and **William Russell** evidently looks at the microphone for a few seconds.
5. During "The Screaming Jungle" the camera seems to collide with the set whilst the camera-operator carries out a sweeping tracking shot around **Edmund Warwick** (Darrius).
6. During "The Snows of Terror" one of the actors playing an Ice Soldier blinks a few times before closing his eyes after the main characters enters the room where he is positioned.
7. The icicles seen in "The Snows of Terror" are made of polystyrene, this becomes evident when Ian uses one of them to make a bridge to get over the chasm.
8. After dematerialising at the end of "The Sea of Death", The Doctor's shadow remains on the wall behind him.
9. During "The Keys of Marinus", the Voord trips over his feet and almost takes a door off its tracks.
10. **Stephens Dartnell**'s eyes and mouth can be seen through his mask during a close-up shot on Yartek.
11. There appears to be some contradictory information with regards to Marinus and its true name. According to **COMIC:** *The World Shaper*, Marinus later became Mondas, which made its first appearance in **The Tenth Planet**. This means that Marinus *could* be Earth's twin-planet and the home to the original Cybermen. However Marinus has also been referred to as Planet 14. The Twelfth Doctor mentions that the Cybermen evolved on various planets; Marinus, Mondas, and Planet 14 in **The Doctor Falls**, making it sound like that Marinus and Mondas are two different planets. It has never been confirmed that Marinus is Mondas, and **COMIC:** *The World Shaper* seems to complicate the timeline and continuity of *Doctor Who*.
12. The model Tardis is missing from the recycled model shot of the island surrounded by the sea of acid towards the beginning of "The Keys of Marinus".
13. It's a little difficult to believe that Susan, Ian, Barbara, Altos and Sabetha all failed to notice that the Ice Soldiers had changed positions after they entered and left the ice cave that the Soldiers occupy. One of them suggests that the Ice Soldiers are permanently frozen, unable to move, so the sudden change of position of the Soldiers should have been an indicator that something is not right.

PUBLICITY

- The *Radio Times* (11-17 April 1964) included a photograph of The Doctor, Ian, Barbara and Susan with Arbitan to promote the new serial. The photograph was taken in front of the Conscience of Marinus.
- Thursday 9 April saw the *Daily Mail* run a piece called *New TV Monsters Will Rival the Daleks* whilst the *Daily Mirror* ran a piece called *A Voord from Outer Space*.
- Saturday 11 April saw the appearance of a photograph of Susan in the hands of a Voord **(Peter Stenson)** on the cover of the *Daily Mail*.
- An interview with **Carole Ann Ford** appeared in *Reveille* (23-29 April) as well as an interview with **William Hartnell** in many papers including the *Yorkshire Evening Press* on Monday 27 April.

WORKING TITLES

- [no known working titles]

VERDICT: The first adventure quest in the show's narrative, **The Keys of Marinus**, is made of up of, not one, not two, but rather several mini-episodes tied together with one basic end goal. Whilst the entire story is somewhat fragmented, there is a whimsical but likeable similarity in the six episodes, where the story and narrative are never taken too seriously.

The plot explores various old and recycled science fiction tropes (mind control, hypnotic powers, aliens resembling giant brains etc.), which only appear for a single episode, play their part in the narrative, and disappear without a trace. Writer **Terry Nation** will later do a similar thing when writing many of his *Doctor Who* scripts over the years, which perhaps says something about his overall enthusiasm for the show. The best episode of the six 'The Snows of Terror' is intensely shot and is your basic survival-of-the-fittest storyline, with **Francis de Wolff** providing a memorable performance as Vasor. The weakest is 'Sentence of Death' which centres round a poorly realised trial narrative with a pretty obvious villain working silently in the background.

The costume and sets design are generally remarkable but the supporting characters, especially *most* of the villains are rather weak. Yartek is the show's first bland and forgettable antagonist. Yartek and the rest of the Voords can be summed up in one word – boring. Yartek's weak personality traits and characteristics are an indication that Terry Nation probably forgot all about him, and just threw in some last minute ideas to give viewers an 'intense' confrontation and 'climatic showdown'. Thankfully Yartek is only in one episode. It's interesting that the production team tried to cash in on the Voords (Terry Nation's second race of aliens for *Doctor Who*), but failed to create another nationwide phenomenon. It's not that surprising that the Voords faded away from the public's hearts and imagination, an indicator for how forgettable they are.

The Keys of Marinus has all the potential for being big and epic, but there's only thing missing – money. Good story ideas with plenty of potential require a decent budget and various production blunders indicate a missed opportunity. Whilst this one is not entirely brilliant, it makes for good compelling entertainment, and that's all *Doctor Who*, at the best of times, is meant to be. ***

6) THE AZTECS

Plot: In fifteenth-century Mexico Barbara is mistaken as the reincarnated high priest Yetaxa. With her newfound position Barbara attempts to change the ways of the Aztecs for the better. However, The Doctor warns her that history must never be tampered with.

CAST

Dr Who	William Hartnell
Ian Chesterton	William Russell
Barbara Wright	Jacquline Hill
Susan Foreman	Carole Ann Ford
Autloc	Keith Pyott
Tlotoxl	John Ringham
Ixta	Ian Cullen
Cameca	Margot van der Burgh
First Victim	Tom Booth
Tonila	Walter Randall
Perfect Victim	Andre Boulay
Aztec Captain	David Anderson
Aztec Warriors	Paul Duval, James Fitzgerald, Alan Viccars, Andrew Jacks, John Beavis, Brian Baker
Old Aztec Lady	Alice Greenwood
Aztec Ladies	Eileen Brady, Stella Wilkinson
Aztec Man	John H Moore
Old Aztec Men	William Rayner, Lionel Gadsden
Stunt Double for Ixta	David Anderson
Stunt Double for Ian Chesterton	Billy Cornelius

CREDITS
Written by John Lucarotti
Title Music by Ron Grainger with the BBC Radiophonic Workshop
Incidental Music by Richard Rodney Bennett
Conductor: Marcus Dods
Fights Arranged by David Anderson, Derek Ware
Costumes by Daphne Dare
Make-up supervisor: Jill Summers
Story Editor: David Whitaker
Designer: Barry Newbery
Associate Producer: Mervyn Pinfield
Producer: Verity Lambert
Directed by John Crockett

ACTOR BIOGRAPHIES: **John Ringham** played various characters in *An Age of Kings* (1960), semi-regular and regulars roles came with *The Railway Children* (1968), and *Dad's Army* (1970); **Ian Cullen** is best known as Warren Kent in *Emergency-Ward 10* (1966-67), Det. Con. Skinner in *Z-Cars* (1969-75) and Angus Hart in *Family Affairs* (1997-99); **Keith Pyott** landed movie roles in *Operation Amsterdam* (1959), and *Village of the Damned* (1960).

BEHIND-THE-SCENES

- **Number of Production Days:** 6
- The names of the Aztec characters were not based on or derived from historical figures. Instead **John Lucarotti** used prefixes and suffixes to create Aztec-sounding names. 'Ixta' comes from an Aztec city called Ixtapalpa.
- Whilst writing the scripts for "The Temple of Evil", **John Lucarotti** based the Perfect Victim sacrifice scene on sacrifices made to the Aztec god Tezcatlipoca.
- Apparently set designers at the BBC were assigned to projects based on their talents and skills, the only factor which guaranteed work on a show was if a designer was free from other commitments. Set designer **Barry Newbery** would discover the negative sides to this recruitment process in later years.
- Set Designer **Barry Newbery** claimed that *The Aztecs* was the most challenging *Doctor Who* serial he had worked on. Very little was known about Aztec culture and society during pre-production and Newbery's research came mostly from BBC books and a then recent documentary made by a Mexican archaeologist.
- Due to the large sets that would be required for the serial **Barry Newbery** asked if filming could take place in Television Centre Studio 3 or 4. His request were declined; but when technical problems arose in Lime Grove Studio D, Television Centre 3 was used for "The Warriors of Death" and "The Bride of Sacrifice".
- The set dressings used for the serial (pots and vases) were painted with Aztec designs by Art students. The shields and clubs used for the serial were made of fiberglass and plywood. **Barry Newbery** avoided using metal for props for historical accuracy.
- For the tomb scenes in "The Temple of Evil" and "The Day of Darkness" a real skeleton was used to represent Yetaxa which wore a mask based on one in the British Museum.

- "The Temple of Evil" was originally going to end with a shot of rain falling on the sacrifice stone. However, due to problems with water being used in a studio, this idea was dropped.
- The tomb entrance seen in "The Temple of Evil" and "The Day of Darkness" proved to be a challenge for **Barry Newbery**. The prop had to look massive but be light enough to be lifted in and out of the studio. The designer ultimately made the tomb door open up horizontally and supported it with weights.
- The fight scene between Ixta and the warrior proved very difficult to look convincing for both actors. The props were very fragile and could break easily with enough force. Fight arranger and stunt double **David Anderson** also had problems with the fight scene in "Warriors of Death".
- During recording for "The Warriors of Death" some of the required scenery had been disposed of previously much to the frustration to **Barry Newbery**. The set designer instead recycled parts of Susan's cell and hired plants from Greenery Hire of Hampton.
- The recording for "The Bride of Sacrifice" did not have a recording break at all. This was very unusual for *Doctor Who*, since recording breaks allowed actors to move between sets and/or change costumes for preceding scenes.
- The cliff-hanger to "The Bride of Sacrifice" did not incorporate real water; instead the illusion was created with the use of lighting and sound effects.
- During the editing process, the solar eclipse was created by cross-fading photo-captions of the moon passing in front of the sun.

BROADCAST

EPISODE	DATE	TIME	VIEWING FIGURE	CHART POSITION	APPRECIATION INDEX
1: *The Temple of Evil*	23/5/1964	5:15-5:40pm	7.4M	25th	62
2: *The Warriors of Death*	30/5/1964	5:15-5:40pm	7.4M	34th	62
3: *The Bride of Sacrifice*	6/6/1964	5:15-5:40pm	7.9M	19th	57
4: *The Day of Darkness*	13/6/1964	5:15-5:40pm	7.4M	34th	58

CLIFFHANGERS

1. After stopping the sacrifice of the First Victim, Barbara is branded as a false goddess by Tlotoxl and threatens to destroy her.
2. Tlotoxl urges Ixta to kill Ian but when Barbara arrives she orders for the fight to be stopped. Tlotoxl challenges Barbara to save her servant if she is indeed a goddess.
3. Venturing through an underground tunnel which leads to Yetaxa's tomb Ian stops in his tracks as the sound of running water can be heard somewhere in the tunnel.
4. Inside The Tardis The Doctor ponders over the console. It seems that he is getting two contradictory messages; one insists that The Tardis has stopped, whilst the other claims The Tardis is still in motion.

COMMERCIAL RELEASES

- **AUDIOBOOK:** August 2012
- **DVD:** October 2002; **[Special Rerelease]** – March 2013
- **NOVELISATION:** **[Hardback]** – 21 June 1984; **[Paperback]** – 20 September 1984; **[Reissue]** – 1992
    - *Target Doctor Who Library Number:* **88**
- **VIDEO:** November 1992

CONTINUITY NOTES

- *The Aztecs* marks a popular trend in various *Doctor Who* serials by focusing on The Doctor describing the disastrous results that could come with interfering with time. The Doctor briefly spoke about this in *An Unearthly Child* commenting on the possibilities that might arise if, the Romans had the weapon of gunpowder and Napoleon had the secret of the airplane. The Doctor also refers to the dangers of meddling with time in *Time-Flight, The Waters of Mars,* and *The Wedding of River Song*. During *The Waters of Mars*, The Doctor knowingly interferes with time, and is left to contemplate the disastrous results which arise because of his meddling.

- The Doctor later meets a band of Mexican Warriors in *The War Games*, whilst a Mexican Cowboy spends a brief spell in Tombstone, Arizona in *The Gunfighters*
- The serial marks the first time where the Tardis lands in North America in a televised serial. Other trips to North America occur in ***Dalek, Daleks in Manhattan/Evolution of the Daleks, The Impossible Astronaut/Day of the Moon***, and ***A Town Called Mercy*** plus others.
- Barbara mentions that the Aztec-period is one of her favourite periods in history. In **SHORT STORY:** *Nothing at the End of the Lane* it is revealed that Barbara wrote her dissertation on the Aztecs, and in **PROSE:** *Who Killed Kennedy?* Barbara became a University History Lecturer, specialising in Aztec and Central American history after travelling with The Doctor.
- The Doctor and Cameca become engaged to be married to each other after The Doctor accepted a drink of cocoa from her. This is the not the last time The Doctor has romantic feelings for a human. He has romantic-feeling towards Madame de Pompadour in ***The Girl in the Fireplace***. The Doctor also falls in love with Joan Redfern in ***Human Nature/The Family of Blood*** whilst disguised as a human called John Smith. The Doctor also marries Queen Elizabeth I in ***The Day of the Doctor***.
- The antagonists of this serial are interesting because their 'evil' personality and 'bad' intentions are simply a result of thousands of years of Aztec tradition and honour.
- Barbara Wright is the first character in the *Doctor Who* universe who is a 'fake god', disguising herself as a reincarnation of Yetaxa. Polly Wright later pretends to be the goddess Amdo in ***The Underwater Menace*** to rescue The Doctor from being sacrificed. Other 'fake' gods who appear in the show include, the Menoptra in ***The Web Planet***, Xoanon in ***The Face of Evil*** who turns out to be a spaceship computer gone mad, and Kroll in ***The Power of Kroll*** who is converted into the fifth segment of the key to time by the Fourth Doctor.

CRITICAL RESPONSE

- **Review Range:** Positive
- *Doctor Who Magazine 2014 Poll*: 61st/241st
- **Bill Edmund** from *Television Today* praised the characters of Ixta and Tlotoxl and **Barry Newbery's** sets praising their historical accuracies after the broadcast of "The Temple of Evil".
- **Bob Lesson** from *Daily Worker* praised the serial's charm, the tighter plot, and the attempt to showcase a historically accurate adventure.
- **Mark Braxton** of the *Radio Times* described the serial as one of the show's best adventures.
- **Morgan Jeffrey** of *Digital Spy* named ***The Aztecs*** as the tenth-best *Doctor Who* story of all time.

DEATHS

DEATH	CHARACTER	TIME OF DEATH	CAUSE OF DEATH
1	First Victim	00:21:34	Jumps off pyramid
2	Aztec Captain	01:32:07	Killed by Ixta
3	Ixta	01:34:44	Thrown off a pyramid by Ian
4	Perfect Victim	01:35:53	Sacrificed by Tlotoxl

FILMING LOCATIONS

- Ealing Film Studios
- Lime Grove Studio D
- Television Centre Studio 3

INFLUENCES

- **BOOK:** *The Man Who Would Be King* (1888, Rudyard Kipling)
- **PLAY:** *Richard III* (c.1593, William Shakespeare)
- **PLAY:** *The Royal Hunt for the Sun* (1964, Peter Shaffer)

PRODUCTION ERRORS

1. There are a few problems with the background drapes throughout the serial. Some of them evidently have creases and folds which reveal they are not constructed set pieces.
2. Some of the actors' voices clearly 'clip' throughout "The Temple of Evil". There are also some problems with background noises whenever the actors speak.
3. **William Hartnell** interrupts **William Russell** mid-sentence in 'The Temple of Evil' when the latter tells the former about the impending sacrifice at the end of the episode.
4. During "The Temple of Evil" the camera which moves closer to the sacrifice stone jerks after hitting the set dressing. This happened because the cameras at Lime Grove Studio D were unable to zoom in manually, so the camera operator had to move the camera himself.
5. There is no one correct way of pronouncing Tlotoxl's name due to numerous cast members all pronouncing his name differently throughout the serial.

PUBLICITY

➢ The *Radio Times* once again promoted the serial. A photograph of The Doctor and Barbara (in her Yetaxa get-up) was accompanied with a short description of the adventure viewers could look forward to.

WORKING TITLES

➢ [no known working titles]

VERDICT: "But you can't rewrite history! Not one line!" *The Aztecs* marks the first time in show's history which directly addresses the implications which come with time travel. From a third-party standpoint it's easy to side with both The Doctor and Barbara about whether or not it is morally acceptable to change history for the better. For The Doctor, he only wants to explore the Universe and never interfere; for Barbara, a history teacher, she only wants to help the Aztecs for the better.

Perhaps what's most interesting about *The Aztecs* aren't the gorgeous sets and costumes, the eerie soundtrack, the excellent use of camera angles, the special effects or the performances, but rather, the antagonists themselves. *Doctor Who* villains tend to be driven by textbook desires and goals, but here, they only want to uphold Aztec honour and tradition. Tlotoxl's only motivation is to prove that Barbara is a false goddess to the point where he plans to poison Barbara to prove his point. Can we really hate the guy? After all, Barbara exploits Aztec religious beliefs just to keep herself and her friends alive. Can we really blame Tlotoxl for wanting to expose Barbara as an imposter?

The Aztecs teaches us that travelling with The Doctor can be tough, and sometimes moral obligations and humanitarian feelings must be sacrificed in order to survive for another day. The Doctor falls in love, unknowingly proposes, and unwittingly parts ways with Cameca in a short space of four-episodes, with only a single broach to remember her by. Whilst historical-based narratives slowly phased out of the show's format as time went on, *The Aztec* is a fine piece of television that does more than just educate. ****

7) THE SENSORITES

Plot: Arriving on a spaceship with a small crew lingering between life and death, The Doctor must venture down to the mysterious Sense-Sphere to obtain some answers

CAST

Dr Who	William Hartnell
Ian Chesterton	William Russell
Barbara Wright	Jacqueline Hill
Susan Foreman	Carole Ann Ford
John	Stephen Dartnell
Carol	Ilona Rodgers
Maitland	Lorne Cossette
Commander	John Bailey
First Human	Martyn Huntley
Second Human	Giles Phibbs
First/First Scientist	Ken Tyllsen
Second/Second Scientist/Warrior	Joe Greig
Third	Peter Glaze
Fourth	Arthur Newall
First Elder	Eric Francis
Second Elder	Bartlett Mullins
Sensorite	Anthony Rogers
Sensorite	Gerry Martin

CREDITS

Written by Peter R Newman
Title Music by Ron Grainger
with the BBC Radiophonic Workshop
Incidental music composed and conducted
 by Norman Kay
Costumes supervised by Daphne Dare
Make-up supervised by Jill Summers
Story Editor: David Whitaker
Designer: Raymond P Cusick
Associate Producer: Mervyn Pinfield
Producer: Verity Lambert
Directed by Mervyn Pinfield, Frank Cox

ACTOR BIOGRAPHIES: Ilona Rodgers appeared in *The New Adventures of Black Beauty* (1990-92); **Bartlett Mullins** appeared in *The Likely Lads* (1964-66), *Nicholas Nickleby* (1968) and *Bright's Boffin* (1970-72); **Anthony Rogers** can be seen in *Camelot* (1967) and appeared in *El Dorado* (1967) but went uncredited; **Joe Greig** had various one-off roles in *Dr. Finlay's Casebook* (1962-71) and *Z Cars* (1963-74) and appeared in five episodes in *Gamble for a Throne* (1961); **Peter Glaze** appeared in over 300 episodes of *Crackerjack* (1960-79).

BEHIND-THE-SCENES

- **Number of Production Days:** 8
- **Peter R Newman** began to write to develop *The Sensorites* in January 1964 and was commissioned by script editor **David Whitaker** to submit the first script and a storyline for the other five on Tuesday 25 February.
- The target delivery of for the first scripts was Tuesday 3 March. **Newman** submitted the scripts early, episode two was accepted on Tuesday 3 March, and episode three arrived at the production office on Wednesday 25 March. The further three scripts had a deadline of Friday 3 April. Newman was a little late submitting the scripts for episodes five and six, arriving on Friday 24 April and Thursday 21 May respectively
- It seemed for a while that *The Sensorites* would be the final televised serial of the show's first season. **Verity Lambert** put forward an idea on Tuesday 7 April that the show should take a six week break after transmission of episode six. However Lambert later suggested that the show should remain in production so the programme could be ahead of schedule when the second season began in later autumn
- Recording for the serial was due to be entirely shot at Lime Grove Studio D. However **Verity Lambert** expressed her dislike of the studio citing technical and working conditions, and restrictive studio space as problems which would affect production of *The Sensorites*. The matter was resolved when recording for the serial in Television Centre Studio 3 and 4 was granted. However "Hidden Danger", "Kidnap" and "A Desperate Venture" were all recorded at Lime Grove Studio D.
- **Martyn Huntley** and **Giles Phibbs**, who played First Human and Second Human, respectively, were close friends of uncredited director's secretary **Cordelia Crawshaw** who managed to get them interviews to appear on the series.
- **Raymond Cusick's** set designs bore a lot of similarities to the Spanish Architect **Antoni Guadí** who was famous for designing buildings without using right angles.

- The Sensorite masks were made by stretching an orange-coloured fabric over a wire framework. Ears were later attached to the masks, whilst the costumes were a one-piece jumpsuit. The Sensorites' flat feet (made out of cardboard discs) caused the actors great difficulty walking on the sets, sometimes causing actors to step on each other's feet. Frank Cox recalled one time where one Sensorite actor said to another, 'Get off my foot, you fool' causing the entire studio to burst out laughing.
- Because recording for the serial was conducted in the middle of the summer, the masks were extremely hot to wear. The actors playing the Sensorites generally did not wear the masks during camera rehearsals.
- During rehearsals it was decided that actor **Brian Proudfoot** would double for **William Hartnell** in film sequences for the following serial, *The Reign of Terror*. Hartnell was initially annoyed with the stand-in actor who was following him around the sets in order to mime his mannerisms but assisted him nonetheless.

BROADCAST

EPISODE	DATE	TIME	VIEWING FIGURE	CHART POSITION	APPRECIATION INDEX
1: *Strangers in Space*	20/6/1964	5:15-5:40pm	7.9M	17th	59
2: *The Unwilling Warriors*	27/6/1964	5:40-6:05pm	6.9M	39th	59
3: *Hidden Danger*	11/7/1964	5:15-5:40pm	7.4M	22nd	56
4: *A Race Against Death*	18/7/1964	5:15-5:40pm	5.5M	58th	60
5: *Kidnap*	25/7/1964	5:15-5:40pm	6.9M	29th	57
6: *A Desperate Venture*	1/8/1964	5:15-5:40pm	6.9M	39th	57

CLIFFHANGERS

1. A frightening whistle sound fills the spaceship which suddenly stops. As silence kicks in, a Sensorite appears outside of the spaceship which glares into the ship.
2. Susan, under the control of the Sensorites, approaches Maitland's ship control room hatch revealing two more Sensorites behind it. She informs the others to stay where they are, and that she has agreed to accompany the Sensorites to their planet. The hatch closes, leaving everyone utterly helpless.
3. Ian drinks some water which comes from a nearby aqueduct but soon collapses to the floor. The First Elder announces that Ian is dying.
4. The Doctor sets off to find out the cause of the poisoned water. During his search, the roar of animals echo somewhere in the surrounding darkness.
5. Carol sets off to find out what has happened to The Doctor and Ian when someone puts a hand over her mouth and drags her away.
6. The Time Travellers watch Maitland's ship depart on the Tardis scanner. Ian jokingly comments that at least Maitland knows where he is going, which The Doctor takes offence to.

COMMERCIAL RELEASES

- **AUDIOBOOK:** 3 May 2012
- **DVD:** January 2012
- **ELECTRONIC MUSIC/SOUND EFFECTS**
    - **5 July 1993:** *Doctor Who: 30 Years at the BBC Radiophonic Workshop*
    - **May 2000:** *Doctor Who at the BBC Radiophonic Workshop Volume 1: The Early Years 1963-1969*
- **NOVELISATION: [Hardback]** – February 1987; **[Paperback]** – July 1987
    - *Target Doctor Who Library Number:* **118**
- **SOUNDTRACK**
    - **10 July 2008**: original release
    - **5 September 2013**: *The TV Episodes – Collection Six*
    - **9 December 2013 – 29 September 2014**: *Doctor Who: The 50th Anniversary Collection*
- **VIDEO:** November 2002

CONTINUITY NOTES

- The serial marks the first time The Doctor declares his dislike of weapons, a trend that will be revisited during the tenure of the Tenth Doctor in **The Sontaran Stratagem, The Doctor's Daughter** and **The End of Time**.
- The Doctor visits the Ood-Sphere in **Planet of the Ood** which is in the same star system as the Sense-Sphere.
- The Tardis materialises on board a ship vessel for the first time in the show's history. The Tardis will materialise on many, many spaceships throughout history notably in **The Wheel in Space, Frontier in Space, The Ark in Space, Underworld, Nightmare of Eden** and **Terminus**.
- The Sensorites are the first telepathic race of aliens to feature in the show. Other telepathic aliens who feature in the show are the Nestenes in **Spearhead from Space** and **Terror of the Autons**, the Osirans (mostly Sutekh) in **Pyramids of Mars**, the Metebelis III Spiders in **Planet of the Spiders**, the Haemovores in **The Curse of Fenric**, and the Vespiform in **The Unicorn and the Wasp**.
- The model shot at the end of "A Desperate Venture" marks the first time that a model spaceship (seen in space) appears in the show. The show will go to have a whole showcase of model spaceships in flight notably in **The Claws of Axos, The Mutants, Frontier in Space, Pyramids of Mars** and **The Invisible Enemy**.
- It is revealed that The Doctor and Susan's home planet is very similar to Earth. However Susan reveals that the skies burn orange and tree leaves are bright silver. The Tenth Doctor later uses these exact descriptions whilst describing Gallifrey to Martha in **Gridlock**.
- Sometime before meeting Ian and Barbara, The Doctor and Susan encountered a telepathic race of plants on the planet Esto. The planet is also home to a race of physics parasites who appear in **SHORT STORY:** *Number 1, Gallows Gate Road*. Esto is also mentioned in **PROSE:** *The Tomorrow Windows*.
- The Doctor mentions that he once quarrelled with King Henry VIII in order to get back to the Tardis which was parked in the Tower of London. The infamous King later appeared in **AUDIO:** *Recorded Time*, **SHORT STORY:** *The Tudor Engagement*, and **The Power of Three**.

CRITICAL RESPONSE

- **Review Range:** Generally Positive
- *Doctor Who Magazine 2014 Poll:* 225th/241st
- **Mark Braxton** of the *Radio Times* praised the realisation of the Sensorites (their appearances and their society), the performances of **Stephen Dartnell, William Hartnell,** and **Carole Ann Ford** and the relationship between The Doctor and Susan.
- **Arnold T. Blumberg** praised the suspense of the first two episodes, set design and lighting.
- **Nick Setchfield** of *SFX* felt the serial was ambitious and that the slow-paced first episode worked well, although he felt that the Sensorites lost their fear-factor as the story progressed.
- **John Sinnott** of *DVD Talk* also praised the set designs as well as Susan's increased importance to the plot. However he felt there was nothing overtly unique about the serial.

DEATHS

DEATH	CHARACTER	TIME OF DEATH	CAUSE OF DEATH
1	Second Elder	[01:49:30]	Murdered by the Engineer

FILMING LOCATIONS

- Ealing Film Studios
- Lime Grove Studio D
- Television Centre Studio 3
- Television Centre Studio 4

INFLUENCES

- **HISTORY:** *Yangtze Incident* (1949)
- **TV:** *Fireball XL5* (1962-63, Gerry and Sylvia Anderson)

PRODUCTION ERRORS

1. The Doctor calls Ian Chesterton, 'Ian Cheston' at the end of "Strangers in Space", and Maitland as 'John'.
2. During the serial, The Doctor claims that he and Susan have never argued before. This is incorrect as The Doctor berated Susan for allowing Ian and Barbara to discover their secret in *An Unearthly Chid*
3. During "A Race Against Death" a couple of boom mics enter the frame as well as one entering above a Sensorite Servant in "Hidden Danger"
4. The note Carol is forced to write for the City Administrator is noticeably different to the one that Barbara reads in the next scene.
5. During "Strangers in Space", The Doctor and Maitland react to a sound effect that is not actually heard.
6. During "A Desperate Venture", The Doctor reads the shoulder flash test he finds as 'I-N-N-E-R', but when the camera tilts to reveal the prop it reads I-N-E-E-R'.
7. If the Sensorites are meant to be a peace-loving species why is there a character called Warrior, and why are they armed with weapons? Did they build their weapons after the first humans arrived on earth, or did they build them just in case threatening situations would arise?

PUBLICITY

- The *Daily Mail* carried a headline entitled 'Look out – the Sensorites are coming' on Monday 15 June with **Mervyn Pinfield** commenting that mothers worry more about the show's monsters than children.
- The *Radio Times* carried a photo of The Doctor, Ian, Carol, and Maitland on the spaceship sets.
- On Monday 22 June, the *Daily Telegraph* carried a comment made by **Verity Lambert** where she revealed no protests had been received from parents regarding the dangers the main characters find themselves in.
- The *Radio Times* dated Thursday 17 July carried an interview with **William Hartnell**.
- University of York Lecturer **Edward Blishen** wrote an article where he declared the series was nothing but 'compulsive nonsense'.

WORKING TITLES

- [no known working titles]

VERDICT: Whilst the first two episodes are long winded and tiresome, the rest of the story does not fare any better. Whilst the Sensorites are excellent in design and are portrayed with flair, too much time is spent overemphasising their weakness and flaws its makes one want to shout 'WE GET IT, MOVE ON! at the TV. The plot is laden with far too may expositional moments which heavily distract viewers from anything interesting, if one can indeed find anything interesting in the first place. The music is either too clichéd or overdramatic at specific points, and never seems to improve. The only saving grace is the spaceship sets, which are astutely designed and filmed, but this highlight gets old, fast. Fluffed lines, repetition of ideas in quick succession, poorly written drawn-out scenes and poor sound quality result in the shows' first real let down. Whilst not the absolute worst, this is still pretty dull. **

8) THE REIGN OF TERROR

Plot: The time travellers find themselves separated in the middle of the French Revolution. With both factions closing in around them they must find their way out before time runs out

CAST

Dr Who	William Hartnell
Ian Chesterton	William Russell
Barbara Wright	Jacqueline Hill
Susan Foreman	Carole Ann Ford
Jailer	Jack Cunningham
Jules Renan	Donald Morley
Lemaitre	James Cairncross
Léon Colbert	Edward Brayshaw
Jean	Roy Herrick
Robespierre	Keith Anderson
Danielle	Caroline Hunt
Small Boy	Peter Walker
Rouvray	Laidlaw Dalling
D'Argenson	Neville Smith
Sergeant	Robert Hunter
Lieutenant	Ken Lawrence
Soldier	James Hall
Judge	Howard Charlton
Shopkeeper	John Barrard
Webster	Jeffry Wickham
Road Works Overseer	Dallas Cavell
Peaseant	Dennis Cleary
Physician	Ronald Pickup
Soldier	Terry Bale
Paul Barras	John Law
Napoléon Bonaparte	Tony Wall
Soldier	Patrick Marley
Soldiers (at Farmhouse)	Bob Berry, Rex Dyer, Gerry Wain, Tony Bates
Knitting Ladies	Eleanor Dalling, Leila Forde
Soldiers (at Prison)	John Sackville West, Don Cavendish, Sid Deller, Don Simons, Nigel James, Jay McGrath, Adrian Drotskie
Prisoner	David Banville
Citizens	Jack Le White, Brian Proudfoot, Ralph Katterns, Jill Howard, Helene Cutt, Eleanor Dalling
Soldiers	Maurice Selwyn, Len Russell, David Anderson, Terry Wallace, Al Raymond, Adrian Drotskie, Brian Proudfoot, Roy Curtis, Bob Berry, Sid Deller, Bill Nicholas, Joseph Cohen, Maurice Leon, Tony Lampdon
Double for Dr Who	Brian Proudfoot

CREDITS

Written by Dennis Spooner
Title Music by Ron Grainer
 with the BBC Radiophonic Workshop
**Incidental music composed
 and conducted by** Stanley Myers
Film Cameraman: Peter Hamilton
Film Editor: Caroline Shields
Costumes Supervised by Daphne Dare
Make-up Supervised by Sonia Markham
Lighting by Howard King
Story Editor: David Whitaker
Designer: Roderick Laing
Associate Producer: Mervyn Pinfield
Producer: Verity Lambert
Directed by Henric Hirsch

ACTOR BIOGRAPHIES: Donald Morley appeared in *The Railway Children* (1957), *Destination Downing Street* (1957), *Coronation Street* (1961/1974), *Compact* (1962-63), *Emergency Ward-10* (1966), *Freewheelers* (1972), *Emmerdale* (1974/1978), *Westway* (1976); **Edward Brayshaw** appeared in *Rentaghost* (1976-84); **Peter Walker** had previously appeared in 15 episodes of *The Arthur Haynes Show* (1962); **Caroline Hunt** played Claire Bell in *199 Park Lane* (1965) and landed a small role in film *The Remains of the Day* (1993); **Jack Cunningham** was a popular face on TV making numerous appearances in *Z-Cars* (1962-65), *Dixon of Dock Green* (1963-64), and *The Wednesday Play* (1965) plus a notable appearance in *Time Lock* (1957); **Tony Wall** landed a part in *Licensed to Kill* (1965); **Jeffrey Wickham** was a regular in *An Age of Kings* (1960); **John Barrard** landed a small role in *Santa Claus: The Movie* (1985); **Roy Herrick** can be seen in *The Regiment* (1972-73); **Ronald Pickup** appeared in *Holby City* (2006-07), *Young Dracula* (2014), *The Crown* (2016), and played Neville Chamberlain in *Darkest Hour* (2017); **Patrick Marley** played Barry Hughes in *Crossroads: Kings Oak* (1966).

BEHIND-THE-SCENES

- **Number of Production Days:** 10
- **Terry Nation** was originally going to write the eighth serial for the season. The serial in question, 'The Red Fort', would have been set during the Indian Mutiny of 1857. However when Nation failed to deliver the scripts, the idea was subsequently dropped, and the writer outlined *The Keys of Marinus* instead.
- Another idea that was considered for Serial H was a story involving the Spanish Armada. The scripts would have been written by **David Whitaker** and directed by **Gerald Blake**.
- Before writing the scripts for *The Reign of Terror*, **Dennis Spooner** expressed interest in writing a science-fiction based narrative; however **David Whitaker** wanted another historical-based serial for the series. Dennis Spooner was presented with four-possible subjects, and after carrying out some research at a library, Spooner informed Whitaker about his preference to write a serial set during the French Revolution.
- This serial replaced a potential six-part story which would have been set in sixteenth century Spain. The scripts were being written by **David Whitaker** and would have been directed by **Gerald Blake**. However the scripts never arrived and *The Reign of Terror* filled in the empty slot.
- The scenes involving The Doctor walking down a country road were not performed by **William Hartnell**, series extra **Brian Proudfoot** performed the scenes. According to **Carole Ann Ford**, Proudfoot followed William Hartnell around the studio to copy his mannerisms, much to his annoyance.
- The locations used for "A Land of Fear" were scouted out by uncredited production assistant **Timothy Combe** who looked for locations which he believed were 'French-looking' and ideally had trees growing in the area. Timothy Combe was also a major help during the casting process for the serial. He had previously worked with **Neville Smith**, he was a fellow student at drama school with **Roy Herrick**, he noticed **John Barrard** on an episode of *Z-Cars*, and was familiar with **Tony Wall** and his theatre work.
- The production team spent Tuesday 16 June 1964 at Ealing Film Studios recording scenes involving Ian's imprisonment and the death of Webster. **Jeffrey Wickham** recorded his death scene as Webster before the lunch break, and believing that all of his scenes were completed, he left the studios and met up with a friend for a drink. However, Wickham was still required for the scene when Lemaitre inspected his dead body. The actor was called back to the studios and eventually fell asleep on set. He woke up to find the studio empty, as everyone has gone home after work had been completed.
- Throughout the recording of the serial, **Henric Hersch** had great difficulty coping with the project. **Carole Ann Ford** recalls that the director left the cast to their own devices instead of directing the scene as he wanted. The director would later criticize the cast for not giving him what he envisioned.
- Filming on Friday 24 July 1964 covered the scenes where a live-horse was required in studio. Thankfully, the horse selected to appear was very familiar with television work, and was not frightened when the scene required firearms going off. **Carole Ann Ford**, a great horse lover, loved working with the animal.
- Director **Henrich Hirsch** was taken ill during the recording of "A Change of Identity". He began to complain about a headache and was later found by **Timothy Combe** outside the recording gallery: the director had collapsed. Instructed to call **Verity Lambert** production secretary **Ann Earl** informed the producer of the situation. Combe took temporary charge of the situation until a placement could be appointed. There is some confusion about who took over. The paperwork credits **John Gorrie**; however he does not recall directing the episode and later believed that either **Verity Lambert** or **Mervyn Pinfield** must have handled the episode.
- On Thursday 6 August 1964, **David Whitaker** announced that he would be leaving his post as the script editor, **Dennis Spooner** was selected to replace him.
- On Friday 14 August 1964, **Carole Ann Ford's** daughter visited the studio, and apparently refused to speak with **Jack Cunningham** because he was responsible for 'locking mummy up'.
- The scene where the time travellers return to the Tardis by a horse-drawn carriage was taken from *The French Revolution*. The film was provided by Gateway Films.

BROADCAST

EPISODE	DATE	TIME	VIEWING FIGURE	CHART POSITION	APPRECIATION INDEX
1: *A Land of Fear*	8/8/1964	5:15-5:40pm	6.9M	37th	58
2: *Guests of Madame Guillotine*	15/8/1964	5:15-5:40pm	6.9M	35th	54
3: *A Change of Identity*	22/8/1964	5:30-5:55pm	6.9M	34th	55
4: *The Tyrant of France*	29/8/1964	5:15-5:40pm	6.4M	36th	53
5: *A Bargain of Necessity*	5/9/1964	5:30-5:55pm	6.9M	39th	53
6: *Prisoners of Conciergerie*	12/9/1964	5:30-5:55pm	6.4M	38th	55

CLIFFHANGERS

1. The Doctor, who lies unconscious in a locked room, remains unaware that a fire is spreading all around him.
2. Imprisoned in the Conciergerie Prison, Ian watches on, from his prison cell, as Barbara and Susan are taken away to be executed by the guillotine.
3. The Shopkeeper who provides The Doctor with his disguise arrives at the Conciergerie Prison and informs the Jailer that he has information about a traitor. The Shopkeeper then holds out The Doctor's ring.
4. Ian meets up with Léon Colbert in a disused church when they are suddenly surrounded by Revolutionary Soldiers. Ian has walked into a trap because Colbert is aiming a pistol at Ian.
5. Arriving at Jules Renan's house, The Doctor has brought Lemaitre with him. Jules exclaims that "they have been betrayed by The Doctor."
6. The episode ends with a shot of a starry landscape, with The Doctor's voice exclaiming that they must find their destiny in the stars.

COMMERCIAL RELEASES

- **AUDIOBOOK:** June 2022
- **DVD:** January 2013
- **NOVELISATION: [Hardback]** – 19 March 1987; **[Paperback]** – August 1987
  - *Target Doctor Who Library Number*: **119**
- **SOUNDTRACK**
  - **6 February 2006:** *BBC Audio*
  - **5 August 2010:** *The Lost TV Episodes – Collection One*
- **VIDEO:** November 2003

CONTINUITY NOTES

- The French Revolution was previously mentioned in *An Unearthly Child* when Barbara lent Susan a book on the subject and the latter noted some historical inaccuracies.
- The Doctor later revisits Paris in the sixteenth century in *The Massacre* and coincidently arrives during another period of violence in French History.
- Napoleon Bonaparte later appears in **PROSE:** *World Game* and **AUDIO:** *The Curse of Davros*.
- This is the first time where The Tardis materialises without making its trademark wheezing noise. According to River Song in *The Time of Angels* the Tardis is not supposed to make a noise. Variations of the Tardis materialising can be seen in; *The Keys of Marinus, The Aztecs, Colony in Space, Planet of Evil, The Brain of Morbius,* and *The Invasion of Time.*
- The Doctor comments that The Tardis has only ever displayed two major faults; the chameleon circuit, a call back to *An Unearthly Child* and the fast return switch, a reference to *The Edge of Destruction*.
- Whilst incarcerated, Barbara is reminded of her imprisonment in the Cave of Skulls. Barbara also claims that she has learned her lesson about interfering with time from her experiences in fifteenth-century Mexico.
- The Doctor assumes a guise of a Regional Officer of the Provinces during the story; other disguises The Doctor will go to use include: a Monk in *The Time Meddler,* Zephon in *The Daleks' Master Plan,* a Redcoat, Washer Woman, and German

- Doctor in *The Highlanders*, an alien student in *The War Games*, a Milkman in *The Green Death*, a Robot Mummy in *Pyramids of Mars*, Harrison Chase's Chauffuer in *The Seeds of Doom*, Hieronymous in *The Masque of Mandragora*, a Sea Base guard in *Warriors of the Deep*, a Miner in *The Mark of the Rani*, a Pilot Fish in *The Runaway Bride*, plus many, many others.
- The serial marks the first time where The Tardis lands in a country of Europe. Further travels in Europe occur in Italy in *The Romans* and *The Masque of Mandragora*, Scotland in *The Highlanders*, Hungary in *The Enemy of the World*, Wales in *The Green Death* and *Delta and the Bannermen*, Holland in *Arc of Infinity*, Spain in *The Two Doctors*, France in *The Girl in the Fireplace,* and Germany in *Let's Kill Hitler*.
- The serial marks the first time in the show's history where alcohol is consumed on-screen. Alcohol will later be consumed by Romans in *The Romans*, Salamander in *The Enemy of the World*, Morgan in *Colony in Space*, Irongron in *The Time Warrior*, and The Third Doctor in *Day of the Daleks* plus others.

CRITICAL RESPONSE

- **Review Range:** Negative-Mixed
- *Doctor Who Magazine 2014 Poll*: 170th/241st
- MMG Oborski, secretary of the Napoleon I Society wrote a letter to the production office which was received on Saturday 12 September 1964. Oborski was heavily critical of the historical inaccuracies of the depiction and portrayal of Napoleon in the serial, also commenting that the BBC should not 'miseducate children'.
- Another letter of complaint commented on the fact that everyone in the serial spoke with English accents. Script Editor **David Whitaker** responded to the letter soon afterwards.
- The *Daily Worker* carried a piece written by **Stewart Lane** on Saturday 31 October negatively commenting on the serial during publicity for *Planet of Giants*.
- Further reviews praised the humour and **Hartnell's** increased role in the narrative but have criticized the over-long story, and the presumption that all viewers have an extensive knowledge of the Revolutionary War.
- One review commented that **Susan Foreman** was at her weakest during the story.

DEATHS

DEATH	CHARACTER	TIME OF DEATH	CAUSE OF DEATH
1	Rouvray	00:17:41	Shot dead by a Soldier
2	D'Argenson	00:18:08	Shot dead by a Soldier
3	Webster	00:35:18	Dies from his wounds
4	Soldier	00:56:06	Shot dead by Jules Renan
5	Soldier	00:56:15	Shot dead by Jean
6	Soldier	00:56:29	Shot dead by Jules Renan
7	Soldier	01:47:35	Shot dead by Jules Renan
8	Soldier	01:48:01	Shot by Leon Colbert
9	Léon Colbert	01:48:15	Shot by Jules Renan

FILMING LOCATIONS

- Ealing Film Studio Stage 3
- Ealing Film Studios Stage 3A
- Isle of Wight Farm, Gerards Cross, *Bucks*
- Lime Grove Studio G
- Television Centre Studio 4
- White Plains, Denham Green, *Buck*

INFLUENCES

- **BOOK:** *A Tale of Two Cities* (1859, Charles Dickens).
- **BOOK:** *The Scarlet Pimpernel* (1905, Baroness Orczy).

PRODUCTION ERRORS

1. There are historical misrepresentations of both Napoleon and Robespierre throughout the serial particularly the meeting scene where Napoleon and Barras plan to overthrow Robespierre.
2. Before the Tardis lands in the countryside the hum noise in the control room can be heard seconds prior.
3. The dying message which Webster gives to Ian consists of 'Le Chien Oris' and Jules Renan', yet Ian passes on the message with additional information consisting of a sinking ship and Paul Barrass.
4. At one point during the story, Danielle mistakenly refers to Jean as 'John'.
5. Jules Renan claims that his escape line works on first name basis only, then why does he know two of the people on it as D'Argenson and Rouvray?
6. During the story, Léon Colbert mentions the 'fall of the Bastille', and says that the historical fortress fell six years ago. This is incorrect as the fortress was stormed and captured on 14 July 1789, whilst the rest of the story takes place over a few days in July 1794.
7. Coincidentally the clothes found by The Time Travellers during "A Land of Fear" fit them perfectly.
8. For some odd and strange reason everyone in the serial speaks with English accents – this has been commented on by many, many reviewers.
9. What are the odds that the clothes the Time Travellers find fit them perfectly?
10. There are couple of technical difficulties during "A Land of Fear" when the time travellers explore the country house. A camera clearly collides with an object off-screen, and a boom mic shadow can be seen.

PUBLICITY

- The serial was promoted in the *Radio Times* (8-14 August 1964) with a quarter-page review and illustrated with a photograph showing The Doctor in combat with a revolutionary soldier.
- The final episode of the serial "Prisoners of Conciergerie" was also promoted in the *Radio Times* and included a black and white photograph of **William Hartnell**. The photograph was, however, from the publicity session for *100,000BC*, and not *The Reign of Terror*.

WORKING TITLES

- Episode 2: Guest of the Guillotine

VERDICT: An entertaining story with plenty of plot twist and surprises, where regular changes of location keeps things highly entertaining, but is a let-down in terms of its historical inaccuracy. The serial is a mixture of highs and lows which is a shame because **The Reign of Terror** is a 'fine' piece of television, but the final result is far from being perfect. It is here where Susan Foreman becomes exceedingly tiring, and the quirky way she calls The Doctor 'grandfather' becomes a tiring writing tool which results in some very dated plot devices. Not good, considering the show was only a few months old at the time. There is some excellent practical effects work at the helm here, as well as some experimental camera work. The writing at time feels very chaotic and rather confused, which is no surprise considering the serial has the 'misfortune' of carrying a large-sized cast, most of whom only appear for a maximum of two episodes. A chaotic storyline and a massive list of characters will continually be a terrible mix for the show over the years. There is also a hidden subplot concerning the violence and rising tension amidst the French Revolution, which although never actually depicted onscreen can be felt throughout; the falling guillotine blade at the start of episode two, Barbara and Susan being escorted for execution off-screen, the deaths of D'Argenson and Rouvray by gunfire etc. The villains of the piece are just typically power hungry and money driven, only in it for themselves revolutionaries, clichéd motivations seen many times before. These not the worst villains by any means, some of them are brilliantly acted, just bland. **The Reign of Terror** also has some witticism here and there resulting in some very funny moments, which brings the serial back to the surface level despite its many flaws. As for the Napoleon side of the story, that should have ended up on the cutting room floor. ***

9) PLANET OF GIANTS

Plot: The Tardis doors open mid-flight and the crew find they have been shrunk down in size to a mere few inches.

CAST

Dr Who	William Hartnell
Ian Chesterton	William Russell
Barbara Wright	Jacqueline Hill
Susan Foreman	Carole Ann Ford
Forester	Alan Tilvern
Smithers	Reginald Barratt
Farrow	Frank Crawshaw
Hilda Rowse	Rosemary Johnson
Bert Rowse	Fred Ferris

CREDITS

Written by Louis Marks
Title Music by Ron Grainger
  with the BBC Radiophonic Workshop
Incidental music by Dudley Simpson
Costumes supervised by Daphne Dare
Make-up supervised by Sonia Markham
Lighting: Howard King
Sound mixing by Alan Fogg
Story Editor: David Whitaker
Designer: Raymond P Cusick
Producer: Verity Lambert
Directed by Mervyn Pinfield, Douglas Camfield

ACTOR BIOGRAPHIES: **Alan Tilvern** was a successful movie actor who appearance in *Captain Horatio Hornblower R.N.* (1951), *Bhowani Junction* (1956), *Tank Force* (1958), *Rasputin: The Mad Monk* (1966), *The Frozen Dead* (1966), *Love and Death* (1975), *Superman* (1978), *Firefox* (1982), *Little Shop of Horrors* (1986), *A Time of Destiny* (1988) and *Who Framed Roger Rabbit* (1988); **Reginald Barratt** landed semi-regular roles in *The Three Musketeers* (1954) and *Gamble for a Throne* (1961); **Fred Ferris** appeared in *The Plane Makers* (1963-64).

BEHIND-THE-SCENES

- **Number of Production Days:** 6
- The idea of a serial involving The Doctor and his companions being shrunk down in size was sought out by **Sydney Newman** during the show's development process. The serial in question 'Nothing at the End of the Lane' would have featured the show's main character being shrunk down in size inside the Doctor's ship.
- On Thursday 16 May 1963, the idea was refined and became known as 'The Giants'. The four-part story would have featured the time travellers being shrunk down in size in Ian Chesterton's school laboratory. The time travellers would have battled many dangers in the classroom. However on Monday 10 June 1963, **Sydney Newman** rejected the scripts citing character development problems, and the 'bug-eyed monsters' (giant spiders in the script) that appeared in the scripts.
- However the production team were still very keen to keep the 'miniscule' serial idea alive, and in September 1963 writer **Robert Gould** was approached to come up with an idea for the proposed serial. Gould began scripting on Friday 27 September 1963 but by January 1964, the serial was dropped from its original slot, and by February, Gould approached **David Whitaker** about submitting another story idea. Producer **Verity Lambert** dismissed the idea fearing it would be too similar to *The Day of the Triffids*. The writer subsequently withdrew his name to write for the series, and nothing was carried forward.
- Still keen to produce a 'miniscule' story, **David Whitaker** called writer **Louis Marks** about the possibility of writing for the show. On Monday 23 March, Whitaker contacted Marks about writing a serial where the main characters are shrunk down in size and by April, Marks was commissioned to write the storyline only,
- Whilst writing his storyline, **Louis Marks** was heavily influenced by the book *Silent Spring* written by **Rachel Carson** The book documented numerous uses of toxic chemicals produced in the USA in the 1950s, and the terrible consequences they had on the environment and wildlife.
- Friday 14 August 1964 marked the first time composer **Dudley Simpson** worked on the show. **Simpson** would go onto work as the regular music composer until 1980.
- Shawcraft Models, the regular model builders for the show, were required to mend the doors to the Tardis props as they had been damaged during the recording for the first episode
- **Douglas Camfield**, who would go onto become a regular director on the show until 1976, directed his very first episode on the show with the fourth and final part to the story "The Urge to Live". Douglas Camfield made quiet the impact on the show

as **Verity Lambert** praised his work and commitment and informed **Donald Wilson** that she would like to work with him again.
- ➤ *Planet of Giants* would prove to be quite a strain on the crew during the post-production process, as on Monday 19 October, **Donald Wilson** decided that the serial would be cut down to three episodes.
- ➤ Vigorous editing trims were made to all four episodes, resulting in numerous scenes being cut. One scene which was cut from the final version consisted of the Cat (seen at the cliffhanger of episode one) succumb to the effects of DN6. The cat would have featured predominantly in the serial until its demise.
- ➤ It was originally intended that *Planet of Giants* would be the penultimate story for the first season, however the serial was pushed back to open the second season.

BROADCAST

EPISODE	DATE	TIME	VIEWING FIGURE	CHART POSITION	APPRECIATION INDEX
1: *Planet of Giants*	31/10/1964	5:15-5:40pm	8.4M	37th	57
2: *Dangerous Journey*	7/11/1964	5:15-5:40pm	8.4M	45th	58
3: *Crisis*	14/11/1964	5:15-5:40pm	8.9M	33rd	59

CLIFFHANGERS

1. Forester murders Farrow to prevent him revealing the truth about DN6. As the Time Travellers approach Farrow's corpse, Susan realises they are being watched by a giant cat.
2. The Doctor and Susan hide in an overflow pipe attached to a laboratory sink. Smithers fills the sink with water, washes his hands, and pulls the plug out.
3. With Forster's plans now at an end, the Time Travellers return to the Tardis where The Doctor looks forward to discovering their next destination.

COMMERCIAL RELEASES

- ➤ **AUDIOBOOK:** May 2017
- ➤ **DVD:** August 2012
- ➤ **NOVELISATION:** [Paperback] – 18 January 1990
    - ➤ *Target Doctor Who Library Number*: **145**
- ➤ **VIDEO:** January 2002

CONTINUITY NOTES

- ➤ Before the Time Travellers discover they have been shrunk down in the size, Ian ponders what kind of planet would support giant-insects, he later finds out in **The Web Planet** with the giant-ant Zarbi.
- ➤ *Planet of Giants* marks the first time where The Doctor is shrunk down in size, but it isn't his last. The Doctor is later shrunk down in size in **Carnival of Monsters, The Invisible Enemy,** and **The Armageddon Factor** plus others whilst The Master himself is no more than a few inches high in **Planet of Fire**.
- ➤ An emergency klaxon can be heard in The Tardis which is similar to the cloister bell first heard in **Logopolis** and again in **The Waters of Mars** which alerts the Doctor to imminent danger.
- ➤ The Doctor mentions he once experienced an air raid during the First World War. The Doctor will later land during an air raid in **The Empty Child/The Doctor Dances** in his ninth incarnation.
- ➤ The exact location of the serial in not wholly evident, however Farrow's comments about 'going on holiday to France' would suggest the story takes place somewhere along the south coast.

CRITICAL RESPONSE

- ➤ **Review Range:** Mixed
- ➤ *Doctor Who Magazine 2014 Poll*: 214th/241st
- ➤ At a BBC Programme Review Board meeting, **Hugh Greene** noted his dissatisfaction with the first episode, and was equally unimpressed with the second, Greene stressed that he hoped the Daleks would return soon.

- ➢ Further reviews have praised the story's ambitious nature and set designs, but the characterisation of Barbara, the music score and the pacing and structure of the episodes have been criticised.
- ➢ Writing in *The Discontinuity Guide*, **Paul Cornell, Martin Day,** and **Keith Topping** found the series to be a mixed bag of elements paying close attention to the mixture of ecological science, cops and gangsters. They found the serial to be 'fun' but felt that the serial didn't really represent the series as a whole.
- ➢ Writing in *The Television Companion*, **David J. Howe** and **Stephen James Walker** concluded they didn't understand why the serial was considered to be important to the production team. They described the plot as slow but praised **Jacqueline Hill**'s performance, they weren't taken-in by **Carole Ann Ford**.
- ➢ For *DVD Talk*, **John Sinnott** wrote that the serial was solid but wrote 'negatively' on the fact that the main characters never interact with the antagonists.
- ➢ Writing for *SFX*, **Dave Golder** concluded the plotting and pacing were slow, the scripts were heavy in dialogue, and lacked overall excitement. He criticised **Jacquline Hill**'s realisation of Barbara.

DEATHS

DEATH	CHARACTER	TIME OF DEATH	CAUSE OF DEATH
1	Earthworm	00:06:38	Victim of DN6
2	Ant	00:07:51	Victim of DN6
3-8	Ants	00:09:30	Victim of DN6
9	Bee	00:18:48	Victim of DN6
10	Farrow	00:20:00	Shot dead by Forester
11	Fly	00:41:02	Victim of DN6

FILMING LOCATIONS

- ➢ Ealing Film Studios
- ➢ Television Centre Studio 4

INFLUENCES

- ➢ **BOOK:** *Gulliver's Travels* (1726, Jonathan Swift)
- ➢ **BOOK:** *Silent Spring* (1962, Rachel Carson)
- ➢ **FILM:** *The Incredible Shrinking Man* (1957, Jack Arnold)
- ➢ **TV:** *Dixon of Dock Green* (1944-76, Ted Willis)

PRODUCTION ERRORS

1. The Doctor mentions that he has never been to Africa. This may have been incorrect if the Tribe of Gum did, in fact, live in Africa, a possibility The Doctor cannot confirm or deny.
2. Two more boom mics enter the frame throughout the serial.
3. Frank Crawshaw blinks a few times after his character Farrow has been murdered.
4. The Time Travellers sees first-hand the devasting effects DN6 has on the environment and wildlife, so why dose Barbara without the fact that she has been infected?
5. Could Forester really disguise his voice as Farrow's by holding a handkerchief over the telephone?
6. At the end of "Dangerous Journey", Smithers unplugs the sink plug and leaves it outside of the sink. However, in "Crisis", when Ian and Barbara go to check for the Doctor and Susan, the plug is in the sink.
7. When investigating the garden, Ian and Barbara find a matchbox between the garden slabs, but when Forester picks it up later, it is on the grass.

PUBLICITY

- The new season was promoted in the *Radio Times* as a one-page article which previewed many of the serials from the previous year. The article included a picture of Ian and Susan face-to-face with the 'giant' ant.
- *The Daily Sketch* also carried a photograph of Ian and Susan and the 'giant' ant as part of an article entitled *Dr Who is Back Again*.

WORKING TITLES

- The Miniscules
- Episode 2: Death in the Afternoon

VERDICT: An ambitious idea brought to life by super-sized sets and props, **Planet of Giants** is both something to be desired, and a giant creative mess. The plot opens up well with the Time Travellers believing they must have landed on an alien planet with giant Insects; only to discover they are actually on Earth, in the middle of an ordinary garden. Things then go at a tangent where a greedy businessman wants to make a quick buck by exploiting a dangerous new chemical for his own selfish needs. Not exactly the most original idea that could have come from this highly experimental three-part series. A far better story would have pitted the time travellers in a garden full of dangers whilst trying to find a way to restore them to full size. The direction is generally all around top notch – **Douglas Camfield** helmed 'Crisis' and will go onto to become the show's top billing director of all time, and there are some great production values with the puppet insects, but on the whole **Planet of Giants** is nothing that special. ***

10) THE DALEK INVASION OF EARTH

Plot: In the twenty-first century the Daleks are the masters of Earth who plan to replace Earth's core with a powerful engine, thus allowing the Daleks to steer the planet Earth around the cosmos to invade and conquer other planets.

CAST

Dr Who	William Hartnell
Ian Chesterton	William Russell
Barbara Wright	Jacqueline Hill
Susan Foreman	Carole Ann Ford
Carl Tyler	Bernard Kay
David Campbell	Peter Fraser
Dortmun	Alan Judd
Robomen	Martyn Huntley, Peter Badger
Daleks	Robert Jewell, Gerald Taylor, Nick Evans, Kevin Manser, Peter Murphy
An Insurgent	Robert Aldous
Dalek Voices	Peter Hawkins, David Graham
Jenny	Ann Davies
Craddock	Michael Goldie
Thomson	Michael Davis
Baker	Richard McNeff
Larry Madison	Graham Rigby
Wells	Nicholas Smith
Slyther	Nick Evans
Ashton	Patrick O'Connell
The Women in the Woods	Jean Conroy, Meriel Hobson
Roboman in River	Kenton Moore
Robomen	Reg Tyler, Billy Moss, John Caesar, Peter Diamond, Adrian Drotsky
Dalek	Ken Tyllsen
Male Freedom Fighters	Tony Lambden, David Graham, Peter Honeywell, Leonard Woodrow, Nigel Bernard, Pat Gorman, Peter Holmes, Michael Reed, Tony Poole, John Doye, Steve Pokol, Peter Diamond, Joe Hardesty, Roy Curtiss
Female Freedom Fighters	Rosina Stewart, Molly Prescott, Susanne Charise, Roma Milne
Child Freedom Fighter	Patricia Phipps
Slaves/Prisoners Down Mine	Maureen Lane, Jan Wills, Jo Calvert, Margo Hanson, Daphne Green, Stenson Falcke, Don Symons, Tony Walsh, John Sackville West, Rex Rashley, George Dare, Nigel Bernard, Alan Wakeling
Prisoners Down Mine	Janos Kurchi, Peter Norton, Jim Appleby, John Timberlake, Leslie Wilkinson, Fred Taylor, Graham Tunbridge, Steve Pokol, Bill McAllister
Slaves	20 Male and 10 Female Extras
[unknown character]	Ted Merwood
Double for Doctor Who	Edmund Warwick
Stunt Double for Roboman in River	/Peter Diamond
Stunt Double for Ian Chesterton	Peter Diamond
Stuntman	Peter Diamond

CREDITS

Written by Terry Nation
Fights Arranged by Peter Diamond
Title Music by Ron Grainger
  with the BBC Radiophonic Workshop
Incidental Music composed and conducted
  by Francis Chagrin
Film Cameraman: Peter Hamilton
Film Editor: John Griffiths
Costumes Supervised by Daphne Dare
Make-Up Supervised by Sonia Markham
Lighting: Howard King
Sound Mixing: Jack Brummitt
Designer: Spencer Chapman
Associate Producer: Mervyn Pinfield
Producer: Verity Lambert
Directed by Richard Martin

ACTOR BIOGRAPHIES: Alan Judd appeared in the television series Jury (1983); **Nicholas Smith** landed regular roles in *Z-Cars* (1972-75), *Are You Being Served?* (1972-85), *Grace & Favour* (1992-93) and lent his voice to the *Wallace and Gromit* movie *The Curse of the Were-Rabbit* (2005); **Ann Davies** appeared in *Paradise Postponed* (1986); **Michael Goldie** made appearances in various films including *The Horror of Frankenstein* (1970), *The Pied Piper* (1972) and *Robin Hood: Prince of Thieves* (1991); **Peter**

Fraser appeared in *Deadline Midnight* (1961); **Graham Rigby** was Charlie Forward to *Crossroads: Kings Oak* (1965-79); uncredited **John Timberlake** landed uncredited movie roles in *Village of the Damned* (1960), and *An American Werewolf in London* (1981).

BEHIND-THE-SCENES

- **Number of Production Days:** 10
- As *The Dalek Invasion of Earth* would complete the show's first 52 episode run, plans for the show's future were being put forth throughout March 1964. **David Whitaker** suggested that the show should have a senior writer, putting **Terry Nation** forward as a possible candidate for the position. However **Donald Baverstock** was not convinced that the show had sufficient storylines which would warrant another 52 weeks of episodes.
- Nothing more was said about the show's new contract until Wednesday 20 May, when **Sydney Newman** took **Terry Nation**'s storyline -The Return of the Daleks-, to a meeting and called **Donald Baverstock** out, and demanded the show be given adequate studio space if *Doctor Who* was to survive. Newman stressed that if an agreement wasn't met the show should be cancelled instead of being produced with minimal support.
- Further plans for the show's second-year run were being put forth during June 1964. **Donald Wilson** suggested that -The Return of the Daleks- could be followed with another six-part serial with Barbara Wright being dropped altogether. Plans also were being put forward to replace Susan with a younger girl. However, Wilson's plans would only be put in place if the show was to continue after his envisioned six-part serial.
- The draft script for "World's End" was slightly different from the broadcast. During the scene where Susan climbed the girders, an owl flew out towards her causing the character to fall and lose consciousness. **Terry Nation** put forth some location ideas whilst writing the script for "World's End". Terry Nation suggested using Ludgate Hill and Piccadilly Circus during the episode for two separate scenes.
- The character of Jenny was originally named Saida, who was originally going to be revealed to Dortmun's daughter, after the former had been killed by The Daleks. It was envisioned that 'Saida' would be the character who would eventually replace Susan.
- The fourth episode of the serial was originally titled "The Abyss" during which the Slyther made its first appearance. **Terry Nation** originally described the Slythers as 'huge black jellyfish'. There was originally going to be more than one Slyther in the episode since the cliff-hanger would involve Robbie (a character whom Ian rescued early in the episode), and Ian being surrounded by several Slythers.
- The draft script for "The Walking Ally" originally had three women living in the woods (there would eventually be two in the finished programme). **Terry Nation** described them as 'three old crones' linking their appearance to the three witches at the start of *Macbeth*.
- Before recording for the serial began, there were still problems behind-the-scenes involving the show's future. **Verity Lambert** was concerned that **Donald Baverstock** had not given the show an adequate extension. On Tuesday 11 August 1964, Verity Lambert outlined her problem to Baverstock. Since a four-part serial was scheduled to precede the six-part Dalek serial, there would be little point in writing out Susan, since another actress would only be contracted for a short period. This would result in **Carole Ann Ford** being re-contracted against her wishes. Verity Lambert also suggested that unless a resolution could be sorted, the show should be cancelled outright.
- On Wednesday 12 August, **Baverstock** was given three options on the show's future. 1) The ending of the six-part Dalek story should be rewritten to end the show entirely. 2) Extending the show until the end of January or 3) Granting the show an extra thirteen episodes until the end of March. Donald Baverstock *eventually* granted a further thirteen episodes on Friday 14 August.
- With the show's foreseeable future now certain, plans went ahead to cast the show's new regular. **Verity Lambert** wished to cast **Pamela Franklin** in the role of 'Saida'. However, the decision was made that the new companion would be introduced in the next serial.
- Sunday 23 August 1964 marked the very first MAJOR film shot for the show. Whilst recording on location, **Ann Davies** wore a balaclava to disguise the fact that her hair had yet to be dyed blonde for studio recording. Recording on the serial proved to be a difficult affair for the actors operating the Daleks. Since it took a long time to get the actors in and out of the Dalek casings, the actors pedalled themselves between locations.
- The cliff-hanger for the first episode, "World's End", was shot on location with **Robert Jewell** operating the aquatic Dalek. Robert Jewell had great difficulty performing the scene, so a cable was attached to the Dalek casing, the cable was of course hidden off-camera.

- Location filming also marked the very first time a quarry was used in the show. John's Hole Quarry in Dorset was used for the Dalek mine sequences.
- During camera rehearsals for "Day of Reckoning", **William Hartnell** was briefly paralysed after colliding with a camera steering wheel. Whilst rehearsing a scene, **Richard McNeff's** leg buckled without warning when he was carrying William Hartnell down a ramp causing Hartnell to fall. It turned out that the ramp had been damaged due to extras playing Prisoners and Robomen not breaking their step when walking up and down the ramp. Hartnell continued to rehearse regardless but required bed rest soon afterwards. However, William Hartnell was in no shape to appear in "The End of Tomorrow", the episode was rewritten, and **Edmund Warwick,** who previously appeared in *The Keys of Marinus*, was hired as a stand-in.
- Observant viewers will notice that various signs reading VETOED appear all over the place. This in an in-joke by the design team. At the BBC, the word VETOED would be stamped across set designers' plans if they were felt to be too ambitious for a show's budget, a common problem faced by **Raymond Cusick**.

BROADCAST

EPISODE	DATE	TIME	VIEWING FIGURE	CHART POSITION	APPRECIATION INDEX
1: *World's End*	21/11/1964	5:40-6:05pm	11.4M	12th	63
2: *The Daleks*	28/11/1964	5:40-6:05pm	12.4M	10th	59
3: *Day of Reckoning*	5/12/1964	5:40-6:05pm	11.9M	10th	59
4: *The End of Tomorrow*	12/12/1964	5:40-6:05pm	11.9M	11th	59
5: *The Waking Ally*	19/12/1964	5:40-6:05pm	11.4M	18th	58
6: *Flashpoint*	26/12/1964	5:55-6:20pm	12.4M	12th	60

CLIFFHANGERS

1. The Doctor and Ian are surrounded by Robomen. The Doctor instructs Ian to dive into the Thames to escape. As they turn around, a Dalek emerges from the river, preventing them from escaping.
2. The Doctor lies on a bench beneath a robotising machine; the Dalek Commanders gives the order for The Doctor to be turned into a Roboman.
3. The Doctor, Susan and David wait anxiously to make their escape. Unknown to them two Robomen place a deadly explosive on walkway above them. The explosive begins its countdown.
4. Ian and Larry are trapped at the top of a mine shift as the vicious Slyther closes in on them.
5. Ian hides inside a capsule which he finds in the Dalek control room. What Ian does not realise is, the capsule is a deadly bomb which begins to descend underground.
6. Having decided that Susan should remain on Earth, The Doctor dematerialises the Tardis. Susan drops her Tardis key to the ground and walks away. An image of a starscape closes the episode.

COMMERCIAL RELEASES

- **AUDIOBOOK:** November 2009
- **DVD:** June 2003
- **ELECTRONIC MUSIC/SOUND EFFECTS**
  - **5 July 1993:** *Doctor Who: 30 Years at the BBC Radiophonic Workshop*
- **NOVELISATION:** [Hardback/Paperback]- 24 March 1977; [Reissues] 1980; 1983; 1990; 1991
  - *Target Doctor Who Library Number*: **17**
- **VIDEO:** May 1990

CONTINUITY NOTES

- Susan Foreman becomes the first regular to leave the series, having grown tired of her character's slow development over the last year. Carole Ann Ford later reprises Susan in *The Five Doctors*.

- The Robomen are very similar to the Cybermen introduced in ***Rise of the Cybermen/The Age of Steel*** whereby once the Daleks' mind control wears off, the converted humans go insane and take their own lives. When a Cyberman is given its humanity back, it ends up dying from the pain caused by their upgrade.
- This is the first Dalek story where the Daleks have a circular disc added to their casing, which explains how they are able to function outside of their city on Skaro, since the Daleks required a steady flow of electricity to function inside of their city.
- Whilst they don't appear again on TV, other Slythers appear in **PROSE:** *War of the Daleks*, **PROSE:** *Legacy of the Daleks*, the **GRAPHIC NOVEL:** *The Only Good Dalek* and **AUDIO:** *Master of Earth*
- The Slyther is the first alien creature native to Skaro who is used by The Daleks for their own gain and needs. Other Skaro creatures used by the Daleks include the Varga Plants in ***Mission to the Unknown***. Other creatures that are subject to the devastating actions by both Thal and Kaleds (who later became the Daleks) include the Mutos and other Animal Mutations in ***Genesis of the Daleks***.
- The Robomen mark the first time where the Dalek employ the use of humans for their own evil gains. The Dalek will later 'recruit' humans voluntarily or involuntarily in ***Resurrection of the Daleks***, ***Remembrance of the Daleks*** and ***Daleks in Manhattan/Evolution of the Daleks*** with the Human Dalek Army.
- The Daleks are commanded by a Supreme Controller, which has a black casing. This is the first time where the Daleks differ by their colour, and every subsequent Dalek story will go on to have at least one Dalek who is different from all the others, This Dalek is always the Dalek Controller or the Supreme Dalek.
- It turns out that The Daleks conquered the Earth by spreading a plague across the Earth. The Daleks will later partake in germ warfare, and other nasty business in: ***Planet of the Daleks, Death to the Daleks***, and ***Resurrection of the Daleks*** where the Daleks hope to find a cure to the Movellan virus.
- It is later revealed in **AUDIO:** *The Wanderer* that The Doctor, Ian, Barbara, and Susan were forewarned by Rasputin that they would later battle strange beings who will invade Earth in the future.
- The Tenth Doctor later recounts the events of the serial in ***The Stolen Earth*** where he comments 'someone tried to move the Earth before', when trying to figure out what how the Earth disappeared.
- Carl Tyler is the first character in the show's history to call The Doctor 'Doc', which The Doctor takes a great dislike to. The Doctor will later berate companions Steven Taylor and Tegan Jovanka for calling him Doc.
- In **PROSE:** *Return of the Living Dead* The Seventh Doctor is menaced by a Dalek agent who plans to make sure the Dalek's invasion of Earth occurs earlier.
- In **PROSE:** *GodEngine* The Seventh Doctor returns to the place where Susan drops her Tardis key after departing from her grandfather. In **PROSE:** *A Time & a Place* The Seventh Doctor also deliver's Susan broken shoe, now mended, to her.
- The Third Doctor will later discover in ***Day of the Daleks*** that The Daleks launched a successful invasion of Earth in the 22nd century. Whether or not these two invasion are the same or different remains unknown.

CRITICAL RESPONSE

- **Review Range:** Generally Positive
- *Doctor Who Magazine 2014 Poll*: 47th/241st
- The serial was highly regarded at a BBC Programme Review Board meeting on Wednesday 25 November and the Audience Research Report dated Tuesday 22 December highlighted viewers thoroughly enjoyed "World's End" although there were some complaints about the lack of Dalek action.
- **Paul Cornell, Martin Day,** and **Keith Topping**, writing in *The Discontinuity Guide,* praised the exterior shots with the Daleks but were less than impressed with the Slyther.
- **David J. Howe** and **Stephen James Walker** writing in *The Television Companion* considered the serial as one of the all-time greats. They praised the script and location filming but felt that the direction was a weak point.
- **Mark Braxton** of *The Radio Times* praised the supporting cast, location filming, and the emotional ending between Susan and The Doctor. However he noted that there were some continuity problems and pointed to the serial's lack of ambition as a result of some production shortcomings.
- **Charlie Jane Anders** of *io9* considered the first cliff-hanger as one of best in the show's history.
- One notable negative review came from **Christopher Bahn** who criticised the slow pacing, the Robomen, and felt that Susan's departure lacked emotional integrity. However, he wrote favourably on the first episode, and cliff-hanger, and praised The Doctor's characterization.

- In another wholly negative review, **Mark Campbell** awarded the serial a 4/10 in his *Doctor Who: The Episode Guide*. He wrote that the serial had clumsy direction and dire modelwork and the whole thing was overambitious for its own good. He praised the built-up in the first episode and Susan's farewell scene, but wrote that the movie version was superior.

DEATHS

DEATH	CHARACTER	TIME OF DEATH	CAUSE OF DEATH
1	Roboman	[00:01:08]	Walks into River Thames
2	Roboman	[00:12:25]	Stabbed in back
3	Thompson	[00:31:46]	Exterminated a Dalek
4	Resistance Fighter	[00:46:41]	Exterminated a Dalek
5	Roboman	[00:49:38]	Stabbed in the back
6	Resistance Fighters	[00:50:53]	Exterminated by a Dalek
7	Resistance Fighter	[00:50:53]	Exterminated by a Dalek
8	Resistance Fighter	[00:51:40]	Shot by a Roboman
9	Resistance Fighter	[00:52:02]	Exterminated by a Dalek
10	Craddock	[00:56:44]	Electrocuted
11	Unknown Character	[00:59:17]	Exterminated by a Dalek
12	Baker	[01:02:13]	Exterminated by a Dalek
13	Dortmun	[1:09:30]	Exterminated by a Dalek
14	Dalek	[1:28:20]	Rundown by a Van
15	Ashton	[1:37:37]	Killed by the Slyther
16	The Slyther	[1:39:51]	Falls down a cliff
17	Roboman	[1:42:24]	Shot dead by Tyler
18	Phil Madison	[1:51:43]	Strangled by Larry Madison
19	Larry Madison	[1:51:46]	Shot dead by Phil Madison
20	Dalek	[2:15:44]	Destroyed from within
21	Dalek	[2:17:16]	Broken in half
22-?	Daleks	[2:18:18-2:18:40]	Destroyed in explosions

FILMING LOCATIONS

- Albert Embankment, *London*
- Albert Memorial, *London*
- Butler's Wharf, Southwick, *London*
- Hammersmith Bridge, Hammersmith, *London*
- Houses of Parliament, *London*
- Irongate Wharf, Tower Hamlets, *London*
- John's Hole Quarry, Stone, *Kent*
- Kew Bridge, Hounslow, *London*
- Palace of Industry, Engineers Way, *Wembley*
- Riverside Studio 1
- Royal Albert Hall, *London*
- St Katherine's Dock, *London*
- Third Way, *Wembley*
- Trafalgar Square, *London*

- Westminster Bridge, *London*
- Wood Lane Underground Station, *London*

INFLUENCES

- **BOOK:** *The War of the Worlds* (1898, H. G. Wells)
- **FILM:** *Things to Come* (1936, William Cameron Menzies)

PRODUCTION ERRORS

1. The dead Roboman in the warehouse can be seen moving at various times.
2. When the Daleks are in Trafalgar Square a van can be seen driving past in the background, when all transportation has been banned.
3. During the "Day of Reckoning" and "Flashpoint" boom mic shadows are visible
4. A couple of crewmember can be seen outside the Dalek's saucer during a scene in "The Daleks".
5. During "The End of Tomorrow" Ashton's shed has windows during interior shots but they are strangely missing during exterior shots.
6. Whilst Barbara is distracting the Dalek Supreme, Jenny is simply miming to do damage to the control instead of actually doing it.
7. When the Tardis lands at the start of "World's End" some of the Tardis windows have caved inwards and no-one seems to notice the damage.
8. When Ian and Larry attack Craddock, Craddock's Roboman helmet falls to pieces.
9. As The Doctor and Tyler climb down the edge of the crater some of the rocks wobble.
10. The Dalek which escorts Barbara and Jenny across the control room of the Dalek saucer can be seen bumping into the Black Dalek.
11. During "Flashpoint", Barbara and Jenny hold their neck manacles in place to stop them from falling off.
12. The dial on the firebomb visibly changes position between scenes.
13. During the scene when Baker and a group of rebel are confronted by a Dalek, a bomb microphone can be seen entering the frame before pulling away.
14. What exactly was a Dalek doing in the Thames in the first place?
15. One camera fails to reach its position after the fight sequence in "The Waking Ally".

PUBLICITY

- On Thursday 12 March 1964, *Television Today* announced that **Carole Ann Ford** would be leaving the series later on in the year. The actress was dissatisfied with Susan's development over the previous months.
- A twenty-second trailer promoted the serial on Saturday 14 November 1964, immediately after the third and final episode of **Planet of Giants**. **Peter Hawkins** narrated the trailer, dating the serial to 2000. The trailer was repeated on Friday 20 November at 8:26pm,
- *The Daily Mirror* ran a small news piece entitled *The Daleks Are Back*. **Verity Lambert** was interviewed for the pieces, and she too dated the serial to the year 2000.
- *The Radio Times* dated Thursday 19 November promoted the serial with a cover of the Daleks, and a half-page article written by **Peter Blake** entitled *The Daleks are Here!*.
- Appearing on *Junior Points of View*, **William Russell** and **Verity Lambert** answered questions about the show as part of the promotion for the upcoming Dalek serial.
- With Dalekmania growing, **David Whitaker** novelized *The Daleks* as *Doctor Who in an exciting adventure with the Daleks*. The novelisation was published by Frederick Muller Ltd on 12 November 1964.
- *Kine Weekly* carried a short-piece which announced that movie producer **Milton Subotsky** was putting forth plans to adapt *The Daleks* for the big-screen. The movie would eventually become *Dr. Who and the Daleks* starring **Peter Cushing** as The Doctor.

WORKING TITLES

- Doctor Who and the Daleks
- The Invaders

➢ The Return of the Daleks

VERDICT: The show's first sequel-ish story demonstrates all lessons from the previous season and goes to great length to produce an overtly brilliant looking production, which is only let down by some silly put together model shots. A larger budget and wider resources are evident in the extensive location shoot, and a wider variety of camera shots all thanks to the move to Riverside Studios, with director **Richard Martin** capturing some intense scenes.

There is some heavy symbolism at play here, continuing on from where *The Daleks* left off, with labour camps, prison escorts, resistance fighters all playing their part. However the symbolism is not the prime focus of the serial, that distinction is where it should be, The Daleks. Writer **Terry Nation** expands the Dalek Universe, rather than repeating it, adding the Robomen and the lumbering Slyther into the mix, giving the Daleks the ability to travel under water, flying spaceships, everything that should be included in a Dalek sequel.

The model work is less than impressive, still bursting with effort, but compared to other serials of the 1960s, they don't quite pop off the screen as they should. The writing at times does feel a little rushed, The Dalek's ultimate goal is not wholly satisfying, in which they plan to hollow out Earth's core, so the planet can be driven throughout the Universe, allowing The Daleks to conqueror and enslave other planets. Okay, but why choose Earth to pilot around the Universe? Why not go for a planet a little closer to Skaro? Despite the totally out there plot, the serial is able to stand-up on its own just because of how bold and ambitious everything is. It was an exciting time back in 1964, The Daleks returned, bigger and better than ever. An instant classic. *****

11) THE RESCUE

Plot: On the planet Dido the survivors of a crashed rocket are held captive by the mysterious Koquillion, but when The Doctor and his companions arrive to help all is not as it seems.

CAST

Dr Who……………………….William Hartnell
Ian Chesterton……………….....William Russell
Barbara Wright……………….   Jacqueline Hill
Vicki……………………….Maureen O'Brien
Bennett……………………….....Ray Barrett
Space Captain……………………...Tom Sheridan
Sand Monster Sandy………………Tom Sheridan
Robed Figures………....John Stuart, Colin Hughes

CREW

Written by David Whitaker
Title Music by Ron Grainger
  with the BBC Radiophonic Workshop
Incidental music by Tristram Cary
Costumes supervised by Daphne Dare
Make-up supervised by Sonia Markham
Designer: Raymond P Cusick
Associate Producer: Mervyn Pinfield
Producer: Verity Lambert
Directed by Christopher Barry

ACTOR BIOGRAPHIES: Ray Barrett appeared in *Emergency-Ward 10* between (1960-61) and *The Troubleshooters* (1965-72). He voiced many characters in *Stingray* (1964-65) and *Thunderbirds* (1965-66). **Maureen O'Brien** made brief appearances in *Emergency-Ward 10* (1966), *The Poisoning of Charles Bravo* (1975), *The Squirrels* (1976-77), and *The Lost Boys* (1978), regular work came with 7 episodes of *The Legend of King Arthur* (1979) and 15 episodes of *Casualty* (1987). Despite being uncredited **John Stuart** was a prolific movie actor whose work includes *Atlantic* (1929), *The Pointing Finger* (1933), *The Black Abbot* (1934), *Abdul the Damned* (1935), *Man on the Run* (1949), *Raiders of the River* (1950), *Quatermass 2* (1957), *Revenge of Frankenstein* (1958), *Blood of a Vampire* (1958), *The Mummy* (1959), *Sink the Bismark!* (1960), *Village of the Damned* (1960), and *Superman* (1978).

BEHIND-THE-SCENES

- **Number of Production Days: 4**
- Much like **The Dalek Invasion of Earth; The Rescue**, also faced pre-production problems due to a lack of communication from **Donald Baverstock** concerning the future of the show. **Verity Lambert** stressed that the offer of a sole four-part story would cause contractual issues for the series regulars. During the confusion, **William Hartnell** was being offered other work, and **William Russell**'s agent was under the impression that the actor would be available for future work at the end of October.
- When the show's future was assured, **Verity Lambert** set about casting **Pamela Franklin** as the new companion. The producer asked for a 19 episode contract to be drawn up for actress, however on Wednesday 19 August 1965, Lambert changed her mind and instead the new-companion would be introduced in a two-part serial written by **David Whitaker**.
- Whilst writing the scripts for **The Rescue**, **David Whitaker** considered naming Vicki, "Valerie" and "Millie". Whitaker originally rejected "Millie" because he felt it would be connected with **Millicent Martin** an actress known for appearing in *That Was the Week That Was* at the time. The character was subsequently renamed "Tanni" and then "Lukki" on Thursday 12 November 1965.
- The original draft scripts for the *Doctor Who and Tanni* (soon to become known as **The Rescue**) were slightly different from the broadcast version. Bennett was originally nastier towards Vicki, yelling at her on multiple occasions, accusing her of antagonising him
- The casting for Vicki was a relatively short process. **Verity Lambert** requested camera-tests for **Maureen O'Brien** and **Denise Upson**. The camera tests were held at Television Centre on Monday 14 September 1965, concluding with Maureen O'Brien being offered the part.
- For the part of Bennett, **Christopher Barry** considered **Bernard Archer** and **John Cronin** before offering the part to **Ray Barrett** who had recently found television stardom during his time on *Emergency-Ward 10*.
- Before production on the serial, **Maureen O'Brien** was 'asked' by **Sydney Newman** to dye her hair black (supposedly so Vicki would look similar to Susan). The actress refused, and blatantly asked Sydney Newman "why don't you just get Carole Ann Ford back?"

- The first scenes to be recorded for the serial were the model sequences of the crashed spaceship. Director **Christopher Barry** worked closely with uncredited film cameraman **Dick Bush** to capture the scenes. Dry ice was used for the mist which surrounded the ship, and sawdust was used for the sandy landscape.
- It was during recording for the serial that, **Mervyn Pinfield** left his role as associate producer, although he would be credited as the Assistant Producer on both *The Rescue* and the succeeding serial *The Romans*.
- The crashed spaceship was made up of three interior compartments; **Raymond Cusick** reused set dressings and props from both *The Daleks* and *The Sensorites*.
- Whilst playing Koquillion, **Ray Barrett** used a high-pitched voice, similar to ones he had previously used during his time on *Stingray*, a popular stop-motion puppet show where he voiced various characters.
- During the recording of "Desperate Measures", **Jacqueline Hill** had to be treated for shock after the powder concealed inside a prop pistol the actress was holding detonated. After recovering from the mishap, **Hill** continued to record the scene where 'Sandy the Sand Monster' emerged from a nearby cave.

BROADCAST

EPISODE	DATE	TIME	VIEWING FIGURE	CHART POSITION	APPRECIATION INDEX
1: *The Powerful Enemy*	2/1/1965	5:40-6:05pm	12.0M	11th	57
2: *Desperate Measures*	9/1/1965	5:40-6:05pm	13.0M	8th	59

CLIFFHANGERS

1. The Doctor and Ian discover a narrow ledge within a cave system after being trapped by Koquillion. As they walk along it, Ian is accidently trapped between two sets of deadly spikes. More spikes emerge from the cave wall pushing Ian towards a cliff edge where a horrific monster waits below.
2. The Tardis dematerialises from Dido and arrives on an edge of the cliff. The Tardis shakes from side to side before falling off-screen, with the Time Travellers still inside.

COMMERCIAL RELEASES

- **AUDIOBOOK:** April 2013
- **DVD:** February 2009
- **NOVELISATION:** [Hardback] – 20 August 1987; [Paperback] – 21 January 1988
  - *Target Doctor Who Library Number*: **124**
- **VIDEO:** September 1994

CONTINUITY NOTES

- During the Tardis scenes, The Doctor mistakenly calls for Susan, forgetting that she is not there. The Doctor goes onto to incorrectly address a companion in *Pyramids of Mars, Castrovalva* and *Attack of the Cybermen*.
- The Doctor, Ian and Barbara talks about their troubles with caves, having battled throughout many systems in *An Unearthly Child, The Daleks, The Keys of Marinus, The Sensorites,* and *The Dalek Invasion of Earth*
- The events of the story could be described as a whodunnit. The Doctor will later be involved in whodunnit scenarios in *The Curse of Peladon, The Robots of Death, Trial of a Time Lord: Vervoids*, and *The Unicorn and the Wasp* (where the culprit in every scenario is so obvious).
- The First Doctor uses the term materialise to explain the Tardis landing for the first time.
- The planet Dido is later mentioned in **AUDIO:** *Maker of Demons,* **PROSE:** *The Empire of Glass,* **PROSE:** *The Tomorrow Windows* whilst the planet Astra (the destination of the crashed spaceship) is later mentioned in **COMIC:** *The Amaryll Challenge*.
- The ending of the serial marks the first 'disastrous' landing of the Tardis, after the ship falls off a cliff edge. Other disastrous landings can be seen in *Fury from the Deep* where the Tardis lands in the middle of the sea, *Inferno* where a test piloting of the console results in The Doctor landing in a rubbish tip, *The Curse of Peladon*, where the Tardis tumbles down a cliff edge, *Warrior's Gate*, where The Tardis lands in a place outside of time and space, *Castrovalva* showcasing the ship landing among vegetation (on its side), *The Trial of a Time Lord: Mindwarp*, where the Tardis lands in water, *Fear Her*, where the

Tenth Doctor lands the Tardis in-between two storage containers, with the door being blocked by one of the containers, and *The Eleventh Hour* where the Tardis crashes into a garden shed.
- Vicki is the first orphan companion to join The Doctor on his travels. Other orphan companions who will later join The Doctor are Victoria Waterfield, Leela, Adric and Nyssa.

CRITICAL RESPONSE

- **Review Range:** Generally Positive
- *Doctor Who Magazine 2014 Poll*: 171st/241st
- After the broadcast of "Desperate Measures", **Sydney Newman** praised the impact **O'Brien** had on the serial, and highlighted that her acting abilities would be a great asset to the show.
- In *The Discontinuity Guide,* **Paul Cornell, Martin Day,** and **Keith Topping** wrote positively on the serial but felt the story was a little inconsequential to have any real impact.
- In *The Television Companion*, **David J. Howe** and **Stephen James Walker** praised the character of Vicki but noted that some story elements were not explained.
- In the *Radio Times*, **Patrick Mulkern** noted the improved production style and commented that the story was a strong debut for Vicki. However he noted that the 'mystery' side to the story was too obvious.
- After the broadcast of "The Powerful Enemy", **T. C. Worsley** writing in the *Financial Times* wrote that Koquillion wasn't on par with The Daleks but appreciated the name of the characters.

DEATHS

DEATH	CHARACTER	TIME OF DEATH	CAUSE OF DEATH
1	Sandy the Sand Monster	[00:31:07]	Shot and killed by Barbara
2	Bennett	[00:44:36]	Falls down a cliff

FILMING LOCATIONS

- Ealing Film Studios Stage 2
- Riverside Studio 1

INFLUENCES

- **FILM:** *It! The Terror from Beyond Space* (1958, Edward L. Cahn)

PRODUCTION ERRORS

1. During, "Desperate Measures", a stagehand can be seen behind Sandy the Sand Monster.
2. The Doctor mentions that he never obtained a medical degree when questioned about his qualifications. However during *The Moonbase*, The Second Doctor tells Polly he achieved a degree whilst studying under Joseph Lister in 1888. The Doctor goes onto provide contradictory information regarding his medical qualifications throughout his incarnations.
3. When exiting The Tardis, the cave wall is visible since The Tardis has no back to it.
4. Throughout the serial, one of the Tardis windows falls inwards. Evidently it had not been fixed from the previous serial where the prop suffered the same issues.
5. The Doctor mentions that the Didoans are a peaceful race that does not understand violence. If that is correct, then why is there a place called the Hall of Justice, and why is there a trap wall with lethal spikes attached? Was the Hall of Justice erected in a small period of time, after Bennett killed a vast majority of the population? This seems unlikely since only two seemingly survived.
6. It's plainly obvious that Bennett is not in the room when Koquillion opens his room door.
7. When Barbara fires a shot at Sandy, the firework, which is the shot, falls off the back of the gun.
8. How did Bennett find out what the 'Koquillion' mask was used for? He couldn't have known about Didoan customs since the *UK-201* was heading for a different planet. Did he ask a Didoan before blowing everyone up to cover up his crime? And what are the odds, that the costume fits him almost perfectly?
9. When Koquillion goes into Bennett's room to speak to him, time passes, and Bennett emerges saying that Koquillion has left. Shouldn't it have seemed odd to Vicki that Koquillion has vanished into thin air? There is no back door in Bennett's

room, and the control room and Bennett's room are connected by a corridor, with no door on either side. How did Koquillion get out without Vicki seeing him?

PUBLICITY

- On Christmas Eve 1964, *Television Today* included an article about **Maureen O'Brien** which promoted her as the new *Doctor Who* companion.
- To disguise the fact **Ray Barrett** played both Bennett and Koquillion. The cast listings for "The Powerful Enemy" created Sydney Wilson as Koquillion. A pseudonym created by coming the first name of **Sydney Newman** and the surname of **Donald Wilson**.

WORKING TITLES

- Doctor Who and Tanni

VERDICT: *The Rescue* marks the first time where *Doctor Who* tries and *fails* to do a whodunnit narrative, where the big reveal at the end is neither surprising nor wholly satisfying. For such a short narrative, very little actually happens, where the plot hangs on a thread, hoping and *failing* to convince the audience that Koquillion is a genuine alien, and not 'some bloke' playing dress up.

Vicki's introduction is squeezed in between the bloke under the mask narrative, but she shows promise to be a worthy successor to Susan. The Doctor has always been made out to be a heroic and highly intelligent being, using his wits and intelligence to save the day. Here, The Doctor doesn't actually solve the mystery behind Koquillion and the crashed spaceship, but rather he just stumbles upon clue after clue as if he's just guessing what he should do next. On a more positive note, The Doctor is shown to be a person of many emotions, hurting at the loss of Susan, but then adopting Vicki who has no family left to return to later on, the pair of them going hand-in-hand. The direction is generally solid, the model shots and sets, the Sand Monster, and Koquillion 'himself' is a solid character and a would-be-monster for the children to be frightened of, but sadly the budget just wouldn't stretch far enough to allow Koquillion to be used in a more fitting manner. *The Rescue* just about works and could have worked, but on the whole feels more like a filler adventure, than proper drama. Still worthy of a watch. ***

12) THE ROMANS

Plot: Whilst having a short relaxing break in first-century Rome, The Doctor and Vicki are separated from Ian and Barbara as the Great Fire of Rome draws near.

CAST

Dr Who	William Hartnell
Ian Chesterton	William Russell
Barbara Wright	Jacqueline Hill
Vicki	Maureen O'Brien
Sevcheria	Derek Sydney
Didius	Nicholas Evans
Centurion	Dennis Edwards
Stall Holder	Margot Thomas
Slave Buyer	Edward Kelsey
Maximus Pettulian	Bart Allison
Ascaris	Barry Jackson
Delos	Peter Diamond
Tavius	Michael Peake
Woman Slave	Dorothy-Rose Gribble
Gallery Master	Gertan Klauber
1st Man in Market	Ernest Jennings
2nd Man in Market	John Caesar
Court Messenger	Tony Lambden
Nero	Derek Francis
Tigilinus	Brian Proudfoot
Poppaea	Kay Patrick
Locusta	Ann Tirard

Women in Market.................Rosemary Devitt
Rilla Madden, Gladys Bacon, Barbara Mansfield
Pat Ambrose, Ursula Granville

Men in Market............John Fay, John de Marco
Frank Wheatley, Harry Davies, George Dale
David Brewster, Ronald Adams, Jack Collins
John Sagar, Nigel Clayton

Children in Market......Dawn Pyke, Gillian Smith
Johnny Wainwright, John Langley

Slaves.................Pat Ambrose, Ursula Granville
Ronald Adams, Jack Collins, John Sagar
Nigel Clayton, Gillian Smith

Woman Slaves............Alison Leney, Terri Dean
Sandra Harris, Tina Kennedy

Gallery Slaves............Vez Delahunt, Roy Reeves
Pat Donoghue, Jim Appleby, Paul Andrews
Tony Lee, Les Wilkinson, Richard Wilding

Woman in Market....................Francesca Bertorelli
Bunty Garland

Men in Market.................Fred Taylor, Terry Leigh
John Little, Tom Sye, Jerry Vidal, John Scammell

Courtiers......................Jim Appleby, Paul Andrews
Soldiers........................Roy Reeves, Pat Donoghue
Guards..........Paul Duval, Janos Kurucz, Allan Selwyn
Gordon Cave, Bill Burridge, Derek Calder
Fred Haggerty, Gerry Wain, Eric Bird, Ross Thomas
James Norton
Gladiators......................Paul Duval, Janos Kurucz
Woman Slaves at Banquet..............Diana Chapman
Alison Leney
Men Slaves at Banquet......Paul Blomley, Steve Peters
Women at Banquet..........Anne Marzeil, Sara Negus
Men at Banquet..............George Fisher, James Lyon
Fred Davies, Dickie Martyn, Ronnie Meade
Michael Essex, Douglas Abercrombie
Rabble............John Day, Frank Sussman, Paul Duval
Tony Poole, Yasha Adams, Michael Baker
Derek Martin, David Cannon, Michael Buck
David Brewster, Bill Richards, Philip Moore
Alfred Morgan, Len Saunders, Alan Jones
Double for Dead Centurion................Vez Delahunt
Double for Dr Who's Hand..................Albert Ward
Stuntmen......................Fred Haggerty, Gerry Wain

CREW

Written by Dennis Spooner
Title music by Ron Grainger
 with the BBC Radiophonic Workshop
Incidental music composed and conducted
 by Raymond Jones
Fight Arranger: Peter Diamond
Costumes Supervised by Daphne Dare
Make-up Supervised by Sonia Markham
Lighting: Howard King
Sound: Richard Chubb
Designer: Raymond P Cusick
Associate Producer: Mervyn Pinfield
Producer: Verity Lambert
Directed by Christopher Barry

ACTOR BIOGRAPHIES: Derek Sydney was best known for his role as Captain Rodrigo in *Sword of Freedom* (1957-59); **Barry Jackson** had a prolific career in Film and TV but is best known for playing Dr. George Bullard in *Midsomer Murders* (1997-2011); **Derek Francis** had a successful Film and TV career and appeared in *The Criminal* (1960), *The Inspector* (1962), *Captain Clegg* (1962), *Bitter Harvest* (1963), *Ring of Spies* (1964), *The Tomb of Ligeia* (1964), *Rasputin: The Mad Monk* (1966), *Carry on Doctor* (1967), *Carry on Camping* (1969), *Man of Violence* (1970), *Scrooge* (1970), *Carry on Henry* (1971), *To the Devil a Daughter* (1976), *Jabberwock* (1977), and *The Wicked Lady* (1983); **Edward Kelsey** lent his voice to many characters in *Danger Mouse* (1981-92); **Bart Allison** appeared in *The Canterbury Tales* (1969).

BEHIND-THE-SCENES

- **Number of Production Days:** 6
- The idea of a *Doctor Who* serial being set in Roman times dates back to the spring of 1964, whilst the production team were putting ideas together for the second season.
- During the planning process, it was intended that **The Romans** would be more comedic and humorous in style, the production team intended for the serial to be a spoof of *Quo Vadis*. However, it soon transpired that *Carry on Cleo* (the tenth film of the popular *Carry On* franchise) was already intended as a spoof of *Quo Vadis*. The film was already in production, as the first day of recording was Monday 20 July 1964.
- The director originally assigned to the serial was **Richard Martin**. However, when the decision was made to produce both **The Rescue** and **The Romans** as one production block, **Christopher Barry** was appointed director, in October 1964.
- Director **Christopher Barry** considered a few actors for the role of Nero before settling on **Derek Francis**, considerations included **Paul Whitsun-Jones, George A. Cooper** and **Dick Emery**.
- The style and tone of the serial was very much liked by **William Hartnell** who enjoyed the opportunity to act in a piece of comedy. The serial also became a firm favourite for **William Russell**.
- To help keep production costs down, many of the set dressings were reused from previous serials. A wall divider frame previously constructed for **The Keys of Marinus** was reused for Nero's palace scenes.
- After the recording of "The Slave Traders" on Friday 18 December 1964, the cast and crew departed for a week's holiday. The decision meant that future episodes of the show would only be recorded three weeks in advance.
- During rehearsals for a fight scene for "All Roads Lead to Rome", **William Hartnell** sustained a slight injury when **Barry Jackson** (Ascaris) accidently hit Hartnell's knuckle with a wooden sword which he wielded. Also during production, **William Russell** also sustained a slight injury, a cut to his left wrist, whilst rehearsing a fight scene alongside stuntman **Peter Diamond**..
- Director **Christopher Barry** went to great length for the recording of the ship gallery scenes caught in the lightning storm. Lighting effects were used to represents the lightning storm, the studio cameras were moved from side to side to stimulate choppy water, and buckets of water were dumped on the cast off-camera to represent sea water crashing into the ship gallery.
- The decision was made to hire Gallery Slave extra, **Vez Delahunt** to stand-in for the corpse of a centurion (originally played by **Dennis Edwards**) to avoid rehiring the actor for a short period of time.
- The third episode of the serial, "Conspiracy" was recorded on Friday 8 January 1965, which happened to be **William Hartnell's** 57th birthday.
- During rehearsals for "Inferno" it was formally announced that **Mervyn Pinfield** had now left the series as associate producer, although he would go on to receive a credit for his work. He would return to the show to direct future serials.

BROADCAST

EPISODE	DATE	TIME	VIEWING FIGURE	CHART POSITION	APPRECIATION INDEX
1: *The Slave Traders*	16/1/1965	5:40-6:05pm	13.0M	7th	53
2: *All Roads Lead to Rome*	23/1/1965	5:40-6:05pm	11.5M	15th	51
3: *Conspiracy*	30/1/1965	5:40-6:05pm	10M	28th	50
4: *Inferno*	6/2/1965	5:40-6:05pm	12M	13th	50

CLIFFHANGERS

1. The Doctor (now posing as Maximus Pettulian) plays a few notes on the dead musician's lyre unaware that a mute assassin, Ascaris is approaching him with a knife in his hand.
2. Ian and Delos are imprisoned and have been informed that they will be trained as Gladiators to fight in the arena. Ian wonders *what* they will be fighting. His queries are answered when he notices a pride of hungry lions outside his cell.
3. Ian and Delos engage in their first fight with each other, in-front of Nero and Barbara. During the fight, Ian loses his balance and Delos holds his sword to Ian's neck. Nero orders Delos to execute Ian.
4. During mid-flight the Tardis is trapped by an unknown force dragging it down to an unknown location.

COMMERCIAL RELEASES

- **DVD:** February 2009
- **NOVELISATION: [Hardback]** – 16 April 1987; **[Paperback]** – 17 September 1987
  - *Target Doctor Who Library Number*: **120**
- **SOUNDTRACK**
  - **8 May 2008**: *BBC Audio*
  - **5 September 2014**: *The TV Episodes - Collection Six*
- **VIDEO:** September 1994

CONTINUITY NOTES

- The Great Fire of Rome is later brought up by The Tenth Doctor in **The Fires of Pompeii** when he tells Donna the fire was not *technically* his fault.
- Emperor Nero is the first monarchical historical figure to feature in the show. Other monarchs who The Doctor goes on to meet include Richard the Lionheart in **The Crusade**, Queen Victoria in **Tooth and Claw**, and Elizabeth I in **The Shakespeare Code** and **The Day of the Doctor**. The Doctor previously mentioned that he met King Henry VIII, who appears very briefly in **The Power of Three**.
- In **AUDIO:** *Starborn*, Vicki refers to her time in Nero's Palace, and comments that 20th century London was not that much advanced to 1st century Rome. Barbara takes great offence to her remark.
- The Doctor assumes the identity of Maximus Pettulian, the first time he openly and willingly acquires a false identity. The Doctor will later assume false identities in **The Power of the Daleks** as an Earth Examiner, **The Curse of Peladon** as a representative from Earth, and **Black Orchid** where he poses as someone also referred to as 'The Doctor'.
- It is later revealed that **PROSE:** *Byzantium!* and **PROSE:** *Romans Cutaway* are set sometime prior to the beginning of **The Romans**, but after the time travellers arrived at the end of **The Rescue**.

CRITICAL RESPONSE

- **Review Range:** Mixed
- *Doctor Who Magazine 2014 Poll*: 131st/241st
- The original response to the serial was somewhat negative. An audience research report dated Tuesday 2 March 1965 found that audience did not enjoy historical stories compared to science-fiction ones. Audiences said that the serial would only be suitable watching for morons, and that it was ridiculous and a bore.
- After the broadcast of "The Slave Traders", **Mary Crozier** wrote negatively towards the episode; describing the dialogue as patchy and the quality as uneven.
- A journalist writing for *The Times* was positive towards the serial calling *Doctor Who* as a great weapon within the BBC. They wrote the adventure promises, and the production was flawless.
- A newspaper article written by a journalist of *The Times* praised "All Roads Lead to Rome" with particular praise for **Verity Lambert** and her team.
- Retrospective reviews have been positive praising the witty dialogue, slapstick comedy, the characterisation of Nero, the comedic direction the serial took, and **William Hartnell's** acting.
- **Christopher Bahn** of *The A.V. Club* wrote that the serial was not overtly interested in being historically accurate but wrote that the serial succeeded with its comedic style and tone.
- Following the broadcast of "Conspiracy", young viewers sent in letter which pointed out that Ian's costume was heavily historically inaccurate.

- An audience report was compiled following the broadcast of "Inferno", where it became obvious that historical serials were not a favourite amongst audiences. Overall the serial was felt to be corny and amateurish, but **William Hartnell** and **Derek Francis'** performances were praised.

DEATHS

DEATH	CHARACTER	TIME OF DEATH	CAUSE OF DEATH
1	Maximus Pettulian	00:08:16	Killed by Ascaris
2	Gallery Master(?)	00:34:47	*death unconfirmed*
3-(?)	Gallery Slaves(?)	00:34:47	*deaths unconfirmed*
4	Centurion	00:45:36	Murdered under the orders of Tavius
5	Tigilinus	01:05:00	Poisoned
6	Guard	01:15:10	Stabbed and Killed by Delos
7	Guard	01:16:19	Stabbed and Killed by Nero
8	Sevcheria	01:29:07	Killed by Delos with a fire torch

FILMING LOCATIONS

- Ealing Film Studios Stage 2
- Riverside Studio 1

INFLUENCES

- **FILM:** *Spartacus* (Stanley Kubrick, 1960)
- **FILM:** *Quo Vadis* (Mervyn Leroy, 1951)
- **FOLKTALE:** *The Emperor's New Clothes* (Hans Christian Andersen, 1837)

PRODUCTION ERRORS

1. A white line appears across the screen after falling wood hits the camera during the ship gallery scene.
2. A boom mic enters the frame when Nero and his wife pick out jewellery.
3. A lens flare occurs across the screen when some of the studio lighting is captured by the camera.
4. During episode one Didius attempts four times to put his sword away before doing so.
5. Ian and Barbara appear to have a plastic-lined fountain.
6. The Fire Staters appear to be paid in metal-washers by Nero.
7. Nero was a much younger man in 64AD, roughly 26-28, and not older as seen in the serial.
8. Nero wasn't in Rome when the fire began, he was in Actium, so the fire was almost certainly an accident.
9. Locusta, although a real historical person, and a maker of poisons, wasn't an 'official poisoner'.
10. The swords used in the serial, are historically inaccurate, they aren't the right shape.
11. When Barbara hugs Ian after being reunited, a zipper can be seen on the back of her dress.

WORKING TITLES

- [no known working titles]

VERDICT: Unlike its historical predecessors, *The Romans* manages to blend both comedy and drama to create scenes intended to give the audience a laugh. **William Hartnell** and **Derek Francis** are the best comedy duo pairing in the show's history, continually playing off on and other, and always trying to outwit the other through visual and verbal jokes. **Dennis Spooner** goes for a more subtle approach to the comedic elements of the story; The Doctor playing the lyre and Nero painstakingly trying not to look like a common fool, the poisoning of the mute Tigilinus, and Nero's reaction are just a couple of highlights. Comedy aside, there is also a darker side to the story, with no cheerfulness in the depiction of slavery and slave labour or gladiator combat. Ian for a while is sold as slave, and is almost killed in a freak storm, we don't find out that Ian survived the shipwreck until later on. It's a haunting image that Ian could have died, and The Doctor would be none the wiser as to the fate of his closest friend. The burning of Rome is also a haunting moment. Firstly, it is The Doctor who inadvertently gives Nero the idea to burn Rome down so he can build a new one, revealing that The Doctor's exploration across space and time does have its consequences. Secondly, Nero is portrayed as a man who can be calm and collective one moment, and diabolically insane the next. Look at the way he cackles whilst playing a lyre as Rome burns. He's the epitome of all villains.

The plot is both sleek and highly engaging, where The Doctor/Vicki and Ian/Barbara continually miss each other, as they venture through Rome, with both pairs remaining oblivious to the other's presence. There's a funny idea at the end, where each pair presumes that the other has been waiting for them to return to the Villa which they have been *borrowing*, without any second thought as to another explanation for their short-term absence. There are a few timing issues, now and again, but it's the comedy which keeps the story afloat.

The Romans is a beautiful piece of television buts it not without its shortcomings. Whilst sets like Nero's palace and the Ship's gallery are a success, others like the country path and market are rather underwhelming and not that visually stunning to look at. Again, these are forgivable due to the brilliant cast, gorgeous costumes, and impressive visual effects: arguably the best historical narrative in *Doctor Who* history. ****

13) THE WEB PLANET

Plot: On the planet Vortis the Animus has taken control and The Doctor and his companions find themselves caught up in a battle between the Zarbi and the Menoptra. If the Animus is to be defeated then both races need to come together

CAST

Dr Who	William Hartnell
Ian Chesterton	William Russell
Barbara Wright	Jacqueline Hill
Vicki	Maureen O'Brien
Vrestin	Roslyn de Winter
Hrostar	Arne Gordon
Hrhoonda	Arthur Blake
Prapillus	Jolyon Booth
Hlynia	Jocelyn Birdsall
Hilio	Martin Jarvis
Hetra	Ian Thompson
Nemini	Barbara Joss
Zarbi	Robert Jewell, Hugh Lund, Kevin Maser, Jack Pitt, John Scott Martin, Gerald Taylor
Animus Voice	Catherine Fleming
Slave Menoptra	Ken McGarvey, Sid Della
Optera Guards	Len Russell, Jane Bowman
Menoptra	Ken McGarvey

CREDITS

Written by Bill Strutton
Insect Movement by Roslyn de Winter
Title Music by Ron Grainger with the BBC Radiophonic Workshop
Film Cameraman: Peter Hamilton
Film Editor: Gitta Zadek
Costume supervised by Daphne Dare
Make-Up supervised by Sonia Markham
Lighting: Ralph Walton
Sound: Ray Angel
Story Editor: Dennis Spooner
Designer: John Wood
Producer: Verity Lambert
Directed by Richard Martin

ACTOR BIOGRAPHIES: Martin Jarvis has had a very successful career making regular appearances in many television series including *The Forsyte Saga* (1967), *Nicholas Nickleby* (1968), *Little Women* (1970), *The Moonstone* (1972), *David Copperfield* (1974), *Rings on Their Fingers* (1978-80), *Breakaway* (1980), *Chelworth* (1989), and 8 episodes of *Eastenders* (2010). Film credits include *Taste the Blood of Dracula* (1970), *First Strike* (1996), *Titanic* (1996) and *United Passions* (2014). Also a prolific voice-actor, the actor has lent his voice for many films and TV Shows including *Man Steel* (2000), *The Grim Adventures of Billy & Mandy* (2003-07) and *Wreck it Ralph* (2012). Video Game voice-over credits include *The Legend of Spyro: The Eternal Night* (2007), *The Legend of Spyro: Dawn of the Dragon* (2008), *Dragon Age: Origins* (2009), *Batman: Arkham City* (2011), *Mass Effect 3* (2012), *Batman: Arkham Origins* (2013) and *Batman: Arkham Night* (2015).

BEHIND-THE-SCENES

- **Number of Production Days:** 12
- Since the Daleks were a major hit with audiences, the production team wasn't interested in writers coming up with another race of 'robotic' monsters for The Doctor to face. So when **Bill Strutton** expressed an interest to write for the show he was asked to come up with 'something different'.
- **Bill Strutton** was commissioned to write his six-part serial on Monday 28 September 1964 by outgoing script editor **David Whitaker**. The writer was not required to write and submit a storyline prior to writing the scripts. The writer was required to submit all six scripts by Friday 13 November 1964.
- **Bill Strutton** was apparently inspired by the idea of insects fighting each other, after witnessing two bull ant engage in a fight in his garden when growing up in Australia. He also took inspiration from his two stepson who would often fight each, and 'lock heads'.
- **Bill Strutton** began to write his scripts whilst moving home, and interestingly the name 'Zarbi' was actually arrived at by his wife. Many of the character's names were inspired by Greek words; for example both Menoptra and Optera derived from the word 'lepidoptera' – the Greek word for the order of insects. Whilst Carsenome came from 'carcinoma' which translates as 'cancerous growth'.
- Some of the characters' names changed during the writing process, Hrostar was originally called Rostar, and Prapillus was named Papillus. The latter's name was inspired by the word 'papilionaceous' which is a Latin word used for butterfly terms.

- In the closing week of 1964, **Dennis Spooner** responded positively to Strutton's scripts but objected to the idea that the Zarbi could spit venom. Eventually Spooner came up with the idea of the larvae guns and gave the new characters the ability to spit venom.
- The director assigned to the serial; **Richard Martin**, was somewhat disappointed with Strutton's scripts, feeling that the dialogue was 'not good' and worked closely with **Dennis Spooner** to amend the scripts. **Richard Martin** believed the serial had great visual potential, but this would be somewhat hampered by the restricted studio space. The director went over budget, and this did not sit well with **Verity Lambert**.
- It was during the pre-production process that a third designer was appointed to work on the show. **John Wood** was appointed as designer after **Raymond Cusick** and **Barry Newbery** requested another designer to work on the second production block.
- In an interesting turn of events the costumes of the Zarbi were actually designed by **John Wood** whilst **Daphne Dare** designed the costumes for the Menoptra. This was because sometimes the monsters of a serial were clearly more like pieces of technical hardware than costumes and were assigned to the designer, such as the Daleks in *The Daleks*, so John Wood was required to construct the Zarbi costumes.
- On Monday 30 November 1964, **Peter Purves** auditioned for a Menoptra role, but **Richard Martin** felt he would be wasted and instead kept him in mind for other roles later in the run.
- The recording of "The Zarbi" was beset with numerous problems which resulted in seven retakes, and production overrunning by sixteen minutes. The recording of "Escape to Danger" would also meet with technical problems which resulted in recording stretching to 10:52pm, an overrun of over thirty minutes. Due to the late finish the cast had to navigate their way out of Riverside Studios in complete darkness.
- During the recording of the serial it came to **Verity Lambert's** attention that cast members were changing their dialogue without permission. The producer criticized **Richard Martin** for not controlling the cast citing that **William Hartnell** could be awkward when scripts were changed.
- The characters of Hetra and Nemini (the Optera) were developed by **Ian Thompson** and **Barbara Joss**. The actors worked closely with together to develop the Optera's dialogue and behaviour.
- Since the character of Hrhoonda was killed off in "The Zarbi" the costume were reused for **Ken McGarvey** who played a Menoptra slave in later episodes.
- It was originally intended to hire both **Catherine Fleming** (Animus Voice) and **Ken McGarvey** (Menoptra) to appear in "Invasion". However, the actors weren't required due to rewrites omitting their characters.

BROADCAST

EPISODE	DATE	TIME	VIEWING FIGURE	CHART POSITION	APPRECIATION INDEX
1: *The Web Planet*	13/2/1965	5:40-6:05pm	13.5M	7th	56
2: *The Zarbi*	20/2/1965	5:40-6:05pm	12.5M	12th	53
3: *Escape to Danger*	27/2/1965	5:40-6:05pm	12.5M	11th	53
4: *Crater of Needles*	6/3/1965	5:40-6:05pm	13M	9th	49
5: *Invasion*	13/3/1965	5:40-6:05pm	12M	12th	48
6: *The Centre*	20/3/1965	5:55-6:20pm	12M	14th	43

CLIFFHANGERS

1. Vicki who has been left alone in the Tardis activates the dematerialisation circuit, after the ship lurches violently. As Ian is covered in a cobweb substance, The Doctor returns to the place where the Tardis landed to get help, only to discover that it has vanished.
2. The Doctor, Vicki and Ian, who have been captured by the Zarbi, are taken to a control centre. The time travellers attempt to communicate with the Zarbi, but their attempts fail. The Doctor is surrounded by a circular device when a voice asks why The Doctor has come to the planet.
3. Ian and Vrestin are forced to hide in a cleft in the rocky landscape to escape from the Zarbi. Whilst inside the land gives way and Ian and Vrestin fall.

4. The Menoptra, who are part of an invasion force landing on the planet, begin to battle the Zarbi. In the middle of the battle, Barbara and Prapillus are trapped and find themselves surrounded.
5. The Doctor and Vicki are herded into a chamber where they are covered in a sticky web-like substance.
6. With the Animus defeated, The Doctor and his companions depart from the planet. Prapillus promises they will never be forgotten and the remaining Menoptra are summonsed back to the planet.

COMMERCIAL RELEASES

- **AUDIOBOOK:** November 2005
- **DVD:** 3 October 2005
- **LP (soundtrack):** 13 December 2019
- **NOVELISATION: [Hardback]** – 16 September 1965; **[Paperback]** - May 1973; **[Reissues]** -1978; 1990; 2016
    - *Target Doctor Who Library Number:* **73**
- **SOUNDTRACK**
    - **1 October 2020**: *BBC Audio*
- **VIDEO:** September 1990

CONTINUTY NOTES

- The Doctor explains that Vortis is located in the Isop Galaxy, the same galaxy where the popular revived series character, 'The Face of Boe' originated from.
- The fifth instalment of ***The Web Planet*** is entitled "Invasion" the same title used for the first part of ***Invasion of the Dinosaurs*** to keep the identity of the monsters [Dinosaurs] a secret.
- Despite saying otherwise, The Doctor has actually made three previous visits to Vortis in the past in **PROSE:** *The Lost Ones*, **PROSE:** *The Lair of the Zarbi Supremo*, and **COMIC:** *On the Web Planet*.
- The Doctor revisits Vortis many times; The Second Doctor returns in **PROSE:** *Twilight of the Gods*, the Fourth Doctor in **COMIC:** *The Naked Flame* and the Fifth Doctor in **AUDIO:** *Return to the Web Planet.*
- Barbara is still wearing the bracelet that Nero gave to her in the previous serial and, because Vicki was unaware that the former was taken to Rome, she asks her about it.
- The Zarbi are first monsters to appear on the show who resemble Earth animals. The Macra who appear in ***The Macra Terror*** and ***Gridlock*** resemble Crabs, the Weed Creature in ***Fury from the Deep*** is a parasitic creature made of weed, and the Racnoss is a giant spider in ***The Runaway Bride***.
- The Animus is the first 'fake god' who is also a monster, to feature on the show, other fake gods who are worshipped throughout the show include Xoanon in ***The Face of Evil,*** Kroll in ***The Power of Kroll*** and Logar in ***Planet of Fire***.

CRITICAL RESPONSE

- **Review Range:** Mixed
- *Doctor Who Magazine 2014 Poll*: 219th/241st
- Early reviews of the serial were generally negative; **Patrick Skene Catling** writing in *Punch* considered the serial as "ludicrous bathos", **Bill Edmund** of *The Stage and Television Today* criticised the lighting effects, summarizing them as both pointless and annoying. **Reggie Phillips** of *The Scotsman* called it a "flop".
- An edition of *Junior Points of View* (19 February 1965) revealed that young viewers felt the story was both exciting and hair-raising, but complaints centred on Zarbi's bleeping noises which were felt to be pointless.
- An audience research report (Friday 24 April 1965) contained many criticisms of the serial. Whilst the resolution was praised, many viewers felt that, as the serial progressed it became evident that ideas were running out. Some viewers were left confused by the narrative, children were critical of the costumes, and the choice of lenses had apparently made viewing rather uncomfortable for some viewers.
- **Mark Braxton** of *The Radio Times* appreciated the costumes and atmospheric sets, despite the fact that they are a product of their time. He felt the story lacked excitement, but appreciated the good vs. evil narrative.
- Writing in *The Independent,* **Neela Debnath** wrote that the serial was "enjoyable", and praised the ambitious writing but cited the poor quality of the visuals as a problem.
- *Den of Geek* considered ***The Web Planet*** as "underrated", and praised it for being somewhat "different".

DEATHS

DEATH	CHARACTER	TIME OF DEATH	CAUSE OF DEATH
1	Hrhoonda	00:44:42	Shot and killed
2	Zarbi	01:25:43	Killed by Prapillus – *unconfirmed*
3	Larvae Gun	01:25:43	Squished against a wall
4	Menoptra	01:33:49	Killed by a Larvae Gun
5-6	Menoptras	01:34:10-01:34:14	Killed by Zarbi
7	Menoptra	01:34:22	*death unconfirmed*
8	Zarbi	01:34:41	Killed by a Menoptra
9	Nemini	01:53:11	Killed by an acid flow
10	Hrostar	02:08:48	Killed by a Larvae Gun
11	Larvae Gun	02:08:54	Crushed to death
12	Animus	02:18:13	Collapses

FILMING LOCATIONS

- Ealing Film Studios Stage 2
- Riverside Studio 1

INFLUENCES

- **BOOK:** *The Sword in the Stone* (T. H. White, 1938).
- **BOOKS:** *Lord of the Rings* (1954-55, J. R. R. Tolkien).
- **FILMS:** Giant Insect Movies of the 1950s.
- **PLAY:** *The Insect Play* (Josef Ĉapek, Karel Ĉapek, 1922).
- **TV:** *The Outer Limits:* "The Zanti Misfits" (Leonard Horn, 1963).

PRODUCTION ERRORS

1. At several times during the story some actors miss their cues to move around the sets
2. Barbara mistakenly gives Vicki aspirin when the latter asks for a sedative.
3. When Ian and The Doctor first hear the Zarbi, the structure they stand beside is just a standing set piece.
4. The Doctor mistakenly refers to ultrasonic as 'extra-sonic' in "The Web Planet".
5. During "Escape to Danger" one of the Zarbi runs directly into the camera.
6. During "Invasion" a cough can be heard off-screen from a production team member.
7. During "Invasion" a stagehand can be seen opening a door for The Doctor and Vicki to enter.
8. During the scenes when Ian is buried in a rock fall someone off-camera can be heard laughing.
9. Hroonda's wings notably fall off after the character is killed in "The Zarbi".
10. One of the Zarbi's abdomens dangles towards the floor throughout the serial.
11. One of Menoptra's prisoners appears to be 'relaxed', judging by their body expressions.
12. Shadows are notably cast on the sky repeatedly throughout the story, even though there is no sky.
13. The GIANT Zarbi for some reason are scared of TINY **DEAD** spiders.
14. During "The Zarbi" one of the Tardis window is leaning inwards.
15. During "The Centre" an Optera can be seen walking normally, after they stop hopping.
16. Some of the Menoptra masks are different between studio work and filming work.
17. Kirby wires are clearly visible whenever the Menoptra fly across the sky
18. For some reason Hetra has a FRENCH accent.

PUBLICITY

- A 104-second trailer for the serial was shown directly after the broadcast of the final episode of **The Romans**. The trailer hit the TV screen at 6:05pm. **Richard Martin** was not happy with the trailer because he felt it "undermined" his work before the serial was even broadcast.
- *The Radio Times* (dated Thursday 11 February 1965) promoted the serial with a cover, half-page feature, and a photograph of The Doctor and Ian on the planet Vortis.
- *The Children's Newspaper* (dated Saturday 13 February 1965) carried an article titled *From Outer Space*, and also carried a photograph of a Zarbi at a bus stop to promote the serial.

WORKING TITLES

- Doctor Who and the Webbed Planet

VERDICT: The most bizarrely put together serial in the entire history of *Doctor Who*, and no, that's not a good thing here. There's an original story here but FROM the first second it becomes plainly obvious that money was a no-no word throughout the production process. The whole thing looks and sounds ridiculous, with silly looking aliens who move and speak in the most annoying ways, (you're off the hook for now Alpha Centauri), which makes one wants to cover up one's ears in sheer annoyance. The story is filled with repetitious moments and has a serious lack of direction and enthusiasm from everyone involved. Ian Chesterton doesn't seem that keen on returning to Vortis, and for good reason, 'Oh, I doubt it, Vrestin. But, knowing the Doctor, you can never be sure'.

The sets and hazy lenses are an eyesore, which could have helped transport viewers to a far off alien world, but fail to do so. **The Web Planet** is over ambitious for its own good where it remains blissfully unaware of its own ridiculousness and where everything becomes ensnared in the farcical narrative. The aliens are just awful, but the Zarbi are marvellous creations, but the Zarbi continually 'bleep, bleep, bleep' all day long, which just becomes bothersome rather than a creative alien language, the Menoptra's vocal cords only stretch to one octave, the Optera are severely restricted in movement, and the Animus is a typical sci-fi mind controlling parasite. There's an interesting idea buried underneath the ill-directed production, it's just a matter of sweeping away the endless cobwebs of misconceived production values, to find that supposed shining light.*

14) THE CRUSADE

Plot: Set in Palestine, 1191, The Doctor and his friends find themselves in the middle of the Third Crusade.

CAST

Dr Who	William Hartnell
Ian Chesterton	William Russell
Barbara Wright	Jacqueline Hill
Vicki	Maureen O'Brien
Richard the Lionheart	Julian Glover
William des Preaux	John Flint
El Akir	Walter Randall
Reynier de Marun	David Anderson
William de Tornebu	Bruce Wightman
Ben Daheer	Reg Pritchard
Thatcher	Tony Caunter
Saphadin	Roger Avon
Saladin	Bernard Kay
Saracen Warriors	Derek Ware, Valentino Musetti
Joanna	Jean Marsh
Chamberlain	Robert Lankesheer
Sheyrah	Zohra Segal
Luigi Ferrigo	Gabor Baraker
Saracen Warriors	Chris Konyils, Raymond Novak
Haroun	George Little
Safiya	Petra Markham
Earl of Leicester	John Bay
Turkish Bandit	David Brewster
Saracen Warrior	Anthony Colby
Maimuna	Sandra Hampton
Fatima	Viviane Sorrel
Hafsa	Diane McKenzie
Man-at-Arms	Billy Cornelius
Saracen Warriors	Edward Haroutunian, Oscar James, Peter Johnson, Sam Shendhary, Roy Fletcher, Roy Stewart, Peter Johnson, Abbas Haschen
Richard's Squire	Andy Brewer
Falconer	John Holmes
Priest	Rikki Patterson
Men-at-Arms	Henry Garcia, John Galahar, Michael Guest, Walter Mann
Ladies-in-waiting	Carole Brett, Maureen Lane
Knights	Michael Hart, Winston Marsh
Concubines	Cicely Joseph, Mei Ling, Cleo Sylvestre, Evelyn Ong
Double for Ian Chesterton (arm)	Viktors Ritelis

CREDITS

Written by David Whitaker
Fight Arranger: Derek Ware
Title Music by Ron Grainger and the BBC Radiophonic Workshop
Incidental music composed and conducted by Dudley Simpson
Film Cameraman: Peter Hamilton
Film Editor: Pam Bosworth
Lighting: Ralph Walton
Sound: Brian Hiles
Costumes supervised by Daphne Dare
Make-up supervised by Sonia Markham
Story Editor: Dennis Spooner
Designer: Barry Newbery
Producer: Verity Lambert
Directed by Douglas Camfield

ACTOR BIOGRAPHIES: Julian Glover has appeared in many high-budget films including *Tom Jones* (1963), *Quatermass and the Pit* (1967), *Alfred the Great* (1969), *Antony and Cleopatra* (1972), *Luther* (1974), *Juggernaut* (1974), *Star Wars: Episode V – The Empire Strikes Back* (1980), *Indiana Jones and the Last Crusade* (1989), *Harry Potter and the Chamber of Secrets* (2002) and *The Young Victoria* (2009); **Tony Caunter** is best known as Roy Evans in *Eastenders* (1994-2003); **Jean Marsh** landed regular roles in *The Informer* (1966-67), *Nine to Five* (1982-83); film roles include *Return to Oz* (1985), *Willow* (1988); she is best known as Rose in *Upstairs, Downstairs* (1971-75); **John Flint** appeared for a brief spell in *Emergency-Ward 10* (1961); Uncredited **Oscar James** played the shopkeeper in *Charlie and the Chocolate Factory* (2005); **Zohra Segal** was a regular in *The Indian Tales of Rudyard Kipling* (1964) and *Tandoori Nights* (1985-87) and appeared in many film produced in Bollywood; **Chris Konyils** landed a small role in *The Bed Sitting Room* (1969); **George Little** played Rev. Edward Ruskin in 100 episodes of *Emmerdale* (1973-83) and Dicker in 5 episodes of *Poirot* (1989-94); **Petra Markham** was Rose Chapman in 13 episodes of *EastEnders* (1993), and landed a small role in *Get Carter* (1971).

BEHIND-THE-SCENES

- **Number of Production Days:** 7
- After leaving his post as script editor, **David Whitaker** was commissioned by **Verity Lambert** to write a four-part historical-based serial on Sunday 1 November 1964. The target delivery date for the scripts was Friday 8 January 1965. Verity Lambert wished to have a good balance of both historical and science fiction narratives.
- The setting for the serial (the Third Crusade 1189-1192) was a period of history which greatly fascinated **David Whitaker**. Whitaker later commented that the relationship between Richard the Lionheart and his sister which he defined as 'incestuous' greatly intrigued him.
- The individual episode titles were very different from the broadcast version; "The Lion" remained the same throughout the production process, "The Knight of Jaffa" was originally "Damsel in Distress", "The Wheel of Fortune" was entitled "Changing Fortunes", and "The Warlords" was entitled "The Knight of Jaffa".
- After delivering the scripts, **Dennis Spooner** was greatly impressed, defining them as both 'adult' and compared them to the works of William Shakespeare. The serial became a firm favourite for director **Douglas Camfield** who later commented that it was the best work he ever did on the show.
- As much as he greatly enjoyed the scripts, they required some trimming. One element of the scripts centred on a possible sexual relationship between Richard the Lionheart and his sister. This did not sit well with **William Hartnell** and the material was eventually omitted by **Dennis Spooner**.
- Whilst researching material to design the sets, **Barry Newbery** referred to *Behind the Veil of Arabia*, a 1962 book written by the Danish author **Jørgen Bisch**.
- Production of the serial began with a three-day shoot between Tuesday 16 to Thursday 18 February 1965 at Ealing Film Studios, which concentrated on numerous shots. During these three days, a shot was required to have ants crawl up **William Russell's** arm. The actor firmly refused to do this and uncredited production assistant **Viktor Ritelis** doubled for **William Russell**. Assistant Floor Manager **Michael** Briant, who was also uncredited, arranged for a colony of ants, supplied by London Zoo, to be specially used for the shot. Unfortunately, many of the ants died under the hot studio lights.
- Whilst casting for the serial, **Douglas Camfield** considered **Nicholas Courtney** for the part of Richard the Lionheart. Since Courtney proved to be unavailable, **Julian Glover was** cast instead. Upon receiving the scripts however, Glover was disappointed that the sexual relationship between Richard and his sister had been removed.
- For the part of Joanna, actress **Adrienne Hill** was considered. Hill would go onto play the short-lived companion, Katarina in *The Myth Makers* and *The Dalek's Master Plan*.
- It was during rehearsal that **Verity Lambert** announced her intention to leave the series.
- The serial saw another use of a live-animal for certain scenes, this time a hawk. The hawk in question was supplied by Formakin Animal Centre, and **John Holmes** who played the uncredited falconer, was in fact an animal trainer who trained animals to appear in Film and TV.
- The director originally intended to capture a shot of **William Russell** through the rib cage of animal and a cow carcass was brought in for these shots. After a short while under the studio lights, the stench coming off the carcass was unbearable and soon attracted flies.

BROADCAST

EPISODE	DATE	TIME	VIEWING FIGURE	CHART POSITION	APPRECIATION INDEX
1: *The Lion*	27/3/1965	5:40-6:05pm	10.5M	16th	51
2: *The Knight of Jaffa*	3/4/1965	5:40-6:05pm	8.5M	29th	50
3: *The Wheel of Fortune*	10/4/1965	5:40-6:05pm	9M	32nd	40
4: *The Warlords*	17/4/1965	5:40-6:05pm	9.5M	27th	48

CLIFFHANGERS

1. King Richard the Lionheart refuses to help the time travellers save Barbara, stating that she can rot in a Saracen prison.
2. Barbara escapes from El Akir's men and runs down a dark alleyway where someone appears behind her and someone clasps a hand over her mouth.
3. Barbara is brought before El Akir who informs her that the only pleasure for her is death. He goes on to say that death is very far away.
4. The Tardis console room is suddenly plunged into darkness where the only light comes from the central column which continues to fall and rise. The time travellers are seen to be motionless.

COMMERCIAL RELEASES

- **AUDIOBOOK:** 7 November 2005
- **DVD:** November 2004
- **NOVELISATION: [Hardback]** - 24 February 1966; **[Paperback]** - May 1973; **[Reissues]** – 1985; 2011
  - *Target Doctor Who Library Number*: **12**
- **SCRIPTS:** 17 November 1994
- **SOUNDTRACK**
  - **5 August 2010:** *The Lost TV Episodes - Collection One*
- **VIDEO:** June 1991; **[Rerelease]** - June 1999

CONTINUITY NOTES

- The Fifth Doctor meets, Richard the Lionheart's brother, King John in **The King's Demons** who turns out to be a robot named Kamelion, owned and controlled by The Master.
- The Doctor mentions that he wishes to be a Knight one-day; his wishes are eventually granted in **Tooth and Claw** when Queen Victoria knights The Tenth Doctor and companion Rose Tyler.
- During the story's events, Vicki disguises herself as a boy, something which she will later do in **PROSE:** *The Plotters* after meeting King James I in November 1605.
- The Doctor tells Vicki that history must be allowed to run its natural course, since he cannot tell King Richard anything about the future, just as he told Barbara during their visit to 16th century Mexico in The Aztecs. The Doctor does tell King Richard that he will see Jerusalem, but misses out on all important details.
- Barbara refers to various adventures when talking to Saladin, she refers to her visit to the far future in **The Dalek Invasion of Earth**, her encounter with Emperor Nero in **The Romans**, and her visit to Vortis in **The Web Planet** recalling her counter with the Zarbi.
- The Third Doctor later recalls his meeting with King Richard in **AUDIO:** *The Warren Legacy*, and refers to the famous monarch as a 'lovely chap'.
- The Doctor apparently gave Hans Christian Anderson the idea to write *The Emperor's New Clothes*. If this is true, this wouldn't be the first time that The Doctor has provided inspiration to writers. The Tenth Doctor goes onto give Agatha Christie ideas for future crime novels in **The Unicorn and the Wasp**.
- King Richard is the first British monarch to feature in the show. Other British Kings and Queens to make an appearance include Queen Victoria, King James VI and I, Queen Elizabeth I and Queen Elizabeth II.

CRITICAL RESPONSE

- **Review Range:** Mixed
- *Doctor Who Magazine 2014 Poll*: 128th/241st
- **John Holmstrom** of *The New Statesman* responded negatively, writing that the series was failing because of the 'charmlessness' of the serials, especially the historical ones.
- **Bill Edmund** of *Television Today* praised the dialogue and the overall story, and commented that **Julian Glover** was a great asset to the story.
- A review in *Television Mail* (Friday 23 April 1965) commented negatively about the dialogue and called the whole thing 'unhistorical nonsense' which would only be appreciated by young children.
- **Patrick Mulkern** of *The Radio Times* commented that the serial was the first time where every production aspect was 'perfect'. Mulkern praised the story, cast, and **Walter Randall's** performance.

- Recalling his time on the show, **Douglas Camfield** called the scripts for *The Crusade* the best out of all of the serials he directed on the show. He called the scripts 'beautiful' and was impressed with the meticulous and accurate historical research that went into the writing process. Working on a costume drama was another highlight and described the whole experience as great fun.
- Writing in *A Critical History of Doctor Who* (1999), **John Kenneth Muir** wrote negatively towards the serial. He wrote that the serial was missing suspense, humour, and complexity compared to other historical adventures. He felt that ***The Crusade*** was the beginning of the end of pure historical adventures. He enjoyed, and praised the performances of **Julian Glover** and **Jean Marsh**.

FILMING LOCATIONS
- Ealing Film Studios
- Riverside Studio 1

INFLUENCES
- **BOOK:** *Gulliver's Travels* (1726, Jonathan Swift).
- **FAIRYTALES** (Hans Christian Andersen).
- **FOLKTALES:** *Arabian Nights* (various authors).
- **LITERATURE:** *Epipsychidion* (1821, Percy Bysshe Shelley).
- **PLAY:** *Henry IV Part I* (c.1597, William Shakespeare).
- **PLAY:** *King Lear* (c.1606, William Shakespeare).
- **PLAY:** *Romeo and Juliet* (1597, William Shakespeare).
- **PLAY:** *The Merchant of Venice* (c.1605, William Shakespeare).

PRODUCTION ERRORS
1. During "The Lion", Julian Glover refers to Sir William Des Preaux as Sir Richard.
2. At the end of "The Wheel of Fortune", after El Akir says "And death is very far away" to Barbara, you can hear someone call "Cue!" just before the credits roll.

PUBLICITY
- The *Radio Times* (Thursday 25 March 1965) promoted the serial with a photograph of The Doctor and Richard the Lionheart. The articles paid particular attention to guest stars, **Julian Glover** and **Bernard Kay**.
- *Television Today* (Thursday 1 April 1965) also promoted the serial, again paying attention to **Julian Glover**.
- *Daily Telegraph* (Friday 2 April 1965) covered the impending departure of **William Russell** and **Jacqueline Hill**.
- *Daily Sketch* (Friday 2 April 1965) carried a photograph of **Jacqueline Hill** and **Raymond Novack**.
- The *Radio Times* (8-14 April 1965) carried a photograph of The Doctor at a marketplace.

WORKING TITLES
- Doctor Who and the Saracen Hordes
- The Lion-heart
- Episode 2: Damsel in Distress
- Episode 3: Changing Fortunes
- Episode 4: The Knights of Jaffa

15) THE SPACE MUSEUM

Plot: When The Tardis jumps time tracks, The Doctor, Barbara, Ian and Vicki get a brief glimpse of their futures, ending up as exhibits in a space museum.

CAST

Dr Who……………………………William Hartnell	**Morok Voices**…..……………………...Salvin Stewart
Ian Chesterton…………………...William Russell	**Double for Dr Who**…………………...Brian Proudfoot
Barbara Wright…………………..Jacqueline Hill	
Vicki……………………….Maureen O'Brien	**CREDITS**
Sita…………………………………..Peter Sanders	**Written by** Glyn Jones
Dako……………………………...Peter Glaze	**Story Editor:** Dennis Spooner
Third Xeron…………………………..Bill Starkey	**Fight Arranger:** Peter Diamond
Morok Guards……...Lawrence Dean, Ken Morris	Title Music by Ron Grainger
Lobos…………………………………..Richard Shaw	with the BBC Radiophonic Workshop
Tor…………………...Jeremy Bulloch	**Lighting:** Howard King
Morok Messenger………………….Salvin Stewart	**Sound:** Ray Angel, George Prince
Morok Technician………………..Peter Diamond	**Costumes supervised by** Daphne Dare, Tony Pearce
Morok Commander…………………...Ivor Slater	**Make-up supervised by** Sonia Markham
Morok Guards….. Salvin Stewart, Peter Diamond	**Designer:** Spencer Chapman
Billy Cornelius	**Producer:** Verity Lambert
Xerons………..Michael Gordon, Edward Granville	**Directed by** Mervyn Pinfield
David Wolliscroft, Bill Starkey	
Dalek Voice………………………../Peter Hawkins	
Dalek……………………Murphy Grumbar	

ACTOR BIOGRAPHIES: Peter Diamond was a successful actor, stunt man and stunt co-ordinator who often played small roles in movies that went uncredited. His uncredited appearances include *Star Wars: Episode IV – A New Hope* (1977), *Star Wars: Episode V – The Empire Strikes Back* (1980), *Superman II* (1980), *Raiders of the Lost Ark* (1981), *Star Wars: Episode VI – Return of the Jedi* (1983), and *Superman IV: The Quest for Peace* (1987); **Jeremy Bulloch** is best known for playing Boba Fett in *Star Wars: Episode V – The Empire Strikes Back* and *Stars Wars: Episode VI – Return of the Jedi*, and also for playing Philip Cooper in *Compact* (1965-68); **Richard Shaw** played Ryan in *Freewheelers* (1971) and Dan Johnson in *Coronation Street* (1980).

BEHIND-THE-SCENES

- **Number of Production Days:** 5
- It would seem that **Glyn Jones** delivered his scripts for *The Space Museum* in mid-November 1964. Apart from the first episode which was titled "The Four Dimensions of Time", the other three did not have titles. By the new year, the fourth episode was titled "Zone Seven", the first episode became "The Space Museum", whilst the second and third episodes were called "The Dimensions of Time" and "The Search".
- Whilst writing the scripts, **Glyn Jones** named the Morok as such because of their 'moronic' attitude towards lesser species than themselves. Lobos derived from the word 'lobotomy' and the Xerons were originally called the Tharls.
- It would seem that the draft scripts for the serial were originally more humorous since **Dennis Spooner** removed a lot of comedic material from the scripts. **Glyn Jones** was unhappy about the changes, but Spooner stressed that the scripts were an intellectual science fiction narrative.
- It was decided early-on that the serial would be a budget saving narrative since **The Web Planet** would be expensive to produce. The technically minded **Mervyn Pinfield** was brought on to direct since his knowledge and expertise would bring production costs down.
- Just before filming began, **Dennis Spooner** carried out further rewrites to the last episode which later became "The Final Phase". Spooner instructed that the final scene should link to the next serial **The Chase**.
- The actors hired to play the Moroks wore fake eyebrows as well as having their own eyebrows hidden by make-up. The fake eyebrows were not easy to work with as they had the habit of falling off.

- Doubling for **William Hartnell** for certain scenes, was **Brian Proudfoot**, who had previously doubled for the show's star in *The Reign of Terror* and played Tigilinus in *Romans*, was hired again.
- During recording for the serial, a scene requiring Barbara to hide in a cupboard was taped for "The Search". Inside the cupboard set were two dummies which wore spacesuits. The spacesuits were reused props from *Quatermass II* (1955).

BROADCAST

EPISODE	DATE	TIME	VIEWING FIGURE	CHART POSITION	APPRECIATION INDEX
1: *The Space Museum*	24/4/1965	5:40-6:05pm	10.5M	16th	51
2: *The Dimensions of Time*	1/5/1965	5:50-6:15pm	9.2M	23rd	53
3: *The Search*	8/5/1965	6:00-6:25pm	8.5M	22nd	56
4: *The Final Phase*	15/5/1965	5:40-6:05pm	8.5M	27th	49

CLIFFHANGERS

1. Having discovered the future fate of being turned into museum exhibits, time snaps back on the correct track. The Moroks discover the Tardis and the time traveller's footprints in the sand. The Doctor announces that he and his companions have now arrived.
2. The Morok interrogation process fails as The Doctor refuses to give them any useful information. The Morok leader, Lobos has The Doctor taken away to be turned into a museum exhibit.
3. Ian forces a Morok Guard to take him to Lobos. The Guard takes Ian to Lobos and informs him that The Doctor is in the middle of the conversion process, and nothing can save him. Ian insists on seeing on The Doctor, Lobos complies, and Ian is astounded at what he sees.
4. On an unknown planet, a Dalek reports that the Tardis has left the planet Xeros. A Dalek voice states that the Dalek's own time machine will soon be in pursuit of the Tardis. The Doctor will soon be exterminated.

COMMERCIAL RELEAESES

- **AUDIOBOOK:** February 2016
- **CASSETTE:** September 1987
- **DVD:** March 2010 – released along with *The Chase*
- **NOVELISATION: [Hardback]** – 15 January 1987; **[Paperback]** – 18 June 1987
    - *Target Doctor Who Library Number:* **117**
- **SOUNDTRACK**
    - **7 May 2009:** *BBC Audio*
    - **5 September 2013:** *The TV Episodes - Collection Six*
- **VIDEO:** June 1999

CONTINUITY NOTES

- The Tardis later jumps time tracks in **PROSE:** *Festival of Death* and in **PROSE:** *Prisoners of the Daleks*. The Doctor later believes that The Tardis might have jumped time tracks in *Amy's Choice* to explain why Amy, Rory and himself appear to be jumping between two timelines.
- The Space Museum is the first time where The Doctor visits a 'space museum'. The Doctor will later visit other space museums in *The Seeds of Death, Dalek* and *The Time of Angels*.
- It is later revealed in **PROSE:** *No Future* that The Meddling Monk was once an advisor to the Moroks.
- For the first time in the show's history; The Doctor witnesses what could be a possible future (he and his companions becoming museum exhibits). Other examples of The Doctor witnessing 'possible futures' include a war ravaged earth after World War 3 in *Day of the Daleks*, The Doctor himself murdering the Time Lord President in *The Deadly Assassin*, to some degree his venture on Hyperion III in *Trial of a Time Lord: Terror of the Vervoids*, and a possible future incarnation of himself in *The Next Doctor*

- The Xeons are first major alien race who have been enslaved by another species to appear in the series (if you exclude the Humans in *The Dalek Invasion of Earth* and the Slave Menoptra in *The Web Planet*). Other notable alien species who are slaves who go onto appear in the show include the Mutos in *Genesis of the Daleks*, the Tharils in *Warrior's Gate*, Thoros-Alphans in *Trial of a Time Lord: Mindwarp*, the Vervoids perhaps in *Trial of a Time Lord: Terror of the Vervoids*, and the Ood, mainly in *Planet of the Ood*.
- The Doctor is shown to fix the Time-Space Visualiser which will feature predominantly in *The Chase*. The Visualiser will later be seen in **AUDIO:** *The Fourth Wall*, and **AUDIO:** *The One Doctor*.

CRITICAL RESPONSE

- **Review Range:** Mixed
- *Doctor Who Magazine 2014 Poll*: 232nd/241st
- **Mark Campbell** awarded the serial a 2/10 calling it nothing more than a run-around affair.
- **Howe-Stammers-Walker** writing in *The Handbook: The First Doctor* responded negatively towards the serial giving it 3/10. He described the rebellion storyline as dull and wrote that the only character, apart from the regulars, who makes any impact, is Lobos. Overall he felt that *The Space Museum* was the weakest of the First Doctor stories. He did however call the first episode 'promising'.
- Writing in *Dreamwatch*, **Jonathan Wilkins** called the first episode 'great' but felt that the rest of the serial was dull. He stressed that the serial was not overly terrible but not exciting either.
- Writing in the *Doctor Who Magazine*, **Graham Kibble-White** wrote negatively towards the serial. He wrote that the first episode was a false indicator for what was to come over the next three episodes [high-concept plotting]; where instead everything becomes monotonous instead. He praised **William Hartnell**'s charm.
- **John Sinnott** of *DVD Talk* wrote positively about the serial, stating that there are plenty of memorable plot points which kept viewers guessing what happens next, and also noted the subtle comedy.
- **Charlie Jane Anders** of *io9* wrote that the first cliff-hanger is amongst the very best in the show's history.
- **Cliff Chapman** of *Den of Geek* called the first episode slow which doesn't really reward the audience. He did not favour the performance of the series regular but praised the cinematography, effects, and main cast.

DEATHS

DEATH	CHARACTER	TIME OF DEATH	CAUSE OF DEATH
1	Morok Guard	01:20:38	Shot dead by Sita
2	Sita	01:21:36	Killed by the Morok Commander
3	Morok Guard	01:25:07	Shot dead
4	Morok Guard	01:25:07	Shot dead
5	Morok Guard	01:25:14	Shot dead by Tor
6	Morok Guard	01:25:27	Shot dead
7	Armoury Guard	01:26:10	Shot and killed by Xeron Rebels
8	Lobos	01:26:42	Shot and killed
9	Morok Commander	01:26:42	Shot and killed

FILMING LOCATIONS

- Ealing Film Studios
- Television Centre Studio 4

INFLUENCES

- **PLAY:** *The Broken Heart* (1633, John Ford).
- **PLAYS** written by J. B. Priestly
- **THEORY:** *The Theory of Relatively*
- **TV:** *The Twilight Zone* – time line narratives (1959-64, Rod Serling)

PRODUCTION ERRORS

1. The main characters' shadows can be seen across the mountains in the background as they leave the Tardis.
2. The Doctor brands both Ian and Vicki's suggestions that the Moroks are mute and speak on a higher frequency as doubtful. However, The Doctor has no reason to be sceptical, and doesn't provide his own suggestion as to why he and his companions are unable to hear the Moroks at first.
3. After the time travellers discover they cannot touch any of the museum exhibits they all clearly collide with a statue as they hide from the Moroks
4. During 'The Search' Ian picks up what appears to be a stone and throws it over the Tardis to distract the Morok guarding the ship. However no noise can be heard which would distract the Morok.

PUBLICITY

- *The Radio Times* (Thursday 22) included an article entitled *Dr Who and the Space Museum* which carried a photograph of Lobos interrogating The Doctor. The article included a small synopsis about the upcoming serial.
- A special item appeared in *The Radio Times* written a Miss Alice Englefield who reported that whilst on holiday, a group of people were watching the serial in a Hotel television room, which included 1 child. She reported that the only person to leave half-way through was the child.

WORKING TITLES

- The Four Dimensions of Time
- Zone Seven

VERDICT: Upon first viewing this one, it's easy to see that **The Space Museum** was the budget saving story of the season, with recycled sets and everything in-between, but unlike other serials around it, *The Space Museum* uses its disadvantages to better itself. The story although very simple, and one that does require a lot of attention at the best of times, has many layers to it which makes it more intelligent than its counterparts. Writer **Glyn Jones** throws in some humour (The Doctor mimicking a Dalek, and subsequent interrogation by the Moroks), in amongst a story which could be rightfully seen as an antiapartheid narrative, since **Glyn Jones** was born in South Africa, and the Morok and Xeon's costumes emphasise the difference between Master and Slave.

The story has some pacing issues especially in the two parts where it feels like one big run around, heck it is one, with very little variety throughout, and a lack of scene change can make for some tedious viewing. Writer **Glyn Jones** should be congratulated nonetheless in writing a four-episode serial that largely takes place in one building, something many future *Doctor Who* writers attempt, and almost always succeed at. Impressive model shots emphasise a grand scale of things and the final two episodes are much more focused and direct, with moments of heroism, action and visually stimulating set pieces, and some very oddly put together scene transitions. **The Space Museum** is a very clever idea (not too clever mind!), using time travel as a primary plot device, one of very few stories to do so resulting in what is perhaps **William Hartnell**'s most underrated adventure. The cliff-hanger and closing moments to episode one are superb. ***

16) THE CHASE

Plot: The Daleks chase The Doctor and his companions throughout time and space trying to exterminate them.

CAST

Dr Who	William Hartnell
Ian Chesterton	William Russell
Barbara Wright	Jacqueline Hill
Vicki	Maureen O'Brien
Abraham Lincoln	Robert Marsden
Francis Bacon	Roger Hammond
Queen Elizabeth I	Vivienne Bennett
William Shakespeare	Hugh Walters
Television Announcer	Richard Coe
Daleks Voices	Peter Hawkins, David Graham
Daleks	Robert Jewell, Kevin Manser, John Scott Martin, Gerald Taylor
Mire Beast	Jack Pitt
Malsan	Ian Thompson
Rynian	Hywel Bennett
Prondyn	Al Raymond
Guide	Arne Gordon
Morton Dill	Peter Purves
Albert C Richardson	Dennis Chinnery
Capt. Benjamin Briggs	David Blake Kelly
Bosun	Patrick Carter
Willoughby	Douglas Ditta
Cabin Steward	Jack Pitt
Frankenstein	John Maxim
Count Dracula	Malcolm Rogers
Grey Lady	Roslyn de Winter
Robot Dr Who	Edmund Warwick
Mechonoid Voice	David Graham
Mechonoids	Murphy Grumbar, Jack Pitt, John Scott Martin
Steven Taylor	Peter Purves
Bus Conductor	Derek Ware
Fungoids	Jack Pitt, John Scott Martin, Ken Tyllson
Aridian	Brian Proudfoot
Stout Tweedy Woman Tourists	Barbara Bruce, Kathleen Heath, Sally Sutherland
Beautiful Woman	Monique Lewis
Crew Cut Youth	Shaun Ryan
Bald Fat Man	Jim Tyson
Sailors on *Mary Celeste*	Bill Richards, Terry Leigh, David Pelton, Marc Laurence, Fred Haggerty, Gerry Wain, David Cannon
Mrs. Briggs	Marilyn Gothard
Dalek/Mechonoid	Michael Summerford
Double for Ian Chesterton	David Newman
Double for Vicki	Barbara Joss
Stuntmen	Fred Haggerty, Gerry Wain, David Cannon

CREDITS

Written by Terry Nation
Fight Arranged by Peter Diamond
Title Music by Ron Grainger and the BBC Radiophonic Workshop
Incidental Music Composed and Conducted by Dudley Simpson
Film Cameraman: Charles Parnall
Film Editor: Norman Matthews
Costumes Supervised by Daphne Dare
Make-Up Supervised by Sonia Markham
Lighting: Howard King
Sound: Ray Angel
Sound Supervisor: Brian Hiles
Story Editor: David Spooner
Designers: Raymond Cusick, John Wood
Producer: Verity Lambert
Directed by Richard Martin

ACTOR BIOGRAPHIES: Roger Hammond's later film credits include *The Madness of King George* (1994), *Around the World in 80 Days* (2004) and *The King's Speech* (2010); **Hywel Bennett** played James Shelley in *Shelley* (1979-84), and *The Return of Shelley* (1988-92); **John Maxim** had a memorable performance in an episode of *The Prisoner* (1967) playing the Second Judge; **Ken Tyllson** played a Telegraph Boy in a couple of episodes of *Dixon of Dock Green* (1962-63); **Ian Thompson** was a regular on *A Family at War* (1970-72) and has appeared on 4 separate episodes of *The Bill* (1991/93/95/97); **Malcolm Rodgers** landed a small role in *Joan of Arc* (1999); **Peter Purves** went on to be a regular presenter of *Blue Peter* between 1967 and 1977.

BEHIND-THE-SCENES

- **Number of Production Days:** 13
- During production of **The Dalek Invasion Earth**, **Terry Nation** was commissioned to write another serial for the show by incoming script editor **Dennis Spooner**. The target delivery date for the scripts was Saturday 30 January 1965 with filming

planned for the end of April. The details about the story are unknown and were eventually abandoned. Instead Terry Nation concentrated on writing a third Dalek serial.

- **Terry Nation** submitted a five-page synopsis which detailed that the serial would be made of a series of mini adventures. The storyline was originally about The Daleks, who, using their time machine saw a time when The Doctor would defeat their plans for universal domination.
- **Terry Nation** suggested many possible landing sites which could feature throughout the serial; Ancient Egypt was a possibility where the Ancient Egyptians would build the Great Pyramid where one of the Daleks would be destroyed, the Planet Stygian where all living matter is invisible due to the different light waves on the planet, and the planet Vapuron, known as the land of mists.
- The Fungoids who appear "The Death of Doctor Who" and "Planet of Decision" was originally the name for the Mire Beasts who appeared in "The Executioners" and "The Death of Time"
- It was also suggested by **Terry Nation** that the Beatles, the biggest name in pop music at the time, could appear, dressed as old men, for a fiftieth anniversary reunion. It later transpired that the group's manager, **Brian Epstein** was not keen on the idea and believed the idea would ruin the band's reputation.
- In **Terry Nation's** original scripts Ian and Vicki were to be dragged down into the underground tunnels on Aridius by a colony of Mire Beasts. This was changed during the script editing process and **Dennis Spooner** changed it so a trapdoor would open allowing Ian and Vicki to venture down below the surface.
- The Aridians were originally envisioned wearing clothes made out of the skin of Mire Beasts, and originally had a second set of eyes on their foreheads. They originally had black hair and only had four fingers on each hand. Their arms were supposed to dangle on the floor. **Verity Lambert** was not happy with the description of the Aridians and requested that their grotesqueness be toned down.
- For the scenes involving the Haunted Fun House, it was originally intended that everything that happened in the haunted house, was going to take place outside of time and space. The Fun House did not appear in **Terry Nation's** original scripts so The Doctor's explanation that the house was the product of the dark side of human imagination was to remain. However **Verity Lambert** was not happy about this and stressed that the use of Frankenstein and Dracula would show a lack of imagination from the production team. It was eventually decided that the events took place in a Haunted House Attraction.
- For the scenes involving the main characters propelling down from the Mechanus City, Barbara was to knock Vicki out unconscious after she panicked at the beginning of the scene.
- The production team went through yet another change during the pre-production process. **Terry Nation** was invited to take up the post as script supervisor on a new ITC show *The Baron*, and Nation invited **Dennis Spooner** to be a co-writer and assistant editor on the show. Keen to work on shows which would have a US market, Spooner was to end his contract on the show after completion of *The Chase*. The serial was also going to mark the departure of Ian Chesterton and Barbara Wright. The departure of another close friends, **William Russell** and **Jacqueline Hill** upset **William Hartnell**.
- The Mechonoids were inspired by the geodesic designs of architect, **Richmond Buckminster Fuller**, and the three props cost a total of £812 to construct. They were made by Shawcraft Models.
- The scenes involving Ian and Vicki walking across the sandy landscapes required the use of **David Newman** and **Barbara Joss** who doubled for Ian and Vicki, respectively.
- Production on the show saw the first use of a water tank which doubled for the ocean in which the Mary Celeste crossed during "Flight through Eternity". Stuntmen **Fred Haggerty, Gerry Wain, David Cannon**, and stuntwoman **Marilyn Gothard** performed stunt falls into the tank off a mock-up of the side of the ship.
- The montage of shots which heralded Ian and Barbara's return home to Earth was handled by **Douglas Camfield** as part of the pre-filming process for the following serial *The Time Meddler*.
- For the destruction of the Dardis (the Dalek's Time Machine) in "Planet of Decision" the production team used a bright flash of light, a camera roll and sound effects to illustrate the explosion of the ship.
- A total of eight Dalek props were used for the serial, many of them used to swell the number of Daleks in the background, instead of having an actor operating the Dalek casing for recording.
- The Mechonoids were met with a mixed reception from the crew, **William Hartnell** in particular did not like the demands expected of him with regards to his movements around the props. As the Mechonoid casings were difficult to move around, *The Chase* would mark their first and only appearance on the show.

BROADCAST

EPISODE	DATE	TIME	VIEWING FIGURE	CHART POSITION	APPRECIATION INDEX
1: *The Executioners*	22/5/1965	5:40-6:05pm	10M	14th	57
2: *The Death of Time*	29/5/1965	5:40-6:05pm	9.5M	12th	56
3: *Flight Through Eternity*	5/6/1965	5:45-6:10pm	9M	12th	55
4: *Journey into Terror*	12/6/1965	5:40-6:05pm	9.5M	8th	54
5: *The Death of Doctor Who*	19/6/1965	5:40-6:05pm	9.0M	11th	56
6: *Planet of Decision*	26/6/1965	5:40-6:05pm	9.5M	7th	57

CLIFFHANGERS

1. Emerging from a pile of sand, The Doctor and Barbara duck out of sight as a Dalek pushes its way to the surface of Aridius.
2. The Tardis dematerialises from the planet Aridius. The Dalek Supreme gives orders for the time travellers to be followed through time and space until they are all exterminated.
3. The Tardis dematerialises from the Mary Celeste. The Tardis inflight through the space/time vortex is swiftly followed by The Dalek's own time machine.
4. The Daleks finish creating their robot duplicate of The Doctor. The Leader of the Daleks asks the robot if it understands its orders. The Robot does, announcing it must infiltrate and kill.
5. A door opens in the wall of a cave where the Time Travellers are hiding from the Daleks, to reveal a strange robot. The robot orders the Time Travellers to step inside.
6. The Doctor and Vicki watch Ian and Barbara's return home to Earth. The Doctor says that he will miss them. The Tardis flies through the space/time vortex heading for its next destination.

COMMERCIAL RELEASES

- **AUDIOBOOK:** August 2011
- **ELECTRONIC MUSIC/SOUND EFFECTS**
  - **5 July 1993:** *Doctor Who: 30 Years at the BBC Radiophonic Workshop*
  - **May 2000:** *Doctor Who at the BBC Radiophonic Workshop Volume 1: The Early Years 1963-1969*
- **EP:** April 1966
- **DVD:** March 2010 – released along with ***The Space Museum***
- **NOVELISATION: [Paperback]** - July 1989; **[Reissue]** – 1991
  - *Target Doctor Who Library Number:* **140**
- **SOUNDTRACK**
  - **9 December 2013 - 29 September 2014:** *Doctor Who: The 50th Anniversary Collection*
- **VIDEO:** September 1993 – along with ***Remembrance of the Daleks***

CONTINUITY NOTES

- The Daleks' replication technology features in ***Resurrection of the Daleks*** where the alien menaces plan to send duplicates of The Doctor, Tegan Jovanka and Turlough to Gallifrey to kill the Time Lord High Council.
- Queen Elizabeth became an important character in the revived series featuring in ***The Shakespeare Code*** played by **Angela Pleasance** and ***The Day of the Doctor*** played by **Joanna Page.**
- The serial marks the first time where a model shot of the Tardis flies throughout time and space. Further Tardis model shots will later be seen in ***Pyramids of Mars***, plus others.
- This is the first time in which viewers see the Daleks travel through time and space.
- The Robot Duplicate of The Doctor marks the first time where The Doctor battles an exact double of himself. Such other encounters of The Doctor battling/meeting doubles of himself can be seen in ***The Massacre, The Android Invasion, Meglos,***

- *Arc of Infinity, The Kings Demons, Resurrection of the Daleks, The Caves of Androzani, Journey's End,* and ***The Rebel Flesh/The Almost People***.
- The Daleks are later revealed to have played a part in the construction of the Empire State Building in ***Daleks in Manhattan/Evolution of the Daleks*** using the building as a tool to create a new race of Human Daleks.
- The Mechonoids went on to feature prominently in a series of comic strips whilst battling The Daleks. Notable appearances include **COMIC:** *The World That Waits*, **COMIC:** *Eve of War*, and **COMIC:** *Impasse*. Davros later resurrects the Mechonoids in **AUDIO:** *Juggernauts*.
- 'Flight through Eternity' marks the first time where the show answers a baffling historical mystery - *Mary Celeste* and the disappearance of its crew. The show will later answer other baffling historical mysteries throughout The Doctor's incarnations. Such mysteries include; the truth behind the Abominable Snowmen in ***The Abominable Snowmen***, the building of the Peruvian Temples in ***Death to the Daleks***, the truth behind the Loch Ness Monster in ***Terror of the Zygons***, the scientific explanation about haunted houses in ***Image of the Fendahl***, an explanation about the construction of a stone circle in ***The Stones of Blood***, the event which caused the Great Fire of London in ***The Visitation***, the mass extinction event which killed the Dinosaurs in ***Earthshock***, and the destruction of Atlantis, although a different explanation is given in ***The Underwater Menace, The Daemons***, and ***The Time Monster*** respectively.
- **Peter Purves** is the first actor to play a different character and a companion in the show. Other actors to achieve this are, **Ian Marter**, **Lalla Ward**, **Freema Agyeman**, **Karen Gillian**, and **Jenna-Louise Coleman**.
- The Fifth Doctor meets the historical Dracula, Vlad III in **AUDIO:** *Son of the Dragon* while The Sixth Doctor encounters his vampiric literary namesake in **AUDIO:** *Legend of the Cybermen*.
- The Robot Double of The Doctor marks the first time where a robot is a villain in a *Doctor Who* serial. Other memorable robots include the Yeti in ***The Abominable Snowmen*** and ***The Web of Fear***, the Quarks in ***The Dominators***, the K1 Robot in ***Robot***, most famously the Sandminer Robots in ***The Robots of Death*** and the Osirian Service Robots in ***Pyramids of Mars***.
- To mark the departure of Ian and Barbara, a montage of the pair celebrating their return to London features towards the end of "Planet of Decision". A montage of villains he defeated and companions who travelled with him is used moments before The Fourth Doctor regenerates. Just before regenerating, The Fifth Doctor hallucinates seeing his previous companions who all urge him to regenerate and live on.
- Steven mentions that the planet Mechanus was forgotten about when the human race found themselves being dragged into interplanetary wars. This could be reference to the Dalek/Draconian Wars seen in ***Frontier in Space***, or possible the second and third Daleks wars as mentioned in ***Frontier in Space*** and ***Death to the Daleks***, or even the War with Cybermen as mentioned in ***Earthshock***
- Mechanus is the first jungle planet which The Doctor visits on his travels. Other jungle planets visited by The Doctor include Kembel in ***Mission to the Unknown*** and ***The Daleks' Master Plan***, Zeta Minor in ***Planet o Evil***, Tigella in ***Meglos*** to name a few,
- The time path detector makes it first and only appearance on the show since it disappeared from the console in preceding serials. In **AUDIO:** *Daughter of the Gods*, The Second Doctor claims that he removed it because he believed it wasn't very useful, thus explaining it abrupt disappearance. The detector makes two further appearance in **PROSE:** *Timewyrm: Genesys* and **PROSE:** *Timewyrm: Exodus*.
- The Mire Beasts later feature or are mentioned in **PROSE:** *The Crystal Bucephalus* where the Gubbage Cone empire kept Mire beasts in pits for the purpose of hunting.

CRITICAL RESPONSE

- **Review Range:** Mixed
- *Doctor Who Magazine 2014 Poll*: 175th/241st
- Writing in the *Sunday Telegraph*, **Philip Purser** responded negatively towards the serial and commented that the Daleks were using their fear factor.
- Writing for *Television Today*, **Marjorie Morris** described the final episode as very successful in terms of drama. She praised the Dalek/Mechonoid battle sequences, the soundtrack, and production design, and the performances of **William Hartnell** and **Peter Purves**.
- At a review board (Wednesday 16 June 1965) Director of Television **Kenneth Adam** responded negatively towards the inclusion of Dracula and Frankenstein's Monster.
- Following the production of "Planet of Decision", **Sydney Newman** responded positively towards the serial, calling it one of the best thus far, and responded positively towards Ian and Barbara's departure.

- An audience research report (22 July 1965) contained mixed responses to "Journey into Terror". Some people enjoyed the blend of science fiction and horror. Some viewers felt the whole serial was a jumble and believed that some children suffered nightmares after watching it. Some viewers felt that the show and The Daleks themselves were losing their appeal. Negative comments were centred on production values particularly the miming of the robot double of Doctor Who.
- Writing in the *Radio Times*, **Patrick Mulkern** was not impressed with the serial. He felt that the mini-adventures were altogether a mixed bag. He praised the first, second, and sixth episodes but felt that the middle episodes were mixed, in particular "Journey into Terror" which he labelled as disappointing.
- The premise of "Journey into Terror" and the Robot Duplicate of The Doctor were named as two of the silliest moments in the show's history in *SFX*.
- *SFX*'s also named Ian and Barbara's departure as the eighth best companion departure.
- Reviewing the serial in *SFX*, **Steve O'Brien** called the haunted house segment and the android Doctor as a couple of the silliest moments in the show's history.
- Also reviewing the serial for *SFX*, **Nick Setchfield** described the serial as 'entertaining' but was overall disappointed when comparing it to other serials which were far superior. The serial, in his eyes, was better in quality compared to ***The Space Museum***, mainly due to its energy, which will never bore audiences.
- In another mixed review, **John Kenneth muir** wasn't as impressed with *The Chase* compared to other serials around it, calling it 'weak' by comparison. He noted there were a few droll and dead-end plot points. He did however praise The Dalek/Mechonoid fight sequence and Ian and Barbara's departure scene.

DEATHS

DEATH	CHARACTER	TIME OF DEATH	CAUSE OF DEATH
1	Aridian	00:28:30	Exterminated
2	Mire Beast	00:31:44	Caught up in an explosion
3-4	Aridians	00:37:30	Exterminated
5	Aridian	00:42:47	Eaten by a Mire Beast
6	Dalek	00:47:10	Falls into a Pit
7	Albert C Richardson	01:10:13	*Death unconfirmed*
8	Capt. Benjamin Briggs	01:10:13	*Death unconfirmed*
9	Bosun	01:10:13	*Death unconfirmed*
10	Willoughby	01:10:13	*Death unconfirmed*
11-17	Sailors	01:10:13	*Deaths unconfirmed*
18	Mrs Briggs	01:10:13	*Death unconfirmed*
19	Cabin Steward	01:10:58	*Death unconfirmed*
20	Dalek	01:11:02	Falls off *Mary Celeste*
21	Dalek	01:28:20	Smashed to pieces
22	Fungoid	01:47:51	Exterminated
23	Robot Doctor Who	01:53:44	Deactivated
24	Mechonoid	02:13:57	Exterminated
25	Dalek	02:14:30	Killed in an explosion
26	Mechonoid	02:17:26	Exterminated
27	Dalek	02:17:38	Destroyed
28	Mechonoid	02:17:47	Killed by a Dalek
29	Dalek	02:17:48	Destroyed

| 30 | Dalek | 02:17:58 | Destroyed |
| 31-? | Daleks/Mechonoids | 02:18:54-02:19:21 | Destroyed in battle |

FILMING LOCATIONS

- Albert Embankment, *London*
- Black Lion Gate, Kensington Gardens, *London*
- Camber Sands, Camber, *Sussex*
- Ealing Film Studios Stage 3
- Ealing Film Studios Stage 3A/B
- Houses of Parliament, *London*
- Hyde Park, Bayswater Road, *London*
- Piccadilly Circus, *London*
- Regent Street, *London*
- Riverside Studio 1
- Trafalgar Square, *London*
- White City Underground Station, *London*

INFLUENCES

- **FILM:** *Max Sennett Movies*
- **FILM:** *Universal Horror Films of the 1930s*
- **TV:** *Cheyenne* (1955-62, Roy Huggins).
- **TV:** *The Beverly Hillbillies* (1962-71, Paul Henning).

PRODUCTION ERRORS

1. During "The Executioners", Barbara clearly invites Vicki to sit down on a chair with the tray and coffee on it, which Barbara then shouts at Vicki for knocking over. And how does Vicki not notice them?
2. How does the Time-Space Visualizer know to show the Time Travellers Abraham Lincoln's famous speech, just with the location of Pennsylvania alone? Wouldn't the machine need a more precise location?
3. The leg of a crew member can be seen as The Daleks enter their Time Machine.
4. As Ian and Vicki emerge on the surface of Aridius they cast shadows on the mountains in the distance
5. Vicki's hair style changes between the scenes set on the surface of Aridius. She has hair tied up either side during one scene, and then short-cut hair the next. This is because **Barbara Joss** doubled as Vicki for certain scenes during pre-filming recording days.
6. The Dalek that pushes itself out of the sand at the end of "The Executioners" can be heard grunting.
7. During the scene where a couple of Aridian slaves are exterminated, one of them can be seen throwing himself on the rocks, waiting for his cue to fall to the studio floor.
8. After Vicki knocks down an Aridian in "The Death of Time", the actor can be seen walking off the set.
9. Barbara is clearly nowhere near the wall which the Mire Beasts knocks down in one shot, yet in the following shot she is standing in front of it so she can perform her pratfall.
10. When the Dalek falls into the pit it is clearly night, but seconds later it appears to be day.
11. When entering the Tardis on Aridius, the time travellers appear to enter the Tardis from the side.
12. Vicki claims in "Planet of Decision" that she is afraid of heights. Yet in "Flight through Eternity" she is clearly staring down at the streets below when she is over **1,400** feet above the ground.
13. The Bald Fat Man's behaviour is both inexplicable and unnecessary.
14. The model prop of the Mary Celeste doesn't displace water during the model shots.
15. When Vicki knocks Ian out cold, it seems to take Barbara a few seconds to realise what has happened.
16. There is literally no reason why a Dalek falls off the Mary Celeste, apart from *comedic* writing.
17. When a Dalek falls into the water during "Flight through Eternity" there is clearly nothing inside the casing even though, it was confirmed in **The Daleks** that there is a living creature inside the casing.
18. It is never explained how one Dalek got on the upper level of the Mary Celeste, when they can't CLIMB stairs. Ian confirms this in "Journey into Terror" when he says stairs are a Dalek's worst enemy.

19. As a History Teacher, you would think that Barbara would get the pronunciation of Mary Celeste right. She doesn't, instead she calls it the 'Marie Celeste' even though Ian called it the 'Mary Celeste' seconds prior.
20. When the Tardis arrives in the Haunted House, the shadow of a crewmember can be seen on the prop
21. A candelabra is clearly seen disappearing inside the Tardis when it lands in the Haunted House, yet the high angle shot which comes next, clearly shows that the candelabra has moved a few inches.
22. The Wires which operate the bats in the Haunted House are clearly visible,
23. The skeleton prop which falls in front of Barbara and Vicki clearly breaks when it falls, as the skull is separated from the rest of the body.
24. A boom mic and its operator are clearly visible when The Doctor and Ian descend the stairs to the laboratory set. He moves out of shot soon afterwards.
25. A Dalek can clearly be seen behind a set of bars during the first laboratory scene before the Daleks have arrived. The prop had been positioned in place ready for the recording of the following laboratory scene.
26. Frankenstein's Monster clearly gains a jacket between scenes.
27. If Frankenstein's Monster is robot, why does it attack people?
28. The final shot of the Haunted House clearly states that it costs $10 to enter. However the Haunted House is in Ghana and the currency of Ghana is the Ghanaian Cedi.
29. After the Haunted House sequence, Vicki can be heard asking a question in the following scene, when she it not onboard the Tardis.
30. Why would Vicki think she could contact the Tardis from the Dalek's Time Machine?
31. During episode four a Dalek can be seen moving infront of a scanner which has a countdown on it. As the Dalek moves infront of the scanner, the countdown appears on top of the Dalek casing.
32. The Robot Duplicate of The Doctor is pretty unconvincing. This becomes evident when a shot of **Edmund Warwick** cuts to a shot of **William Hartnell**.
33. A hand belonging to a crewmember can be seen coming into shot during "The Death of Doctor Who".
34. A camera can also be seen during the jungle scenes in "The Death of Doctor Who".
35. A boom mic can be seen entering the frame when The Doctor, Ian, Barbara and Vicki exit the lift that takes them up to the Mechanus City.
36. One of the pursuing Daleks mistakenly calls the Mechonoids, the Mechons. This is because the Dalek voices were recorded before the Mechons became the Mechonoids.
37. The camera wobbles at one point during "Planet of Decision".
38. When Barbara nearly falls off the Mechonoid City, Ian grabs hold of her pants and almost rips them off.
39. You would think that the Dalek execution squad would leave at least one Dalek to guard their Time Machine, instead of leaving it open and unguarded so anyone can walk in.

PUBLICITY

- Publicity for the serial dates back to Monday 28 December 1964 with the *Daily Mail* promoting a third Dalek serial after the broadcast of **The Dalek Invasion of Earth**.
- The *Radio Times* (22-28 May 1965) promoted the new serial with a one-page article called *Dr Who and the Chase*. The article was written by **Michael Williams** which contained a photograph of three Daleks standing outside The Tardis. The photo was from studio session for "The Death of Time".
- A photocall held for the Daleks and Mechonoids promoted various newspaper stories on Thursday 15 April 1965. The *Daily Mail* included an article titled *Mechanoids Challenge The Daleks.*
- The *Daily Express* promoted the new-robots with a photograph of Mechonoid lighting up **Verity Lambert's** cigarette, with a caption reading *Me? I'm a Mechanoid.*
- The front cover of *Television Today* consisted of The Doctor, Dracula and Frankenstein's Monsters which promoted the broadcast of "Journey into Terror".
- The casing of **Peter Purves** as Steven Taylor was announced on Friday 18 June 1965. His début was given as Saturday 3 July. His character was described as a 'wrecked space-adventurer'.

WORKING TITLES

- The Pursuers

VERDICT: *The Chase* is a similar idea to *The Key of Marinus*, no, wait a minute, scratch that, reverse it, it's a direct copy. The serial only succeeds in emphasising just how boring the jumping-around-between-various-locations in quick succession becomes when watching all six episodes in one sitting, and how long winded it can be when watching episodes week by week.

The Chase is a mixture of greatness and frustration. There is a sense of fun from the four regulars, and the Dalek vs. Mechonoid battle scene (another failed attempt to cash in on a new *Doctor Who* monster) is decent for 1960s standards, but everything else is dumbed down where the plot becomes a mockery of what made The Daleks so special in the first place. Perhaps **Terry Nation** never believed his creations would remain as popular for long as they did. The direction is muddled and confused, with a list of seemingly endless production errors which suggest a rushed and poorly directed production. The writing is poor and somewhat juvenile and amateurish, going back and forth between serious hard-hitting drama, slapstick comedy, woe-is-me soap opera acting and hammy monster movie acting. Whether it was a lack of discipline from **Dennis Spooner**, or enthusiasm from Terry Nation doesn't excuse how lazy the plot gets. There is clearly effort from time to time to create something memorable (the use of stock footage of New York, cutting between model shots and footage from studio recordings etc.) but again why not concentrate on one setting for the entire story? Why **Terry Nation**?

This is the Daleks' worst showing, in terms of being a menace and threat, becoming the laughing stock for most of the story, instead of the run-and-hide-behind-the-sofa menaces children fell in love with following their introduction. The departure of Ian and Barbara is hard hitting, and marks the first major change for the show, and fans can only agree when The Doctor says 'I shall miss them. Yes, I shall miss them'. Steven Taylor meanwhile shows promise, the show's first companion not to officially join The Doctor through a request or invite.

As a whole, *The Chase* has aged terribly, but is memorable, nonetheless. The serial will always be a guilt-pleasure and does make for some light hearted entertainment, but deeply flawed on a number of levels. If you're looking for something which doesn't require a lot of attention, this one will satisfy. If you're looking for a solid, well-structured, intellectually stimulating adventure then take a 'Flight through Eternity' and look elsewhere. **

17) THE TIME MEDDLER

Plot: In Saxon England, a mysterious Monk is obsessed with the upcoming Battle of Hastings but why is this? The Doctor soon discovers the Monk is planning to divert the course of history down another path.

CAST

Dr Who	William Hartnell
Vicki	Maureen O'Brien
Steven	Peter Purves
Monk	Peter Butterworth
Edith	Alethea Charlton
Eldred	Peter Russell
Wulnoth	Michael Miller
Saxon Hunter	Michael Guest
Ulf	Norman Hartley
Viking Leader	Geoffrey Cheshire
Sven	David Anderson
Gunnar the Giant	Ronald Rich
Saxons	Fred Haggerty, Tim Condren, Lyn Turner, Ken McGarvie, Peter Brooks, Freddy Parsons, Derek Chafer, Vic Taylor, John Evans
Viking	James Hamilton
Saxons Boys	Don Simons, Duggie Dean
Stuntmen	Fred Haggerty, Tim Condren

CREDITS

Written by Dennis Spooner
Fight Arranger: David Anderson
 Title Music by Ron Grainger
  with the BBC Radiophonic Workshop
Percussion played by Charles Botterill
Costumes supervised by Daphne Dare
Make-up supervised by Sonia Markham
Lighting: Ralph Walton
Sound: Ray Angel, Brian Hyles
Story Editor: Donald Tosh
Designer: Barry Newbery
Producer: Verity Lambert
Directed by Douglas Camfield

ACTOR BIOGRAPHIES: Michael Miller made three separate appearances in *The Prisoner* (1967-68) and played Jailer at Chateau d'If in *The Count of Monte Cristo* (1964) and M. de Treville in *The Three Musketeers* (1966-67); **Peter Russell** was Rufus Wright in *Swizzlewick* (1964); **Ronald Rich** can be seen in *You Only Live Twice* (1967); **Peter Butterworth** was a popular face on the big-screen appearing in *Murder at the Windmill* (1949), *Mr Drake's Duck* (1951), *Appointment with Venus* (1951), *Tom Thumb* (1958), *The Prince and the Pauper* (1962), *Robin and Marian* (1976), *The First Great Train Robbery* (1978), plus many of the popular *Carry-On* films; **Alethea Charlton** played 7 separate characters in *Z Cars* (1962-71) and was a regular on *Sam* (1973-75); **John Evans** appeared very briefly in *The Adventures of Tom Sawyer* (1960) and landed a small role in *101 Dalmatians* (1996).

BEHIND-THE-SCENES

- **Number of Productions:** 5
- During production of *The Chase* it became evident that script-editor **Dennis Spooner** was not going to extend his contract to work on the show. At the beginning of March it was announced that the soap opera *Compact* was to be cancelled with production finishing in late July. Incoming script-editor **Donald Tosh** was given the option of working on the successor of *Compact* or *Doctor Who*. He eventually chose the latter.
- It was also known that **Verity Lambert** would be moving on from the series and would be replaced by **John Wiles**. Lambert was originally assigned to *199 Park Lane* but she was released from the project, and was instead asked by **Sydney Newman** to helm a new series which eventually became *Adam Adamant Lives!*
- To help **Donald Tosh** and **John Wiles** familiarise themselves with the show they were given a document called *The History of Doctor Who* which contained details of every commissioned serial broadcast thus far, including a stand-alone Dalek episode which had been ordered in February, and **Dennis Spooner's** as yet untitled serial which was to be set in 1065 about a time traveller who plans to divert the course of history by defeating William the Conqueror.
- The first episode of *The Time Meddler* was originally called "The Paradox". In the original scripts, Vicki was originally more abrupt towards Steven for not believing her about the Tardis. She was also going to mention to The Doctor that he failed to close the Tardis doors whilst on Mechanus, commenting that a Dalek possibly got into the ship.
- Whilst naming his Viking and Saxon characters, **Dennis Spooner** borrowed names of the members of the royal family; Edith (King Harold's sister), Wulnoth (derived from Wulfnoth, King Harold's grandfather), Ulf (brother to King Harold's mother Gytha), and Sven, originally Sweyn (one of King Harold's brothers).

- It transpired that **Donald Tosh** had very little to do on his first script-editor credit. Since **Dennis Spooner** was familiar with the series, little work had to be carried out during the script editing process. However there was a lengthy speech in "A Battle of Wits" that **Donald Tosh** was unhappy about and he planned to omit the dialogue on the recording day for the episode.
- It was originally intended to record the serial in Riverside Studio 1 in Hammersmith; however the decision was made to move recording back to Television Centre.
- The overall title for the serial was not arrived at until June. The uncredited production assistant **David Maloney** (later a director on the show) apparently joked that the serial was called *The Vikings*, until the crew realised that there were more Saxon extras than Viking extras. From then on the serial became known as *The Saxons*. The title *The Time Meddler* was arrived at in early June when promotional material was being put together.
- The second change of production personnel did not sit well with **William Hartnell**. The actor would often throw fake tantrums to get his own way. Apparently Hartnell told the cast and crew he was only joking.
- Much like many early serials, the decision was made to use library music instead of paying an artist to compose a score and conduct a group of musicians. **Eric Siday**'s work was used, as it had been for *The Edge of Destruction*. However there was room in the budget to pay a solo musician to provide some percussive drumbeats. This was **Charles Botterill** who had played percussion for *Marco Polo* under **Tristram Cary**.
- The recording for the serial required the assistance of the BBC Catering Department who provided three portions of roast chicken for the rehearsals at 4pm and recording at 8pm.
- For the recording of "Checkmate" the Viking actors were replaced with dummies for the sequences where the Saxon mob overpowered and killed the unwanted invaders.
- Director **Douglas Camfield** originally intended to credit the actors playing the Saxon extras. The actors were originally going to be credited as Saxon Villagers, this idea was eventually dropped.

BROADCAST

EPISODE	DATE	TIME	VIEWING FIGURE	CHART POSITION	APPRECIATION INDEX
1: *The Watcher*	3/7/1965	6:55-7:20pm	8.9M	15th	57
2: *The Meddling Monk*	10/7/1965	5:40-6:05pm	8.8M	19th	49
3: *A Battle of Wits*	17/7/1965	5:40-6:05pm	7.7M	28th	53
4: *Checkmate*	24/7/1965	5:40-6:05pm	8.3M	24th	54

CLIFFHANGERS

1. The Doctor ventures into the nearby monastery and discovers that the 'Monk's chanting is actually a recording played on a gramophone. The Doctor has walked into a trap, as bars descend from the ceiling trapping The Doctor in an alcove. The Monk approaches and laughs hysterically.
2. Vicki and Steven explore the monastery and also discover the gramophone. They eventually arrive at the cell where The Doctor has been imprisoned. They open it and discover that The Doctor has disappeared.
3. Vicki and Steven continue exploring the monastery that might lead them to The Doctor's whereabouts. Vicki discovers a wire that leads to an altar. Vicki and Steven discover a door on the altar; they pass through and find themselves in another Tardis.
4. Having thwarted The Monk's plans, the Time Travellers depart from Saxon England. The faces of The Doctor, Vicki, and Steven appear across a star landscape.

COMMERCIAL RELEASES

- **AUDIOBOOK:** October 2016
- **CASSETTE:** September 1987
- **DVD:** February 2008
- **NOVELISATION:** [Hardback] - 15 October 1987; [Paperback] - 17 March 1988; [Reissue] – 1992
    - *Target Doctor Who Library Number*: **104**
- **SOUNDTRACK**
    - **1998:** *Space Adventures: Music from Doctor Who 1963-71*

- **VIDEO:** November 2002 – released with *The Sensorites* and *The Gunfighters*

CONTINUITY NOTES

- Steven Taylor is the first companion who isn't initially invited to join The Doctor on his journeys, due to Steven stowing away in the Tardis. Other companions who join The Doctor without permission include Sarah Jane Smith in *The Time Warrior*, Leela in *The Face of Evil*, Romana in *The Ribos Operation*, Adric in *Full Circle*, Tegan in *Logopolis*, and Turlough in *Mawdryn Undead*.
- The Meddling Monk is the first character to appear on the show who is of the same race as The Doctor (excluding his granddaughter, Susan Foreman) and is also the first villain (excluding the Daleks) to make a second appearance on the show in *The Daleks' Master Plan*, for three episodes.
- The Meddling Monk is also the first villain Time-Lord character to appear in the show. Other rogue Time Lords who make appearances on TV include The War Chief in *The War Games*, Drax in *The Armaggedon Factor*, Borusa in *The Five Doctors*, Azmael in *The Twin Dilemma*, The Valeyard in *Trial of a Time Lord*, Omega in *The Three Doctors* and *Arc of Infinity* and The Master and The Rani in various serials.
- The Meddling Monk's Tardis is the first appearance of another Tardis to feature in the show. Other Tardises which appear throughout the show including those owned by The Master in *Terror of the Autons* and many others, and the Rani's in *The Mark of the Rani* and *Time and the Rani*.
- The Doctor proclaims that he does not like to be called "Doc" and displays his dislike for the title in *The Five Doctors*, *The Twin Dilemma*, the animated special release *Dreamland* and others.
- The Doctor describes The Meddling Monk as a menace rather than evil due to his obsession with meddling with time. The plot to the story is reminiscent of The Doctor's continual position that history should never be meddled with as seen in *The Aztecs*, *The Reign of Terror* and *The Crusade*.
- The Doctor's race is finally identified as Gallifreyan, however his home planet is not revealed as Gallifrey until *The Time Warrior* written by **Robert Holmes**.
- The Doctor and Vicki had previously visited a monastery in **AUDIO:** *The Doctor's Tale*, along in the company of Ian and Barbara.
- Eldred the Saxon will not be the last character to have such a name. Another Eldred appears in *The Seeds of Death* and another Eldred will serve as the antagonist in *The Hand of Fear*.
- The Doctor will later visit many monasteries throughout his incarnations. Notable monasteries appear in *The Abominable Snowmen, The Rebel Flesh/The Almost People* and *The Bells of Saint John*. Much like in *The Time Meddler* troubles always seems to find The Doctor any time he is near a monastery.
- King Harold II appears in **SHORT STORY:** *The Real Hereward* and **AUDIO:** *Mary's Story*. The tale that King Harold was killed when an eye struck him in the eye is later brought up in *The Sarah Jane Adventures* two-part serial *Lost in Time* where Rani mentions that some historians dispute the fate of the Saxon King.
- The Doctor's handwriting appears to have drastically changed from *The Sensorites*.
- For the second time in the show's history, the acronym of the T.A.R.D.I.S is explained by Vicki to Steven, the first time since the show's debut. However Vicki says 'D' stands for Dimensions rather than Dimension, the first time a character does so, Dimensions will later be the norm.
- HiFi, Steven's stuffed Panda mascot makes his second and last appearance in the show, apparently HiFi stayed on the Tardis after Steven's departure, and fully left the ship during The Second Doctor's trial in *The War Games*.

CRITICAL RESPONSE

- **Review Range:** Generally Positive
- *Doctor Who Magazine 2014 Poll*: 77th/241st
- An Audience Research Report (Thursday 5 August 1965) contained positive comments on "The Watcher". Some viewers found the concept of finding a wrist-watch and gramophone in 1066 fascinating, with some viewers speculating that The Monk was another time traveller. Other viewers enjoyed the return to a historical setting and Steven Taylor's character. There was a consensus that Ian and Barbara would be missed.
- One viewer apparently missed the point of the serial entirely commenting that the wrist watches and gramophones weren't around in 1066 and called watching the serial a waste of time.

- A report released on "The Meddling Monk" contained comments from viewers with many finding the story uneventful and slow. Others were confused by the inclusion of toasters and frying pans, and wonder what they had to with early Britons living in the 11th century. Again the point of the story was missed.
- Writing in *The Handbook: The First Doctor,* **David J. Howe, Mark Stammers,** and **Stephen James Walker** awarded the serial a 6/10. They commented that the serial had both good and bad points. They praised the character of the Monk and **Peter Butterworth's** performance but commented that the fight scenes and the Viking elements of the story were low points.
- Writing in *The Discontinuity Guide,* **Paul Cornell, Martin Day,** and **Keith Topping** commented that the serial was a major change for the show commenting that The Doctor's Tardis is no longer unique in the *Doctor Who* universe. They also praised **William Hartnell** and **Peter Butterworth** but felt that the characters of Sven and Ulf were a little tacky.
- **Simon Brew** of *Den of Geek* awarded the serial 3 stars out of 5 commenting favourably on the sparring between The Doctor and The Monk but felt that the story did not have enough material to warrant four episodes.
- **Jonathan Wilkins** of *Dreamwatch* described **The Time Meddler** as a forgotten gem and commented that the performances were generally good. He felt the weakest part of the story were the "stereotypical" villagers.

DEATHS

DEATH	CHARACTER	TIME OF DEATH	CAUSE OF DEATH
1	Gunnar the Giant	[00:44:52]	Killed in an ambush
2	Sven	[01:30:06]	Killed in an ambush
3	Ulf	[01:30:06]	Killed in an ambush

FILMING LOCATIONS

- Ealing Film Studios Stage 3A/B
- Television Centre Studio 3
- Television Centre Studio 4

INFLUENCE

- **BOOKS:** *A Connecticut Yankee in King Arthur's Court* (1889, Mark Twain).

PRODUCTION ERRORS

1. The blankets seen at the beginning of "A Battle of Wits" do not match those seen "The Meddling Monk".
2. Shortly after arriving, The Doctor, Vicki and Steven discover a Viking helmet with horns; this is historically inaccurate due to a lack of archaeological evidence that Vikings did indeed have horns on their helmets.
3. During "The Watcher", Steven wonders what a wristwatch is doing in the 10th century, even though The Doctor clearly told him early they had arrived in the 11th century.
4. The middle two episodes turn into a run-around going back and forth between the monastery and village.
5. It still a little vague whether or not Eldred worked for the Meddling Monk or not. She is taken food to him, but the close relationship would suggestion something a little more complex.
6. It's a little odd that Steven doesn't ask where Ian and Barbara are during "The Watcher" since he wasn't present when the two decided to go home at the end of **The Chase**.
7. During "The Watcher" the monastery door has a deadbolt lock attached to it despite having no handles.
8. Why would The Doctor monologue to himself about important historical information, concerning events to come, when Edith can evidently hear him? Doesn't The Doctor look negatively on this kind of thing?
9. Vicki's fear of heights is yet again contradicted during "A Battle of Wits" when she looks down at the beach from a considerable height. Her fear of heights is brought up when she dismisses the idea of climbing up to the cliff edges during "The Watcher".
10. The Monk is a little bit careless concealing the cannons he plans to use to wipe out the Vikings. He places somewhere where any passing wanderer could accidentally tamper with them, and render them useless.

PUBLICITY

- ➢ The *Radio Times* provide a preview on the serial with a photograph of The Doctor, Vicki, and Steven outside the Tardis, as The Doctor inspects a Viking helmet.

WORKING TITLES

- ➢ The Monk
- ➢ The Vikings
- ➢ The Saxons
- ➢ Episode 1: The Paradox

VERDICT: *The Time Meddler* is unique in many ways, where we are introduced to a character who is of the same species as The Doctor (excluding Susan Foreman), who just like The Doctor loves travelling through time and space, but for very different purposes. The Meddling Monk, perfectly portrayed by the equally perfect **Peter Butterworth**, provides another category of villain The Doctor faces. The Meddling Monk is not evil, The Doctor himself admits that much himself, rather he's a menace who loves altering history which in his eyes, will result in a much more prosperous future. **William Hartnell** continues to shine as The Doctor bringing more childish charisma in performance, where young viewers are always reminded that The Doctor always has a trick up his sleeve no matter how desperate the situation is. **Peter Purves** slides into the role as the new regular companion, and Steven both ironic and perplexed at the best of times provides a much more solid platform for **William Hartnell** to play off of. **Douglas Camfield** proves to be a very talented director using a mixture of stock footage and studio recordings to create a grand scale of things with a much more varied camera angles and shots. This is a true delight which continues to be held in high regard. *****

18) GALAXY 4

Plot: The Tardis lands on a disintegrating planet where escape is the uppermost priority, but who are the mysterious Rills and what secrets do the Drahvins hold with time running out?

CAST

Dr Who	William Hartnell
Vicki	Maureen O'Brien
Steven	Peter Purves
Maaga	Stephanie Bidmead
Drahvin One	Marina Martin
Drahvin Two	Susanna Carroll
Drahvin Three	Lyn Ashley
Rill Voice	Robert Cartland
Chumbley Operators	Jimmy Kaye, William Shearer, Angelo Muscat, Pepi Poupee, Tommy Reynolds
Garvey	Barry Jackson
Rills	Bill Lodge, Brian Madge, Peter Holmes, David Brewster
Dead Drahvin	Lyn Ashley

CREDITS

Written by William Emms
Title Music by Ron Grainger and the BBC Radiophonic Workshop
Costumes supervised by Daphne Dare
Make-up supervised by Sonia Markham
Lighting: Ralph Walton
Sound: George Prince
Story Editor: Donald Tosh
Designer: Richard Hunt
Producer: Verity Lambert
Directed by Derek Martinus

ACTOR BIOGRAPHIES: Lyn Ashley can be seen in *Compact* (1963-65) as Valerie Peters and has played various roles in *Monty Python's Flying Circus* (1970-72); **William Shearer** landed one-off roles in *The Avengers* (1963), and *Blake's 7* (1978); **Angelo Muscat** is best remembered for playing The Butler in *The Prisoner* (1967-68), and also played one of the Oompa-Loompas in *Willy Wonka & the Chocolate Factory* (1971). Other roles include the TV movies, *Alice in Wonderland* (1966) and *Magical Mystery Tour* (1967) but Angelo went uncredited both times; **Pepi Poupee** was also an uncredited Oompa-Loompa in *Willy Wonka & Chocolate Factory* (1971), and landed an uncredited role in *The Mutations* (1974).

BEHIND-THE-SCENES

- **Number of Production Days:** 9
- Writer **William Emms** first involvement with the show began when he submitted an unsolicited storyline to the production office, in early 1965, and was taken on as a writer by producer **Verity Lambert** and script editor **Dennis Spooner**.
- The story would have focused on two different alien species – one being beautiful and the other ugly. The message of the serial would be the classic 'don't judge by appearances' and 'appearances can be deceiving'. The scripts were written with the involvement of Barbara Wright and Ian Chesterton since Emms began writing his scripts before **William Russell** and **Jacqueline Hill** announced their intentions to leave the show.
- The Drahvins were originally male and were called the 'Dravians' however **Verity Lambert** supposedly came with the idea of making the antagonists of the serial female, **William Emms** concurred with the change.
- Commissioned to write his four-part serial on Monday 1 March 1965, **William Emms** was required to deliver his scripts by Thursday 15 April.
- Despite being commissioned by **Verity Lambert** and **Dennis Spooner**; a majority of the production would be overseen by incoming script editor **Donald Tosh** and producer **John Wiles**. Donald Tosh handled most of the rewrites, and John Wiles spent most of his time with Verity Lambert.
- **William Emms** was not best pleased with the amendments made to his script. Since the regular cast reduced from 4 (The Doctor, Ian, Barbara, and Vicki) to 3 (The Doctor, Vicki, and Steven) over the last few months, the character of Steven was given Barbara's dialogue and role in the story. This caused continuity problems; during the serial. Steven is trapped in an air lock and struggles to escape, even though his character was established as that of a highly skilled and trained astronaut during **The Chase**.
- *Galaxy 4* was originally going to end the second series of *Doctor Who*, since the serial went into production immediately after **The Time Meddler**. However the decision was made to delay the broadcast, and instead, *Galaxy 4* opened the third season.

- The director assigned to the serial was originally ex-associate producer **Mervyn Pinfield**. The director's expertise and extensive knowledge was a key factor to his appointment, since *Galaxy 4* was going to prove to be a highly complicated and technical serial to produce. However, soon into production, **Meryn Pinfield** became gravely ill and was removed from the project. **Verity Lambert** called upon **Derek Martinus** (who was also under consideration to direct *The Myth Makers*) to handle the serial.
- The four Rill costumes were constructed using fiberglass and rubber, and were actually greyish-green in colour. The costumes were big enough to house an actor who was able to operate the Rill's tiny arms.
- In total four Chumbley costumes were constructed for the story made from a fibreglass shell which was then attached to castors, this allowed the actors inside to move around the studio floor easily. One special dummy Chumbley was used in certain shots whenever one of the robots was attacked or deactivated.
- During rehearsals it became obvious that the script were not a favourite of the series regulars. **Peter Purves** was upset that **Dennis Spooner** (the man who helped create his character) was leaving the show, shortly after he arrived. **Maureen O'Brien** was displeased with her dialogue and asked many times for her lines to be amended. Sensing that the actress was unhappy with her time on the show, **John Wiles** decided that O'Brien's time on the show would be coming to an end. **William Hartnell** was not happy with the script, and John Wiles supposedly threatened to fire the leading actor if he did not follow the scripts.
- During production, actor **Anthony Paul**, hired to voice the Rills, dropped out of the project and was eventually replaced by **Robert Cartland**. **Cartland** had already been cast as Malpha in *Mission to the Unknown*, the serial due to proceed *Galaxy 4*.
- Since *Galaxy 4* was going to be **Derek Martinus**' first directing stint on *Doctor Who*, the director was quickly sized up by **William Hartnell**. The director commented in later years that Hartnell liked to be an imposing figure, since he had a great record in the world of film, and would often give new directors on the show a 'hard time'.
- The final shot of the exploding unnamed planet, which served as the main location for the story, was achieved simply by playing the footage in reverse to achieve the desired effect.

BROADCAST

EPISODE	DATE	TIME	VIEWING FIGURE	CHART POSITION	APPRECIATION INDEX`
1: *Four Hundred Dawns*	11/9/1965	5:40-6:05pm	9M	23rd	56
2: *Trap of Steel*	18/9/1965	5:50-6:15pm	9.5M	22nd	55
3: *Air Lock*	25/9/1965	5:50-6:15pm	11.3M	13th	54
4: *The Exploding Planet*	2/10/1965	5:50-6:15pm	9.9M	20th	53

CLIFFHANGERS

1. Inside the Tardis, The Doctor fiddles about with controls when he discovers that the planet has less time left than originally thought. The planet has two dawns left until it is destroyed.
2. The Doctor and Vicki venture through the Rill centre whilst being pursued by a Chumbley. Entering a chamber, they discover a deactivated Chumbley and Vicki screams when she sees a pair of eyes looking at them through a glass partition
3. Steven is locked inside an air-lock on the Drahvin's ship, and Maaga has the air sucked out of the air-lock.
4. Following the destruction of the planet, The Doctor, Steven, and Vicki relax inside the Tardis. Vicki notices a planet on the scanner and wonders what could be happening on it. On the said planet, a man called Garvey is lying in the middle of an alien jungle. A terrifying animal screech can be heard, and Garvey wakes muttering, I must …. I must kill … I must kill … I must kill …

COMMERCIAL RELEASES

- **AUDIOBOOK:** 6 July 2017
- **DVD:** November 2004; **[Releases]** 11 March 2013; 15 November 2021
- **ELECTORNIC MUSIC/SOUND EFFECTS**
    - **15 July 1993:** *Doctor Who: 30 Years at the BBC Radiophonic Workshop*

- ➢ **2000:** *Doctor Who at the BBC Radiophonic Workshop Volume 1: The Early Years 1963-1969*
- ➢ **LP (soundtrack):** 13 April 2019
- ➢ **NOVELISATION: [Hardback]** - 14 November 1985; **[Paperback]** - 10 April 1986
  - ➢ *Target Doctor Who Library Number:* **104**
- ➢ **SCRIPTS:** 14 July 1994
- ➢ **SOUNDTRACK**
  - ➢ **June 2000:** *BBC Audio*
  - ➢ **5 August 2010:** *The Lost TV Episodes - Collection One*
- ➢ **VIDEO:** November 1998

CONTINUITY NOTES

- ➢ The Drahvins are among the alien races who band together with other alien creatures to imprison, The Doctor inside the Pandorica in *The Pandorica Opens* although they do not appear on-screen.
- ➢ The Rills never feature on the show again, but they are mentioned by name in **PROSE:** *Timewyrm: Apocalypse*, and **PROSE:** *Infinite Requiem*.
- ➢ The unnamed planet which features in the serial is the first planet to be entirely destroyed. Other planets which meet similar fates include Mondas in *The Tenth Planet*, the unnamed planet in *Underworld*, Traken in *Logopolis* and *technically* pre-historic Earth in *Earthshock*.
- ➢ The planet is also the first unnamed planet to feature in the show. Other planets which The Doctor later lands on include the Savages' home world in *The Savages*, the planet used by the War Lords in *The War Games*, Leela's home world in *The Face of Evil*, and planet featured in *The Robots of Death*, plus many others.
- ➢ The astral map which made its debut appearance in *The Web Planet* makes its second and final appearance during the classic era. It will not pop up again until *Twice Upon a Time*. The prop will later feature in Eldred's space museum in *The Seeds of Death*.
- ➢ Vicki refers to the possibility that the Tardis might have jumped time-tracks again as it did in *The Space Museum*, The Doctor however believes that the Tardis has not jumped time-tracks again
- ➢ Maaga refers to the Drahvins as a clone race ready for war, this is similar to *Doctor Who*'s most iconic clone-race the Sontarans introduced in *The Time Warrior*.
- ➢ The Drahvins are the show's first major female antagonists to feature in the show (if you exclude Kala from *The Keys of Marinus* and the Animus from *The Web Planet*). Other notable female antagonists include the Metebelis III Spiders in *Planet of the Spiders*, Eldred (for a while) in *The Hand of Fear*, Camilla in *State of Decay*, Captain Wrack in *Enlightenment*, The Rani in *The Mark of the Rani* and *Time and the Rani*, Tilda and Tabby in *Paradise Towers*, Helen A in *The Happiness Patrol*, the Carrionites in *The Shakespeare Code*, Mother and Daughter of Mine in *Human Nature/The Family of Blood*, the Fortune Teller in *Turn Left*, Rosanna Calvierri in *The Vampires of Venice* and Ganger Jennifer in *The Almost People*.
- ➢ The Rills are the first monsters in the show's history to be falsely identified as the antagonists due to their 'hideous' appearance. Other monsters and characters to be falsely accused of being the enemy, for numerous reasons, include the Martian Ambassadors in *The Ambassadors of Death*, the Ice Warriors Izlyr and Ssorg in *The Curse of Peladon*, the Draconians and Humans in *Frontier in Space*, the Citizens of Zeos in *The Armageddon*, the Mandrels in *Nightmare of Eden* and Commander Lytton in *Attack of the Cybermen*.
- ➢ There is an uncomfortable 'possible' turn of events regarding The Rills as it is never actually made wholly clear who is telling the truth. The Drahvins say one thing, and the Rills say the **exact** opposite. It could be that The Rills toyed with The Doctor to escape the destruction of the exploding planet, and the Drahvins were actually telling the truth all along. The Drahvins says the Rills killed one of the soldiers, whilst the Rills say they saw Maaga kill the soldier. There is one flashback scene which puts the unseen event into context, but again there is no proof to determine which side told the absolute truth. If so, it wouldn't be the first time The Doctor has been on the wrong-side when dealing and resolving with the adventures he finds himself entangled in.
- ➢ The guns that the Drahvins use will later be reused for *Genesis of the Daleks* in another capacity.

CRITICAL RESPONSE

- **Review Range:** Mixed
- *Doctor Who Magazine 2014 Poll*: 210th/241st
- Thursday 23 September 1965 saw a review from *Television Today* critic **Bill Edmund** commenting on the regular characters being rather 'sluggish' and felt that the story was rather slow.
- Wednesday 29 September 1965 saw television controller **Huw Wheldon** praising the Chumblies at a BBC Programme Review Meeting
- A critic in *The Listener* commented that the scene when Maaga sucked the air out of the air lock Steven was trapped in was troubling. The critic commented it would raise trouble among feminists and psychiatrists alike.
- The Chumblies were subject to scrutiny on Friday 8 October 1965 when presenter **Sarah Ward** received various comments from children on the robot servants. One comment was unfavourable likening the Chumblies to jellies whilst another child wrote that they would beat The Daleks any day. The child in question expressed an interest in seeing the Chumblies return to the show
- Writing in *The Handbook: The First Doctor*, **David J. Howe, Mark Stammers**, and **Stephen James Walker** commented that the serial contained one of the greatest shock moments in the show's history. They praised the costumes, sets and the Rills but were not entirely convinced by the Drahvins. They also wrote that the serial was too simple to warrant a four-part narrative.
- Writing in *Doctor Who: The Episode Guide*, **Mark Campbell** awarded the serial a healthy 6/10 summing up the production as confident, but called the whole thing clichéd.

DEATHS

DEATH	CHARACTER	TIME OF DEATH	CAUSE OF DEATH
1	Dead Drahvin	[01:00:40]	Killed by Maaga
2-9	Rills	[01:06:41]	Killed in Crash
10	Chumbley	[01:35:57]	Falls into Lava
11	Drahvin	[01:36:00]	Falls into Lava
12	Maaga	[01:36:20]	Falls into Lava
13	Drahvin	[01:36:20]	Killed when Planet explodes

FILMING LOCATIONS

- Ealing Film Studios Stage 3
- Television Centre Studio 3
- Television Centre Studio 4

INFLUENCES

- **BOOK:** *Brave New World* (1932, Aldous Huxley)
- **FAIRY TALE:** *Beauty and the Beast* (1740, Gabrielle-Suzanne de Villeneuve)
- **FILM:** *Queen of Outer Space* (1958, Edward Bernds)
- **PLAY:** *Lysistrata* (c.411BC, Aristophanes)
- **RADIO:** *Journey into Space* (1953-58, Charles Chilton)
- **TV:** *The Avengers* (1961-1969, Sydney Newman) – [strong female characters]

PRODUCTION ERRORS

1. In "Air Lock", the Rill twice refers to the robots as "Crumblies"
2. During "Trap of Steel", Steven comments on the fact that Maaga was knocked out cold when she and her fellow Drahvins crashed on the planet. Steven can't possibly know this since the dialogue which brought this plot point up was cut from the final edit of the first part "Four Hundred Dawns".

3. During "Four Hundred Dawns", the Drahvins tell The Doctor, Vicki and Steven they come from a planet in Galaxy 4 (not the planet The Tardis has landed on). In the same episode, Stevens asks if the planet they have landed on is the Drahvins' home planet. Did he forget what he was told, or did he fail to listen?
4. Whilst The Doctor tampers with the air converter, a Chumbley can be seen approaching Vicki on her right, but for some reason it stops moving and remain stationary for a brief period.
5. The sound effect used for the Rill centre can be heard throughout the scene when Steven attempts to escape the Drahvin spaceship
6. It seems unlikely that Steven, a trained and highly qualified astronaut would be so easily tricked into getting himself trapped inside an air lock.
7. At the end of "Four Hundred Dawns", The Doctor tells Steven that the planet only has two dawns left, and tomorrow be the final day the planet sees. This is incorrect as the planet still has two days left. If the Tardis arrived on Monday for say, then two dawns would take the planet to Wednesday. If the following day is the last day for the planet, then it would be destroyed on Tuesday.
8. During "Four Hundred Dawns", The Doctor says 'As a matter of fact, I think we shall get some long-deserved, undisturbed peace for once' but then goes onto say, 'my dear young man, this isn't a joy ride. This is a scientific expedition.' So are they here for peace and quiet or carry out scientific research?
9. During "Trap of Steel" Maaga announces that Steven will soon be disposed of and Steven doesn't seem disturbed by this when he is in the same room when Maaga makes it clear what is to become of him.
10. Whilst speaking to one of the Rills, Vicki comments that it would be easier to talk to them if she could see them. The Rill declines the suggestion, commenting that Vicki might find their appearance 'disturbing'. However Vicki can clearly see what the Rills roughly look like since one of them is looking at her through a transparent mirror.
11. It is an incredibly stupid idea to build the Chumblies with the inability to detect anything approaching behind them. Did they take inspiration from the Sontarans and their provic vent or what?
12. It is shown that The Rills are able to communicate via the Chumbley, so why don't they do so and tell Steven he will come to no harm if he opens the Drahvin ship's exterior door?

PUBLICITY

- During rehearsals for the serial, **William Emms** was profiled by **Shaun Usher** of the *Daily Sketch*. The profile was published on Tuesday 13 July 1965
- The *Daily Sketch* also promoted the serial with a photograph of **Lyn Ashley** and **William Emms** where the writer of the serial commented on the creation of the Drahvins.
- The *Radio Times* (Thursday 2 September) previewed the upcoming serial with a photograph of the Drahvins.
- *The Daily Telegraph* (Monday 6 September) promoted the return of *Doctor Who* with a photo of the Drahvins
- An article appeared in *Television Today* (Thursday 9 September) with the title "New four-part Dr Who". The article gave a brief synopsis of the upcoming adventure and credited the producer as **Verity Lambert**. However the following week the paper printed a letter of apology since most of the production work was handled by **John Wiles** during the production process.
- To promote the return of *Doctor Who* after the summer break, a 1'45" trailer promoted *Galaxy 4* on BBC1 at 8pm on Friday 10 September 1965. The trailer was narrated by **Shaw Taylor**
- Some publicity notices were responsible for ruining the plot twist (The Drahvins being the real villains and not the Rills). Some of these notices described the Drahvins as having an 'evil nature'.

WORKING TITLES

- Doctor Who and the Chumblies

VERDICT: A derivative, slow-paced, long-winded story at the best of times, *Galaxy 4* is nonetheless an intelligently written beauty and the beast tale whose duty is to entertain the viewer, but also to set the mind to think. The Drahvins are the personification of true beauty and feminism. The Drahvins are admirable villains, a species whose society is based on hierarchy where the biggest and boldest lead, and the smaller, home-grown soldiers sole purpose is to fight and ultimately die. The Drahvins under Maaga are the product of brainwashing and draconian upbringing, never questioning what they are told, and always relaying on Maaga, which said continually throughout a scene, ends up sounding suspiciously like 'Mother' for support, guidance, and survival.

The story is laden with xenophobia, closemindedness and false perception imagery where the Drahvins, the femme fatales are exposed for their crimes, and left to face the consequences of their actions. It's a bold move *not* to have The Doctor being fooled by the beautiful Drahvins, rather the plot allows him to form his own judgement which eventually leads him to the ultimate truth. The Rills, the 'ugly' villains of the piece, are honourable secondary monster characters, confined to their spaceship, and hidden away out-of-sight with nothing but a booming disembodied voice for viewers to form their own imaging of their 'grotesque' appearance. The production values and directorship are generally on-par with later First Doctor episodes, with several silent stilted scenes thrown in, and toss and catch dialogue at the best of the times, and some of the more *interesting* sound effects from the Radiophonic Workshop of all time. ***

19) MISSION TO THE UNKNOWN

Plot: On the planet Kembel, The Daleks are planning to take over the Galaxy.

CAST

Jeff Garvey	Barry Jackson
Marc Cory	Edward de Souza
Gordon Lowery	Jeremy Young
Malpha	Robert Cartland
Dalek Voices	David Graham, Peter Hawkins
Daleks	Robert Jewell, Kevin Manser, John Scott Martin, Gerald Taylor
Vargas	Tony Starn, Roy Reeves, Leslie Weekes
Planetarians	Ronald Rich, Sam Mansary, Johnny Clayton, Pat Gorman, Len Russell

CREDITS

Written by Terry Nation
Title Music by Ron Grainger
with the BBC Radiophonic Workshop
Costumes supervised by Daphne Dare
Make-up supervised by Sonia Markham
Lighting: Ralph Walton
Sound: George Prince
Story Editor: Donald Tosh
Designers: Richard Hunt, Raymond Cusick
Producer: Verity Lambert
Directed by Derek Martinus

ACTOR BIOGRAPHIES: Jeremy Young has had many television roles; Neville Crane in *Deadline Midnight* (1960-61), Athos in *The Three Musketeers* (1966-67) and *The Further Adventures of the Musketeers* (1967), Bennis Lewis in *Coronation Street* (1972), Alec Shawcross in *On the Line* (1982) and Officer Stone in *Eastenders* (1989); **Edward de Souza** played Colin Grimshaw in *Coronation Street* (2008-09); **Johnnie Clayton** played Reg Cox in the very first episode of *Eastenders* (1985) giving him the unique distinction of playing the very first character to be killed-off on the show; **Sam Mansary** landed a small role in *The Beast Must Die* (1974).

BEHIND-THE-SCENES

- **Number of Production Days:** 2
- *Mission to the Unknown* effectively came into being when **Planet of Giants** was cut down from four episodes to three. To make up for the 'missing' episode, **Sydney Newman** allowed an extra episode to be commissioned which would be recorded in August 1965.
- With **The Chase** transmitted over May and June 1965, producer **Verity Lambert** and then script-editor **Dennis Spooner** granted their 'approval' for **Terry Nation** to write another six-part Dalek story which would be transmitted over November and December 1965. The original goal with the fourth Dalek serial was to recreate the major success of **The Dalek Invasion of Earth**.
- During the planning process, the new Dalek serial evolved into a 12-part epic narrative. The decision was made to produce the extra episode as a cutaway trailer which would focus primarily on the Daleks. In a turn of events the decision was made that the episode would not feature The Doctor or his companions.
- The protagonist and 'hero' of the single episode, Marc Cory was crafted around the image of James Bond. *Goldfinger* (the third James Bond film) received box-office success and was popular amongst audiences during September 1964, so **Terry Nation** described Marc Cory as a space-age Bond.
- The script for the cutaway episode reached the production office on Friday 14 May 1965. The planet where the episode takes place was originally called Varga, the native planet of the Varga plants. However during rewrites in July, the name of the planet was changed to Kemble, and then Kembel. It turned out that the name Kemble, had been used by **Dennis Spooner** in his script 'Space Vacation' for *Fireball XL5*.
- The first draft of *Mission to the Unknown* (although it was still to be called this during rewrites) originally had seven delegates present at the conference. One of the delegates was eventually omitted, possibly due to budgetary restraints, and would not appear in the episode. The omitted delegate Zephon would go onto to appear as a secondary character in **The Daleks' Master Plan**.
- In his scripts, **Terry Nation** made it very clear that each alien delegate should have its own personal design and appearance, wanting as much variety as possible.
- The original setting for both the single and 12-part epic serial was originally going to be 1,000,000 AD. This was eventually changed to 4000 AD.

- Much like *Galaxy 4*, the production credit was given to **Verity Lambert**, when infact incoming producer **John Wiles** handled most of the work on the serial.
- The three Varga Plant costumes were covered with fireproof paint. These were left to dry outside the recording studio whilst the camera rehearsals were underway.
- Designer **Raymond Cusick** drew inspiration from Nuremberg Rallies when designing the Conference Room.

BROADCAST

EPISODE	DATE	TIME	VIEWING FIGURE	CHART POSITION	APPRECIATION INDEX
1: *Mission to the Unknown*	9/10/1965	5:50-6:15pm	8.3M	37th	54

CLIFFHANGER

1. Learning about the impeding Dalek Invasion, Marc Cory records a message to warn the planet Earth. Before he can send the message, the Daleks exterminate him. Meanwhile inside the conference room, both the Daleks and the alien delegates chant 'victory'.

COMMERCIAL RELEASES

- **AUDIOBOOK:** 6 May 2010
- **LP (soundtrack):** 1 March 2019
- **NOVELISATION: [Paperback]** - 21 September 1989
  - *Target Doctor Who Library Number*: **141**
- **SOUNDTRACK**
  - **22 October 2001:** *BBC Audio*
  - **14 February 2011:** *The Lost TV Episodes - Collection Two*

CONTINUITY NOTES

- The Varga plants became popular recurring monsters throughout Doctor Who merchandise appearing in, **AUDIO:** *Purity*, **AUDIO:** *Dalek Empire II: Dalek War*, **AUDIO:** *Masters of Earth*, **GAME:** *City of the Daleks* and **COMIC:** *The Only Good Dalek*.
- Lowery recalls that The Daleks had invaded Earth once before thousands of years ago, a reference to ***The Dalek Invasion of Earth*** which occurred in the 22nd century.
- The planet Kembel makes it first 'proper' appearance on the show, despite being briefly seen at the end of *Galaxy 4*. The planet goes onto feature or is mentioned by name in **AUDIO:** *The Perpetual Bond*, **AUDIO:** *The Sontarans*, **AUDIO:** *Daughter of the Gods* and **AUDIO:** *The Dalek Defence*.
- This is the first story in which the Tardis does not appear. There are 11 other stories in which the Tardis also does not appear at all which include, **Doctor Who and the Silurians, The Sea Devils, The Sontaran Experiment, Genesis of the Daleks, Midnight** and **The Lie of the Lands.**
- The Space Security Service was formed roughly sometime in the 20th century. According to **NOVELISATION:** *The Ambassadors of Death* was a new organisation, and headed by General Carrington roughly at the time of Mars Probe 7 incident.
- The Galactic Council was around in the 21st century, in **PROSE:** *The Tomorrow Window*, the Council allowed the Vorshagg membership which helped found the Galactic Heritage. During the 20th century a group of Judoon were fooled into using 'illegal' device on Earth in **PROSE:** *Revenge of the Judoon*.
- The Galactic Council is the subject point of an episode of the TV spin-off series *K9*. In the episode ***The Bounty Hunter***, K-9 is almost framed by bounty hunter Arab, for murdering the head of the Galactic Peace Commission, Zanthus Pia, which turns out to be false.

CRITICAL RESPONSE

- **Review Range:** Mixed
- *Doctor Who Magazine 2014 Poll*: 169th/241st

- Writing in *Television Today* (Thursday 14 October 1965), **Bill Edmunds** praised the episode, commenting that the adventure was exciting whilst looking forward to the rest of the story.
- However there was some confusion amongst fans when the adventure did not continue the following week (during the broadcast of **The Myth Makers**). Various letters came from confused families living in Coventry and Yorkshire. These letters were read out on *Junior Points of View* (Friday 29 October 1965).
- One viewer shared their opinions that the Daleks had lost their fear factor and were now quite silly.
- Another letter of complaint came from a concerned mother who thought that the alien delegates were too frightening for children. The letter was published in the *Radio Times* (Thursday 11 November 1965). Further comments were received on Thursday 2 December 1965 when the magazine's editor noted that the timeslot allocated for *Doctor Who* was not suitable for child viewing.

FILMING LOCATIONS

- Ealing Film Studios Stage 3
- Television Centre Studio 4

INFLUENCES

- **FILM:** *Goldfinger* (1964, Guy Hamilton).
- **BOOK:** *The Day of the Triffids* (1951, John Wyndham).

PRODUCTION ERRORS

1. Marc Cory fluffs a line, announcing himself as "Marc Cory, Special Security Service" instead of saying "Space Security Service".
2. During the episode Lowery comments that the Daleks had previously invaded Earth 1000 years ago. If he is referring to the events of **The Dalek Invasion of Earth** then he is off by 900 years, and he can't be referring to the events of **Day of the Daleks** since again Lowery would be off by roughly 900 years. It's possible that Lowery could be referring to another Dalek invasion (which occurred off-screen) but this seems unlikely.
3. During the episode, one Dalek confirms that all 7 alien delegates will arrive for the conference on time. However, one delegate (Zephon) fails to turn up on time, meaning that only 6 delegates are actually present.
4. The Daleks for some reason announce their supposedly secret and diabolical plans on a loudspeaker system for any passer-by to hear, Cory hears it himself.

PUBLICITY

- The *BBC Press Service* issued a small bulletin on Friday 6 August which outlined a short synopsis of the episode. The bulletin gave brief details about the plot and names of the alien delegates who were due to appear in the episode as – GEARON, TRANTIS, MALPHA, SENTREAL, BEAUS and CELATION. The bulletin noted that the regular cast would not appear and the episode was to act as a forerunner for an upcoming 12-part epic adventure later on in the year.
- Saturday 7 August 1965 saw items from the *Daily Express* and *Daily Mail* covering both the departure of **Verity Lambert** and the comments from Varga Plant extra **Leslie Weekes**.
- Another report featured in the *Daily Express* carried a photograph of **Verity Lambert** with the alien delegates which outlined their names as being – Gearon, Trantis, Sentreal, Beaus and Celation. Comments from **Leslie Weekes** revealed that his costume was being fired proofed, explaining his absence from the photo.
- The *Daily Telegraph* published a short news pieces with the title 'Dr Who v Vargas' which outlined that the episode was due for transmission on Saturday 9 August 1965.
- The *Radio Times* promoted the single episode with a half-page feature. The article contained two photographs of the Daleks and the alien delegates which outlined that The Doctor would not appear in the episode.
- On Thursday 12 August 1965, *Television Today* released a photograph of **Verity Lambert** with the alien delegates. The article also announced the producer's departure from the show.

WORKING TITLES

- Dalek Cutaway

20) THE MYTH MAKERS

Plot: Arriving in Ancient Greece, The Doctor is mistaken for the god Zeus and Steven and Vicki are taken into the great city of Troy. In order to get them back, The Doctor needs one thing – a giant wooden horse

CAST

Dr Who	William Hartnell
Vicki	Maureen O'Brien
Steven	Peter Purves
King Priam	Max Adrian
Paris	Barrie Ingham
Cassandra	Frances White
Achilles	Cavan Kendall
Hector	Alan Harwood
Odysseus	Ivor Slater
Agamemnon	Francis de Wolff
Menelaus	Jack Melford
Cyclops	Tuttle Lemkow
Messenger	Jon Luxton
Troilus	James Lynn
Katarina	Adrienne Hill

4 Greek/3 Trojan Soldiers............Russell Scott, Peter Stewart, James Hamilton, Gary Wyler, Ken Morris, Michael Stevens, Paul Barnes

Young Girl Servant in Agamemnon's Tent......…Michelle Barry

Young Boy Servant in Agamemnon's Tent......…Stephen Ubels

Greek Soldiers.........Pat Gorman, Michael Wilder, Peter Roy, Derek Chafer, John Freeman, Tony Hennessy, Mike Reid, Graham Hardy, Norton Clark, Ralph Carrigan, Roy Douglas, Christopher Stephens, Derek Chafer

People in Square of Troy...........Joanna Smithers, Doreen Ubels, Cara Stevens, Margaret Bass, Victor Bailey, Walter Henry, Ian Anton, John Moyce, Jack Roland, John Moore, John May, Michael Osborne, David Greneau, Eric Blackburn, Darrell Richards

Trojan Soldiers.........Jack Duggan, Lesley Bryan, Gerry Alexander, Ricky Lancing, Steve Pokol, Peter Day, Donald Simons, Ralph Carrigan, Roy Douglas, Christopher Stephens, Derek Chafer, Derek Ware

People in Square..........Ralph Carrigan, Roy Douglas, Christopher Stephens, Derek Chafer, Beverley Stephens, Pat Stephens

Trojan Women in Square................Daphne Green, Mary McMillan

Stuntman......................................Derek Ware

CREDITS

Written by Donald Cotton
Fight Arranged by Derek Ware
Title Music by Ron Grainger
with the BBC Radiophonic Workshop
Film Cameraman: Peter Hamilton
Film Editor: Caroline Shields
Costumes by Daphne Dare
Make-up Supervised by Elizabeth Blattner, Sonia Markham
Lighting: Ralph Walton
Sound: Dave Kitchen, Bryan Forgham
Story Editor: Donald Tosh
Music composed and conducted by Humphrey Searle
Designer: John Wood
Producer: John Wiles
Directed by Michael Leeston-Smith

ACTOR BIOGRAPHIES: Barrie Ingham landed regular television roles in *Hine* (1971) and *Funny Man* (1981) and voiced Basil of Baker Street in the Disney animated film *The Great Mouse Detective* (1986); **Frances White** played Kate Hamilton in *Crossroads: King Oak* (1977-78); **Max Adrian** was Sen. Ludicrus Sextus in *Up Pompeii* (1969-70); **Ivor Salter** was a regular face on TV making many one-off appearances in countless popular TV dramas with regular work with *Honey Lane* (1967-69), *Westway* (1976) and *Jangles* (1982); **Alan Haywood** was Eric Lake in *Crossroads: Kings Oak* (1966); **Jack Melford** landed a small role in *A Shot in the Dark* (1964); **Cavan Kendall** appeared for a brief spell in *Softly Softly* (1966).

BEHIND-THE-SCENES

- **Number of Production Days:** 10
- Landing the post as story editor of *Doctor Who* in April 1965, **Donald Tosh** was keen to take the show in new directions, wishing to produce and commission scripts which blended humour and horror. Tosh was very keen to utilise both forms of writing for historical-based serials.
- As it turned out **Donald Tosh** was to oversee three already commissioned serials by old script editor **Dennis Spooner** (*The Time Meddler, Galaxy 4,* and *Mission to the Unknown*), so **Tosh** was very keen to recruit new writers as soon as possible.
- Both **Donald Tosh** and writer **Donald Cotton** were old friends from their time at the Guildhall School of Music during the 1950s, and Tosh invited Cotton to submit a story idea to the production office. Originally reluctant to write for the show, **Donald Cotton** eventually agreed to submit a storyline provided he could chose the subject matter and cast and crew of his Third Programme Plays
- Primarily a writer for radio dramas, **Donald Cotton** had written various plays which were heavily influenced by Greek myths and legends. This eventually led to the writer choosing the Wooden Horse of Troy legend as his plot point for his scripts. His idea was accepted by **Donald Tosh** and **John Wiles**.
- One actor who would appear in the serial was **Max Adrian** who had played various role in **Donald Cotton's** radio plays. Composer **Humphrey Searle** had previously worked with the writer on radio.
- Whilst writing his scripts, **Donald Cotton** carried out extensive research, utilising various work such *Cambridge Ancient History, History of Greece, The Origins of Greek Civilizations* and *A Companion to Greek Studies*. The writer felt that he was met with many historical contradictions during his research.
- With the show fully under the control, **Donald Tosh** and **John Wiles** formed a strong working relationship. Just like Donald Tosh, John Wiles had his own ideas about how the show should progress and develop. The new producer liked historical based serials but was also an admirer of science fiction works from the likes of **Isaac Asimov** and **Ray Bradbury**.
- During the writing process, **Donald Tosh** intended to give his four episode titles which would be puns. The fourth and last episode appeared to be called 'A Doctor in the Horse' or 'Is There Doctor in the Horse?'. Apparently **John Wiles** rejected the titles but 'Small Prophet, Quick Return' survived.
- During a script conference for the third episode, the title 'Death of a Spy' was apparently put upon **Donald Tosh** for the broadcast. This supposedly caused the introduction of the character of Cyclops into the storyline, although Tosh's original storyline would seem to suggest otherwise.
- The biggest change for the serial came over the summer break when the decision was made to drop Vicki's character entirely. During rehearsals for *Galaxy 4* **Maureen O'Brien** had argued about her lines, and **John Wiles** took the decision to write her character out of the series. During production break Maureen O'Brien returned from holiday expecting to be in regular employment. She was 'glad' that she would be able to move onto other aspects of her career but was shocked at the short notice of her departure from the show.
- The end of the fourth episode would introduce Katarina, a handmaiden whom The Doctor would rescue from the story's events. However it transpired that a 'Vicki' character was already being used by **Terry Nation** for his scripts for *The Daleks' Master Plan*. This would causes further problems down the line.
- Designer **John Wood** was assigned to the serial during the recruiting process. To understand Greek architecture a little better, Wood visited the British Museum. He soon discovered that Greek architecture was not very complex, and buildings were generally made out of large stones.
- The beginning of the recording process was met with a necessary remount at Frensham Ponds in Surrey. Whilst recording fight sequences, **Alan Haywood** and **Cavan Kendall** received minor grazes and cuts, and a remount for some of Cavan Kendall's scenes were carried out on Monday 30 August 1965. The production was met with yet another necessary remount when **James Lynn** cut his hand whilst performing some scenes, thus work for the day was carried over to Wednesday 1 September 1965.
- The rehearsal process was not an easy time for the leading star **William Hartnell**. After sustaining a bruised shoulder after being hit by a mole crane camera platform, Hartnell was fearful that he was being upstaged by the guest stars of the serial, particular **Max Adrian**. It was also during rehearsals that Hartnell's Aunt Bessie, to whom he was really close, passed away, and Hartnell was unable to attend her funeral.
- One of the guest stars of the episode, **Frances White** asked that her name be removed from the *Radio Times* listings for every episode that she would appear in.

- The cell set in which Steven and Vicki were imprisoned, was a clever design from **John Wood**. The cell looked out across a raised set which allowed the extras to walk across. This gave the impression that Steven and Vicki were lower down in the ground compared to the passers-by who would walk by the window.

BROADCAST

EPISODE	DATE	TIME	VIEWING FIGURE	CHART POSITION	APPRECIATION INDEX
1: *Temple of Secrets*	16/10/1965	5:50-6:15pm	8.3M	34th	48
2: *Small Prophet, Quick Return*	23/10/1965	5:50-6:15pm	8.1M	40th	51
3: *Death of a Spy*	30/10/1965	5:50-6:15pm	8.7M	33rd	49
4: *Horse of Destruction*	6/11/1965	5:50-6:15pm	8.3M	38th	52

CLIFFHANGERS

1. Captured by Odysseus, Steven is brought into Agamemnon's tent where The Doctor denies knowing who Steven is, but The Doctor has a plan to escape. The Doctor says that Steven should be sacrificed in his temple [The Tardis] tomorrow. However, Cyclops arrives with news that the 'temple' has gone.
2. When Vicki calls Steven by his proper name, Cassandra declares that Vicki has provided proof that she is a spy. She orders for Vicki and Steven to be killed.
3. Paris arrives with great news – he has found the Great Horse of Asia in the sandy plains. King Priam gives orders for the horse to be brought into the city. The citizens of Troy watch eagerly as the horse sits outside Priam's palace.
4. Inside the Tardis, Katarina tends to Steven, and The Doctor tells her that he is not a God. The Doctor hopes that they land somewhere so Steven can make a full recovery.

COMMERCIAL RELEASES

- **AUDIOBOOK:** April 2008
- **DVD:** November 2004
- **LP (soundtrack):** 27 August 2021
- **NOVELISATION: [Hardback]** - 11 April 1985; **[Paperback]** - 12 September 1985; **[Reissue]** – 1989
  - *Target Doctor Who Library Number*: **97**
- **SOUNTRACK**
  - **8 January 2001:** *BBC Audio*
  - **4 August 2003:** *Adventures in History*
  - **5 August 2010:** *The Lost TV Episodes - Collection One*

CONTINUITY NOTES

- It is later explained in **PROSE:** *Byzantium* that The Doctor knew Vicki would eventually become Cressida in circa 13th Century BC Greece before leaving her travels with him.
- Vicki later appears in **PROSE:** *Apocrypha Bipedium* where she meets the Eight Doctor. Unfamiliar with regeneration she assumed that the Eighth Doctor was a younger version of the First Doctor
- Vicki is the first companion who leaves The Doctor for love. Future companions who stay behind and marry are Jo Grant in **The Green Death** and Leela in **The Invasion of Time**
- **The Myth Makers** is the first example of The Doctor interfering directly (The Doctor giving Nero the idea to burn Rome down so her can build another one was a mistake), if unwillingly with historical events. The Fifth Doctor accidently causes the Great Fire of London in **The Visitation** while The Tenth Doctor and Donna cause Vesuvius too erupt in **The Fires of Pompeii** and subconsciously gives Agatha Christie ideas for future books and characters in **The Unicorn and the Wasp**.
- The High Priestess Cassandra is the first seer in the show's history who accurately predicts the future. Other seers and fortune tellers who succeed in predicting the future include Miss Hawthorne in **The Daemons**, Hieronymous in **The Masque of Mandragora**, the Sisterhood of Karn in **The Brain of Morbius**, The Seeker in **The Ribos Operation**, Aukon in **State of Decay** and Elizabeth Rawlinson in **Battlefield**.

- For the first time The Doctor is mistaken for someone, in the serial's case the Great God Zeus. The Doctor will later be mistaken for many people over his incarnation who include Salamander in *The Enemy of the World*, Sir Reginald Styles in *Day of the Daleks*, The Evil One in *The Face of Evil*, plus many others.
- *The Myth Makers* marks the first time where the show delves into Greek Myths and Legends. Other Greek myths and legends which the show will later explore include, the Medusa in *The Mind Robber*, the god Kronos in *The Time Monster*, and the mystery of Atlantis, most predominant in *The Underwater Menace*.

CRITICAL RESPONSE

- **Mixed Range:** Mixed
- *Doctor Who Magazine 2014 Poll*: 145th/241st
- "Horse of Destruction" was reviewed at a BBC Programme Review Board on Wednesday 10 November 1965 and was met with not-so-positive comments. **Michael Peacock**, controller of BBC1, called the serial 'brutal'; **Tom Sloan**, Head of Television Light Entertainment, felt that the subject of the Trojan War was too complex for young children, and **Huw Wheldon** said that children made up a fair majority of the show's audience.
- "Temple of Secrets" was reviewed on Wednesday 17 November in an audience research report. A total of 176 comments were not that great. Some viewers were confused as to why the narrative to **Mission to the Unknown** was not continued. This led to many believing that the episodes were transmitted in the wrong order. Some further comments highlighted that the confusion between the broadcasted episodes resulted in the show no longer making sense. There were positive notes on the comedic style of the serial, and some viewers welcomed the historical setting. However the acting and production were not well received.

FILMING LOCATIONS

- Frensham Little Pond, Frensham, *Surrey*
- Ham Polo Club, Petersham Road, Ham, *Middlesex*
- Riverside Studio 1

INFLUENCES

- **MUSICAL:** *A Funny Thing Happened on the Way to the Forum* (1962, Stephen Sondheim).
- **PLAY:** *Troilus and Cressida* (1602, William Shakespeare).
- **PLAY:** *Troilus and Criseyde* (mid 1380s, Geoffrey Chaucer).
- **POEM:** *Iliad* (c.8th century BC, Homer).
- **POEM:** *Odyssey* (c.8th century BC, Homer).
- **RADIO PLAYS:** written by **Donald Cotton** and starring **Max Adrian**.

PRODUCTION ERRORS

- No known production errors as all episodes are missing from the BBC Archives.

PUBLICITY

- The *Radio Times* published a half-page feature on the upcoming *Doctor Who* serial with a photograph of Vicki meeting Trojans, Paris and Steven fighting, and **Max Adrian** in his King Priam costume.
- On *Junior Points of View* (Friday 15 October 1965) a letter from a young fan was read, with the young fan declaring their 'liking' of the show despite it being a bit confusing.

WORKING TITLES

- The Mythmakers
- The Trojans
- The Trojan War
- Episode 1: Deus ex Machina
- Episode 3: Is There a Doctor in the Horse?

21) THE DALEKS' MASTER PLAN

Plot: The Daleks and Mavic Chen, Guardian of the Galaxy are planning to conquer the Universe but when The Doctor steals the vital taranium core he must travel across space/time to escape The Daleks

CAST

Dr Who	William Hartnell
Steven	Peter Purves
Mavic Chen	Kevin Stoney
The Meddling Monk	Peter Butterworth
Bret Vyon	Nicholas Courtney
Sara Kingdom	Jean Marsh
Katarina	Adrienne Hill
Kert Gantry	Brian Cant
Lizan	Pamela Greer
Roald	Philip Anthony
Interviewer	Michael Guest
Zephon	Julian Sherrier
Trantis	Roy Evans
Kirksen	Douglas Sheldon
Bors	Dallas Cavell
Garge	Geoffrey Cheshire
Karlton	Maurice Browning
Daxtar	Roger Avon
Borkar	James Hall
Froyn	Bill Meilen
Rhynmal	John Herrington
Station Sergeant	Clifford Earl
First Policeman	Norman Mitchell
Second Policeman	Malcolm Rogers
Detective-Inspector	Keneth Thornett
Man in Mackintosh	Reg Pritchard
Blossom Lefavre	Sheila Dunn
Darcy Tranton	Leonard Grahame
Steinberger P Green	Royston Tickner
Ingmar Knopf	Mark Ross
Assistant Director	Conrad Monk
Arab Sheik	David James
Vamp	Paula Topham
Clown	Robert G Jewell
Professor Webster	Albert Barrington
Prop Man	Buddy Windrush
Cameraman	Steve Machin
Celation	Terence Woodfield
Trevor	Roger Brierley
Scott	Bruce Wightman
Khepren	Jeffrey Isaac
Tuthmos	Derek Ware
Hyksos	Walter Randall
Malpha	Bryan Mosley
Dalek Voices	Peter Hawkins, David Graham
Daleks	Kevin Manser, Robert Jewell
Technix Engineer	John Cam
Technix Pilot	Dennis Tate
Cory's Voice	Peter Hawkins
Criminals	Beatrice Greetz, Rene Heath, Jack Le White, MJ Matthews
Visian	Francis Whilley
Chaplin	MJ Matthews
Charlie	Jack Le White
Keystone Kops	Paul Sarony, Malcolm Leopold
Make-up Man	Harry Davies
Cowboy	William Hall
Saloon Bar Girl	Jean Pestell
Cricket Umpire/Cricketeers	Peter Holmes, Ken McGarvie, John Bohea, Geoffrey Witherick
Revellers	Peter Holmes, Ken McGarvie, John Bohea, Geoffrey Witherick, Pat McDermott, Andrea Cameron
Egyptian Soldiers	David Anderson, Rocky Taylor, Valentino Musetti, Keith Sanderson, Steven Campbell, David Brewster, Gerry Videl, Kevin Leslie, John Crawford, Eric Mills, Agit Chauhan, Bruno Castagnoli, David Shaurat, John Caesar, Clay Hunter, Terry Leigh, Peter Johnson, Ray Mrioni, Ali Hassan, Andrew Andreas, Michael Lawrence, Russell Scott, John Daye, Paul Sinclair, Alan Walling, Barry Noble
Egyptian Slaves	Anthony Lang, Len Russell, Paul Bahadur, Paul Phillips, Glenn White
Old Sara	May Warden
Double for Kirksen	Rob Walker

CREDITS

Written by Terry Nation, Dennis Spooner
From an idea by Terry Nation
Story Editor: Donald Tosh
Fight Arranger: Derek Ware, David Anderson
Title Music by Ron Grainger
 and the BBC Radiophonic Workshop
Incidental music by Tristram Cary
Special Photographic Transparencies
 by George Pollock
Special sound effects by the
 BBC Radiophonic Workshop
Costumes by Daphne Dare
Make-up supervised by Sonia Markham
Lighting: Geoff Shaw
Sound: Robin Luxford

Gerald Taylor, John Scott Martin	**Production Assistant:** Viktor Ritelis
Technix Operators........,Hugh Cecil, Gary Peller	**Designer:** Raymond Cusick, Barry Newbery
John Cam, David Freed, Dennis Tate	**Producer:** John Wiles
Ashley Brown	**Directed by** Douglas Camfield

Gearon...Jack Pitt
Celation.......................................Ian East
Malpha................................Brian Edwards
Beaus.......................................Gerry Videl
Dalek......................................Jack Pitt

ACTOR BIOGRAPHIES: Douglas Sheldon is perhaps best known as Arthur Parker in *Triangle* (1981); **Norman Mitchell** was a very successful film actor landing roles in *The Price of Silence* (1960), *Invasion* (1965), *Half a Sixpence* (1967), *Oliver!* (1968), *Atlantic Wall* (1970), *Lady Caroline Lamb* (1972), *Frankenstein and the Monster from Hell* (1974), *Legend of the Werewolf* (1975), *The Pink Panther Strike Again* (1976), *The Return of the Soldier* (1982) and *Revenge of Billy the Kid* (1991); **Bryan Mosley** played Alf Roberts in *Coronation Street* (1961-99); **Pamela Greer** landed a small role in *They Came from Beyond Space* (1967) and appeared very briefly as WPC Shepherd in *Z Cars* (1967); **Maurice Browning** played in Elliot Morrow in *Compact* (1965); **Bill Meilen** had a small role in *Scooby Doo 2:Monsters Unleashed* (2004); **Kenneth Thornett** can be seen in *The Adventures of Black Beauty* (1972-74); **John Scott Martin** landed small roles in *The Little Shop of Horrors* (1986) and *Erik the Viking* (1989); **John Herrington** landed small roles in *A Shot in the Dark* (1964) and *Billion Dollar Brain* (1967); **Geoffrey Cheshire** can be seen in *On Her Majesty's Service* (1969); **Julian Sherrier** landed three roles in *The Troubleshooters* (1966/70/71); **Francis Whilley** can be seen in *Plague of Zombies* (1966); **Conrad Monk** appeared briefly in *Compact* (1964) and landed four separate roles in *Dixon of Dock Green* (1966/68); **Terence Woodfield** played 7 different characters in *Z-Cars* (1962-68).

BEHIND-THE-SCENES

- **Number of Production Days:** 27
- When an extra episode was allocated to the series, **Terry Nation** delivered the script to *Mission to the Unknown* before working on his third six-part Dalek serial commissioned by **Verity Lambert** and **Dennis Spooner**. However during a Programme Review Board meeting held on Wednesday 26 May various comments from **Huw Wheldon** and **Kenneth Adam** resulted in the six-part Dalek serial being extended to 13 weeks.
- The request for a 12-part serial was noted by Head of Drama **Sydney Newman**, who through the help of **Donald Wilson** persuaded then-producer **Verity Lambert** that the next Dalek serial should be 12 episodes.
- **Verity Lambert** agreed to the change but outlined that the Dalek serial could only be 12 episodes long if the script were jointly written by **Terry Nation** and **Dennis Spooner**. The producer also indicated that recording would need to be pushed back from Friday 15 October 1965 since two weeks of film work would be required instead of the usual one allocated to serials. The budget of the serial would also be as low as possible, although it was expected that **Terry Nation**'s scripts would be expensive to realise.
- At the next BBC Programme Review Board meeting on Wednesday 9 June 1965, it was confirmed that the next Dalek serial would be 12 episodes long, and not 13 as requested by **Kenneth Adam**.
- However the 12-part Dalek serial would prove to cause incoming story editor **Donald Tosh** problems of his own. **Donald Tosh** was very keen on bringing onboard new writers for the show including **Hugh Whitemore** (a writer on *Compact*) and **Alex Miller** (who submitted two story ideas which went unproduced). With the new Dalek serial being 12 parts long he was unable to commission scripts for two regular 4-parts serials. Another writer whom **Donald Tosh** approached was **Keith Dewhurst** (a writer on *Z Cars*). Keith Dewhurst refused the invitation to write for *Doctor Who*.
- Despite a meeting being held where **Terry Nation** and **Dennis Spooner** discussed the storyline, both writers would end work working independently.
- During the handover of production personnel, incoming producer **John Wiles** was not happy with the 12-part serial, and threatened to resign from the show. The producer was persuaded otherwise by **Donald Tosh** over lunch. Donald Tosh himself believed the climax of the serial would see the final end of the Daleks.
- Whilst outlining the scripts, episode five was to take place on the Planet of Mists which was inhabited by invisible beings. This idea was left over material from **Terry Nation**'s third Dalek serial, *The Chase*.
- The storyline for episode nine was to take place in Ancient Egypt (it still does in the broadcasted episode) where the Egyptians built a pyramid as a monument for conquering the Daleks. This idea was also leftover material from *The Chase*.

- Further along the writing process, **Dennis Spooner** requested that The Meddling Monk should be included in episode nine, whom the writer created whilst writing *The Time Meddler*.
- In early June, the director assigned to the project was **Douglas Camfield**. Due to the large production it was thought that another director should be appointed to help Douglas Camfield with the workload. The decision was eventually made to allow one director to handle the entire production.
- When the storyline was completed and commissioned, **Donald Tosh** commissioned episodes 1-6 from **Terry Nation**, and episodes 7-12 from **Dennis Spooner**. However the writers swapped assignments on episodes six and seven. The writers did this as a means of setting a challenge for themselves. For example, with Terry Nation writing episode five, Dennis Spooner would write the resolution to episode five's cliffhanger for episode six. Terry Nation would then write the resolution to **Spooner's** cliffhanger to episode six for episode seven. However, Dennis Spooner later claimed that Terry Nation ignored the situation that he set up.
- **Terry Nation** eventually delivered his six scripts to **Donald Tosh's** flat one evening. However the scripts were rather short, running to only 15 minutes each. Donald Tosh carried out extensive work to flesh out the script to bring them up to around 25 minutes each.
- During the pre-production process, **Terry Nation** gave his opinion about how the interview with Mavic Chen should look. Heavily inspired by a BBC2 adaption of **Isaac Asimov's** *The Cave of Steel*, Nation envisioned the interview should be played on a trimencolvision screen with a flickering light above the actors.
- During the writing process a major change was to be made to The Doctor and his travelling companions. Having been introduced in *The Myth Makers*, the decision was made to kill Katarina off in the fourth episode for shock value. It was discovered that Katarina was a little 'unsophisticated' and would be very hard to identify with. Other writers who were busy with their scripts were finding it difficult to include Katarina in their storylines. It was decided that another character would accompany The Doctor and Steven for the remainder of the serial, only to be killed off at the climax. The new companion was named as Sara Kingdom who would be Bret Vyon's brother (originally the characters would be lovers). Sara Kingdom was heavily inspired by Cathy Gale from *The Avengers*.
- The fifth episode was originally called 'There's Something Just Behind You'. Coincidentally **Terry Nation** and **Dennis Spooner** called one of their scripts for *The Baron*, 'There's Someone Close Behind You'.
- Episode 9 was originally called 'Land of the Pharaohs' and many of Egyptian character names were heavily inspired by people from Ancient Egyptian history; Khepren was named after Chephren who supposedly erected the Second Great Pyramid of Giza in around 2650BC; Hyksos was named after a tribe who were expelled from Egypt around 1575BC, and Tuthmos, derived from Tuthmose, was named after several Pharaohs who ruled over Egypt.
- With the scripts finalised, it was hoped that four actors from *Z Cars* could do a cross-over episode for 'The Feast of Steven'. The production team expressed an interest in, **Colin Welland, Joseph Brady, James Ellis,** and **Brian Blessed** making an appearance in the episode – playing their characters from *Z Cars*. However, *Z Cars* producer **David Rose** did not grant his permission to releases the actors and the idea was dropped.
- The first day of production was on Monday 27 September 1965 which was devoted largely to various effects sequences. **Adrienne Hill** performed Katarina's death scene in the afternoon along with **Douglas Sheldon** who played Kirksen. Both actor and actress were filmed in slow motion whilst jumping on trampolines against a projected starscape. Both actors were supervised by trampoline expert **Rob Walker** who also doubled for Kirksen during certain sequences.
- Wednesday 6 October 1965 was devoted largely to a number of model shots and the death of Sara Kingdom in the final episode. Actress **May Warden** was hired to double as 'Old Sara', and **Douglas Camfield** was inspired by the death of the title character in **H Rider Haggard's** novel *She*, for Sara's death scene.
- Friday 8 October 1965 focused on model work involving the erupting volcano. Steam and compressed air were used to achieve the effect but proved unsatisfactory since the volcano was out of scale with the Tardis. It is decided to try the effect out on another day. Monday 18 October saw the second attempt to get the desired model shot but various technical problems again resulted in a remount. Thursday 21 marked the third attempt to get the desired shot but ultimately proved unsatisfactory again. Monday 15 November 1965 saw the fourth attempt to get the volcano shot complete, and proved successful.
- Rehearsals for the serial commenced on Monday 18 October 1965 and it was discovered that the production of the serial was not going to be an easy one. Many cast members concurred that the scripts were not at a high standard, and the story was rather weak. **Douglas Camfield** would often perform rewrites during rehearsals thus preventing read-throughs taking place in the following weeks. Above all, Douglas Camfield was not that fond of the Daleks. He believed they were weak villains – always threatening but doing very little.

- To achieve the effect of an Invisible Visian examining Sara's hair was a simple affair. **Jean Marsh**'s hair was placed across a metal wire which was then lifted and lowered on cue.
- To play the part of the Cowboy, **Douglas Camfield** hired **William Hall**, who was actually a film critic for the *Evening News*. The Saloon Bar Girl role went to **Jean Pestell** who was a poet by profession.
- After transmission of 'Counter Plot', the production office received a surprising phone call from the production team working on **Stanley Kubrick**'s upcoming science-fiction epic *2001: A Space Odyssey*. The team wanted to know how the effect of corpses floating in space was achieved. They also expressed an interest to know how **Douglas Camfield** achieved the molecular dissemination sequences.
- During recording for 'Golden Death', **Sam Rolfe** the creator of MGM's *The Man from U.N.C.L.E* visited the studios and was photographed beside the Daleks. Sam Rolfe believed that the Daleks had real potential to be a massive hit back in the United States.
- Overall the production for **The Daleks' Master Plan** had been a real challenge for both cast and crew alike. Since he was heavily assisted by production assistant **Viktor Ritelis**, **Douglas Camfield** requested that he should be given an on-screen credit for 'Destruction of Time'. Up to this point production assistants always remained uncredited, so Viktor Ritelis was given a unique privilege.
- The pressure and demanding production schedule also took its toll on **Donald Tosh** and **John Wiles** who both sent in their requests to leave the show.
- When production concluded on Friday 14 January 1966, **Douglas Camfield** decided he would distance himself from *Doctor Who* for a while. He would return to direct many times for the show, and would ultimately become the top billed director for the classic era.
- It was discovered that 'Destruction of Time' underrun. This was because **John Wiles** had to cut two shots during Sara's death scene for sensory reasons.

BROADCAST

EPISODE	DATE	TIME	VIEWING FIGURE	CHART POSITION	APPRECIATION INDEX
1: *The Nightmare Begins*	13/11/1965	5:50-6:15pm	9.1M	35th	54
2: *Day of Armaggedon*	20/11/1965	5:50-6:15pm	9.8M	31st	52
3: *Devil's Planet*	27/11/1965	5:50-6:15pm	10.3M	29th	52
4: *The Traitors*	4/12/1965	5:50-6:15pm	9.5M	34th	51
5: *Counter Plot*	11/12/1965	5:50-6:15pm	9.9M	26th	53
6: *Coronas of the Sun*	18/12/1965	5:50-6:15pm	9.1M	40th	56
7: *The Feast of Steven*	25/11/1965	6:35-7:00pm	7.9M	71st	39
8: *Volcano*	1/1/1966	5:50-6:15pm	9.6M	31st	49
9: *Golden Death*	8/1/1966	5:50-6:15pm	9.2M	43rd	52
10: *Escape Switch*	15/1/1966	5:50-6:15pm	9.5M	37th	50
11: *The Abandoned Planet*	22/1/1966	5:50-6:15pm	9.8M	35th	49
12: *Destruction of Time*	29/1/1966	5:50-6:15pm	8.6M	39th	57

CLIFFHANGERS

1. The Doctor discovers Marc Cory's skeleton and warning message about the impending Dalek invasion. Hurrying back to the Tardis, The Doctor discovers that Daleks have surrounded the Tardis.
2. The Doctor has successfully stolen the Dalek's taranium core and heads back to the Spar spaceship. Meanwhile Bret Vyon, who has grown impatient, begins the take-off procedure without The Doctor onboard.
3. The Doctor and his companions successfully escape from the planet Desperus just as the Daleks arrive. The Doctor instructs Katarina to ensure that the airlock door is closed and secure. Whilst checking the airlock, Kirksen appears, holding a knife, and grabs Katarina.
4. The Doctor, Steven, and Bret Vyon are confronted by Sara Kingdom. The Doctor and Steven run and Sara shoots and kills Bret Vyon. Sara summons Borkar and tells him that there are still fugitives on the loose who must be killed on-sight.
5. Arriving on the planet Mira, The Doctor and his companions hide in a cave from both the Visians and the Daleks. The Daleks arrive and drive the Visians away, leaving The Doctor and his companions trapped.
6. Having escaped the Daleks (yet again), the Tardis arrives at its next destination. However there is a slight problem, The Doctor discovers that the atmosphere outside is poisonous.
7. Inside the Tardis, The Doctor, Steven, and Sara celebrate Christmas with a glass of champagne. The Doctor toasts Steven and Sara, turns to the camera and wishes a Merry Christmas to everyone at home.
8. The Tardis crew escape a group of revellers at Trafalgar Square during New Year's celebrations. They remains unaware that the Daleks are on their trail (again).
9. Having landed in Ancient Egypt, the Tardis has materialised inside a tomb. Inside the tomb the lid to a sarcophagus begins to move, and a bandaged hand emerges.
10. The Doctor fits The Meddling Monk's directional circuit inside the Tardis console. The Doctor knows that doing so is a dangerous operation. The Doctor activates the controls, and an explosion rocks the Tardis.
11. The Tardis arrives back on Kembel, where Steven and Sara are captured by Mavic Chen. Mavic Chen marches them into the Dalek base at gun-point.
12. The Daleks have been defeated, but at a terrible cost. With Sara dead, and Kemble reduced to a wasteland. The Doctor and Steven head back to the Tardis and leave Kembel.

COMMERCIAL RELEASES

- **AUDIOBOOK:** June 2010
- **DVD:** November 2004 [Episodes 2,5, and 10]
- **ELECTRONIC MUSIC/SOUND EFFECTS**
  - **2000** – *Doctor Who at the BBC Radiophonic Workshop Volume 1: The Early Years 1963-1969*
- **LP (soundtrack):** 1 March 2019
- **NOVELISATION: [Paperback]** - 19 October 1989; **[Reissue]** – 1990
  - *Target Doctor Who Library Number*: **142**
- **SOUNDTRACK**
  - **22 October 2001:** *BBC Audio*
  - **2003:** *Doctor Who: Devils' Planet – The Music of Tristram Cary*
  - **14 February 2011:** *The Lost TV Episodes - Collection Two*
  - **9 December 2013-25 February 2016:** *Doctor Who: The 50th Anniversary Collection*
- **VIDEO:** July 1992 [episode 5 and 10]

CONTINUITY NOTES

- *The Daleks' Master Plan* marks the first time where a companion dies during the story. Katarina is sucked into space in "The Traitors" while Sara Kingdom ages to death in "Destruction of Time". However Adric became the first full-time companion when killed off in *Earthshock*.
- The Visians are the first invisible creatures to appear on the show: other invisible beings include the Refusians in *The Ark*, the Spiridons in *Planet of the Daleks*, Xoanan (sometimes) in *The Face of Evil*, the Krafayis in *Vincent and the Doctor*, and the Cerebravores in **COMIC:** *Revolutions of Terror*.
- The alien delegates who appear in *Mission to the Unknown* differ very slightly in the serial. Sentreal does not make an appearance and is replaced by Zephon, and Warrien was replaced by Celation.

- The alien delegates: Malpha, Sentreal, Trantis, Beaus, Celation and Gearon all appear in **AUDIO:** *The Prefect Prisoners* starring the Fourth Doctor.
- The Doctor mentions that he was present during the Relief of Mafeking in 1900. The Relief is later brought up by John Smith in *Human Nature*, and Colonel Curbishley in *The Unicorn and the Wasp*.
- The Doctor is artificially aged during the climax of 'Destruction of Time' but the process is reversed. The Doctor is later temporary artificially aged during *The Leisure Hive* and *The Sound of Drums*.
- Although previously featured in *The Time Meddler*, the Meddling Monk's Tardis is the first time where a Tardis changes it appearance to blend in with its surroundings. The Monk's Tardis takes on the form of a motorbike, a stagecoach, a tank, a tree, a biplane, a police box, and a block of ice. Both The Master and The Rani's Tardises continually change their appearance whenever they appear in the series.
- Mavic Chen, whose title is Guardian of the Galaxy; turns out to be working for the Daleks. Stein in *Earthshock* and Mike in *Remembrance of the Daleks* are two other characters who are supposedly aligned with 'the good side' but are later exposed as traitors who have allied themselves with the Daleks.
- The Meddling Monk makes his second and last appearance in the show, but does go to feature in several more of The Doctor's adventures during his eighth incarnation. Future appearances include **AUDIO:** *The Book of Kells*, **AUDIO:** *The Resurrection of Mars*, **AUDIO:** *Lucie Miller* and **AUDIO:** *To the Death*.
- Desperus is the first prison planet to feature in the show, where prisoners are dumped and left to fend for themselves. Other prison planets to feature in the show include Shada in the incomplete *Shada*, Varos in *Vengeance on Varos*, Krop Tor in *The Impossible Planet/The Satan Pit*, Volag-Noc in *The Infinite Quest*, and the Dalek Asylum in *Asylum of the Daleks*. Desperus itself is later mentioned in **PROSE:** *Placebo Affect*.
- The Doctor and his companions briefly land in Ancient Egypt and are soon followed by the Daleks. The Doctor will later revisit the famous country in *Pyramids of Mars* and *Dinosaurs on a Spaceship*.
- To this date *The Daleks' Master Plan* remains as the longest *Doctor Who* serial in the show's run (if you exclude *Trial of a Time Lord* which runs to 14 episodes, but is split into four separate narratives).
- In **PROSE:** *Scribbles in Chalk* it is revealed that Cassandra, who appeared in *The Myth Makers* prophesied Katarina's death, which was the ultimate reason she chose her as her handmaiden.
- Episode 7 'The Feast of Steven' is the first and only classic episode of *Doctor Who* to be set at Christmas, unlike the revived series where it became an annual tradition until 2017 for a Christmas-based episode to be broadcast on Christmas day.

CRITICAL RESPONSE

- **Review Range:** Mixed
- *Doctor Who Magazine 2014 Poll*: 48th/241st
- Friday 19 November 1965 saw various children's comments being shared on *Junior Points of View*. One letter commented that the new series was off to a good start. Another letter outlined their like of the Daleks, but suggested that they should 'take a break'. A more negative letter was received asking why the show cannot have new monsters.
- Friday 29 November 1965 saw comments from **Mary Whitehouse** (somebody whom the *Doctor Who* production office would have regular dealings with). She commented that the Daleks were a bad influence on young children. She outlined there chanting cries of 'Kill! Kill! Kill! as a problem.
- After the broadcast of 'The Traitors' there were major complaints and comments concerning the death of Katarina and Bret Vyon. A mother sent in a letter to the *Daily Mirror* outlining her concerns about a young girl (Katarina) being grabbed and held against her will by a big, hairy man (Kirksen). The concerned mother believed that *Doctor Who* had descended into horror with the scene.
- Tuesday 11 January 1966 saw an audience research report on 'Devil's Planet' with a total of 340 viewers sharing their comments. There was a widespread approval of the Dalek's return, however **William Hartnell**'s performance was largely criticised.
- Before the broadcast of 'Destruction of Time', **Bill Edmunds** review of the serial was not a terribly positive one. He outlined that his respect and awe for the Daleks was waning. He outlined that the Daleks were continually running about the place, chanting threats, but doing very little to overcome their situation.
- Another audience research report appeared on Tuesday 1 February with a total of 177 viewers sharing their views on 'The Feast of Steven'. The episode was meet with a mixed response. One comment stated the episode was one of the worst things the viewer had seen. There were however several comments which praised the direction and festive spirit of the episode.

- Thursday 3 February 1966 saw a review from **Stewart Lane** of the *Daily Worker*. **Lane** outlined that the show was beginning to age and believed that youngsters were beginning to lose interest in the show. **Lane** also believed that the Dalek would return again – much to his dismay.
- A third audience research report appeared on Monday 7 February 1966 with 233 viewers sharing their opinions on 'Volcano'. The episode received 'better' comments compared to other episodes but the Daleks and **William Hartnell** were again criticised.
- Friday 11 February 1966 saw comments on 'Escape Switch' from 255 viewers. There was a generally consensus that viewers were growing bored with the serial and The Doctor. However, The Doctor and The Meddling Monk's double-act received praise.
- Tuesday 8 March 1966 saw a final analysis on 'Destruction of Time' where there was general praise for the serial climax and horrific events.
- Writing in *The Discontinuity Guide*, **Paul Cornell, Martin Day**, and **Keith Topping** responded 'positively' towards the serial. They described the whole thing as epic, but the plot wasn't justified with 12 episodes, 6 would have been fine. The story's ambition was justifiable nonetheless in spite of the pantomimish feel of the seventh episode. They described The Doctor breaking the fourth wall as ahead of its time.

FILMING LOCATIONS

- Ealing Film Studios Stage 2
- Ealing Film Studios Stage 3
- Ealing Film Studios Stage 3B
- Hammersmith Park, Shepherd's Bush, *London*
- Television Centre Studio 3
- Television Centre Studio 4

INFLUENCES

- **CHARACTER:** *James Bond* (1953, Ian Fleming).
- **COMIC BOOK CHARACTER:** *Dan Dare* (1940-53, Fawcett Comics).
- **FILM:** *Flash Gordon* (1936, Frederick Stephani).
- **FILM:** *Silent Hollywood Films of the 1930s*
- **NOVEL:** *She: A History of Adventure* (1887, H. Rider Haggard).
- **TV:** *The Avengers* (1961-69, Sydney Newman).
- **TV:** *Z Cars* (1962-78, Troy Kennedy Martin and Allan Prior).

PRODUCTION ERRORS

1. The Doctor sounds like a Dalek at one point during "Coronas of the Sun"
2. At the beginning of "Volcano" the Tardis background "hum" noise can be heard instead of the usual Dalek control room sounds, one sound quickly cross-fades to the other.
3. During "Escape Switch", The Doctor refers to Mavic Chen as Magic … before correcting himself.
4. Wouldn't a Police Box be very suspicious sitting outside a Police Station?
5. The message tape which Marc Cory left behind in **Mission to the Unknown** is remarkable different to the one heard during the story's events.
6. Kurt Gantry's beard seen in "The Nightmare Beings" is remarkably different compared to other points in the serial; particularly between pre-filmed scenes and scene shot in a studio.
7. During various close-ups, the hair lace on **William Hartnell**'s wig is visible.
8. It seems rather odd to have Grand Alliance in the first place if it is so expendable.
9. Its never explained how The Meddling Monk left England in 1066 considering The Doctor stole his dimensional control. Did a future incarnation of The Doctor gives it back to him at some point? If so, The Monk clearly never learned his lessons from his previous encounter with The Doctor.

PUBLICITY

- To promote the up-coming serial, two film trailers running at 18' and 37' long were released for the serial.

- The *Radio Times* promoted the new serial with various photographs and previews of characters and settings etc. Promotional photographs included The Doctor with two Daleks, Katarina tending to a sick Steven and The Doctor onboard the spaceship *Spar*. There was also a preview of the character of Bret Vyon. Promotional material and photographs varied from region to region.
- The *Daily Mirror* promoted the new serial with a short article by **Clifford Davis** who chatted to regular Dalek voice artiste **Peter Hawkins**.
- The *Daily Express* promoted the new *Doctor Who* companion Sara Kingdom with an article titled 'Look out Daleks! Sara is gunning for you'. The article gave a brief outline and synopsis about the character.
- The *Daily Mail* also promoted the character of Sara Kingdom with a title called 'A Touch of Avengers: The New Girl Linking Up with Dr Who Tonight'. The article was companioned by another outline of the new character courtesy of BBC Publicity.
- The second episode 'Day of Armageddon' was previewed in the *Radio Times* on Thursday 18 November with a photograph Chen with the Daleks. The following week's issue promoted 'Devil's Planet' which carried a photo of The Doctor and Bret with the Daleks' taranium core.
- A short feature in *The Daily Mirror* centred on the actor playing the Technix Operators which include details that three of the actor were already bold, before taking on the part of the bald characters.

WORKING TITLES

- Doctor Who and the Daleks' Master Plan
- A Switch in Time
- Episode 5: There Someone Just Behind You
- Episode 6: Counter Plot
- Episode 9: Land of the Pharaohs
- Episode 11: Return to Varga
- Episode 12: The Mutation of Time
- Episode 12: A Switch in Time

22) THE MASSACRE OF ST BARTHOLOMEW'S EVE

Plot: In Paris 1572 The Doctor mysteriously vanishes and Steven is caught up in tensions between the Huguenots and Catholics. Can The Doctor really be the Abbot of Amboise? Only time will tell

CAST

Dr Who/Abbot of Amboise	William Hartnell
Steven	Peter Purves
André Morell	Marshal Tavannes
Admiral de Coligny	Leonard Sachs
Nicholas	David Weston
Anne	Annette Robertson
Gaston	Eric Thompson
Simon	John Tillinger
Catherine de Medici	Joan Young
Charles IX	Barry Justice
Roger	Christopher Tranchell
Preslin	Erik Chitty
Landlord	Edwin Finn
Teligny	Michael Bilton
Priest	Norman Claridge
Captain of the Guard	Clive Cazes
Servant	Reginald Jessup
Old Lady/Old Woman	Cynthia Etherington
1st Man	Will Stampe
2nd Man	Ernest Smith
Dodo	Jackie Lane
Officer	John Slavid
1st Guard	Jack Tarran
2nd Guard	Leslie Bates
Small Boy	Robert Bartlett
Tavern Customers	Edward Granville, David Ronowski, Emmett Hennessy, Ken McGarvie, Ken Dougall, Leslie Conrad, Charles O'Rourke, Peter Day, Dennis Plenty
Cardinal's Guard	Vic Taylor
Passers-by	Valerie Cox, Katie Heal, Valerie Taylor, Jean Channon, Elizabeth Forbes, Susan Lane, Susan Farr, David J Grahame, Reg Cranfield, John Beerbohm, Ernest Smith, John Lawrence, Bill Howes, Charles Erskine, Fred Rawlings, John Pollock, Charles Gilbert, Daryl Richards, David Olive
Old Man	Juba Kennelly
Priest	Hugh Cecil
Guards	Pat Gorman, John Freeman, Denis Plenty, Nigel James, Derek Chafer, Frances Whilley, Montagu Howard, James Haswell, Jeffrey Witterick, Roy Peace, Jim Appleby, Mike Reid, Arthur McGuire
Usher	George Romano
Councillors	Graham Tunbridge, Nigel Bernard, Leslie Shannon, Robert Pearson
Secretary	Norton Clarke
Assassin [Bonbot]	Tom Sye
Citizens of Paris	Ralph Katterns, Derek Martin, Eddie Davis, Yanos Jurchi, Rick Patterson, Peter Stewart, Valerie Stanton, Andre Cameron, Margo Abbot, Elisabeth Digby-Smith, Elaine Laniado, Marguerite Young, Leila Forde, Ursula Granville, Joanna Hobson, Harry Mitchell, Harry Hymes, Gerry Holmes, Barry Noble, Declan Cuff, John Terrell, Alan Wakeling, Pat Leclerc, Len Russell, Edward Phillips, Eric Mills, Donald Campbell, Fred Taylor
Servant	Alan Viccars
Passer-by [on Wimbledon Common]	Marguerite Young
Double for Steven	John Clifford

CREDITS

Written by John Lucarotti and Donald Tosh
Title music by Ron Grainer and the BBC Radiophonic Workshop
Story Editors: Donald Tosh, Gerry Davis
Film Cameraman: Tony Leggo
Make Up Supervisor: Sonia Markham
Costume Supervisor: Daphne Dare
Lighting by Dennis Channon
Sound by Gordon Mackie
Designer: Michael Young
Producer: John Wiles
Directed by Paddy Russell

ACTOR BIOGRAPHIES: André Morell landed films roles in *Ten Days in Paris* (1940), *Flesh and Blood* (1951), *Stolen Face* (1952), *The Man Who Never Was* (1956), *Zarak* (1956), *The Camp on Blood Island* (1958), *Ben-Hur* (1959), *Cash on Damned* (1961), *The Plague of Zombies* (1966), *The Mummy's Shroud* (1967), *10 Rillington Place* (1971), *Pope Joan* (1972) and the animated *The Lord of the Rings* (1978); **Edwin Finn** landed small roles in *Julius Caesar* (1970) and *Time Bandits* (1981); **Barry Justice** was Dr. Bill Conrad in *The Doctors* (1969-71); **Eric Thompson** was the narrator on *The Magic Roundabout* (1964); **Chris Tranchell** appeared briefly in *Survivors* (1975-76); **Jackie Lane** can be seen as Rosemary Gray in *Compact* (1963) for 9 episodes; uncredited child actor **Robert Bartlett** went to be appeared in *The Newcomers* (1969) as Michael Robertson.

BEHIND-THE-SCENES

- **Number of Production Days:** 9
- Having written both *Marco Polo* and *The Aztecs*, **John Lucarotti** was invited by script editor **Dennis Spooner** to submit another historical-based idea for the show on Wednesday 24 February 1965. After some discussions it was decided that an Indian historical setting would form the basis for a good story.
- There was no urgency to deliver the scripts since there was some doubts as to whether or not **Jacqueline Hill** and **William Russell** would renew their contracts in May 1965.
- In the meantime, **John Lucarotti** began research for his potential story idea and met with **Waris Hussein** on Tuesday 22 March 1965 to form ideas. However it transpired that there was very little interest in producing a story focusing on Indian history prior to the seventeenth-century. **Waris Hussein** instead suggested the Indian Mutiny of 1857. It transpired that the Indian Mutiny has already formed the basis of an unused script 'The Red Fort' which would have been written by **Terry Nation**.
- Pushing the Indian Mutiny idea further, it soon transpired that the production office did not like producing historical based stories with a setting after 1600. This decision had obviously come into place after *The Reign of Terror* had entered production in mid-summer 1964. **Dennis Spooner** was impressed with the idea and contacted **Verity Lambert** and **Donald Wilson** to see if an exception could be made for the Indian Mutiny.
- A few days later it was decided that the Indian Mutiny setting could not feature in *Doctor Who*, and **Dennis Spooner** offered **John Lucarotti** the chance to select another time period. John Lucarotti eventually selected the Vikings as the basis of his serial, which would cause further problems down the line.
- Whilst researching for his Viking storyline, the *Doctor Who* production office changed hands with **Verity Lambert** and **Dennis Spooner** being replaced by **John Wiles** and **Donald Tosh** respectively. During the handover, Donald Tosh invited **John Lucarotti** to submit a storyline, with the writer explaining that he had already been commissioned to write for the series by Spooner.
- Towards the end of May 1965, **John Lucarotti** meet with **Donald Tosh** to discuss his Viking storyline despite the fact that **Dennis Spooner** was working on *The Time Meddler* which also featured Vikings. Lucarotti's story would have focused primarily on Erik the Red discovering Newfoundland, and would have featured Ian, Barbara, and Vicki.
- On Tuesday 8 June, **John Lucarotti** met with **John Wiles** and **Donald Tosh** to discuss his storyline further. Both producer and script editor wanted to take the show in new directions, wishing to install more mystery into The Doctor and the series. Taking onboard on their comments John Lucarotti sent about writing the storyline over the next 10 days. During this time John Lucarotti kept in regular contact with Donald Tosh who sounded very excited about the changes the writer was making.
- The Viking storyline was put into doubt on Thursday 24 June 1965 when **John Lucarotti** received a letter of rejection, despite handing in a 12-page storyline with the amendments requested included. **Donald Tosh** felt that, among other reasons, the new storyline was too similar to the already in-production *The Time Meddler*.
- With two storylines rejected and a promise of writing for the show, a promise was made that the next storyline **John Lucarotti** submitted would be purchased and commissioned. During discussions, the idea of using the Massacre of the Huguenots on St Bartholomew's Day was arrived at. Apparently it was **Donald Tosh** who came up with the idea, and **John Wiles** was very interested in producing a story which focused on the negative sides of religious conflict.
- During the writing process for the new serial, **William Hartnell** suggested an idea that he could play a different character in the serial – this idea was rejected by the production office. The basis for this idea would have featured in a story called 'The Son of Doctor Who' which would have centred on The Doctor encountering his evil son who also roamed through time and space inside a Tardis. Although the idea was never taken up, **John Wiles** was very keen in producing a story which involved a double for Doctor Who.
- Having produced the four-scripts for his new serial they were formerly accepted by **Donald Tosh** but the script editor requested rewrites on all four episodes on Tuesday 3 August 1965.
- It is not certain why rewrites were requested but the likely answer possibly lay with the change of companions. Having reached the decision to drop Vicki, it was decided that Katarina introduced in *The Myth Makers*, would be the new full-time companion. However these plans were quickly changed when it was decided that a companion from ancient times would not quite work in stories set in the future. Sara Kingdom was then created to be the full-time companion only to die at the end of *The Daleks' Master Plan*. The new companion for a time looked like it was going to be Anne Chaplet, a character who

would accompany Steven, and who would ultimately be saved from certain death during the climax. However it was decided that the use of Anne Chaplet would causes certain problems. **Donald Tosh** rejected the idea of having Anne as the new companion because he believed the character would go against the show's principles about not altering established Earth history. Anne Chaplet was also quite similar to Katarina, since she came from a period of Earth history and thus using her in futuristic settings would be problematic.

- During Autumn 1965, **John Wiles** and **Donald Tosh** didn't believe that **John Lucarotti** was giving them what they wanted from his scripts. They eventually paid him off and Tosh would make further changes. It didn't help when Donald Tosh believed he found many historical inaccuracies throughout the scripts.
- The end of the final episode would introduce the new companion, Dodo Chaplet, whose French heritage would suggest that she is a distant relative of Anne Chaplet.
- Before production commenced on the episode, both **John Wiles** and **Donald Tosh** would be leaving the series in the near future. Both men had their own difficulties settling into the show, and had their own runs in with **William Hartnell** who was proving to be difficult to work with. During this time, **Gerald Savoy**, whom Donald Tosh did not get on well with at Granada Television, had taken up the position as Head of Serials.
- It was later decided that **Donald Tosh** would receive a co-credit with **John Lucarotti**, since the script editor had written most of the final episode and had carried out extensive rewrites on the main story. Incoming story editor **Gerry Davis**'s first duty as script editor also came with the final episode.
- The third day of filming, Wednesday 5 January 1966, saw work on a Paris street set. Since **Peter Purves** was busy with rehearsals for *The Daleks' Master Plan*, extra **John Clifford** was hired to double for Steven.
- Friday 7 January 1966 saw **Jackie Lane** perform her first scenes as Dodo at Windmill Road. It was hoped that **Jacqueline Hill** and **William Russell** could make cameo appearances as Barbara and Ian, but the idea was dropped.
- Director **Paddy Russell** wished to create an authentic feel during the scenes set in the Paris street. Background noises of horses, carts, hustle and bustle and birdsong were all added throughout the serial.
- The part of the 1st Man went to **Roy Denton** (previously a Tribesman in *An Unearthly Child*) but he was taken ill shortly afterwards. He was replaced by **Will Stampe**, however the change of actors happened after the *Radio Times* went to print, meaning **Roy Denton** was not removed from the billings.
- During episodes where **William Hartnell** played the Abbot of Amboise throughout, **Paddy Russell** gave **Hartnell** advice when she felt that his performance as the Abbot was too close to his performance as The Doctor. The director believed that both characters should act and behave differently from one and other.
- During rehearsals for 'Bell of Doom', **William Hartnell** expressed concerns about a long soliloquy he was required to perform towards the end of the episode. However **Donald Tosh** praised Hartnell's performance during the readthrough, and the actor subsequently agreed to perform the entire speech later on.

BROADCAST

EPISODE	DATE	TIME	VIEWING FIGURE	CHART POSITION	APPRECIATION INDEX
1: *War of God*	5/2/1966	5:15-5:40pm	8M	45th	52
2: *The Sea Beggar*	12/2/1966	5:15-5:40pm	6M	96th	52
3: *Priest of Death*	19/2/1966	5:15-5:40pm	5.9M	92nd	49
4: *Bell of Doom*	26/2/1966	5:15-5:40pm	5.8M	94th	53

CLIFFHANGERS

1. Simon Duvall brings the Abbot of Amboise news that Anne Chaplet has taken refugee inside Admiral de Coligny's house. The Abbot demands that the girl should be brought to him tomorrow. As the episode end, viewers see that the Abbot is a spitting image of The Doctor.
2. Returning to his residence Admiral de Coligny informs his assistant Nicholas Nuss that he has successfully convinced the King to ally with the Netherlands against Spain. The King has also informed de Coligny that he will go down in history as the Sea Beggar. Little does de Coligny realises is that The Abbot and Marshal Tavannes have hired an assassin to kill 'The Sea Beggar'.

3. Finding the Abbot of Amboise dead in a gutter, Steven attempts to convince the Catholics that the Huguenots were not responsible. A man called Roger Colbert incites the crowd against Steven, and Steven is forced to run for his life.
4. Landing in 1966, Steven storms out of the Tardis, angry that The Doctor did not save Anne Chaplet. A young girl called Dodo Chaplet enters the Tardis believing it to be a real police box. Steven runs back in to inform The Doctor that two policemen are coming. Steven is astounded at Dodo's surname and believes that she might be a descendant of Anne's. The Tardis leave with its new crew member on its next journey.

COMMERCIAL RELEASES

- **AUDIOBOOK:** June 2015
- **CASSETTE:** September 1987
- **LP (soundtrack):** 29 August 2020
- **NOVELISATION: [Hardback]** - 18 June 1987; **[Paperback]** - 19 November 1987; **[Reissue]** – 1992
  - *Target Doctor Who Library Number*: **122**
- **SOUNDTRACK**
  - **1999**: *BBC Audio*
  - **4 August 2003**: *Adventures in History*
  - **14 February 2011**: *The Lost TV Episodes - Collection Two*

CONTINUTY NOTES

- When meeting Dodo for the first time, The Doctor asks Steven if he thinks she has a resemblance to his granddaughter Susan. Steven informs The Doctor that he cannot comment on that since he joined him on his travels after Susan departed him – see **The Dalek Invasion of Earth** and **The Chase**.
- For the first time in the show's history, The Doctor has an exact double roaming about the place. The Doctor will later meet exact doubles of himself throughout his incarnations, The Second Doctor/Salamander in **The Enemy of the World** and The Eleventh Doctor/Ganger Doctor in **The Rebel Flesh/The Almost People**, and to an extent The Third Doctor in **Day of the Daleks** where a future projection of himself is sent back in time.
- The Doctor will also have the unfortunate pleasure of witnessing various aliens and enemies using his image to disguise themselves; The First Doctor/Robot Dr Who in **The Chase**, The Fourth Doctor/Xoanon in **The Face of Evil**, The Fourth Doctor/Meglos in **Meglos**, and The Fifth Doctor/Omega in **Arc of Infinity**.
- Steven refers to his brief visit to Egypt from **The Daleks' Master Plan**
- The serial marks the second time where The Doctor is caught up in the violent events in French History. The first instances being **The Reign of Terror** set during the French Revolution.
- Steven is the first companion to berate The Doctor for not stepping in to save a certain someone (Anne Chaplet) from established historical events. Tegan Jovanka pleads with The Fifth Doctor to save Adric from the Freighter which wiped out the dinosaurs in **Earthshock**, and Donna Noble continually attempts to make The Tenth Doctor save the city of Pompeii from certain destruction from Mount Vesuvius in **The Fires of Pompeii**. The Tenth Doctor does eventually give in, and saves the Caecilius family from certain death.

CRITICAL RESPONSE

- **Review Range:** Positive
- *Doctor Who Magazine 2014 Poll*: 100th/241st
- *The Massacre*, as it is called nowadays, is one of only three serials where there is no surviving footage (the other two being **Marco Polo** and **Mission to the Unknown**). Most reviews have come from listening to the soundtrack, and many reviews have only been compiled in recent years.
- *The Daily Telegraph* placed the serial in 10th place among the shows 56 greatest stories and episodes. The review praised the serial for its educational integrity and linked the story more to adult costume drama than to Saturday teatime children's viewing. The reviews also praised The Doctor's monologue at the end of episode four, calling it one of **William Hartnell**'s finest moments in the show.
- In the *Radio Times*, **Patrick Mulkern** gave the serial 4 stars out of 5, calling it an outstanding piece of drama, highlighting its grim realism as a selling point. He praised **Peter Purves**' performance as Steven, and called the rest of the cast strong. However he was not as taken in by Dodo but showered praise on the ending and The Doctor's monologue

- Writing in his book *Doctor Who: The Complete Guide*, **Mark Campbell** gave the serial a 9/10 describing the historical story as complex and engaging, and praised Steven's increased dominance in the story.

FILMING LOCATIONS
- Ealing Film Studios Stage 3
- Riverside Studio 1
- Windmill Road, Wimbledon Common, *London*

INFLUENCES
- [no known influences]

PRODUCTION ERRORS
1. It seems very unlikely that Dodo is indeed a direct descent from Anne Chaplet, since both characters have the same surname. If Anne married in later life wouldn't she have taken her husband's name? Or maybe Anne was in the early stages of pregnancy with an illegitimate child, and gave her [son?] the surname Chaplet.
2. If Anne Chaplet is supposed to be a working-class French citizen, why doesn't her accent reflect this?
3. Steven's turnaround in forgiving The Doctor for his actions seems a little rushed and unconvincing. If he was that mad with The Doctor why would the appearance of two policemen change anything?

PUBLICITY
- The *Radio Times* (5-11 February 1966) promoted the serial with a short article accompanied with a photograph of The Doctor and Steven sitting inside a tavern.
- The *Daily Worker* (Thursday 3 February 1966) contained comments from critic **Stewart Lane** who wrote that the show was showing signs of age, and gave a brief synopsis about the upcoming adventure. He also states his 'dislike' of the Daleks commenting that he feared they would make yet another appearance.

WORKING TITLES
- The Massacre
- The Massacre of St Bartholomew
- The War of God

23) THE ARK

Plot: An ark travels through space to a distant planet carrying the last of the Human Race and Monoids but when Dodo develops a cold it may be the Ark will never reach its destination.

CAST

Dr Who	William Hartnell
Steven	Peter Purves
Dodo	Jackie Lane
Commander	Eric Elliott
Zentos	Inigo Jackson
Manyak	Roy Spencer
Mellium	Kate Newman
Rhos	Michael Sheard
Baccu	Ian Frost
1st Guardian	Stephanie Heesom
2nd Guardian	Paul Greenhalgh
Maharis	Terence Woodfield
Monoid Two	Ralph Carrigan
Yendom	Terence Bayler
Monoid One	Edmund Coulter
Dassuk	Brian Wright
Venussa	Eileen Helsby
Monoid Three	Frank George
Monoid Four	John Caesar
1st Monoid	Edmund Coulter
2nd Monoid	Frank George
Monoid Voices	Roy Skelton, John Halstead
Refusian Voice	Richard Beale
Monoid [Slaves]	Eric Blackburn, Chris Webb, Raymond Byrom, Bernard Barnsley
Male Guardian [Miniaturised]	David Greneau
Male Guardians	Bill Hunter, George Gibbs, Roy Douglas, Trevor Griffiths, Mark Allington, Ron Gregory, Tony Kemp
Female Guardians	Judith Webb, Jackie Salt, Jackie Duval, Sheila McGrath, Jan Williams, Terry Cashfield, Diane Chapman, Iris Fry
Child Guardians	Hazel Graham, Jacqueline Lewis, Philips Harris, Paul Johnson
Monoids [6, 9, 21, 33, 45, 63, 77]	Eric Blackburn, Chris Webb, Raymond Byrom, Bernard Barnsley, Denis Marlow, Bill Richards
Male Guardians [slaves]	John Moyce, Paul Linley, Royston Farrell, Victor Hunt, Alan Norburn, Michael Osborn
Female Guardians [slaves]	Sara Negus, Andrea Beddows, Rosemary Chalmers, Gloria Williams, Rosemary Lord, Deryn Fisher

CREDITS

Written by Paul Erickson & Lesley Scott
Title Music by Ron Grainer and the BBC Radiophonic Workshop
Incidental music by Tristram Cary
Film Cameraman: Tony Leggo
Film Editor: Noel Chanan
Costumes designed by Daphne Dare
Make-up by Sonia Markham
Lighting: Howard King
Sound: Ray Angel
Story Editor: Gerry Davis
Designer: Barry Newbery
Producer: John Wiles
Director by Michael Imison

ACTOR BIOGRAPHIES: Terence Bayler landed small roles in various films including *Macbeth* (1971), *Time Bandits* (1981), *Brazil* (1985) and *Harry Potter and the Philosopher's Stone* (2001); **Eileen Helsby** played Prudence Penrose in *The Newcomers* (1967); **Roy Skelton** went on to voice both Zippy and George in *Rainbow* (1973-92); **Ralph Carrigan** landed a small role in *The Body Stealers* (1969); **Bright Wright** appeared briefly in *The Young Doctors* (1977); **John Halstead** appeared in *General Hospital* (1973-75); uncredited **Bill Hunter** went on to have a very successful film career landing roles in *Stone* (1974), *The Man from Hong Kong* (1975), *Mad Dog Morgan* (1976), *Gallipoli* (1981), *Sky Pirates* (1986), *The Adventures of Priscilla, Queen of the Desert* (1994), *Race the Sun* (1996), *Kangaroo Jack* (2003), *The Wedding Part* (2010) and voiced the Dentist in hit animated film *Finding Nemo* (2003).

BEHIND-THE-SCENES

- **Number of Production Days:** 10
- The idea for an adventure set on a large spaceship where cars and bicycles would be required to get around was the brainchild of producer **John Wiles**. The producer discussed his idea with script editor **Donald Tosh** shortly after his arrival on the show in May 1965.
- At first **Donald Tosh** was less than convinced with the idea, believing it would be too ambitious for the show, and linked the idea to science fiction works by **Arthur C. Clarke**. The idea went ahead regardless and **Donald Tosh** contacted writer **Paul Erickson** who was commissioned on Thursday 27 May 1965 to write a four-part story with target delivery dates being set for the beginning of September for episode one and two, and early November for episode three and four.
- With the extended six-part Dalek serial turning into a daunting 12-part story, **Paul Erickson** was informed that his serial would feature later in the show's run, but the production dates were to remain the same.
- **Paul Erickson** delivered his draft scripts for episodes one and two early and they were written under the overall title of *The Ark*. The scripts however were very complex and needed rewriting by **Donald Tosh**. One such change was the character of Katarina who was going to be the full-time companion until the decision was made to kill her off during *The Daleks' Master Plan* and replace her with a new companion.
- It was early on in the production stage when the production team would change once again. **John Wiles** had not settled in his role as producer. Wanting to take the show into more adult themes and storylines (something which **William Hartnell** vehemently disagreed with), Wiles saw himself more as a writer/director than a producer, and expressed a desire to leave the series. John Wiles also did not get on well with the leading actor William Hartnell, the latter would often go to Head of Serials **Gerald Savoy** if he had any complains, and Savoy would often side with Hartnell. Also leaving the series would be **Donald Tosh**, who handed over his script editing duties to **Gerry Davis** during work on *The Massacre of St. Bartholomew's Eve*, would oversee the production side of the serial after **Tosh** accepted **Erickson**'s script shortly before leaving.
- The director assigned to *The Ark* was **Michael Imison** who was aware that the serial would be very expensive to produce. This meant that the following serial *The Celestial Toymaker* would be a budget saving story.
- The first scene to be recorded for the serial was the miniaturisation effect for the male guardian played by extra **David Greneau**, who was not hired to appear in the next instalment as another guardian.
- During the pre-filming process which took place between Monday 31 January to Thursday 3 February 1966, incoming producer **Innes Lloyd** trailed **John Wiles** to get a better understanding of the show.
- A total of 8 Monoid costumes were made for the serial by freelance effect artists **John** and **Jack Lovell**. To increase the number of Monoids onboard the Ark, the printed numbers on the voice collars were continually changed between shots. Clever editing was also used to increase the number of Monoids whereby the same Monoid could appear twice in the same scene thus swelling their numbers.
- The guns which the Monoids carry were fully operational props which could emit puffs of white powder when fired. To stimulate the effect of the guns, a white spotlight was shown over anyone who was hit.
- To stimulate the effect of the Invisible Refusians, wires and other clever techniques were used in various capacities. The foliage of the Refusian jungle was attached to wires which were then moved when a Refusian walked through it, the objects inside the castle on Refusian II were moved with hidden wires, the controls inside Launcher 14 were operated by stagehands hidden outside of the shot, and wires were placed underneath the seats which were then pulled down when a Refusian sat on the cushion.
- The jungle scenes, which opened the first episode, featured a wide variety of animals: a monitor lizard, a snake, a hornbill and a baby Indian Elephant called Monica who born in 1954 and was accompanied by her trainer **Mary Chipperfield**. Director **Michael Imison** was extremely proud of the use of live animals instead of using stock footage which would normally be the case.
- To save money on the sets and set dressings, many of the computer banks were taken from stock, and designer **Barry Newbery** used angles mirrors to increase the number of storage cabinets.
- Freelance designer **Peter Pegrum** provided cut-out models of miniaturised humans to appear in the serial, these would ultimately go unused in the finished programme.
- The gates which made up a part of the Castle on Refusian II were actually reused set dressings. The gates had previously be designed by **Barry Newbery** for *The Crusade* the previous year.
- Just before recording commenced on "The Bomb", **Michael Imison** found out that his contract with the drama series and serial department was not being renewed. The director believed this was because the recording of episodes always overran.

BROADCAST

EPISODE	DATE	TIME	VIEWING FIGURE	CHART POSITION	APPRECIATION INDEX
1: *The Steel Sky*	5/3/1966	5:15-5:40pm	5.5M	102nd	55
2: *The Plague*	12/3/1966	5:15-5:40pm	6.9M	70th	56
3: *The Return*	19/3/1966	5:15-5:40pm	6.2M	85th	51
4: *The Bomb*	26/3/1966	5:15-5:40pm	7.3M	71st	50

CLIFFHANGERS

1. As Dodo's cold spreads amongst the Monoids and humans alike, one Monoids is brought into the control room and dies. The Commander has also been affected, and Zentos blames the 'strangers' for bringing the strange illness onboard. Zentos orders for The Doctor, Steven and Dodo to be arrested and taken away.
2. Having found a cure to the common cold, The Doctor, Steven, and Dodo are free to go. They leave in the Tardis, but dematerialize back on board the spaceship – but 700 years later. When they arrive in the control room, Dodo discovers that the statue (under construction at the start of the voyage) had been completed. Except it doesn't have the head of a human, it has the head of a Monoid!
3. Monoid Two boards the launcher sent down to Refusian II, and begins to send a message back to the ark with instructions about how to destroy the Refusians. But a Refusian has laid a trap and blows up the launcher, killing Monoid Two. The Doctor and Dodo will have to remain on the planet if a rescue party doesn't arrive ..
4. Onboard the Tardis, The Doctor vanishes in front of Dodo and Steven. Dodo thinks this could be something to do with the Refusians. It isn't. The Doctor tells them it's some sort of an attack!

COMMERCIAL RELEASES

- **AUDIOBOOK:** March 2018
- **DVD:** February 2011
- **NOVELISATION:** [Hardback] - 16 October 1987; [Paperback] - 19 March 1987; [Reissue] – 1992
  - *Target Doctor Who Library Number*: **114**
- **SOUNDTRACK**
  - **7 August 2006**: *BBC Audio*
  - **5 September 2013**: *The TV Episodes - Collection Six*
- **VIDEO:** October 1998

CONTINUITY NOTES

- The Monoids later feature in **AUDIO:** *The Kingdom of the Blind*
- The events of *The Ark* take place during the 57th Segment of Time. *The Romans* and *The Myth Makers* occurred in the 1st Segment of Time as did The Doctor's encounter with The Daleks in *The Daleks*.
- The Silurians, who later appear in *Doctor Who and the Silurians, Warriors of the Deep* and *The Hungry Earth/Cold Blood* and others, constructed an ark for a similar purpose to escape an impending destruction of Earth. The Silurians believed the Earth was going to be destroyed by an approaching planet, which eventually became the Moon millions of years earlier. The ark in question appears in the Eleventh Doctor serial *Dinosaurs on a Spaceship* ransacked by pirate and murderer Solomon.
- The first example of a race bank being used to preserve an entire race of people features during *The Ark*. Other examples of race banks can be seen during *The Power of the Daleks, Invasion of the Dinosaurs, The Ark in Space, The Hand of Fear, The Leisure Hive, Four to Doomsday* and *Victory of the Daleks*.
- The music heard when The Doctor explores Refusian II is the same music which appears in *The Daleks* as The Doctor and his companions explore the Dalek City.
- *The Ark* marks the first time where the destruction of Earth plays an important part in the overall narrative. Other serials which centre around the demise of the Earth can be seen in *The Ark in Space, Trial of a Time Lord: The Mysterious Planet, The End of the World* and *The Beast Below*. All of these provide a different explanation as to fate of the Earth.

- The common cold is later brought up during **Doctor Who: TV Movie** where The Eight Doctor tells Grace Holloway that Leonardo da Vinci was suffering the ailment whilst painting one of his master pieces, and **Dalek** where Henry Van Statten claims he found the cure to the sickness, from a meteor.
- The Monoids make their first and only appearance in the show but The Eleventh Doctor does make a puppet Monoid during *The Time of the Doctor* whilst putting on a puppet show depicting his various adventures throughout time and space.

CRITICAL RESPONSE

- **Review Range:** Generally Positive
- *Doctor Who Magazine 2014 Poll*: 184th/241st
- Critic **Bill Norris** of the *Television Today* wrote positively about the episode on Thursday 31 March 1966. He wrote that he had grown quite fond of the Monoids, and was sorry to see them go. Further praise went towards the costume design from **Daphne Dare** and **Eileen Helsby's** performance as Venussa. He wrote that the story had plenty of imagination but high levels of concentration were required to follow the plot at times.
- Thursday 7 April 1966 saw a review on "The Bomb" from **JC Trewin** who highlighted that he has enjoyed the comedic element of the episode – referring to the ending where The Doctor became invisible after he sneezed. [Quite what was comedic about the moment is anyone's guess].
- A review in the *Radio Times* from **Patrick Mulkern** gave the episode an all-round positive review. He wrote that the whole concept of the serial is fine, but felt that the plot lacked dramatic incidents, and there are a few moments of tedium. He wrote that the Guardians were underdeveloped and was not so keen on the Monoids. He praised the direction, music, and effects, nonetheless.
- Writing for *DVD Talk's*, **John Sinnott** awarded the serial 3 out of 4 stars. He wrote that first half was slow, but the plot became more interesting in the second-half.
- **Arnold T. Blumberg** of *IGN* awarded the serial an 8/10. He praised the pacing of the serial, and production values apart from the Monoids.
- Writing a review for *SFX*, **Ian Berriman** gave the serial 3 out of 5 stars. He described it as 'quaint' but was not so taken in by the Monoids. He praised the story for being ambitious and commented it was much faster-paced compared to other serials of the time. Further praise went to the sets.
- **Charlie Jane Anders** of *io9* wrote positively about the cliffhanger to "The Plague", describing it as one of the great cliffhangers in the show's history.
- Writing in *The Discontinuity Guide*, **Paul Cornell, Martin Day,** and **Keith Topping** wrote positively about the serial. They called the story as clever and tightly constructed, and praised the two-episode built up. They highlighted the opening jungle scene as impressive. They summed *The Ark* as 'not perfect', but held it with high regard since it tries.

DEATHS

DEATH	CHARACTER	TIME OF DEATH	CAUSE OF DEATH
1	Monoid	[00:22:29]	Killed by the common cold
2	Monoid	[00:26:54]	Killed by the common cold
3	Monoid	[00:27:06]	Killed by the common cold
4	Guardian	[00:36:23]	Killed by the common cold
5	Male Guardian	[01:00:35]	Killed by Monoid Three
6	Yendom	[01:11:25]	Killed by Monoid Two
7	Monoid Two	[01:12:11]	Killed in an explosion
8	Monoid 6	[01:30:32]	Shot and Killed
9	Monoid 77	[01:30:36]	Shot and killed by Monoid Four
10	Maharis	[01:31:48]	Shot and killed by Monoid One
11	Monoid 45	[01:32:01]	Shot and killed by Monoid Four
12	Monoid	[01:32:41]	Shot and killed by Monoid Four

FILMING LOCATIONS

- ➤ Ealing Film Studios
- ➤ Riverside Studio 1

INFLUENCES

- ➤ **BIBLE:** *The Book of Genesis* [reference to Noah's Ark]
- ➤ **BOOK:** *The First Men in the Men* (1901, H. G. Wells).
- ➤ **BOOK:** *The Lord of the Rings* (1954-55, J. R. R. Tolkien) – [statue with a head with one eye]
- ➤ **BOOK:** *The War of the Worlds* (1898, H. G. Wells).

PRODUCTION ERRORS

1. When Monoid Two kills a Guardian in "The Return" the Guardian is still breathing afterwards.
2. During "The Bomb" **Edmund Coulter**, who played Monoid One, forgets to switch on his character's communication collar before delivering his lines.
3. During "The Plague", Dodo wonders what is going on outside their prison cell when she hears a drumbeat, and she says 'it sounds like savages'. However when the scene cuts to the Monoid funeral procession, no musical instrument or any other device is present which would have aroused her attention.
4. The Doctor advising that feverish patients warm seems a little questionable.
5. At one point Monoid One declares that Refusis will soon be theirs, when he should have said Refusis II.
6. During "The Bomb", all of the Monoids leave the ark inside capsules and head to Refusis II. During a scene when the Monoids board a capsule there is evidentially four in the launch bay area, but only three are used by the Monoids. This means there is still one left, which could have been used by humans on the ark to escape.
7. If the Guardian, who is miniaturised at the beginning of the serial, did something which threatened life on the ark, then wouldn't the logical punishment be execution? What if he does something even stupider on Refusis II which causes a setback in progress, or a famine, or even the deaths of other humans?
8. If *The Ark* follows directly from *The Massacre of St Bartholomew's Eve* (which it presumably does since Dodo doesn't quite believe that The Tardis can time travel) how did Dodo catch her cold in the first place? She didn't display any symptoms when she entered the Tardis at the end of *The Massacre of St Bartholomew's Eve*, and she didn't catch it from The Doctor and Steven.
9. When entering the castle-like structure in "The Return", Monoid Two trips over his own feet.
10. If The Monoids are so primitive and do not have advanced science or technology of their own, how did they get to Earth, centuries prior, in the first place? Its only after being introduced to the common human cold that they gained some sort of intelligence.
11. When the Monoids depart to Refusis II, the wires operating the capsules can be seen.
12. Towards the end of "The Plague", the Monoid who drives the 'truck' appears to be breaking the fourth wall, since it is staring at the audience. Does it know that we're watching it, and his whole existence is pure fiction?
13. The Doctor brands Dodo at one point during "The Plague" for coming along with Steven and himself on their travels, however Dodo did not join the Tardis crew willingly, since she quite rightly mistook the Tardis for a proper police box, and her departure from 20th century Earth wasn't her choice.
14. When Yendom is killed by Monoid Two he doesn't flinch when shot down.
15. Several of the actor's microphones during "The Steel Sky" appear to be malfunctioning since whenever their deliver their lines they sound like their hissing.
16. Some of the actors playing the Monoids have numerous problems operating the voice collars.

PUBLICITY

- ➤ The Monoids were promoted during a photocall on Saturday 19 February 1966. The *Daily Express* ran an article called 'Something awful hunts the Doc'. The article included comments from Monoid actor **Ray Byrom** and Female Guardian extra **Jan Williams,** who said that the Monoids reminded her of Mick Jagger (a member of The Rolling Stones).
- ➤ The *Radio Times* (5-11 March 1966) previewed the serial with an article called 'Dr. Who and a Space Ark'. A photograph of the regular cast with Monica the Elephant was used to promote the new adventure.

WORKING TITLES

- The Space Ark

VERDICT: The first of many *Doctor Who* serials to provide us with an end of the world narrative, whilst having nothing to do with the end of the world at all. ***The Ark*** in itself is actually two two-part stories which share the same plot, but at two different ends of a space journey. It's a format that will never be revisited, thus making this rare occurrence all the more unique.

     The Ark is the last **William Hartnell** serial where the budget is well spent. The production team were blessed with a whole array of live animals for the opening episode including a real life elephant. The direction is very clever in a sense, where upon first viewing you would believe that stock footage was used for the elephant, but nope, director **Michael Imison** fools us by having The Doctor and his friends go up and stroke its trunk. It's an ambitious few precious moments that even the director cited as his proudest achievement. No understatement. The sets, although minimal at the best of times, are some of the finest in the early years of the show, aided by some of the most imaginative camera movements seen in a while. But this becomes an undoing in a sense, and are exactly the reason Imison never worked on the show again. Over spending on *Doctor Who* is a big no-no. Imison is one of the best all-round directors to work on the show, who will sadly never been seen again.

     The two two-parters are imaginative, but poorly structured at times. There's a lot of talking, sitting around, expositional dialogue, and *very* convenient plot conveniences to keep everything moving. The common cold plot killing the human crew could have served as the main narrative for all four episodes, but what we get in 'The Return' and 'The Bomb' does make for some compulsive viewing. But again, the Monoids descend into a civil war, which is both uncalled for, and uninspired to say the least. Speaking of the Monoids, they are interesting, in that they have a great presence through voice, but lack dominance through body language. They are decent monsters, but ***The Ark*** will see their first and last appearance. It's not hard to see why this is. ***The Ark*** is a great space adventure, and remains up there with commendable 60s *Doctor Who*. ***

24) THE CELESTIAL TOYMAKER

Plot: The Celestial Toymaker has captured The Tardis and brings it to his domain. If The Doctor and his companions wish to escape, they must first win his seemingly innocent games, if not they will become the Toymaker's play things for all eternity

CAST

Dr Who	William Hartnell
Steven	Peter Purves
Dodo	Jackie Lane
Toymaker	Michael Gough
Joey/King of Hearts/Sergeant Rugg	Campbell Singer
Clara/Queen of Hearts/Mrs Wiggs	Carmen Silvera
Knave of Hearts/Kitchen Boy/Cyril	Peter Stephens
Joker	Reg Lever
Ballerina Dolls	Beryl Braham, Ann Harrison, Delia Lindon
Hand Double for Dr Who	Albert Ward

CREDITS

Written by Brian Hayles
  [Script by Gerry Davis, with material by Donald Tosh from an idea by Hayles]
Choreography by Tutte Lemkow
Title Music by Ron Grainger and the BBC Radiophonic Workshop
Incidental music by Dudley Simpson
Costumes by Daphne Dare
Make-up by Sonia Markham
Lighting: Frank Cresswell
Sound: Alan Fogg
Story Editor: Gerry Davis
Designer: John Wood
Producer: Innes Lloyd
Directed by Bill Sellars

ACTOR BIOGRAPHIES: Michael Gough had a successful acting career and appeared in many films including *The Small Back Room* (1949), *The Man in the White Suit* (1951), *Rob Roy: The Highland Rogue* (1953), *Dracula* (1958), *Horror of the Black Museum* (1959), *Black Zoo* (1963), *Berserk* (1967), *Julius Caesar* (1970), *Horror Hospital* (1973), *Venom* (1981), *Batman* (1989), *Batman Returns* (1992), *Batman Forever* (1995), *Batman & Robin* (1997), *Sleepy Hallow* (1999), and provided voice-over performance in *Corpse Bride* (2005) and *Alice in Wonderland* (2010); **Carmen Silvera** is best known as Camilla Hope in *Compact* (1963-65) and Edith Artois in *'Allo 'Allo* (1982-92); **Campbell Singer** was Henry Burroughs in *The Newcomers* (1967-69).

BEHIND-THE-SCENES

- **Number of Production Days:** 6
- Since 1965, writer **Brian Hayles** had attempted multiple times to write for *Doctor Who* when he went into freelance writing full-time. One such story 'Dr Who and the Dark Planet' was submitted to the production office but turned down when it was deemed too similar to another submitted story idea by **Malcolm Hulke**, which was also ultimately unproduced.
- When the production team changed hands, **Brian Hayles** submitted four more story ideas, with **John Wiles** expressing a keen interest for Hayles to write for the show. One idea was ***Doctor Who and the Toymaker*** which **John Wiles** and **Donald Tosh** liked tremendously. Working together, John Wiles and Brian Hayles began developing the idea to turn it into a psychological horror fantasy. The story also allowed John Wiles and Donald Tosh to move the show into fantasy dimensions, instead of setting 'every' story on Earth.
- It was **Donald Tosh** who came up with the idea of calling the Toymaker, the Celestial Toymaker. It was also suggested that the Toymaker could be another figure of The Doctor's own race.
- The idea settled; **Brian Hayles** was commissioned to write the first episode with a target delivery date of Friday 17 September 1965. All going well the remaining three scripts would be taken up by Friday 1 October 1966. It was during this time that serial was also referred to as ***The Trilogic Game***. Brian Hayles delivered his script on Monday 13 September 1965.
- One of the key elements of the first episode was the introduction of two characters called George and Margaret. Both characters came from a successful West End comedy penned by **Gerald Savory**, who had taken over the position as Head of Television Drama Serials at the BBC in 1965. It was originally intended by **Brian Hayles** that George and Margaret would be a jolly aunt and uncle whom Steven and Dodo would play games against. The characters would become increasingly menacing as the story progressed.
- The remaining scripts were formally commissioned on Friday 17 September 1965 with a deadline of all three scripts by Friday 26 November 1965. It was during this time that **Brian Hayles** was commissioned by **Donald Tosh** for two more story ideas 'The White Witch' and 'The Hands of Aten'.

- With the script delivered it was obvious that certain changes would be required to bring the cost of the serial down to within the show's budget. It was also apparent that **John Wiles** wanted the darker elements of the serial to be toned down since the show was often referred to as a family programme. However, **Brian Hayles** would be too busy to perform the extensive rewrites due to heavy workloads on other shows, one being *United!*. Brian Hayles himself confessed some of the darker elements of his scripts frightened him.
- After some discussion **Brian Hayles** granted his permission for **Donald Tosh** to rewrite his scripts with a proposal that Brian Hayles would receive an on-screen credit reading, based on a story by Brian Hayles.
- Another element of the story was the absence of The Doctor from episodes 2 and 3. This in itself was the first attempt by the production office to write **William Hartnell** out of the series It was also announced to the press that William Hartnell was making plans to leave the series but nothing was certain. The final episode would have seen another actor replace The Doctor, leaving Dodo and Steven confused as to whether or not the sudden change in The Doctor was another trick by the Celestial Toymaker. As it turned out, William Hartnell's contract was due to expire with the serial, but the actor was offered a 16 episode extension before any plans to replace him could be put in place.
- As the production team changed hands yet again during the pre-production process, incoming producer **Innes Lloyd** and script editor **Gerry Davis** would oversee the production in its entirety.
- Both **Innes Lloyd** and **Gerry Davis** had new visions about how the series should look resulting in **Brian Hayles** storylines 'Dr Who & The White Witch' and 'Dr Who & The Hands of Aten' being rejected as they did not meet the directions they wished to take the series in. On such vision that Innes Lloyd wished to bring to the series was hiring big name actors to guest star in the show. One such actor **Michael Gough** who had enjoyed earlier episodes of the show was cast as the title character – The Celestial Toymaker.
- The line-up of companions was going to change. **Innes Lloyd** wished to change the companions wanting to make them more contemporary. **Peter Purves** had already been offered an extension of 12 episodes, but another 13 episodes beyond his provisional 12 would not be taken up.
- The production was going to face another setback when **Gerard Savory** (who previously granted permission for his George and Margaret characters to be used in the serial) changed his mind, and rescinded his permission thus causing another rewrite to the scripts.
- Luckily, **Gerald Savory** gave **Gerry Davis** a *carte blanche* (complete freedom to act as one wishes) to create a workable platform for both cast and crew alike. Whilst Gerry Davis kept many of the story elements, he rewrote much of the material from **Brian Hayles** and **Donald Tosh**. Gerry Davis wished to explore the darker sides of the nursery settings of the episode, and apparently wrote one script a day in his garden.
- The second set of rewrites did not go down well with **John Wiles** and **Donald Tosh** believing that the more important elements of the story had been toned down too much. John Wiles later complained about the changes saying that Donald Tosh's scripts were pieces of brilliance, and money was wasted on unnecessary rewrites. He also believed that **Gerry Davis'** scripts did not do **Brian Hayles** or Donald Tosh justice. Interestingly, Brian Hayles would later tell Gerry Davis that he was happy with the finished result.
- To create a menacing and uneasy atmosphere, **Frank Cresswell** designed his lighting to gradually get darker as the game of Blind Man's Bluff progressed. This highlighted that the innocent playground game was turning into something far more dangerous and deadly.
- Since **William Hartnell** would be missing for episode 2 "The House of Dolls", allowed **Peter Purves** and **Jackie Lane** to carry much of the story themselves, although they did miss working with their fellow actor.
- The serial was to face yet another set-back with the character of Cyril. The schoolboy has been described in the script as a 'Billy Bunter' kind of boy, and this comment would causes problems later on. **Gerry Davis** had previously suggested that Cyril should be more in-line with Dodger from **Charles Dicken**'s *Oliver Twist*.
- For the scene when various characters tested 7 chairs with Dolls to find out which one was safe, various filming making techniques were used to stimulate the different effects each chair had. Chair 1 was fitted with a blade which could then spring out behind to cut the already pre-cut Doll in half. Chair 2 had no special effects, **Jackie Lane**'s acting suggested she was freezing to death. Chair 3 was fitted with various flash charges and fireworks which were then detonated on cue. Chair 4's disappearing act was achieved by removing both the chair and the Doll from the set after a recording break. Chair 6 was rigged to collapse after being sat on, and chair 7, which vibrated out of shot, a headless Doll placed on the chair it to make it seem the chair had decapitated it.

BROADCAST

EPISODE	DATE	TIME	VIEWING FIGURE	CHART POSITION	APPRECIATION INDEX
1: *The Celestial Toyroom*	2/4/1966	5:50-6:15pm	8M	44th	48
2: *The Hall of Dolls*	9/4/1966	5:50-6:15pm	8M	49th	49
3: *The Dancing Floor*	16/4/1966	5:50-6:15pm	9.4M	32nd	44
4: *The Final Test*	23/4/1966	5:50-6:15pm	7.8M	36th	43

CLIFFHANGERS

1. Steven and Dodo have won their game of blind man's buff and receive a riddle for the next game 'Four legs, no feet, of arms no lack, it carries no burden on its back. Six deadly sisters, seven for choice, call the servants without voice'. Moving onto the next game, Steven and Dodo leave Joey and Clara behind who have reverted back into lifeless Dolls.
2. After winning their second game, Steven and Dodo are given their next riddle, 'Hunt the key to fit the door that leads out on the dancing floor, then escape the rhythmic beat, or you'll forever tap your feet'. Continuing with their journey, a locked cupboard opens and Steven and Dodo are pursued by three ballerina dolls.
3. After beating the Ballerina's deadly dance, Steven and Dodo are given their third riddle, 'Lady Luck will show the way, win the game or here you'll stay'. Cyril (now dressed as a fat, jolly schoolboy) appears and tells Steven and Dodo they won't find the next game so easy, because he will be their opponent ….
4. The Doctor, Steven, and Dodo escape the Toymaker's domain, and Dodo decides to celebrate with Cyril's sweeties. Steven is not so sure, but The Doctor takes one and winces in pain.

COMMERCIAL RELEASES

- **DVD:** 1 November 2004
- **NOVELISATION: [Hardback]** - 19 June 1986; **[Paperback]** - 20 November 1986; **[Reissue]** – 1992
  - *Target Doctor Who Library Number*: **111**
- **SOUNDTRACK**
  - **2 April 2001:** *BBC Audio*
  - **14 February 2011**: *The Lost TV Episodes - Collection Two*
- **VIDEO:** June 1991

CONTINUITY NOTES

- The Celestial Toymaker later appears in **PROSE:** *Divided Loyalties*, **COMIC:** *Endgame* and **AUDIO:** *The Magic Mousetrap*. The Toymaker was originally going to appear in the original twenty-third season story *The Nightmare Fair* alongside The Sixth Doctor before its untimely cancellation.
- Dodo later recalls her time in the Toymaker's domain in **PROSE:** *Who Killed Kennedy?*
- **The Celestial Toymaker** marks the first time in *Doctor* Who where flashbacks to previous adventures feature in the narrative. Steven sees himself on the planet Kemble and in Paris referring to **The Daleks Master Plan** and **The Massacre of St Bartholomew's Eve**.
- The Celestial Toymaker is the first villain in the shows' history who successfully breaks through the Tardis' supposedly impregnable barriers. Other villains and characters who achieve this goal include the Master of the Land of Fiction in **The Mind Robber**, Kronos in **The Time Monster**, Sutekh in **Pyramids of Mars**, Commander Stor in **The Invasion of Time**, the White Guardian in **The Ribos Operation** and **Enlightenment**, the Black Guardian in **Enlightenment**, Biroc in **Warrior's Gate**, Omega in **Arc of Infinity**, the Malus in **The Awakening**, and several Cybermen in **Attack of the Cybermen**.
- The Celestial Toymaker is the first *Doctor Who* villain who dresses himself in authentic Chinese clothing. The mutated Magnus Greel dresses himself in Chinese Robes in **The Talons of Weng-Chiang** in order to disguise his hideous appearance.
- Technically speaking The Celestial Toymaker is the first villain to appear in the show who is immortal, although this fact is never actually confirmed or denied.

CRITICAL RESPONSE

- **Review Range:** Mixed
- *Doctor Who Magazine 2014 Poll*: 197th/241st
- The inclusion of Cyril as a 'Billy Bunter' wannabe sparked a lot of criticism from **Frank Richard**'s estate, who were not happy that the BBC had not acquired permission to use 'Billy Bunter' as character. The BBC responded saying that they did not intentionally copy Frank Richard's popular character, and Cyril was only pretending to be the character. The BBC later added a message of apology to the estate following the broadcast of "The Final Test".
- Following the use of 'Billy Bunter' as a character, the BBC received many letter from viewers pointing out that the real Billy Bunter wouldn't be so cruel to Steven and Dodo.
- During an edition of *Junior Points of View* (Friday 29 April 1966), presenter **Sarah Ward** read out many comments from children. One such child was not at all impressed with the ending scene. They pointed out that the sweetie The Doctor ate at the end could have been poisoned by the Celestial Toymaker, and The Doctor should have been more cautious.
- Following the broadcast of "The Final Test", an audience research report was compiled with a total of 259 comments from members of BBC1's viewing panel. There was a general consensus that the closing moments lacked excitement and action, but **Michael Gough**'s performance was praised. Most comments highlighted that people did not really care for the fantasy elements which were felt to be heavily drawn out.
- **David J. Howe, Mark Stammers**, and **Stephen James Walker** wrote highly of the serial giving it a top rating of 9/10. They described it as one of the most imaginative stories in the show's first three years. **Michael Gough** was praised as was the rest of the cast. They felt that **Bill Sellar's** direction of the serial which created many dramatic moments was very assured. They also highlighted the contrast between the childish nature of the games, and the Toymaker's menace as highlights.
- Writing in *Doctor Who: The Episode Guide*, **Mark Campbell** awarded the serial a disappointing 4/10. He described the whole thing as weird, but laborious, and summed the whole thing up by saying its reputation was estimated.

FILMING LOCATIONS

- Ealing Film Studios
- Riverside Studio 1

INFLUENCES

- **CHARACTER:** *Arthur Dodger* (Charles Dickens).
- **CHARACTER:** *Billy Bunter* (Charles Hamilton aka Frank Richards).
- **LITERATURE** [the works of Lewis Carroll]
- **OPERA:** *The Love of Three Oranges* (1921, Sergei Prokofiev).
- **PERSON:** *Harpo Marx* [Joey's use of a horn]

PRODUCTION ERRORS

1. Some of the Trilogic Game pieces change angles when the Toymaker advances the game.
2. A camera operator can be seen twice during "The Final Test" as Steven, Dodo and Cyril play hopscotch.
3. Peter Stephens fluffs a line during 'The Final Test'.
4. During a scene where The Doctor plays the Trilogic game, a shadow can be seen which does not belong to either The Doctor or The Toymaker who are the only two characters present in the room.
5. Before Cyril throws his die (which lands on 2), the dice indicator predicats what Cyril will throw.
6. Throughout the Tardis hopscotch game, Steven, Dodo's and Cyril's turns are sometimes out of order. This is particularly evident during the scene when Cyril pretends to be bleeding. Whether or not this is some conjuring trick by the Toymaker or even Cyril remains unknown.
7. Just before Cyril tells Steven that the floor surrounding the Tardis hopscotch board is electrified, a reflection of camera and its operator can be seen on the wall.
8. The shadow of a boom mic can be seen falling across the Robot, which is used as a communication device between the Toymaker and The Doctor, at one point during the serial.
9. Cyril must have an appalling memory if he forgot he booby trapped one of the hopscotch pieces, only to be a victim of his little plan less than two minutes later.

10. If The Toymaker is so powerful and supposedly immortal, why does he look so terrified when The Doctor wins the Trilogic game? It is implied, that although defeated, the Toymaker could recreate his world as many times as he wants, so why does he look like he is about to be defeated indefinitely, and is heading for certain doom? It is also implied that The Doctor has met the Toymaker before, so did The Doctor win the Toymaker's deadly games once before in order to escape? If so, the Toymaker should not be so dramatic since he has experienced defeat previously.
11. Why would The Doctor openly and gladly eat one of Cyril's sweets without a second thought? For all The Doctor knows the sweets could be poisoned and another one of The Toymaker's traps.

PUBLICITY

- The *Radio Times* (2-8 April 1966) previewed the serial under the title 'Dr. Who plays the Trilogic Game'. The article highlighted **Michael Gough** as the main guest star of the story and came with an explanation of what the Trilogic Game is – which The Doctor would be challenged with during the story's events.
- Throughout the transmission of the four episodes, the *Radio Times* did not include a detailed cast listing and only credited the regulars, **Michael Gough**, and the Dancers.

WORKING TITLES

- The Toymaker
- Doctor Who and the Toymaker

25) THE GUNFIGHTERS

Plot: Tombstone 1881, with the battle of the O.K. Corral just days away, The Doctor must overcome his toothache if he, Steven and Dodo are to escape before the first shot is fired.

CAST

Dr Who……………………….William Hartnell	Chinese Storekeepers….....Jackie Ho, Edward Cheekan
Steven……………………….....Peter Purves	Settler's Wife…………………………./Marguerite Young
Dodo…………………………….Jackie Lane	Settler's Daughters……..Jane Tucker, Edwina Salmon
Johnny Ringo…………………Laurence Payne	Savage……………………………………...John Raven
Wyatt Earp…………………….John Alderson	Pianists for Dodo's scenes: off-camera…Tom McCall
Doc Holliday………………….Anthony Jacobs	Winifred Taylor
Ike Clanton…………………..William Hurndell	
Phineas Clanton………………..Maurice Good	**CREDITS**
Billy Clanton……………………….David Cole	**Written by** Donald Cotton
Kate……………………………Sheena Marshe	Title Music by Ron Grainger
Seth Harper…………………….Shane Rimmer	with the BBC Radiophonic Workshop
Charlie………………………….David Graham	**Ballad music by** Tristram Cary
Bat Masterson………………….Richard Beale	**Sung by** Lynda Baron
Pa Clanton…………………....Reed de Rouen	**Film Cameraman:** Ken Westbury
Warren Earp………………….Martyn Huntley	**Film Editor:** Len Newman
Virgil Earp……………………...Victor Carin	**Costumes:** Daphne Dare
Cowboys……..John Doye, Roy Curtis, John Caesar	**Make-up:** Sonia Markham
Bill Smith	**Lighting:** George Summers
Brassy Bar Girls…….Vilma Stuttle, Maureen Lane	**Sound:** Colin Dixon
Maureen Nelson	**Story Editor:** Gerry Davis
Settlers…………….Reg Cranfield, Leslie Shannon	**Designer:** Barry Newbery
Mark Allington, Jonas Kurchi, Kevin Leslie	**Producer:** Innes Lloyd
John de Marco, Derek Chafer	**Directed by** Rex Tucker
Mexican Cowboy…………………..Antony Billing	

ACTOR BIOGRAPHIES: Shane Rimmer is best known for voicing Scott Tracy in *Thunderbirds* (1965-66); **Laurence Payne** is best known for playing Sexton Blake in *Sexton Blake* (1967-71); **Anthony Jacobs** appeared in *War & Peace* (1972); **David Cole** appeared very briefly in *Orlando* (1966) as Dr. Brown; **John Alderson** played 3 separate characters in *Gunsmoke* (1955/57/63), 4 characters in *Maverick* (1959-62), and 2 characters in *Bonanza* (1961/65); **Martyn Huntley** appeared very briefly in *United!* (1966-67); **Maurice Good** played 3 different characters in *The Avengers* (1961/63/68); **Victor Carin** appeared in 20 episodes of *Sutherland's Law* (1973-76).

BEHIND-THE-SCENES

- **Number of Production Days:** 9
- Throughout the later 1950s and early 1960s, American Western TV series were very popular amongst British audiences. Successful shows included **The Life and Legend of Warren Earp, Wagon Train** and **Rawhide**. However in 1964 they were slowly losing their appeal in favour of variety and thriller TV shows which were becoming increasingly popular. With this in mind, the *Doctor Who* production office still wanted to explore the Western genre for the show, and **Donald Cotton** was hired to write the scripts.
- **Donald Cotton** was commissioned by **Donald Tosh** for a four-part serial under the provisional title 'Dr Who and the Gun-Fighters' in late November 1965. The target delivery date for the scripts was set for mid-January 1966. **William Hartnell** would later claim that the idea of doing a Western story originated from him.
- With the first two scripts arriving on Wednesday 15 December 1965 and Friday 14 January 1966 respectively, the *Doctor Who* production office changed hands with **John Wiles** and **Donald Tosh** leaving the series after staying for only a few months. **Innes Lloyd** and **Gerry Davis** were their replacements.

- The change of production personnel did not sit well with **Donald Cotton** who believed he would have less creative freedom writing for **Gerry Davis**. Gerry Davis meanwhile believed that *Doctor Who* was not the right fit for **Donald Cotton**'s skills as a writer, but he admired the writer's cleverness and sophistication.
- Both **Innes Lloyd** and **Gerry Davis** were unhappy with the Western serial that they had inherited. Gerry Davis wasn't taken with the idea of a Western comedy, and Innes Lloyd wanted to take the show into the realms of realistic, science-fiction rather than historical-based narratives. Innes Lloyd also believed that costume dramas were better suited to other departments of the BBC rather than *Doctor Who*.
- The draft scripts for episodes one and two were sent to **Rex Tucker**, the director assigned to the serial on Wednesday 26 January 1966, the same day the script for episode three arrived. The third script required extensive rewrites since **Gerry Davis** believed there wasn't enough action, and too many sets were required. Rex Tucker also expressed concerns about the scripts when the script for episode four arrived on Monday 31 January 1966.
- Whilst casting the serial, many actors were considered for the same role; Canadian actor **Donald Sutherland** was the first choice for Wyatt Earp, **Patrick Troughton** was considered was a possible Johnny Ringo, but was too busy to commit, other possible Ringos were **John Carson, William Dexter, Philip Madoc,** and **John Slater**. Considered for both Pa Clanton and Bat Masteron was **John Bryans**. **Alan Tilvern** was considered for both Seth Harper and Ike Clanton. Other actors considered for Ike Clanton and Virgil were **David Burke, Marne Maitland, Derek Newark,** and **Ewen Solon**. Many actresses were on the short list to play Kate which included **Jeanne Moody, Patricia English, Carol Cleveland, Jill Melford, Delena Kidd, Anita West**, and **Delphi Lawrence**.
- When the cast was finalised it was discovered that apart from **John Alderson, Reed de Rouen,** and **Shane Rimmer** the cast had little experience putting on and working with American accents. This proved to be a constant problem throughout production, with cast members going into hysterics hearing their fellow actors putting on an American brawl. It would seem the production was heading more towards comedy rather than adventure.
- It was originally intended (what would become the cliffhanger to episode one) that Steven would play the piano, and Dodo would sing *The Ballad of the Last Chance Saloon*. However **Jackie Lane**'s singing skills were not what the production was looking for, so she and **Peter Purves** switched roles since the actor had some singing experience previously.
- Production on the serial began at Ealing Film Studios where many of the more expensive scenes were recorded. One such scene was the Clanton brothers ride into Tombstone on horseback. It was decided that the use of live horses would be more practical at Ealing than Riverside. The horses however found it difficult to trot across the studio floor which had been covered in sawdust (to represent the desert sand) and the actors on horseback couldn't ride them very quickly either.
- For the verse of *The Ballad of the Last Chance Saloon* which was going to be played as a voice-over throughout the serial was originally going to be sung by **Sheena Marshe**. It was soon decided that her voice just wasn't right and **Rex Tucker** wanted to use his daughter, **Jane Tucker** instead (who was also booked as an extra for the serial) but it was decided that her voice wasn't right as well.
- The regular cast of **William Hartnell, Peter Purves,** and **Jackie Lane** felt that **Rex Tucker** was not happy working on *Doctor Who* and had little time for them. They believed he was more concerned working with the guest stars, lacked humour, and was very 'old fashioned' in his directional views.
- Many of the props dotted around the sets such as the saloon, the surgery and the jailhouse were hired out from Old Times Props House by designer **Barry Newbery**. The wanted posters for Johnny Ringo placed around the Jailhouse set were made by Newbery.
- For the cliffhanger to episode one, clever camera angles disguised the fact that **Jackie Lane** was merely miming playing the piano whilst **Peter Purves** sang the ballad. Another piano played by **Tom McCall** was placed out of the shot, with McCall playing the song to appear at the end of the episode.
- The cliffhanger to episode two was also a technical affair, another horse was especially brought into the studio and the use of a mole crane camera (looking out of a dummy window) created the illusion of someone looking down on the street below whilst Steven was being taken away to be hanged.
- During production it was announced that **Jackie Lane** and **Peter Purves** would be leaving the show to be replaced by two new companions – Ben and Polly - later on in the run.
- During recording a complaint was made against armourer **Jack Lennox** who was late in delivering firearms to the studio for recording of "The O.K. Corral". This was not the first time that the armourer was late in delivering the firearms (he had previously been late delivering the firearms for the recording of "Don't Shoot the Pianist" a few weeks prior.

BROADCAST

EPISODE	DATE	TIME	VIEWING FIGURE	CHART POSITION	APPRECIATION INDEX
1: *A Holiday for the Doctor*	30/4/1966	5:50-6:15pm	6.5M	50th	45
2: *Don't Shoot the Pianist*	7/5/1966	5:50-6:15pm	6.6M	45th	39
3: *Johnny Ringo*	14/5/1966	5:55-6:20pm	6.2M	51st	36
4: *The O.K. Corral*	21/5/1966	5:50-6:15pm	5.7M	60th	30

CLIFFHANGERS

1. The Doctor has been unknowingly set up by Doc Holliday, and heads to the Last Chance Saloon. Inside the Saloon, Steven and Dodo are held at gunpoint who are forced to play the piano and sing for the Clanton Brothers. The Clanton Brothers plan to kill The Doctor who they believe to be Doc Holliday when he arrives.
2. The Clanton Brothers, who still believe The Doctor is Doc Holliday, captures Steven and take him to be hanged. Outside the jailhouse, the Clanton Brothers threaten to hang Steven if 'Doc Holliday' doesn't come out of the jailhouse.
3. With Phineas Clanton in jail, his fellow Brothers come to rescue him. There is a struggle, and Warren Earp is killed, the Brothers flee, and Warren Earp is left for dead.
4. The Tardis arrives at its next destination. The Doctor believes they have landed in the far future, a time of prosperity. The Tardis crew leave the control room when a savage looking figure appears on the scanner.

COMMERCIAL RELEASES

- **AUDIOBOOK:** February 2013
- **DVD:** June 2011
- **NOVELISATION: [Hardback]** - 11 July 1985; **[Paperback]** - 9 January 1986; **[Rerelease]** – 1988
  - *Target Doctor Who Library Number*: **101**
- **SOUNDTRACK**
  - **5 February 2007**: *BBC Audio*
  - **5 September 2013 – 25 February 2016**: *Doctor Who: The 50th Anniversary Collection*
- **VIDEO:** November 2002

CONTINUITY NOTES

- The Doctor revisits the Wild West in **AUDIO:** *A Town Called Fortune*, **PROSE:** *Peacemaker* and *A Town Called Mercy* where he engages in a gunfight of his own.
- Dodo later recalls her time at the O.K. Corral in **PROSE:** *Who Killed Kennedy?*
- The Torchwood Institute traced The Doctor to Tombstone in **COMIC:** *The Time Machination*
- **The Gunfighters** marks the final time where each individual episode of a serial has a different title.
- **The Gunfighters** marks the final time until *The Mark of the Rani* where real-life historical figures appear in the narrative, The Doctor does continue to mention historical figures on a regular basis.
- Although The Doctor previously announced his dislike of weapons, he does hold and threaten to operate a gun during the serial. The Doctor will go on to use firearms (often in self-defence) for various reasons through his incarnations which include; disposing of Ice Warriors in *The Seeds of Death*, killing an Ogron in *Day of the Daleks*, murdering a giant rat in *The Talons of Weng-Chiang*, firing salt samples at a Fendahleen in *Image of the Fendahl*, killing the Cyber Leader in *Earthshock*, threatening to execute Davros in *Resurrection of the Daleks*, and killing the Cyber Controller in *Attack of the Cybermen*.
- **The Gunfighters** is also the only classic episode of *Doctor Who* to be set entirely in the United States. *The Chase* was briefly set on the Empire State Building. The first episode of the revived series to be set in the USA is *Dalek* underneath the Utah desert.

CRITICAL RESPONSE

- **Review Range:** Negative-Mixed
- *Doctor Who Magazine 2014 Poll*: 202nd/241th

- Various letters from children and young viewers were read out on *Junior Points of View* on Friday 13 May 1966 with host **Sarah Ward** reading them out. One viewer stated they had not enjoyed the programme since Doctor Who landed in the Wild West. Another viewer described the depiction of the Wild West as 'crude', and also said that Steven can't sing.
- Following the broadcast of "The O.K. Corral", **Sydney Newman** wrote a letter of concern to producer **Innes Lloyd**. Whilst **Sydney Newman** felt that the story was well made he described the finished product as ill-conceived. His criticisms mainly lay with the ballad and **Lynda Baron's** realisation of the song.
- An audience research report dated Monday 13 June 1966 saw various comments on the final episode "The O.K. Corral". Complaints were made about dull scripts, the depiction of violence but praise went towards **William Hartnell** and **Anthony Jacobs**.
- Overall response to the entire serial was generally poor and this led to **Innes Lloyd** deciding that historical stories were on their way out. The producer was also aware that producing Westerns was not ideal for small, videotaped studios.
- In a later review, **David J. Howe, Mark Stammers,** and **Stephen James Walker** awarded the serial a 4/10. They wrote that *The Gunfighters* marked the first time where the show tried out something different (comedic Western) but failed. They praised the performance of the cast with various compliments paid to the Clanton Brothers, Doc Holliday, **William Hartnell** and **Peter Purves**. However, they highlighted the small studio space as to why the serial ultimately fails and they were less than impressed with the ballad.

DEATHS

DEATH	CHARACTER	TIME OF DEATH	CAUSE OF DEATH
1	Seth Harper	00:44:42	Killed by Doc Holliday
2	unknown person	00:57:04	*death unconfirmed*
3	Charlie	01:06:20	Killed by Johnny Ringo
4	Warren Earp	01:18:00	Shot by Ike and Billy Clanton
5	Johnny Ringo	01:31:10	Killed by Doc Holliday
6	Billy Clanton	01:32:09	Killed by Doc Holliday
7	Phineas Clanton	01:32:32	Killed by Wyatt Earp
8	Ike Clanton	01:32:48	Shot and killed

FILMING LOCATIONS

- Callow Hill Sandpit, Virginia Water, *Surrey*
- Ealing Film Studios Stage 3
- Riverside Studio 1
- Television Centre Studio 4

INFLUENCES

- **BOOK:** *Impressions of America* (1882, Oscar Wilde).
- **FILM:** *Carry on Cowboy* (1965, Gerald Thomas).
- **FILM:** *Gunfight at the O.K. Corral* (1957, John Sturges).
- **FILM:** *High Noon* (1952, Fred Zinnemann).
- **PERSON:** *Mae West* (1893-1980) – [**Sheena Marshe's** performance as Kate]

PRODUCTION ERRORS

1. The serial has some incredible historical inaccuracies through the narrative.
    a. Bat Masterton, Johnny Ringo, Warren Earp, Phineas Clanton weren't near Tombstone in 1881.
    b. Johnny Ringo and Phineas Clanton did not participate in the gunfight.
    c. Warren Earp died in July 1900 and not 1881.
    d. Ike Clanton was not killed during the gunfight and Pa Clanton died in August 1881 not October.
    e. Doc Holliday was 30 in 1881, however he is portrayed as a much older man in the serial.

      f. Four of the Tombstone gunfight participants aren't mentioned, nor do they appear in the serial; Morgan Earp, Billy Claiborne, Tom McLaury, and Frank McLaury
2. The Doctor mentions that he has never touched alcohol, however in *The Time Meddler* he clearly enjoys a drink of mead and calls it 'delightful'.
3. The K on the O.K. Corral sign has a bullet hole in it before Billy Clanton shoots the sign in the next scene.
4. After being shot dead by Doc Holliday, Harper crashes into the bar which wobbles.
5. Steven and Dodo's accents are inconsistent throughout the serial.
6. During the scene when Kate advances on Johnny Ringo, something can be heard crashing to the ground off-screen. **Sheena Marshe** looks off-camera and continues with the scene.
7. The gunshots heard in "A Holiday for The Doctor", and "Don't Shoot the Pianist" are rather quiet.
8. Certain phrases in the Ballad are actually anachronistic whose origins lie during World War II.
9. When entering the saloon for the first, **Peter Purves** slips, stumbles forward, and looks behind him.
10. When Harper talks to The Doctor in Doc Holliday's dental surgery, Doc Holliday hides behind a door to eavesdrop. As he does so Holliday collides with the doors and has to grabs hold of it to stop it from closing.
11. During the gunfight in "The O. K. Corral", Masteron and Earp appear to walk through gunfire unharmed.

PUBLICITY

> Writing in the *Daily Mirror*, **Jack Bell** included an interview with **William Hartnell** (conducted during rehearsals) which appeared on Friday 23 April 1966. During the interview William Hartnell disclosed that it was his 'idea' of doing a Western story claiming that children will always love playing cowboys and Indians.
>
> The *Daily Mail* ran a short piece about the changes to the show's format. Under the title 'Dr Who is losing his aides', reporter **Brian Dean** covered the news that Stephen and Dodo would soon be leaving the show.
>
> The BBC internal staff magazine *Ariel* covered the serial with a photograph taken during production. The photograph was used as the front cover for the magazine.
>
> The *Radio Times* (30 April-6 May 1966) covered *The Gunfighters* with a half-page article and a couple of photographs including one of Wyatt Earp facing off against the Clanton brothers.

WORKING TITLES

> The Gunslingers

VERDICT: The show's first and perhaps finest parody, *The Gunfighters* takes the gun welding, smooth talking, and wild attributes of the classic Western genre to create a comedic tale, something the show very rarely gets right. You know you're watching a great piece of television when the cast themselves are having tremendous fun. **William Hartnell** is given another opportunity, to provide a performance which calls for both comedy and seriousness, in a story where there is no real threat to face, apart from staying alive from a band of redneck brothers.

    The script is tightly written and brought to life by the highly experienced **Rex Tucker** who for a while was the original producer of the show. It's only fitting that his first and last assignment on the show was to take a vastly growing popular genre and turn *The Gunfighters* into something that is both suitable but educational for children. It's easy to see *The Gunfighters* as a critique of gun violence, the title is a big give away, and all of the characters who die are killed by being shot to death. Compare this to other American Western films and TV shows at the time who glorify gun violence, and look at The Doctor's reaction at being offered a firearm, 'Well, I should hope not. I certainly disapprove of violence', followed by an awkward moment when The Doctor holds a gun for the first time. The Doctor has always been a role model for children, and not some swash buckling cowboy who fires bullets into the air. It's a bold attempt and statement for The Doctor when the entire atmosphere around him is constructed around violence, and the possibility of being killed is more likely than discovering a nugget of gold in the local mine.

    The scripts are the most creative (up-to-this-point) that is, incorporating dark humour for the occasion, cheap joke now and then, impressive camerawork inside a small BBC recording studio, short musical numbers, and a ballad singer who acts like a narrator and commentator at the same time. The entire plot of the story hangs on the whole mistaken identity storyline where 'The Doc' is mistaken for Doc Holliday and The Clanton Brothers fail to listen to Steven and Dodo for the umpteenth time that The Doctor is not Doc Holliday. This is better suited for comedic Silent-movies than *Doctor Who*. The final gunfight is fine, for a small budget, but does appear to be clumsy in places; heck 3 of the Brothers are killed within a 39 second timespan. Thrilling? Entertaining more like. Despite the botched gunfight at the end, *The Gunfighters* is a brave attempt to take the show to new heights and doesn't disappoint.
****

26) THE SAVAGES

Plot: On a distant planet The Doctor is impressed with the advanced civilization of the Elders. Meanwhile, out in the wilderness, Steven discovers the truth and horrible secrets of the Savages.

CAST

Dr Who	William Hartnell
Steven	Peter Purves
Dodo	Jackie Lane
Jano	Frederick Jaeger
Chal	Ewen Solon
Tor	Patrick Godfrey
Captain Edal	Peter Thomas
Exorse	Geoffrey Frederick
Avon	Robert Sidaway
Flower	Kay Patrick
Nanina	Clare Jenkins
Senta	Norman Henry
Wylda	Edward Caddick
First Assistant	Andrew Lodge
Second Assistant	Christopher Denham
Third Assistant	Tony Holland
Savage	John Dillon
Guard	Tim Goodman
Savages	Bill Burridge, Gordon Lang, Robert Pitt, John Raven, Anderson Smith
Male Elders	Keith Ashely, Tony Douglas, Nicholas Edwards, Royston Farrell, Lionel Wheeler
Woman Elders	Fiona Fraser, Lynn Howard, Christina Wass
Guards	David Billa, Alex Doland, Keith Goodman, Scot Hamilton
Citizens	/Michael Earl, David Harford, Keith Ashley, Martin Tozer, Gordon Lang
Lab Assistants	Michael Earl, David Harford
Savages (female)	Nina Ovenden, Olive MacNeil, Jean Gennele Dixon
Savages (children)	Peter Baldwin, Frances Machin, Denise Brown

CREDITS

Written by Ian Stuart Black
Title Music by Ron Grainger and the BBC Radiophonic Workshop
Incidental music composed and conducted by Raymond Jones
Costumes: Daphne Dare
Make-up: Sonia Markham
Lighting: Graham Sothcott
Sound: Norman Greaves
Story Editor: Gerry Davis
Designer: Stuart Walker
Producer: Innes Lloyd
Directed by Christopher Barry

ACTOR BIOGRAPHIES: **Frederick Jaeger** landed regular television roles in *Compact* (1962), *The Inside Man* (1969), *Pretenders* (1972), *Special Branch* (1974), *One-Upmanship* (1974-78), *Highroad* (1980) and *The Onedin Line* (1980), whilst films appearances include in *Voyage of the Damned* (1976) and *Indiana Jones and the Last Crusade* (1989); **Ewen Solon** made regular appearances on TV including *Maigret* (1960-63), *The Revenue Men* (1967-68), and *Section 7* (1972); **Clare Jenkins** can be seen in *Ivanhoe* (1970); **Christopher Denham** appeared in *Z Cars* (1968) as PC Adamson for a while; **Geoffrey Frederick** appeared in *24-Hour Call* (1963) and the film *Lifeforce* (1985).

BEHIND-THE-SCENES

- **Number of Production Days:** 8
- The origins of *The Savages* dates back to when writer **Ian Stuart Black** had watched *Doctor Who* from the beginning with his family. The writer believed that the programme would offer him the chance to write an interesting story, and also impress his family. Ian Stuart Black formally entered the production office headed by **John Wiles** and **Donald Tosh** to ask if he could send in a possible storyline.
- The writer was commissioned to contribute a four-part storyline before Christmas 1965, and the writer delivered the storyline in the middle of January 1966.
- Unforeseen circumstances which threatened *The Gunfighters* meant that **Ian Stuart Black**'s story might appear earlier in the season run and replace **Donald Cotton**'s story. However the problems were soon resolved, and Black's story would follow Cotton's.

- **Ian Stuart Black** delivered his first script towards the end of January 1966 with an overall title of 'Doctor Who and the White Savages' but the individual episodes did not have individual titles. After the production office changed hands, **Innes Lloyd** brought about a change to the show, where each individual episode would not have its own title. Innes Lloyd believed that moving to an overall story title, and using episode numbers – EPISODE 1, EPISODE 2 etc. would help audiences understand when a new adventure was beginning.
- **Innes Lloyd** and **Gerry Davis** had inherited both Steven and Dodo as companions, with the producer and script editor not really seeing their potential. **Ian Stuart Black**'s scripts would also see the departure of Steven Taylor as a companion. Despite enjoying working with **Peter Purves**, **Innes Lloyd** took the actor to one side whilst recording *The Ark* to inform the actor that his contract would not be renewed after his extension of 12 more episodes.
- Upon hearing that news that his time on the show would be coming to end, **Peter Purves** was not terribly upset about his impending departure for various reasons; 1) He was disappointed that Steven's creator **Dennis Spooner**, who in his eyes had created a promising character, had the left the show shortly after his arrival, 2) He felt the character of Steven was underdeveloped whilst **John Wiles** and **Donald Tosh** were in charge, 3) He missed **Verity Lambert** who had also moved on shortly after his arrival. As it transpired the actor was thinking about moving on anyway, but it was feared that his departure would upset **William Hartnell**.
- The director appointed to the serial was **Christopher Barry** who didn't take a liking to **Ian Stuart Black**'s script and felt that *Doctor Who* was well past its time.
- Apparently the animal fur costume worn by **Clare Jenkins** booked to play Nanina was the same one worn by **Raquel Welch** for the prehistoric movie *One Million Years BC* released the previous year.
- Make-up designer **Sonia Markham** designed the appearances of the Savages by applying a thin layer of latex to the actors and extras faces. She then stretched it out and blew it up with hot air in order to wrinkle it. She then scuffed it to make the latex flake.
- Because he was away pre-filming for the next serial *The War Machines*, **William Hartnell** had no dialogue for episode three. Beforehand **William Hartnell** helped **Frederick Jaeger** on how to impersonate him (mannerisms, movement, and walking) for the scenes where Jano is dominated by The Doctor's personality.
- With episode three recorded on Friday 27 May 1966 the decision was made to extend the day's recording to 10:15pm in order to capture all of the scene where dry ice was required in studio. Since episode 4 led on from episode three's climax, the decision was made to capture all of the scenes requiring dry ice on the same day. Since the effect was both troublesome and would result in two weeks' worth of using the same effect, **Christopher Barry** opted to get all of the scene out of the way, and thus save time the following week.
- When recording for the serial wrapped up, **Peter Purves** suggested that a possible sequel could be made where The Doctor returns to the planet where Steven's regime had become corrupt, just like the Elders.
- **Peter Purves'** departure from the show was a sad time for **William Hartnell**. The leading actor had failed to bond with new companions stars **Michael Craze** and **Anneke Wills** during the location shoot for *The War Machines*. All of the changes combined was only the beginning of what was to come ….

BROADCAST

EPISODE	DATE	TIME	VIEWING FIGURE	CHART POSITION	APPRECIATION INDEX
1	28/5/1966	5:35-6:00pm	4.8M	62nd	48
2	4/6/1966	5:35-6:00pm	5.6M	50th	49
3	11/6/1966	5:35-6:00pm	5.0M	66th	48
4	18/6/1966	5:35-6:00pm	4.5M	93rd	48

CLIFFHANGERS

1. Slipping away from the tour, Dodo comes across one of the Savages, his eyes wide open, he stumbles forwards as he walks down towards Dodo. As his arms stretch out towards Dodo, the young girl screams.
2. The Doctor is prepared for the transference process, but Senta protests against using The Doctor. Jano however sees the opportunity as a great experiment. The Doctor is strapped onto a trolley and wheeled into the transference machine. The Doctor's life force begins to be drained out of him.

3. Steven and Dodo attempt to get The Doctor, who is semi-conscious, to safety when the corridor they are in is filled with smoke. Fighting to breathe, armed Guards begin to surround Steven and Dodo, as The Doctor remains oblivious to the danger around him.
4. Agreeing to stay on the planet, Steven bids his farewells to The Doctor, and Dodo. The Doctor and Dodo enter the Tardis, and the Tardis dematerialises.

COMMERCIAL RELEASES

- **AUDIOBOOK:** February 2021
- **DVD:** 1 November 2004
- **ELECTRONIC MUSIC/SOUND EFFECTS**
  - **2000**: *Doctor Who at the BBC Radiophonic Workshop Volume 1: The Early Years 1963-1969*
- **NOVELISATION: [Hardback]** - 20 March 1986; **[Paperback]** - 11 September 1986; **[Reissue]** – 1992
  - *Target Doctor Who Library Number*: **109**
- **SOUNDTRACK**
  - **2 April 2001** – *BBC Audio*
  - **14 February 2011** – *The Lost TV Episodes – Collection Two*
  - **29 September 2014** - *Doctor Who: The 50th Anniversary Collection*

CONTINUITY NOTES

- After travelling with The Doctor, Steven became King of the planet of the Savages and had three daughters, the youngest of whom he named Dodo. In **AUDIO:** *The War to End All Wars,* Steven is the deposed king of the Savages having been deposed by his two eldest daughters. During his time in prison he tells his granddaughter, Sida stories of his time in the Tardis. Steven and Sida also appear in **AUDIO:** *The Founding Fathers* and **AUDIO:** *The Locked Room*.
- The Savages are the first characters in *Doctor Who*, who are regarded as 'outsiders' and somewhat inferior to their superiors. The idea of a band of outcasts and misfits, living and working beyond society will later be revisited in **The Sun Makers** with the Rebels and **The Invasion of Time** with the Outcast Time Lords.
- The Elders are the first characters in *Doctor Who* history who rely on external sources (lifeforces in the serial's case) in order to survive. The idea of aliens and other villains using external energy sources to survive or sustain themselves will later be revisited with the Mondasian Cybermen in **The Tenth Planet**, the Axons in **The Claws of Axos**, Magnus Greel in **The Talons of Weng-Chiang**, the Nimons in **The Horns of Nimon**, and Mawdryn and his fellow Mutants in **Mawdryn Undead**.

CRITICAL RESPONSE

- **Review Range:** Generally Positive
- *Doctor Who Magazine 2014 Poll*: 198th/241st
- An audience research report dated Tuesday 19 July contained comments regarding episode four. There was a generally consensus that **The Savages** worked better compared to 'boring historical' narratives. It was highlighted that children were not losing interest in the show, most of whom found the serial to be one of more exciting adventure to date. The standard of acting was given praise all round.
- Writing in their book *Who's Next*, **Mark Clapham, Eddie Robson**, and **Jim Smith** responded positively to the serial. Praise was given to the soundtrack, Steven's maturity into a leader, impressive sets and direction (judged from surviving production photographs), the pacing and energy of the serial, and the intelligent constructive rather than destructive resolution, whereby Jano realises the mistakes of the Elders after inheriting a piece of The Doctor's conscience, instead of excessive violence being used to save the day.
- Writing in *The Discontinuity Guide*, **Paul Cornell, Martin Day**, and **Keith Topping** wrote positively about the serial highlighting the intelligence games the script plays and science fiction clichés which appear throughout as highlights. The writers felt however that the serial was nothing wholly special but did have an effective atmosphere.
- Writing in *The Handbook: The First Doctor*, **David J. Howe, Mark Stammers,** and **Stephen James Walker** gave the serial a more mixed review and a 5/10. They felt that the story 'fails' due to a lack of identifiable characters and a not 'so' complex plot. They praised the Savages but weren't so taken in by the Elders. Praise however was given to the character of Jano, and the soundtrack describing the music as eerie and different compared to other serials of the time.

FILMING LOCATIONS
- Callow Hall Sandpit, Virginia Water, *Surrey*
- Ealing Film Studios
- Riverside Studio 1
- Shire Lane Quarry, Chalfont St Peters, *Bucks*

INFLUENCES
- [no known influences]

PRODUCTION ERRORS
1. If the Elders are such a threat to the Savages' existence, why do they continually live just outside of the Elder's city? Why not move away?

PUBLICITY
- The *Daily Mirror* ran a feature on the make-up applied to **Ewen Solon's** face under the title 'Just Look what they've done to Lucas'. The article appeared on Monday 23 May 1966.
- The *Radio Times* promoted the new serial with a half-page article with the title 'Dr Who and the Savage'. The article appeared a week prior to the broadcast to episode one.

WORKING TITLES
- Doctor Who & the White Savages
- The White Savages

27) THE WAR MACHINES

Plot: London, 1966 and WOTAN can answer any and all questions put to it, but when it starts to develop a personality of its own the War Machines are constructed and total world domination draws near.

CAST

Dr Who	William Hartnell
Dodo	Jackie Lane
Polly	Anneke Wills
Ben	Michael Craze
Sir Charles Summer	William Mervyn
Professor Brett	John Harvey
Professor Krimpton	John Cater
Major Green	Alan Curtis
Kitty	Sandra Bryant
Flash	Ewan Proctor
American Journalist	Ric Felgate
Interviewer	John Doye
Tramp	Roy Godfrey
Taxi-driver	Michael Rathborne
Worker	Desmond Cullum-Jones
Machine Operator	Gerald Taylor
Worker	Eddie Davis
Captain	John Rolfe
Sergeant	John Boyd-Brent
Corporal	Frank Jarvis
Soldier	Robin Dawson
Television Newsreader	Kenneth Kendall
The Minister	George Cross
Garage Mechanic	Edward Colliver
Man in Telephone Box	John Slavid
Radio Announcer	Dwight Whylie
US Correspondent	Carl Conway
The Voice of WOTAN	Gerald Taylor and **WOTAN**
Policeman	Peter Stewart
Discotheque Customers	Carolee Foss, Janice Hoye, Kathie Fitzgibbon, Tina Simmons, Gloria Forstner, Fiona Fraser, Diana Hallows, Michele Barrie, Valerie Shelton, Ruth Calvert, Nigel James, Victor Munt, Decklan Cusse, Barry Noble, Emmett Hennessy, Steve Hardy, Alan Norburn, Alan Cassell, Chris Reck, Gary Leeman
Taxi driver	W Busell
Steward at Scientific Club [Kennedy]	George Wilder
Professor at Scientific Club	Graham Tonbridge
People at Scientific Club	Sam Mansaray, Mrs S Singh
Reporter	Jack Rowlands
Workers	David Waterman, Vic Taylor, Steve Pokol, Pat Leclerc, Dennis Plenty, Jay McGrath, John Pollock, Peter Day, Pat Gorman, Michael Buck, Roger Bowlder, Geoffrey Witherick, Ray Cooper, Hugh Cecil, Nigel James, Terry Wallis, Stephen Rich, Ken McGarvie
Electric 'Teddy' Driver	John Boddimeade
Army Lorry Driver	Bill Taylor
Soldiers	David Waterman, Vic Taylor, Steve Pokol, Pat Leclerc, Mike Reid, Dennis Plenty, Jay McGrath, John Pollock, Peter Day, Pat Gorman, Barry Noble, Alan Wakeling, Nigel James, Terry Wallis, Robert Pearson, Donald Simmons, Roy Stanton, Paul Andrews, John Cook, John Knott, Chris Reck
'Top Brass'	Bill Byfield, Lewis Alexander
People in Pub	John Pollock, John Doye, Connie Georges, Dolly Brennan
Policeman's Voice	Michael Craze
Pedestrians	Doreen Ubels, David J Grahame
Chauffeur	Stephen Rich

CREDITS

Written by Ian Stuart Black
  [First uncredited draft: Pat Dunlop]
Title music by Ron Grainger
and the BBC Radiophonic Workshop
Based on an idea by Kit Pedler
Costumes by Daphne Dare
Make-up by Sonia Markham
Lighting: George Summers
Sound: Davis Hughes
Film Cameraman: Alan Jonas
Film Editor: Eric Mival
Story Editor: Gerry Davis
Designer: Raymond London
Producer: Innes Lloyd
Directed by Michael Ferguson

ACTOR BIOGRAPHIES: William Mervyn is perhaps best known for playing Justice Campbell in *Crown Court* (1973-76) for 103 episodes. **John Cater** can be seen in the films *The Abominable Dr. Phibes* (1971), *Dr. Phibes Rises Again* (1972), and *Captain Kronos: Vampire Hunter* (1974). **Frank Jarvis** landed a small role in *The Italian Job* (1969). **Eddie Davis** landed a small role in *Chitty Chitty Bang Bang* (1968). **Anneke Wills** is perhaps best known for appearing in *The Railway Children* (1957) for 8 episodes and 4 episodes in *Gamble for a Throne* (1961); **Michael Craze** can be seen in *Target Luna* (1960), four separate episodes of *Dixon of Dock Green* (1962/64/65/66), *Ivanhoe* (1970), and the film *Satan's Slave* (1978); **Desmond Cullum-Jones** played 8 separate one-off characters in *Z Cars* (1962-72), 7 characters in *Dixon of Dock Green* (1963-66), and played an uncredited Platoon Member in *Dad's Army* (1969-77); **John Rolfe** appeared in *Cluff* (1964-65).

BEHIND-THE-SCENES

- **Number of Production Days:** 9
- The origins of the serial date back to when **Innes Lloyd** and **Gerry Davis** planned to get *Doctor Who* into more science-fiction based ideas in Spring 1966. Having decided that historical-based narratives were not as popular amongst audiences, both producer and script editor planned to phase these out in favour of stories being set in contemporary surroundings previous seen in *An Unearthly Child* and *Planet of Giants*. It was during this time that **Gerry Davis** planned to recruit a science consultant to work on the show. He approached many people including **Doctor Alex Comfort, Professor Eric Laithwaite** of Imperial College, and astronomer **Patrick Moore**. However, everyone declined the job offer since they were more interested in science reality rather than science-fiction. However, one man **Christopher Magnus Howard Pedler** (or **Kit Pedler**) was very enthusiastic about the opportunity and put forward many exciting ideas for the show.
- The basic premise of *The War Machines* arose when **Gerry Davis** looked up at the newly constructed Post Office Tower and wondered what would happen if the Tower was to be taken over. Responses to this possible storyline were generally somewhat routine, with nobody really expressing an interest in it. It was **Kit Pedler** who suggested that a rogue computer, who decided that mankind should be replaced, would most likely act as the villain for The Doctor to defeat.
- A storyline was soon drawn up where it was decided that the rogue computer would have the ability to hook itself up to the telecommunications network, and would have the ability to operate through the phone lines. The rogue computer would be stationary within the Post Office itself, thus it would require other robots, under its control to take control of London. The production team believed that the serial would bring *Doctor Who* down to Earth, since ordinary settings and everyday objects would become things in a nightmarish world within the story.
- A storyline was written up and writing duties were assigned to BBC staff writer **Pat Dunlop,** appointed to write four scripts for 'Doctor Who and the Computers' with a target deadline of Monday 4 April 1966. However, after completing a first draft script for episode one, **Pat Dunlop** asked to be removed from the project so he could commit his time and energy to other projects elsewhere.
- Brought into to take over writing duties was **Ian Stuart Black** again with a target delivery date of Monday 4 April 1966. It was up to Ian Stuart Black to find a way of writing out existing companion Dodo. Since her introduction to the show, the character was not exceptionally written for, Dodo's accent was inconsistent throughout her appearance on the show, and it was obvious that **Jackie Lane** was far older than the average teenage schoolgirl. The decision was made by **Innes Lloyd** not to renew Jackie Lane's contract.
- With this mind it was then decided that two new companions would be introduced in the serial. **Innes Lloyd** made further plans to bring the show more down to Earth in the wake of the success of the *James Bond* film series and *The Man from U.N.C.L.E* found with British audiences.
- It was firmly decided that the new female companion would not be an orphan or schoolgirl, but instead would be created with the 'Swinging London of the mid-1960s' in mind. The new girl, Polly, would come from a well-off family and would be a secretary to a successful scientist in London. It was planned that Polly should mirror **Julie Christie** and **Marianne Faithfull** and other popular actresses of the time. Meanwhile the new male companion, Ben, would be an Able Seaman in the Royal Navy and was described as a 'realist, solid, capable, cautious, occasionally shy, loyal, a no-nonsense kind of guy, and would do anything for his two companions'. A full detailed background document was written for Ben during the production process.
- The scripts arrived for the serial, now 'Doctor Who and the War Machines', in little over a month over Monday 21 March to Thursday 28 April 1966.
- It was hoped that a small production crew of 6 people would be able to film inside the Post Office Tower in order to get a high-angle shot for the Tardis materialising and an establishing shot from the exterior. It was hoped filming could take place on Sunday 22 May 1966. Permission was declined since it was believed that filming would cause disruption so close to the Tower's public opening on Thursday 19 May 1966.
- Prior to the response from the Post Office Tower inquiry, director **Michael Ferguson** worked closely with **Mr Pascoe** of ICT and IBM, based in Hammersmith who helped the young director obtain a better understanding of computers and artificial intelligence.

- The new companions of Polly and Ben Jackson were to be played by **Anneke Wills** and **Michael Craze**. Both actors were contracted for four serials, consisting of three four-part serials, and a six-part serial over Wednesday 25 and Thursday 26 May 1966.
- Whilst on-location extra **Peter Stewart**, who played the Policeman in episode one, was mistaken for a real Policeman. A member of public asked him for directions.
- The extensive location shoot for the serial was the first 'proper' chance that the press had to photograph the new monsters due to appear in *Doctor Who*. Filming on-location was a rarity for the show with the only extensive time on location occurring in both *The Dalek Invasion of Earth* and *The Chase*.
- The script stated that a total of 12 War Machines had been constructed but only one prop was made. It was designed in such a way that the number plate could be changed between scenes thus creating the illusion that more than one War Machine was appearing in the programme.
- Some of the computer banks and props were recycled from previous serials in the show's run such as *The Keys of Marinus* and *The Space Museum*. A countdown clock which appears during the story was previously utilised for the spin-off movie *Daleks' Invasion of Earth 2150AD*.
- During recording of the serial The Tardis underwent an extensive refurbishment, the first time since the show's debut. The refurbishment was undertaken ahead of an extensive filming shoot planned for the next serial *The Smugglers*. The height of the Tardis prop was reduced, the sides of the prop were narrowed, and the roof was widened. The window panels would become fixed features with the windows on the door being replaced. The lock to the Tardis was moved to the right and the entire prop was repainted and the St John Ambulance emblem was removed. The removal of the emblem would cause minor continuity errors between scenes shot on location and those shot in the studio.
- To save on production costs, stock music would be used throughout the serial instead of composed music. For the scenes when various characters were hypnotised by WOTAN a piece called *Hypnosis* was selected which was composed by **Eric Siday**. The show had used his works many times before.
- For episode two, a set was constructed to represent the street which contained the entrance to the Inferno nightclub and the doorway into the Warehouse where the War Machines was being assembled, and was big enough for a Taxi to driver in and manoeuvre around.
- Two of the extras within the story **John Boddimeade** and **Bill Taylor** were actually employees of the BBC, both of whom worked as scene men, they were paid a staff contribution fee for the services to the serial.
- When the recording of episode two was completed, **Jackie Lane**'s time on the show came to an end. **Innes Lloyd** thanked the actress for her work and was sorry that Dodo had to be dropped from the show.

BROADCAST

EPISODE	DATE	TIME	VIEWING FIGURE	CHART POSITION	APPRECIATION INDEX
1	25/6/1966	5:35-6:00pm	5.4M	71st	49
2	2/7/1966	6:55-7:20pm	4.7M	76th	45
3	9/7/1966	5:35-6:00pm	5.3M	62nd	44
4	16/7/1966	5:15-5:40pm	5.5M	67th	39

CLIFFHANGERS

1. Having been hypnotised by WOTAN earlier, Dodo returns to the Post Office Tower to receive her orders from the super computer. WOTAN tells her 'Doctor Who. Isss. Re-quired. Bring him here!'
2. The Doctor instructs Ben to do some investigating around the area near the nightclub. Ben enters the Warehouse, where a Machine is being tested. Sensing that an intruder is near, the War Machine slowly advances towards Ben.
3. The Army arrives to deal with a War Machine, but their weapons are useless against it. Retreating from the Warehouse, the War Machine chases after them. The Doctor however steps forward, stands his guard, as the War Machine advances towards him.
4. The Doctor waits for Dodo outside the Tardis, but Ben and Polly arrive to tell him she has decided to stay in London. The Doctor enters the Tardis, alone. Ben however remembers he still has Dodo's key to the Police Box, and together he and Polly enter the Tardis before it dematerialises.

COMMERCIAL RELEASES
- **AUDIOBOOK:** March 2019
- **DVD:** August 2008
- **NOVELISATION: [Paperback]** - 16 February 1989; **[Reissue]** – 1992
  - *Target Doctor Who Library Number*: **136**
- **SOUNDTRACK**
  - **August 2007**: *BBC Audio*
  - **5 September 2013**: *The TV Episodes – Collection Six*
- **VIDEO:** June 1997

CONTIUNUTY NOTES
- The War Machines later make a very brief cameo in **PROSE:** *Earthworld* while in **PROSE:** *The Time Travellers* WOTAN successfully conquers Earth in an alternative timeline.
- **Kenneth Kendall** is the first person to make a cameo appearance in *Doctor Who*. Other celebrities who have appeared as themselves in the show include; **Alex MacIntosh** in *Day of the Daleks*, **Courtney Pine** in *Silver Nemesis*, **Andrew Marr** in *Aliens of London/World War Three*, and **Alan Sugar** in *The Power of Three*.
- The romantic chemistry between Ben and Polly, is later brought up in **COMIC:** *The Love Invasion*, where Ben proposes to Polly. The Ninth Doctor and Rose witness the event, but The Doctor doesn't interact with his two previous companions.
- In **PROSE:** *The Rag & Bone Man's Story*, it is revealed that The First Doctor checked to see if the Hand of Omega has been buried in a nearby cemetery as he instructed in November 1963. To his dismay the Hand of Omega hadn't been buried. The First Doctor decided that one of his future self would deal with the situation at an early point in time. The situation is later resolved in ***Remembrance of the Daleks***.
- WOTAN is the first villain to address The Doctor as 'Doctor Who' when its announces 'Doctor Who is required'. Ian Chesterton is the first companion to call The Doctor by this name in *An Unearthly Child* when he says 'Who is he? Doctor who? Perhaps if we knew his name we might have a clue to all of this'.
- *The War Machines* is the first serial since *An Unearthly Child* where the story is set on contemporary Earth.
- The Tardis lands in Leicester Square at the beginning of the serial, as it had done previous in **AUDIO:** *The Founding Father* in the summer of 1762.
- In **AUDIO:** *The Last Post* it is revealed that some of WOTAN's processing banks were recovered after its destruction. They were used to create the Apocalypse Clock which shared some of WOTAN's characteristic. The Third Doctor recognised the components and realised the danger they pose.
- The Doctor hangs a OUT OF ORDER sign on The Tardis, a sign he still has in his possession during his Twelfth Incarnation as seen in *The Pilot*.
- In **AUDIO:** *Machines* Torchwood One constructed Law Machines, a sleeker version of the War Machines, which are quickly taken over by WOTAN to conquer Earth once more.
- The Doctor display quiet a nack of using hypnosis after Dodo is taken over by WOTAN. The Doctor will later use hypnosis in *The Curse of Peladon* and *The Monster of Peladon* to calm Aggedor down, *Terror of the Zygons* and *The Hand of Fear* on Sarah Jane Smith, and one a Shrieve in *The Ribos Operation* plus many other characters over his incarnations.
- WOTAN is the first mad computer to feature on the show. Other mad computers to feature in the show include BOSS in *The Green Death*, Xoanon in *The Face of Evil*, and the Oracle in *Underworld*.
- WOTAN is the first antagonist who uses the phonelines for its own gain and evil plans. Other examples of villains using the phonelines include The Master who controls a trimphone cable to attack the Third Doctor in *Terror of the Autons*, whilst John Lumic takes control of the population of a parallel-world London in *The Age of Steel* to upgrade people into Cybermen.

CRITICAL RESPONSE
- **Review Range:** Mixed
- *Doctor Who Magazine 2014 Poll*: 133rd/241st
- Thursday 21 July 1966 saw a review from **Bill Norris** who wrote about the serial in his column in *Television Today*. He wrote that *The War Machines* was one of the better stories and **William Hartnell** was supported by a strong cast, particularly **William Mervyn, John Harvey, John Cater** and **Alan Curtis**. Norris also wrote highly about **Anneke Wills** and **Michael Craze** as the new companions.

- An audience research report on episode four was compiled on Thursday 4 August 1966 with mixed responses from audiences. Half of the comments highlighted that the story lacked appeal, with many people finding the concept on a computer taking over humans as ridiculous. Other comments found the whole serial as anti-climactic, and others looked unfavourably upon the War Machines. The acting was felt to be not up to scratch, and one housewife wrote that her two sons could have come up with the idea for the War Machines. It was discovered that children had enjoyed the programme, and welcomed the idea of *Doctor Who* being set in Contemporary London, others found the idea quite unconvincing.
- Writing for *DVD Talk's*, **J. Doyle Wallis** gave the serial 3/5 stars. He called the serial 'serviceable' but felt that WOTAN and his henchmen lacked depth.
- Reviewing the serial, *Den of Geek* also gave the serial 3/5 stars. The review wrote highly on **William Hartnell**'s performance, and felt that the story was 'solid' despite the plot holes the story suffered from.
- Writing in *IGN*, **Arnold T Blumburg** awarded the serial a 7/10. His review highlighted that the story's concept has aged, but was entertaining, nonetheless. Criticism was given to Dodo's off-screen departure, and **William Hartnell,** who seemed a little bit lost at times. Blumberg stated that the story did in fact showcase William Hartnell pretty well.
- In a more positive review, **Jonathan Wilkins** of *Dreamwatch* awarded the serial a 9/10. He felt that the story was a forgotten masterpiece and praised **William Hartnell**'s performance, which he highlighted as the reason behind the story's success. He was not as taken in by the War Machines describing them as dull.
- Writing in *The Daily Telegraph* in 2013, **Ben Lawrence** called *The War Machines* as one of the top adventure to take place in contemporary Earth.

DEATHS

DEATH	CHARACTER	TIME OF DEATH	CAUSE OF DEATH
1	Tramp	[00:33:40]	Killed by hypnotised workers
2	Worker	[00:43:18]	Killed by a War Machine
3-8	Soldiers	[01:05:52-01:07:42]	Killed by a War Machine
9	Garage Mechanic	[01:17:30]	Killed by a War Machine
10	Man in Telephone Box	[01:19:42]	Killed by a War Machine
11	Professor Krimpton	[01:34:27]	Killed by a War Machine

FILMING LOCATIONS

- Bedford Square, *London*
- Berner Mews, *London*
- Charlotte Place, *London*
- Conway Street, *London*
- Cornwall Gardens, *London*
- Cornwall Gardens Walk, *London*
- Covent Garden, *London*
- Ealing Film Studios
- Ealing Film Studios Stage 3
- Gresse Street, *London*
- Maple Street, *London*
- Riverside Studio 1
- Royal Opera House, Bow Street, *London*

INFLUENCES

- **TV:** *Coronation Street* (1960 – present, Tony Warren) – [bar scene in episode three]
- **TV:** *Quatermass and the Pit* (1958-59, Nigel Kneale) – [army's presence]

PRODUCTION ERRORS

1. During episode two, the War Machine misses the Worker it's ordered to kill but the actor drops dead anyway.
2. The test War Machine changes from 9 to 3 during its movement trials.
3. The scene where Ben backs away from an approaching War Machine at the start of episode three, is different from the ending which closed episode two.
4. The year in which **The War Machines** is set is a little elusive. According to **The Faceless Ones** the story is set in July 1966, since Ben discovers at the end of **The Faceless Ones** that The Tardis has landed on the same day that he and Polly left with The Doctor. However this cannot be the case. Sir Charles Summer states that C-Day is in four days' time – Monday 16 July 1966. This isn't possible since the 16 July fell on a Sunday in 1966. The next time the 16 July would fall on a Monday would be 1973. And the story can't be set in 1973.
5. The sound the War Machine makes during its movement tests differs between episodes two and three.
6. WOTAN pronounces it name with a 'w' sound rather than a soft 'v' which is used by other characters.
7. The Tardis design changes between location footage and scenes shot in a studio. This is evident in the opening scene when the St John's Ambulance emblem vanished from the Tardis door between shots.
8. It seems unlikely that the Tramp's death would make front-page news the following morning. Also the Tramp's death occurs at a time when it would be too late for his death to be reported for the morning paper.
9. Why do all of the boxes containing components for the War Machine have WOTAN's 'W' logo on them? WOTAN has only put its plan into action now, but it seems the whole operation has been going on for ages.
10. The Doctor knocks off the end of a War Machine's gun with his cloak, and then he knocks his head against the gun whilst inspecting the robot.
11. It is never explained how the War Machine got to the top floor of the Post Office Tower, considering it must have entered and operated a lift to do so. I don't think the lift would be big enough to house the Machine.

PUBLICITY

- A special preview occurred during an edition of *Blue Peter* (20 June 1966) where a War Machine was presented to the public. Presenters **Christopher Trace** and **Valerie Singleton** demonstrated all the working components of the War Machine ahead of its debut during episode two of the serial.
- The *Radio Times* (25 June – 1 July 1966) promoted the serial with a half-page article and accompanying artwork. The artwork showed The Doctor and the Tardis standing under the shadow the Post Office Tower under the title 'Doctor Who and the War Machines'
- A publicity photo of **Michael Craze** and **Anneke Wills** appeared in *Television Today* (Thursday 7 July 1966) promoting the pair as the new companions who would return to the show for the autumn season.

WORKING TITLES

- Doctor Who and the Computers

VERDICT: At the time of its original broadcast, **William Hartnell**'s personal health was failing, and viewing figures were on the decline, the show was becoming tired and monotonous, the style that worked less than two years ago had run its course, even The Daleks were losing their appeal, the beginning of the end was nigh. **The War Machines** marks the beginning of **Innes Lloyd** and **Gerry Davis**' new vision for the show, phasing out historical-based narratives and whimsical storytelling in favour for nitty gritty science fiction stories.

A mixture of filming locations and studio work blend together to bring *Doctor Who* literally down to Earth, turning everyday objects and locations into vices in a nightmarish world. This was a trend that **Russell T Davies** later resurrected when penning the show for its return in 2004. On saying that the story is not that original, hypnotism, super intelligent computers, these have been seen many times beforehand, but this is *Doctor Who*, a show that is never too scared to experiment with clichéd science fiction tropes, and they work here.

The script is extremely tight and ingenuously written by **Ian Stuart Black**, moving from one plot development to the next, building up the tension bit by bit, whilst juggling various scripting requirements that were thrown onto the writer. The first of these is the departure of Dodo, an easy contender for the absolute worst swansong for a companion. Having decided that he disliked the character, **Innes Lloyd** decided that Dodo should leave the show in favour of Ben and Polly. Dodo's absence occurs halfway through, with her expositional departure being explained towards the final moments. It's a decision that The Doctor himself feels most saddened about, as do the viewers, since Dodo herself was not that much developed as a character, a missed opportunity. Ben and Polly make an impression on their own accord, mirroring the swinging sixties that were predominant at the time in Britain. A bigger variety of angles – high and low angles, tracking and panning shots and close-ups all add up for a claustrophobic tale. **William Hartnell** plays a more confident Doctor using his smarts to save the day, and using the enemy's own weapons against them, a fitting style, and The Doctor's last great stand before his upcoming regeneration. *The War Machines* is the product of changing with the times, and is only the beginning of what is to come. ****

28) THE SMUGGLERS

Plot: In eighteenth century Cornwall The Doctor, Ben and Polly are caught up in a search for buried treasure.

CAST

Dr Who	William Hartnell
Polly	Anneke Wills
Ben	Michael Craze
Cherub	George A Cooper
Captain Pike	Michael Godfrey
Squire	Paul Whitsun-Jones
Churchwarden	Terence de Marney
Jacob Kewper	David Blake Kelly
Tom	Mike Lucas
Spaniard	Derek Ware
Jamaica	Elroy Joseph
Blake	John Ringham
Gaptooth	Jack Bligh
Pirate Daniel	Les Clark
Customers at Inn	Steve Kirby, Tony Madison, Harry Tierney, Ricky Lansing, Roy Stanton, Leslie Bates
Pirates	Steve Kirby, Tony Madison, Harry Tierney, Ricky Lancing, Roy Stanton, Leslie Bates, Richard Courtney, A R Serle, Malcolm Attmere, Dennis Symons, Philip Williams, George Charles, Tony Madison, Gary Wyler, Ray Marioni, Peter Day, Terence Jones
Cabin Boy/John	John Jose
Pirate Rowers	Terry Hawes, Ted Rogers
Squire's Manservant (Birch)	Raymond Bales
Militiamen	Hugh Fraser, John Guest, Bill E Raynor, Daniel Sinclair, David Pelton, Alan Lesley, Ronald Robinson, Leonard Kingston
Stunt Pirates	Richard Courtney, A R Serle, Malcolm Attmere, Reginald Hitchin, Christopher Newman, Allan Matthews, Charles Mitchell, Philip Williams, William Thomas, John Weaver, F W Stoker, Buddy Windrush, Ian McKay, Fred Windrush, Valentino Musetti, Mike Horsburgh
Stunt Militiamen	Bill Weston, Malcolm Douglas, Terry Walsh, Brian Mulholland, David Newman
Double for Dr Who	Gordon Craig
Double for Dr Who's Hands	Albert Ward
Double for Blake	Derek Ware
Double for Jacob Kewper (corpse)	Terence Connolly
[unknown character]	R C F Care

CREDITS

Written by Brian Hayles
Title Music by Ron Grainger and the BBC Radiophonic Workshop
Fight Sequence Arranged by Derek Ware
Film Cameraman: Jimmy Court
Film Editor: Colin Eggleston
Costumes by Daphne Dare
Make-up by Gillian James
Lighting: Cyril Wilkins
Sound: Leo Sturges
Story Editor: Gerry Davis
Designer: Richard Hunt
Producer: Innes Lloyd
Directed by Julia Smith

ACTOR BIOGRAPHIES: Paul Whitsun-Jones played James Fullalove in the television series *The Quatermass Experiment* (1953) and appear in numerous films including *The Masque of the Red Death* (1964) and *Assassin* (1973); **George A. Cooper** played Mr. Griffiths in *Grange Hill* (1985-92); **Michael Godfrey** can be seen very briefly in *Licensed to Kill* (1965) and *The Message* (1976); **Jack Bligh** appeared in *Taxi!* (1964); uncredited **Hugh Fraser** went onto have a very successful career, he is perhaps best known for playing Captain Hastings in *Poirot* (1989-2013) and appeared in *101 Dalmatians* (1996).

BEHIND-THE-SCENES

- **Number of Production Days:** 9
- After submitting a storyline which eventually became **The Celestial Toymaker**, writer **Brian Hayles** continued to submit story ideas to the production office, which were all rejected by **Donald Tosh**. One storyline however 'The Nazis' was commissioned by **Gerry Davis**, when he took over the post as script editor. However the storyline was eventually dropped, and another four-part serial was commissioned instead.
- The new storyline **The Smugglers** was commissioned on Monday 4 April as a four-part serial, with all four scripts required at very short notice, needing to be submitted within a fortnight.
- The new story was to be a historical narrative, with the seventeenth century selected as the setting. Apparently **Brian Hayles** had discussed writing a historical serial with both **Donald Tosh** and **Gerry Davis**, but was also unhappy with writing historical narratives for the series.

- The scripts for the serial arrived at the production office over April and May 1966. Episode one arrived on Thursday 12 April, episode two on Wednesday 20 April, episode three on Thursday 28 April, and the final script arrived on Thursday 5 May.
- Since the scripts took longer to arrive than anticipated the decision was made to push recording back to form the end of the current recording block. The serial would then be broadcasted in Autumn 1966 to begin the new series.
- Appointed as director for the serial was **Julia Smith** who previously had trained as an actress at RADA (The Royal Academy of Dramatic Art). Julia Smith also had an extensive knowledge of Cornwall and the surrounding area, the same setting which the serial would be set in.
- It transpired that *The Smugglers* would be the final series in which costumes would be designed by **Daphne Dare** who had worked on every serial from *The Daleks* onwards.
- Since the serial was to have several fight sequences, **Julia Smith** sought the help of stuntman and stunt arranger **Derek Ware**, who had previously founded HAVOC, a company who supplied stunt people for television and film. Derek Ware was also cast in the role as Spaniard, a character who would be very active in fight sequences, Ware was disappointed that his character had no lines.
- Before recording on the serial began, **Brian Hayles'** other script 'Doctor Who and the Nazis' was formally dropped on Wednesday 15 June 1966. Since both **Gerry Davis** and producer **Innes Lloyd** planned to produce scripts with a futuristic science-fiction setting, the decision was made to drop historical serials entirely. It was felt that the time of the Nazis was too recent to form the narrative for a *Doctor Who* serial.
- Before production began, **Brian Hayles** submitted another possible storyline to the production office entitled 'Doctor Who and the Hounds of Time'. **Brian Hayles** drew up a storyline but no scripts were commissioned.
- The serial would see the first major location shoot for the show, since location filming would be conducted outside of London, the usual location for serials such as *The Dalek Invasion of Earth* and *The War Machines* which also had extensive location shoots. The days at Cornwall were carefully planned out by **Julia Smith** since the serial regulars would still be recording material for *The War Machines*.
- Location filming began on Sunday 11 June 1966 which covered material for episodes 1 and 4. This was the only day where **William Hartnell** would be required on-location. With filming completed at the end of the day, the show's leading star was able to return to London.
- The serial required the use of horses, which were supplied by the Rose Hill School of Riding, located near where filming was completed. **Derek Ware** doubled for **John Ringham** for scenes when Blake rode on horseback. During recording when Blake is thrown from a horse, Derek Ware performed a stunt fall, and landed in some nearby dung.
- Since **William Hartnell** had returned to London earlier in the week, The Doctor was still required to feature in certain shots. **Gordon Craig** was hired to double for **William Hartnell** for certain shots.
- The serial also required the use of two pirate rowers who were played by extras **Terry Hawes** and **Ted Rodgers**. Both men were actually sea cadets in real life.
- The final day on location saw both cast and crew capturing scenes on a motor fishing vessel *Bonny Mary* which was taken out to the sea for the day. The vessel has been redressed for the programme the previous night, and many members of the cast and crew were extremely sea sick including **Julia Smith**.
- When the filming was completed, the team headed back to London to proceed with studio sessions. **Julia Smith** at the time had acquired stock footage to represent establishing shots of the *Black Albatross*. However the prints were not up to scratch, and were ultimately dropped from the programme.
- The studio recordings were not an easy time for both **Julia Smith** and **William Hartnell**. The director was aware that the 40 weeks contract the leading actor was under had begun to take it tool on Hartnell who in turn had reservations about whether or not to continue in the part. It didn't help the matter that William Hartnell was not striking a cord with fellow actors **Michael Craze** and **Anneke Wills**.
- During recording of episode one, **Terence de Marney** slipped up on a line, and incorrectly delivered the rhyme riddle to **William Hartnell** in the wrong order. Instead of saying ''Ringwood, Smallbeer, and Gurney', de Marney said 'Smallwood, Ringwood, and Gurney'. This explains a continuity error later on, when **William Hartnell** stuck to the script when The Doctor passes the riddle on.
- Hand-double **Albert Ward** was once again hired to double for **William Hartnell** during the scene when The Doctor dealt out cards to predict other character's futures.
- Before recording for episode four, **Michael Craze** sustained an injury when he fell through an unsecured trapdoor during morning rehearsals. The actor sustained a bruise and cut on his right elbow.

- Episode four marked the first time stuntman, stunt double and occasional actor **Terry Walsh** appeared in the series. **Terry Walsh** would go on to double for both **Jon Pertwee** and **Tom Baker** in later years, and would go onto to play many characters both speaking and non-speaking.
- Recalling his time on the episode, **Terry Walsh** revealed that in order to increase the number of pirates fighting in the graveyard, extras and stuntmen would crawl from behind a gravestone, after being killed, only to switch hats and wigs, and re-join the battle as a new character.
- With recording complete, the production team parted ways, with **William Hartnell**'s swansong schedule to be recorded after the summer break.

BROADCAST

EPISODE	DATE	TIME	VIEWING FIGURE	CHART POSITION	APPRECIATION INDEX
1	10/9/1966	5:50-6:15pm	4.3M	96th	47
2	17/9/1966	5:50-6:15pm	4.9M	77th	45
3	24/9/1966	5:50-6:15pm	4.2M	96th	43
4	1/10/1966	5:50-6:15pm	4.5M	109th	43

CLIFFHANGERS

1. Onboard the *Black Albatross*, Cherub tells Captain Pike that The Doctor knows the location of Captain Avery's treasure. The Doctor is brought to Captain Pike but refuses to speak. Captain Pike demands that The Doctor speak to him, and slams his hand on the table top. However it's not a hand that Captain Pike slams on the table top, it's a barbed pike.
2. Ben returns to the church crypt having discovered a secret tunnel that leads to the beach, and the Tardis. However Ben is blocked by the Squire, Captain Pike, and Cherub. They have Polly with them, who has been bound, and gagged.
3. The Squire and Jacob Kewper arrive back at the church, to attempt once again to make The Doctor reveal what he knows about the hidden treasure. Before The Doctor can say anything, Kewper and the Squire argue about the best course of action to take. During the argument, Cherub enters and throws a knife into Kewper's back, and a shot rings out. Polly screams.
4. Inside the Tardis, the console room is all of a sudden freezing cold. The Doctor tells Ben and Polly that the Tardis has landed on the coldest place on Earth.

COMMERCIAL RELEASES

- **AUDIOBOOK:** August 2020
- **DVD:** 1 November 2004
- **NOVELISATION:** [Hardback] 16 June 1988; [Paperback] - 17 November 1988; [Reissue] – 1993
    - *Target Doctor Who Library Number*: **133**
- **SOUNDTRACK**
    - **6 May 2002:** *BBC Audio*
    - **4 August 2011:** *The Lost TV Episodes – Collection Three*
- **VIDEO:** 1998 [a short segment]

CONTINITY NOTES

- *The Smugglers* is the first *Doctor Who* story to have only one female character in it (Polly), the next story to have one female character is *The Moonbase* (again Polly being the only female character), then again in *Pyramids of Mars* (Sarah Jane Smith), which was also the last.
- The Doctor encounters all kinds of pirates throughout his incarnations; Blackbeard in *The Mind Robber*, space pirates in *The Space Pirates*, the cyborg robot Captain in *The Pirate Planet*, Kari and Olvir in *Terminus*, Eternals masquerading as Earth pirates in *Enlightenment*, Baltazar in the animated special *The Infinite Quest*, and the infamous Captain Avery in *The Curse of the Black Spot*.
- The Doctor will later revisit Cornwall in the 1970s in *The Stones of Blood*; further adventures in Cornwall occur in **PROSE:** *The Shadow in the Glass*, **AUDIO:** *Beach Head*, **COMIC:** *The Amateur*, plus others.

- During the story it is revealed that everyone is looking for Captain Avery's hidden treasure. Captain Avery himself will later meet The Eleventh Doctor in *The Curse of the Black Spot*.

CRITICAL RESPONSE

- **Review Range:** Generally Positive
- *Doctor Who Magazine 2014 Poll*: 194th/241st
- The first episode was reviewed at a BBC Programme Review Board on Wednesday 14 September 1966. **Huw Wheldon** praised the episode paying particular attention to **William Hartnell** who in his eyes had provided a better and light-hearted performance. Wheldon believed this was because the leading actor knew he would be leaving the show in the near future.
- A critic writing in the *Sheffield Telegraph* wrote highly about the first episode. The critic wrote that the episode was much better written and produced than the show had broadcasted for quite a while.
- Reviewing the serial in *The Listener*, **JC Trewin** was not so keen with the first two episodes calling them sub-par for a serial that was trying to be like *Treasure Island*. However on Thursday 13 October he had a change of heart, writing that he had enjoyed the serial very much.
- Writing in *Doctor Who: The Episode Guide*, **Mark Campbell** awarded the serial a 8/10. He summed the serial up as swashbuckling, and full of characterisation. He wrote that the dialogue was OTT (over the top).

FILMING LOCATIONS

- Bonny Mary, Newlyn Harbour, *Cornwall*
- Bosistow Cliffs, Nanijzal, *Cornwall*
- Church Gove, *Cornwall*
- Nanijzal Bat, Nanijzal, *Cornwall*
- Riverside Studio 1
- St Grada Church, Grade, *Cornwall*
- Trenethick Barton, Helston, *Cornwall*
- Trethewey Farm, Trethewey, *Cornwall*

INFLUENCES

- **BOOK:** *Jamaica Inn* (1936, Daphne de Maurier).
- **BOOK:** *Moonfleet* (1898, J. Meade Falkner).
- **BOOK:** *Treasure Island* (1883, Robert Louis Stevenson).
- **CHARACTERS:** *Dr Syn* and *Captain Clegg* (Robert Thorndike).

PRODUCTION ERRORS

1. The rhyme riddle is different between episodes one and three. In episode one, the Churchwardens says 'Smallwood, Ringwood, and Gurney', instead of 'Ringwood, Smallbeer, and Gurney'. The Doctor passes the message on delivering the riddle in the correct order.
2. During episode four, Gaptooth refers to Pirate Daniel as 'David' for some reason.

PUBLICITY

- After the broadcast of episode four of **The War Machines**, a 45' trailer for **The Smugglers** was broadcast at 5.39pm. The trailer was narrated by **Martin Locke**.
- The serial was promoted in the *Radio Times* on Thursday 8 September. The article contained photographs of The Doctor, Ben, Polly, Captain Pike, and Cherub. A short text piece introduced the plot to the serial.
- On Friday 9 September, *Junior Points of View* promoted the upcoming adventure with poems written by young viewers about how much they were looking forward to the show's return.
- The involvement of locals as extras in the serial was promoted in *The Cornishman* with an article called "Sea Cadets turn to piracy to help time traveller Dr Who".

WORKING TITLES

- Doctor Who and the Pirates

29) THE TENTH PLANET

Plot: Antarctica, 1986; when a mysterious planet identical to Earth approaches, a race of emotionless creatures called The Cybermen come with it as The Doctor's body wears a bit thin

CAST

Dr Who	William Hartnell
Polly	Anneke Wills
Ben	Michael Craze
General Cutter	Robert Beatty
Williams	Earl Cameron
Dyson	Dudley Jones
Barclay	David Dodimead
Schultz	Alan White
Tito	Shane Shelton
American Sergeant	John Brandon
Wigner	Steve Plytas
Radar Technician	Christopher Matthews
Krail	Reg Whitehead
Talon	Harry Brooks
Shav	Gregg Palmer
Geneva Technician	Ellen Cullen
TV Announcer	Glenn Beck
Cyberman Voice	Roy Skelton
R/T Technician	Christopher Denham
Terry Cutler	Callen Angelo
Krang	Harry Brooks
Jarl	Reg Whitehead
Gern	Gregg Palmer
Cybermen Voices	Peter Hawkins
Tracking Room Technicians	Richard Lawrence, Morris Quick, Bill Gosling, Gordon Lang
R/T Technician	Nicholas Edwards
Soldiers	Ken McGarvie, Terence Jones, Nick Hilton, Roy Pearce, Freddie Eldrett, Peter Pocock
Corporal	Alec Coleman
High Ranking Officers	Chris Konyils, Stanley Davies
Geneva Secretary	Sheila Knight
Engineer Haines	Freddie Eldrett
Engineer	Roy Pearce
Cybermen	Reg Whitehead, Harry Brooks, Gregg Palmer, John Slater, Bruce Wells, John Haines, John Knott
Snowcap Base Voices	Glenn Beck, Roy Skelton
Countdown Voice	Roy Skelton
Double for Dr. Who	Gordon Craig
Double for Ben	Peter Pocock

and introducing Patrick Troughton as **Dr Who**

CREDITS
Written by Kit Pedler, and Gerry Davis
Title Music by Ron Grainer
 and the BBC Radiophonic Workshop
Costumes by Sandra Reid
Make-up by Gillian James
Lighting: Howard King
Sound: Adrian Bishop-Laggett
Story Editor: Gerry Davis
Designer: Peter Kindred
Producer: Innes Lloyd
Director: Derek Martinus

ACTOR BIOGRAPHIES: Robert Beatty appeared in high-budget films throughout his career including landing roles in *2001: A Space Odyssey* (1968), *Where Eagles Dare* (1968), *The Pink Panther Stike Again* (1976), *Superman IV: The Quest for Peace* (1987), and played Det. Insp. Mike Maguire in *Dial 999* (1958-59); **Earl Cameron** made a small appearance in *Inception* (2010); **Callen Angelo** played Gary Strauss in *Coronation Street* (1967-70); **Harry Brooks** credits include four uncredited appearances in *Quatermass II* (1955); **Dudley Jones** appeared in 5 episodes of *Treasure Island* (1957); **Steve Plytas'** film credits include *Orion's Belt* (1985), *Superman IV: The Quest for Peace* (1987), and *Batman* (1989); **David Dodimead** landed a small role in *The Honey Pot* (1967); **Alan White** was a regular cast member in *The Flying Doctor* (1959), and *Tell It To the Marines* (1959-69); **John Brandon** landed a small role in *Scarface* (1983); **Glenn Beck** played an astronaut in *2001: A Space Odyssey* (1968); **Freddie Eldrett** featured in *The Adventures of Tom Sawyer* (1960); **William Gosling** can be seen in *Galileo* (1975).

BEHIND-THE-SCENES

- **Number of Production Days:** 8
- The origins of *The Tenth Planet* date back to when the serial was commissioned on Tuesday 17 May 1966. During this time it was not intended that **William Hartnell** would leave the series, and as such this element was not under consideration. The author of the serial was to be **Kit Pedler**, who had been appointed as the show's scientific advisor just a short while prior.
- The concept for *The Tenth Planet* focused on two scientific concepts which writer **Kit Pedler** found interesting. The first of these centred around a space capsule whose energy loss was the result of a race of cyborgs whose own energy sources were running rapidly dry. Both **Gerry Davis** and **Innes Lloyd** liked the space capsule idea since both the US and USSR were in the middle of their space race during the time the story was being conceived. The second was the idea of a race of people called 'Star Monks' who were from Earth's twin planet. However there were certain elements to the second concept which Gerry Davis felt to be too similar to *The Time Meddler*, and *The Daleks' Master Plan*.
- As it turned out a storyline about Earth having a twin planet had been considered and discussed with potential writers for the show from the beginning of the series run. One such storyline 'The Hidden Planet' had been proposed by **Malcolm Hulke** but ultimately went unproduced.
- The scripts for the episode indicated that the design of the Polar Base's tracking room should mirror the design and layout of Cape Kennedy. The capsule that was to feature in the serial, *Zeus IV* was to be identical to a Gemini Capsule, which was used during experiments for the Space Race. The Antarctic Base setting was heavily inspired by the film *The Thing from Another World* (1951), where an American Air Force team are menaced by an alien being from a crashed spaceship.
- After initial planning for the storyline, **Gerry Davis** suggested to **Kit Pedler** that he concentrated on what frightened him the most as a scientist, instead of writing science-fiction. As a doctor, Kit Pedler was both fascinated/frightened by the idea of the replacement of limbs and organs with machines. He discussed the idea with his wife, who was also a doctor, and together they came up with the idea of 'spare part' surgery, taken to extreme levels. Intrigued by the idea of a completely cybernetic man, **Kit Pedler** pondered whether or not if these 'cybernetic men' would still have a soul. The idea was also hit upon by having the 'Cybermen's' arms starting lower down their bodies rather than from the elbow.
- Meeting together at a fish and chip shop at Kensington, **Kit Pedler** and **Gerry Davis** discussed the idea further, with Kit Pedler being formally commissioned to write 'Doctor Who and the Tenth Planet' on Tuesday 17 May 1966, to be delivered by Monday 6 June.
- After the storyline was settled, it became evident that **William Hartnell** would soon be leaving the series. Problems began to arise after the original production team began to depart in 1965. **William Hartnell** had threatened to leave the show, and **John Wiles** had tried (and failed) to replace the leading actor with someone else. Hartnell was concerned about the increasing levels of what he called 'evil' in the series; the actor wanted the series to focus more on whimsical storylines which would be suitable for younger audiences. John Wiles, himself had wanted to take the show down different paths, but Hartnell would often go straight to **Sydney Newman** and make his concerns be known. When **Innes Lloyd** replaced John Wiles, the producer did get some respect from the leading actor, but it became evident that a change was necessary. Since **Shaun Sutton** took over as Head of Drama Series in April 1966, he wanted to see the show continue; suggesting that perhaps a change of actor would be good for the series.
- Since The Doctor was a very old alien, **Gerry Davis** suggested the idea that The Doctor could die and be reborn into a younger body. **Innes Lloyd** enhanced the idea suggesting The Doctor could have an ability allowing him to rejuvenate himself every so often. This idea was eventually worked into *The Tenth Planet*.
- With the change of leading actor imminent, the production team considered various actors for the job; **Michael Horden, Patrick Wymark, Ron Moody** and rock and roll star **Tommy Steele** were all considered. Eventually the production team selected **Patrick Troughton**, and **William Hartnell** apparently approved.
- During the scripting process, **Kit Pedler** was taken ill and admitted to hospital, thus preventing him for completing work on episodes three and four. **Gerry Davis** was cleared to complete work on the final two scripts but was working flat out across three projects (*The Smugglers, The Tenth Planet*, and **Patrick Troughton**'s debut story). An agreement was eventually reached where both Kit Pedler and Gerry Davis would get a 50:50 split for scripting duties, and both men would have copyright clearance on the Cybermen.
- When the script, cast, and crew were all settled, time soon came to designing the Cybermen. It was intended that the halogen lamp in the Cybermen's headwear would illuminate. However after a test shot, the bulb exploded(!) and the idea was subsequently dropped. Although the scripts stated that the Cybermen still obtained their human hands, costume designer

- **Sandra Reid** claimed that she had forgotten to design silver gloves for the actors to wear. Make-up designer **Gillian James** applied silver-blue make-up to the actors' hands instead.
- The voices of the Cybermen were originally intended to be flat and hard in tone, but voice artiste **Roy Skelton** came up with a different idea. He eventually used a more stilted, mechanical-sounding voice, with the pitch intonated and inflected differently from normal human speech.
- Work on *The Tenth Planet* began with various model shots being shot on film at Ealing Film Studios. One such model shot was of the planet Mondas, a polystyrene model shot against a smoky space background. For the planet's destruction in episode four, the model was melted by a blowtorch.
- During the film shots, **William Hartnell** was still enjoying his time in Cornwall, so **Gordon Craig** was hired to double for The Doctor as he had done in *The Smugglers*.
- Wednesday 31 August saw **Michael Craze** and **Anneke Wills** join the cast along with extras; **Alec Coleman, Ken McGarvie,** and **Terence Jones** to perform scenes for episode 1. It was on this day that both Craze and Wills found out that **William Hartnell** would be leaving the show. They young actors had not struck a strong cord with the leading actor, and looked forward to working with Hartnell's successor.
- The polar landscapes were shot at Ealing for various reasons, 1) the production team wanted the icy landscapes to look convincing and Riverside Studios would be too small, 2) the landscapes needed to be constructed on a platform so a trapdoor could be used by ISC personnel, 3) Jabolite was used to represent the snow which was thrown in front of a wind machine, again very difficult to operate in small, recording studios, and 4) a rotating periscope and a set of radio aerials were required to project from under the snow.
- Before working on *Doctor Who*, **Michael Craze** underwent surgery to remove a bone chip from his nose, the operation left his nose very delicate. The Jabolite snow caused him some discomfort. Uncredited production assistant **Edwina Verner** was responsible for throwing the Jabolite in front of the wind machine. After leaving the show, Michael Craze and Edwina Verner married.
- Since many of the extras were required to operate firearms, an armourer was present to oversee all work when the Browning 9mm automatics were fired in the studios.
- The actors who played the Cybermen found working on the serial extremely difficult. The Cybermen costumes were uncomfortable to wear under the hot studio lights causing some of them to faint.
- After episode two was recorded **William Hartnell** was taken ill and advised by his doctor not to work on episode three. He spent the week resting in his cottage at Mayfield. **Gerry Davis** rewrote the script for episode three, and director **Derek Martinus** sent Hartnell a letter wishing him a quick recovery. To make up for **William Hartnell**'s absence, **Gordon Craig** was hired once again to double for The Doctor, collapsing to the studio floor with his face away from the camera.
- To save money on the budget, the *Zeus 4* capsule set was reused for scenes set in *Zeus 5*. **Callen Angelo,** playing Terry Cutler, only appeared on monitors to disguise the recycled sets.
- The final day on *Doctor Who* for **William Hartnell** was on Saturday 8 October 1966 (the same day episode one was broadcast). A leaving party was held at **Innes Lloyd**'s flat, with the producer taking the actor home at 1am. The party was an emotional affair for William Hartnell ….

BROADCAST

EPISODE	DATE	TIME	VIEWING FIGURE	CHART POSITION	APPRECIATION INDEX
1	8/10/1966	5:50-6:15pm	5.5M	77th	50
2	15/10/1966	5:50-6:15pm	6.4M	57th	48
3	22/10/1966	5:50-6:15pm	7.6M	46th	48
4	29/10/1966	5:50-6:15pm	7.5M	48th	47

CLIFFHANGERS

1. After retrieving equipment from the Snowbase to cut open the Tardis, Joe and Tito return to join the American Sergeant. What they think is the American Sergeant, is actually a Cyberman. Two more Cybermen appear, and Tito and Joe are killed. One Cyberman looms over Tito's body, and stares at the camera ….

2. After killing the Cybermen inside the Base, General Cutter discovers that his son, Terry has been sent up into space to help *Zeus IV*. Before Cutler can make any further plans to secure the base, the Radar Technician announces that hundreds of spaceships are approaching the Earth in formation.
3. Ben, who had previously been knocked unconscious, cannot remember if he succeeded in sabotaging the rocket. When the countdown reaches zero, the engines ignite, and the rocket prepares for take-off.
4. The Doctor collapses to the Tardis Console Room floor, Ben and Polly arrive, and watch as The Doctor changes his appearance before their eyes.

COMMERCIAL RELEASES

- **AUDIOBOOK:** December 2017
- **DVD:** 1 November 2004; October 2013
- **ELECTRONIC MUSIC/SOUND EFFECTS**
  - **2000** *Doctor Who at the BBC Radiophonic Workshop Volume 1: The Early Years 1963-1969*
- **NOVELISATION: [Hardback/Paperback]** - 19 February 1976; **[Reissues]** - 1978; 1993; 2012
  - *Target Doctor Who Library Number*: **62**
- **SOUNDTRACK**
  - **1987:** Space Adventures – Music from 'Doctor Who' 1963-68
  - **2000:** *Doctor Who at the BBC Radiophonic Workshop Volume 1: The Early Years 1963-1969*
  - **1 November 2004:** *BBC Audio*
  - **9 January 2006:** *Single Audio CD*
  - **4 August 2011:** *The Lost TV Episodes – Collection Three*
  - **9 December** 2013 - 29 September 2014 : *Doctor Who: The 50th Anniversary Collection*
- **VIDEO:** November 2000 [with a reconstructed episode 4]

CONTINUITY NOTES

- For the first and only time in the show's history the Cybermen have individual names. However their names were never uttered on screen, but were reinstated for the end credits.
- Despite **The Tenth Planet** being the Cybermen's debut appearance, The Doctor seems to display an extensive knowledge about Mondas and the Cybermen. Subsequent audio dramas and books have explored this notation: in **AUDIO:** *The Alchemists* Susan seems to know that gold is deadly to the Cybermen, in **PROSE:** *Byzantium!*, The Doctor recalls a visit to Mondas, in **PROSE:** *The Empire of Glass*, The First Doctor chairs the Armaggedon Convention, which the Cybermen do not attend and **PROSE:** *Salvation*, Steven seems to have met the Cybermen at some point, but this could have occurred before meeting The Doctor.
- The Doctor comments before regeneration 'This body is wearing a bit thin'. This is the same description The War Doctor uses before regenerating into the Ninth Doctor in **The Day of the Doctor**.
- Antarctica features in many of The Doctor's adventures. He later revisits the barren landscape in **The Seeds of Doom**, **PROSE:** *Iceberg*, **COMIC:** *The First*, **AUDIO:** *Frozen Time* and **AUDIO:** *The Word Lord*.
- The Mondasian Cybermen later battle the Second Doctor in **COMIC:** *The Time Museum*, the Fifth Doctor in **AUDIO:** *Spare Parts*, the Seventh Doctor and Ace in **COMIC:** *The Good Soldier*, the Eighth Doctor in **AUDIO:** *The Silver Turk* and the Twelfth Doctor in **World Enough and Time/The Doctor Falls**.
- The Earth later faces a similar problem that Mondas posed, where an approaching Gallifrey (a much larger planet compared to the Earth) threatens to destroy the planet in **The End of Time**.
- The Cybermen later plan to save Mondas from destruction in **Attack of the Cybermen** by destroying the Earth in 1985, before Mondas itself returns to the Solar System in 1986.
- The Antarctic Base is the first base to come under siege in the show's history. Other bases which come under attack include the Moonbase in **The Moonbase**, a Euro Gas Refinery in **Fury from the Deep**, another Antarctica Base in **The Seeds of Doom**, Sea Base in **Warrior of the Deep**.
- The First Doctor's regeneration marks the first time when The Doctor regenerates inside the Tardis, the next Doctor to regenerate inside the Tardis is the Fifth Doctor in **The Caves of Androzani**.

- It is later revealed in **AUDIO:** *The First Wave* that another companion witnessed The Doctor's regeneration into his second incarnation, Oliver Harper. Introduced in the *Big Finish* audio range, Oliver Harper's ghost remained in the Tardis after being killed sometime previously.
- The Spacesuits which feature in the story are later reused for ***The Wheel in Space*** (although in a different capacity).
- In **AUDIO:** *The Silver Turk*, The Eighth Doctor battles Cybermen of the same design seen in the serial, and again in ***World Enough and Time/The Doctor Falls***.

CRITICAL RESPONSE

- **Review Range:** Positive
- *Doctor Who 2014 Magazine Poll*: 85th/241st
- At a BBC Programme Review Board meeting on Wednesday 19 October 1966, BBC Director-General **Hugh Greene** spoke highly of episode two based on the grounds that the episode contained more Cybermen.
- A fortnight later, BBC's Head of Presentation, **Rex Moorfoot** praised episode four to his fellow colleagues.
- A 2009 review from **Patrick Mulkern** was not so convinced with the Mondasian Cybermen, but praised the characters of Cutler and The Doctor nonetheless.
- Episode four was named one of the best 10 'classic *Doctor Who* cliffhangers by *Den of Geek*.
- Writing for *io9*, **Alasdair Wilkins** described the story as solid, and excellent at certain times. He felt that the Cybermen were not as intimidating compared to other Cybermen stories, but wrote that they were definitely at their creepiest with this serial. He placed ***The Tenth Planet*** and The First Doctor's regeneration as the fourth best respectively.
- The serial was awarded 4.5 stars out of 5 by **John Sinnott** of *DVD Talk*. He praised **William Hartnell**'s performance and the Cybermen.
- In a more average review, **Ian Berriman** of *SFX* gave the serial 3 stars out of 5. Praise went towards the Cybermen and to the tension of the situation that the characters found themselves in. However he felt that the regeneration was a little rushed, and Mondas had little background information to make it believable.

DEATHS

DEATH	CHARACTER	TIME OF DEATH	CAUSE OF DEATH
1	American Sergeant	[00:21:36]	Killed by a Cyberman
2	Tito	[00:21:36]	Killed by a Cyberman
3	Joe	[00:21:59]	Killed by a Cyberman
4	Soldier	[00:27:28]	Killed by a Cyberman
5	Williams	[00:36:30]	Killed when *Zeus IV* explodes
6	Schultz	[00:36:30]	Killed when *Zeus IV* explodes
7	Talon	[00:39:24]	Killed by Ben Jackson
8	Shav	[00:40:53]	Killed by General Cutler
9	Krail	[00:40:57]	Killed by General Cutler
10-14	Cybermen	[01:01:09-01:01:17]	Shot down with weapons
15	General Cutler	[01:13:32]	Killed by Krang
16	Jarl	[01:26:07]	Killed by Ben Jackson
17	Cyberman	[01:26:22]	Killed by Dyson
18	Engineer Haines	[01:26:24]	Killed by a Cyberman
19	Krang	[01:26:27]	Killed by Ben Jackson
20-23	Cybermen	[01:28:16-01:28:20]	Disintegrate
24	Gern	[01:28:16]	Disintegrates

FILMING LOCATIONS

- Ealing Film Studios Stage 3
- Riverside Studio 1

INFLUENCES

- **BOOK:** *Cybernetics* (1948, Norbert Weiner).
- **BOOK:** *Frankenstein* (1818, Mary Shelley).
- **BOOK:** *Limbo* (Bernard Wolfe).
- **BOOK:** *Strange Case of Dr Jekyll and Mr Hyde* (1886, Robert Louis Stevenson).
- **BOOK:** *When Worlds Collide* (1933, Philip Wylie and Edwin Balmer).
- **CHARACTER:** *Dan Dare* (1950-1967, Frank Hampson).
- **FILM:** *Dr Strangelove* (1964, Stanley Kubrick).
- **FILM:** *The Day the Earth Stood Still* (1951, Robert Wise).
- **FILM:** *The Thing from Other World* (1951, Christian Nyby).
- **STAGEPLAY:** *R.U.R.* (1920, Karel Ĉapek) – [cyborgs]
- **TV:** *The Avengers* 'The Cybernauts' [1965, Sidney Hayers]

PRODUCTION ERRORS

1. There are a few problems with the opening and closing credits. **Kit Pedler**'s name reads as Kitt Pedler. **Gerry Davis** is credited as Gerry Davies.
2. Some of the Cybermen's dialogue is out of sync with their mouths. This is because the voice actors provided the dialogue off-camera instead of getting the actors who played the Cybermen to perform the lines.
3. The Gaffatape which was used to hold the Cybermen's helmets together is clearly visible.
4. A part of one of a Cyberman's headpiece comes loose during the story.
5. During episode one, one of the Cybermen's ear can be seen flapping about.
6. At one point the Cybermen enter the Antarctic Base by putting on parkas. This would work if it was not for the fact that their headlamps are clearly visible.
7. The Cybermen claim that they have removed all emotions and humanity from themselves because they are 'weaknesses'. However their individual names seem to contradict this statement.
8. If Barclay designed the base why did he construct the ventilation shaft so he could fit through it?
9. During episode four **Michael Craze** accidentally says plonet Mandos instead of Planet Mondas
10. Krail's head-mounted lamp reflects the studio lights during episode two.

PUBLICITY

- The departure of **William Hartnell** was announced on Friday 5 August 1966 and was covered extensively by the British press. The news was covered in *The Times* with an article called "New Dr Who Sought" the following day on Saturday 6 August 1966.
- Writing for the *Daily Mirror*, **Clifford Davies** story "Why I must quit – by Dr Who" contained personal quotes from **William Hartnell** on his departure.
- The *Daily Mail* carried the article "Dr Who to Quit" written by **Brian Dean**, whilst **Martin Jackson** of the *Daily Express* covered the departure of the leading actor with an article titled "A New Who in View, But Who?"
- The *Radio Times* promoted the serial with a half-page article before the broadcast of episode one. The article contained a photograph of seven Cybermen, taken at Ealing Film Studios, standing in the Antarctic landscape. One Cybermen is notably missing its headgear lamp.
- A photograph of **Robert Beatty** in his General Cutter costume appeared in the trade paper *Television Today* on Thursday 6 October 1966 to promote the up-coming adventure.
- Saturday 8 October 1966 saw the *Illustrated London News* run an article entitled "Exploring the Jungle of the Eye". Reporter **Timothy Johnson** visited **Kit Pedler**'s research laboratory on Bloomsbury to discuss his work and research in ophthalmology. The article also promoted that the scientist was the write of the upcoming *Doctor Who* adventure, which was Kit Pedler's first television writing credit.

WORKING TITLES

➢ [no known working titles]

VERDICT: For the first time ever, British Television Drama was about to change. The leading actor, that adults and children alike adored for three years were about to watch his entire appearance change, with no explanation until the next adventure. **William Hartnell** through his highs and lows, his temper and tantrums, the struggles and triumphs, his desire not to let the kids down at home, and his adoration for his show deserved nothing but perfection for his final one and half hours as science fiction's most beloved hero…. Bring on the Cybermen, those pesky contradicting monsters. Over the years, the Cybermen's designs became more refined, more robotic and more 'inhuman'. Here the Cybermen, despite saying otherwise, still possess some of their original selves. It is entirely believable that a flesh and bone being still lurks behind the Cybernetic equipment, and their individual names Karl, Gern, etc. suggests they have a concept of individual identity.

The Tenth Planet is more of a template for future Cybermen stories than anything else, where **almost** every **subsequent Cyberman story** follows the **same basic narrative**, recycled over and over again. Director **Derek Martinus** makes great use of the Snowcap base sets, and the snow polar landscapes do make for some frightening imagery, emphasising the isolation that the main characters find themselves in, which is aided with an excellent soundtrack. The plot makes excellent use of having the story take place all over the world, emphasizing the scale and danger that the cast will soon find themselves in.

For the first few minutes, it would seem that the production team were going all out for William Hartnell. There's only **one** major problem. *The Tenth Planet* is unbelievably, painstakingly, pull your hair out frustratingly slow, and padded out with unnecessary filler and tat. The Doctor disappears for HALF of his final adventure, and the whole Mondas destroying the Earth plotline doesn't really accelerate until EPISODE FOUR. It's also incredibly lazy that The Doctor doesn't actually have to do ANYTHING to save the day. He could lie down and take a nap whilst the Cybermen become the makers of their own destruction. Wait a second, THAT's EXACTLY WHAT HAPPENS! The rest of characters are mostly stereotypes, the trigger happy General Cutler being the most painstakingly obvious, which is fine, if this was a social commentary on culture and society, but *The Tenth Planet* is not a social commentary in the slightest. *Doctor Who* will later go on to do social-commentaries in later years, but most stories in the **Innes Lloyd** and **Gerry Davis** era are pure escapism narratives, nothing more.

As a last adventure for William Hartnell this doesn't hold up compared to other regeneration stories. It's not that original or imaginative, nor is it that intelligently written, it's lazy, very lazy, and The First Doctor's final moments are no fitting departure for *Doctor Who*'s first and most charismatic, whimsical leading actor. ***

END NOTE: Assuming every episode of the **William Hartnell** era was still around today, it would take you a total of 54 hours 24 minutes and 36 seconds to watch the entire First Doctor era.

FIRST DOCTOR: OTHER MEDIA

AUDIO

BBC NEW SERIES ADVENTURES

NO	TITLE	WRITER	RELEASE DATE	COMPANIONS	FEATURING	MAIN ENEMY
1	The Lost Magic	Cavan Scott	3 May 2017	Alex, Brandon	John Dee, Madenia, Gabriel Alvarez, Francis Drake, Ben, Eleventh Doctor, Tenth Doctor, Ninth Doctor, War Doctor, Eighth Doctor, Seventh Doctor, Sixth Doctor, Fifth Doctor, Fourth Doctor, Third Doctor, Second Doctor, First Doctor	Time Storm

DESTINY OF THE DOCTOR

NO	TITLE	WRITER	RELEASE DATE	COMPANION	FEATURING	MAIN ENEMY
1	Hunters of Earth	Nigel Robinson	1 January 2013	Susan	Eleventh Doctor	Colonel Rook

MAIN RANGE

NO	TITLE	WRITER	RELEASE DATE	FEATURING	MAIN ENEMY
1	Master	Joseph Lidster	31 October 2003	First Doctor	The Master, Death

OTHER

NO	TITLE	WRITER	RELEASE DATE	COMPANIONS	FEATURING
1	Men of War	Justin Richards	3 May 2018	Steven, Sara	Mark Steadman

SHORT TRIPS

NO	TITLE	WRITER	RELEASE DATE	COMPANIONS	FEATURING	MAIN ENEMY
1	Rise and Fall	George Mann	5 November 2010	Susan, Ian, Barbara	-	-
2	1963	Niall Boyce	28 February 2011	Ian, Barbara, Vicki	-	-
3	Seven to One	Simon Paul Miller	11 May 2011	-	Second Doctor, Third Doctor, Fourth Doctor, Fifth Doctor, Sixth Doctor, Seventh Doctor	The Entity and RWR Mark II
4	A Star is Born	Richard Dinnick	10 August 2011	Susan, Ian, Barbara	-	Rode
5	Flywheel Revolution	Dale Smith	5 January 2015	-	-	-
6	Etheria	Nick Wallace	24 September 2015	Vicki, Steven	-	Pirates
7	The Toy	Nigel Fairs	21 October 2015	-	Fifth Doctor, Tegan, Adric, First Doctor, Second Doctor, Third Doctor, Fourth Doctor, Sixth Doctor, Seventh Doctor, Eight Doctor, Susan	The Master
8	The Horror at Bletchington Station	Chris Wing	15 March 2016	Dodo	-	The Beast
9	This Sporting Life	Una McCormack	31 May 2016	Steven, Dodo	-	-
10	Falling	Jonathan Barnes	30 May 2017	Polly, Ben	-	-
11	Helmstone	Tony Jones	12 September 2017	Steven Taylor	-	-
12	O Tannenbaum	Anthony Keetch	22 December 2017	Steven	-	-

NO	TITLE	WRITER	RELEASE DATE	COMPANIONS	FEATURING	MAIN ENEMY
13	*A Small Semblance of Home*	Paul Phipps	27 September 2018	Susan, Ian, Barbara	-	Sinensis
14	*Peace in Our Time*	Una McCormack	23 December 2019	Steven	-	Gledhill Family
15	*Out of the Deep*	John Pritchard	30 June 2020	Steven	-	-
16	*Home Again, Home Again*	Felicia Barker	30 June 2020	Susan, Ian, Barbara	-	-

SPECIAL RELEASES

NO	TITLE	WRITER	RELEASE DATE	COMPANIONS	FEATURING	MAIN ENEMY
1	*The Light at the End*	Nicholas Briggs	23 October 2013	Leela, Nyssa, Peri, Ace, Charley	First Doctor, Ian, Susan, Vicki, Steven, Sara, Second Doctor Polly, Jamie, Zoe, Third Doctor, Jo, Tegan, Turlough, Straxus	Decayed Master
2	*The Legacy of Time – Collision Course*	Guy Adams	17 July 2019	Leela, Romana II	Benny, First Doctor, Second Doctor, Third Doctor, Fifth Doctor, Sixth Doctor, Seventh Doctor, Eighth Doctor, Tenth Doctor	Sirens of Time

SUSAN's WAR

NO	TITLE	WRITER	RELEASE DATE	FEATURING	MAIN ENEMY
1	*The Shoreditch Intervention*	Alan Barnes	16 April 2020	Eighth Doctor, Alex, First Doctor	Daleks

THE COMPANION CHRONICLES

NO.	TITLE	WRITER	RELEASE DATE	MAIN CHARACTER(s)	MAIN ENEMY	FEATURING
1	Frostfire	Marc Platt	Feb 2007	Vicki	The Cinder	First Doctor, Steven
2	Mother Russia	Marc Platt	Oct 2007	Steven Taylor	Shape Thief	First Doctor, Dodo, Napoléon
3	Here There Be Monsters	Andy Lane	July 2008	Susan Foreman	-	First Doctor, Ian, Barbara
4	Home Truths	Simon Guerrier	Nov 2008	Sara Kingdom	An Intelligent House	First Doctor, Steven, Robert
5	The Transit of Venus	Jacqueline Rayner	Jan 2009	Ian Chesterton	-	First Doctor, Barbara, Susan
6	The Drowned World	Simon Guerrier	July 2009	Sara Kingdom	-	First Doctor, Steven, Robert
7	The Suffering	Jacqueline Rayner	Jan 2010	Steven Taylor, Vicki	The Suffering	First Doctor
8	The Guardian of the Solar System	Simon Guerrier	July 2010	Sara Kingdom	Mavic Chen	First Doctor, Steven, Robert, Bret Vyon
9	Quinnis	Marc Platt	Dec 2010	Susan	Meedla	First Doctor
10	The Perpetual Bond	Simon Guerrier	Feb 2011	Steven, Oliver	Fulgurites	First Doctor
11	The Cold Equations	Simon Guerrier	June 2011	Steven, Oliver	-	First Doctor
12	Tales from the Vault	Jonathan Morris	July 2011	Ruth Matheson and Charlie Sato	Kali Carash	First Doctor, Second Doctor, Third Doctor, Fourth Doctor, Steven, Dodo, Jamie, Zoe, Jo, Romana I
13	The Rocket Men	John Dorney	Aug 2011	Ian Chesterton	Ashman	First Doctor, Barbara, Vicki
14	The First Wave	Simon Guerrier	Nov 2011	Steven, Oliver	Vardans	First Doctor
15	The Anachronauts	Simon Guerrier	Jan 2012	Steven, Sara	Time Pilots	First Doctor
16	The Wanderer	Richard Dinnick	Apr 2012	Ian, Susan, Barbara	The Dahensa	First Doctor, Grigori Rasputin
17	The Revenants	Ian Potter	May 2012	Ian, Barbara	The Marsh-Wains	First Doctor
18	Return of the Rocket Men	Matt Fitton	Nov 2012	Steven Taylor	Van Cleef, Rocket Mne	First Doctor, Dodo
19	The Flames of Cadiz	Marc Platt	Jan 2013	Susan, Ian, Barbara	Spanish Inquisition	First Doctor
20	The Library of Alexandria	Simon Guerrier	April 2013	Ian Chesterton	The Mim	First Doctor, Barbara, Susan
21	The Alchemists	Ian Potter	Aug 2013	Susan	Pollitt	First Doctor
22	Upstairs	Mat Coward	Sept 2013	Vicki, Steven	The Time Fungus	First Doctor
23	The Beginning	Marc Platt	Nov 2013	Susan	Archaeons, Stoyn	First Doctor
24	The Sleeping City	Ian Potter	Feb 2014	Ian, Barbara, Vicki	Limbus	First Doctor
25	Starborn	Jacqueline Rayner	Mar 2014	Vicki	Stella	First Doctor, Barbara, Ian
26	The War to End All Wars	Simon Guerrier	Apr 2014	Steven Taylor	-	First Doctor, Dodo, Sida
27	The Sleeping Blood	Martin Day	Jun 2015	Susan Foreman	The Butcher	First Doctor
28	The Unwinding World	Ian Potter	Jun 2015	Vicki	Connie	First Doctor, Barbara, Ian
29	The Founding Fathers	Simon Guerrier	Jun 2015	Steven Taylor	-	First Doctor, Vicki
30	The Locked Room	Simon Guerrier	Jun 2015	Steven Taylor	A Vardan	First Doctor
31	Fields of Terror	John Pritchard	Jun 2017	Vicki	-	First Doctor Steven
32	Across the Darkened City	David Bartlett	Jun 2017	Steven Taylor	Chaons	First Doctor, Two-One-Zero
33	The Bonfires of the Vanities	Una McCormack	Jun 2017	Polly, Ben	Bonfire Boys	First Doctor
34	The Plague of Dreams	Guy Adams	Jun 2017	Polly, Ben	Psychoactive Virus	First Doctor, The Player
35	E is for..	Julian Richards	Sept 2019	Susan	Maria Rage	First Doctor
36	Daybreak	John Prichard	Sept 2019	Vicki	The Examiner	First Doctor, Ian, Barbara
37	The Vardan Invasion of Mirth	Paul Morris, Ian Atkins	Sept 2019	Steven Taylor	Michael Hart	First Doctor
38	The Crumbling Magician	Guy Adams	Sept 2019	Polly	Continuity	First Doctor, Ben

THE DIARY OF RIVER SONG

NO	TITLE	WRITER	RELEASE DATE	MAIN CHARACTER	FEATURING	MAIN ENEMY
1	An Unearthly Woman	Matt Fitton	27 August 2019	River Song	First Doctor, Ian, Susan, Barbara	Nightstalker

THE EARLY ADVENTURES

NO	TITLE	WRITER	RELEASE DATE	COMPANIONS	MAIN ENEMY
1	Domain of the Voord	Andrew Smith	4 September 2014	Susan, Ian, Barbara	Voord
2	The Doctor's Tale	Marc Platt	17 October 2014	Ian, Barbara, Vicki	Thomas Arundel, Sir Robert de Wensley
3	The Bounty of Ceres	Ian Potter	14 November 2014	Vicki, Steven	Thorn
4	An Ordinary Life	Matt Fitton	16 December 2014	Steven, Sara	Anemone Changeling
5	The Age of Endurance	Nick Wallace	14 September 2016	Susan, Ian, Barbara	Arran
6	The Fifth Traveller	Philip Lawrence	13 October 2016	Ian, Barbara, Vicki	Jospa
7	The Ravelli Conspiracy	Robert Khan, Tom Salinsky	10 November 2016	Vicki, Steven	Guiliano de Medici
8	The Sontarans	Simon Guerrier	14 December 2016	Steven, Sara	Commander Slite
9	The Dalek Occupation of Winter	David K Barnes	12 September 2018	Vicki, Steven	Daleks
10	An Ideal World	Ian Potter	17 October 2018	Vicki, Steven	Samsara
11	Entanglement	Robert Khan, Tom Salinsky	14 November 2018	Vicki, Steven	Isaiah Hardy, Linus Woolf
12	The Crash of the UK-201	Jonathan Morris	11 December 2018	Vicki, Steven	-
13	Daughter of the Gods	David Barnes	13 November 2019	Jamie Zoe	The Master
14	The Secrets of Det-Sen	Andy Frankham-Allen	17 August 2021	Steven, Dodo	-

THE FIRST DOCTOR ADVENTURES

NO	TITLE	WRITER	RELEASE DATE	COMPANIONS	MAIN ENEMY
1	The Destination Wars	Matt Fitton	25 December 2017	Susan, Ian, Barbara	The Master
2	The Great White Hurricane	Guy Adams	25 December 2017	Susan, Ian, Barbara	-
3	The Invention of Death	John Dorney	25 July 2018	Susan, Ian, Barbara	Sharlan
4	The Barbarians and the Samurai	Andrew Smith	25 July 2018	Susan, Ian, Barbara	Takagi Mamoru, Casper Knox
5	The Phoenicians	Marc Platt	29 January 2019	Susan, Ian, Barbara	Pygmalion
6	Tick-Tock World	Guy Adams	29 January 2019	Susan, Ian, Barbara	Xesto
7	Return to Skaro	Andrew Smith	18 March 2020	Susan, Ian, Barbara	Dalek Supreme
8	Last of the Romanovs	Jonathan Barnes	18 March 2020	Susan, Ian, Barbara	-
9	For the Glory of Urth	Guy Adams	27 April 2021	Susan, Ian, Barbara	Daddy Dominus, Mummy Martial
10	The Holly Crown	Sarah Grochala	27 April 2021	Susan, Ian, Barbara	-

THE LOST STORIES

NO	TITLE	WRITER	RELEASE DATE	COMPANIONS
1	Farewell, Great Macedon	Moris Farhi, **Adapted by** Nigel Robinson	10 November 2010	Susan, Ian, Barbara
2	The Fragile Yellow Arc of Fragrance	Moris Farhi, **Adapted by** Nigel Robinson	10 November 2010	Susan, Ian, Barbara
3	The Masters of Luxor	Anthony Coburn, **Adapted by** Nigel Robinson	16 August 2012	Susan, Ian, Barbara
4	The Dark Planet	Brian Hyles, **Adapted by** Matt Fitton	12 September 2013	Ian, Barbara, Vicki

BOOKS

BBC EIGHTH DOCTOR ADVENTURES

NO.	TITLE	AUTHOR	RELEASE DATE	FEATURING	MAIN ENEMY
1	The Eight Doctors	Terrance Dicks	2 July 1997	Sam, First Doctor, Second Doctor, Third Doctor, Fourth Doctor, Fifth Doctor, Sixth Doctor, Seventh Doctor, Susan, Barbara, Ian, Jamie, Zoe, Jo, Benton, Romana II, Tegan, Turlough	Ryoth

BBC NOVELISATIONS

NO.	TITLE	AUTHOR	RELEASE DATE	COMPANIONS	FEATURING	MAIN ENEMY
1	Scratchman	Tom Baker	24 January 2019	Sarah, Harry	First Doctor, Second Doctor, Third Doctor, Tenth Doctor, Thirteenth Doctor	Scrathman

BBC PAST DOCTOR ADVENTURES

NO.	TITLE	AUTHOR	RELEASE DATE	COMPANIONS	MAIN ENEMY
1	The Witch Hunters	Steve Lyons	2 March 1998	Susan, Barbara, Ian	Samuel Parris, Abigail Williams
2	Salvation	Steve Lyons	4 January 1999	Steven, Dodo	Latter-Day Pantheon
3	City at World's End	Christopher Bulis	6 September 1999	Susan, Barbara, Ian	Monitor, the Taklarians
4	Divided Loyalties	Gary Russell	4 October 1999	Adric, Tegan, Nyssa	Celestial Toymaker
5	Bunker Soldiers	Martin Day	5 February 2001	Steven, Dodo	The Dark Angel
6	Byzantium!	Keith Topping	2 July 2002	Barbara, Ian, Vicki	-
7	Ten Little Aliens	Stephen Cole	3 July 2002	Ben, Polly	The Ten-Strong, Morphieans
8	The Eleventh Tiger	David A. McIntee	3 May 2004	Barbara, Ian, Vicki	Qin Shi Huang, Mandragora Helix
9	The Time Travellers	Simon Guerrier	10 November 2005	Susan, Barbara, Ian	General Louise Bamford

DR MEN

NO.	TITLE	AUTHOR	RELEASE DATE	COMPANION	FEATURING	MAIN ENEMY
1	Dr. First	Adam Hargreaves	25 April 2017	Susan	Water the Worm, Early Bird	CyberFaction

STAND ALONE NOVEL

NO	TITLE	AUTHOR	RELEASE DATE	COMPANIONS	MAIN ENEMY
1	Doctor Who and the Invasion from Space	J. L. Morrissey	1966	George, Helen, Alan, Ida	The One, Aalas

TELOS NOVELLA

NO.	TITLE	AUTHOR	RELEASE DATE	COMPANION	FEATURING	MAIN ENEMY
1	Time and Relative	Kim Newman	23 November 2001	Susan	Mr Chesterton, Miss Wright	The Cold
2	Frayed	Tara Samms	20 November 2003	Susan	-	Iwan Foxes

THE TIME LORD LETTERS

NO.	TITLE	AUTHOR	RELEASE DATE	FROM	TO	DATE
1	Missing Tardis	Justin Richards	29 September 2015	First Doctor	'Whom it May Concern'	unknown
2	A Warning to the Meddlesome	Justin Richards	29 September 2015	First Doctor	The Monk	October 1066
3	Taken to the Tower	Justin Richards	29 September 2015	First Doctor	Henry VIII	July 1543
4	To my Granddaughter	Justin Richards	29 September 2015	First Doctor	Susan Foreman	2167
5	An Application	Justin Richards	29 September 2015	First Doctor	Coal Hill School	June 1963
6	Get Well Soon	Justin Richards	29 September 2015	First Doctor	Dodo	July 1966
7	Lyre Liar	Justin Richards	29 September 2015	First Doctor	Nero	64
8	A Parting Gift	Justin Richards	29 September 2015	First Doctor	Xerons	Unknown
9	Safe Keeping	Justin Richards	29 September 2015	First Doctor	Padmasambhava	1630
10	Unpredictable Times	Justin Richards	29 September 2015	First Doctor	Michel de Nostredame	1555
11	A Painful Extraction	Justin Richards	29 September 2015	First Doctor	Doc Holliday	October 1881
12	England Expects…	Justin Richards	29 September 2015	First Doctor	Horatio Nelson	1798
13	Maintenance Notes	Justin Richards	29 September 2015	First Doctor	-	Unknown
14	Historical Nonsense	Justin Richards	29 September 2015	First Doctor	-	c.1184BC

TIME LORD VICTORIOUS

NO.	TITLE	AUTHOR	RELEASE DATE	COMPANION	FEATURING	MAIN ENEMY
1	The Knight, The Fool and The Dead	Steve Cole	1 October 2020	Brian	Eight Doctor, Ninth Doctor Rose, First Doctor Ian, Barbara, Susan	Kotturuh

VIRGIN MISSING ADVENTURES

NO	TITLE	AUTHOR	RELEASE DATE	COMPANIONS	MAIN ENEMY
1	Venusian Lullaby	Paul Leonard	20 October 1994	Barbara, Ian	Sou(ou)shi
2	The Sorcerer's Apprentice	Christopher Bulis	20 July 1995	Susan, Barbara, Ian	Marton Dhal, Gramling
3	The Empire of Glass	Andy Lane	16 November 1995	Vicki, Steven	Albrellian, Jamarians
4	The Man in the Velvet Mask	Daniel O'Mahony	15 February 1996	Dodo	Minski
5	The Plotters	Gareth Roberts	21 November 1996	Barbara, Ian, Vicki	Robert Hay

VIRGIN NEW ADVENTURES

NO.	TITLE	AUTHOR	RELEASE DATE	COMPANIONS	FEATURING	MAIN ENEMY
1	*Timewyrm: Revelation*	Paul Cornell	5 December 1991	Ace	First Doctor, Third Doctor, Fourth Doctor, Fifth Doctor, K'anpo, Death, The Daleks, Adric, Katarina, Sara Kingdom	The Timewyrm
2	*Nightshade*	Mark Gatiss	20 August 1992	Ace	-	The Sentience
3	*Tragedy Day*	Gareth Roberts	17 March 1994	Ace, Benny	-	Crispin, Friars of Pangloss
4	*All-Consuming Fire*	Andy Lane	16 June 1994	Ace, Benny	Holmes, Watson, First Doctor, Third Doctor, Susan	Azathoth, Baron Maupertuis, Sherringford Holmes
5	*Head Games*	Steve Lyons	19 October 1995	Benny, Roz, Chris	Sixth Doctor, First Doctor, Second Doctor, Third Doctor, Fourth Doctor, Fifth Doctor, Ace, Mel, Norman, The Valeyard, Winifred Bambera, Sabalom Glitz	Jason, Dr. Who
6	*Lungbarrow*	Marc Platt	20 March 1997	Chris	Ace, Leela, Andred, Romana II, K9, Susan	Glospin, CIA

COMICS

CHAD VALLEY

NO.	TITLE	RELEASE DATE	COMPANION	MAIN ENEMY
1	Dr Who in 'Lilliput'	-	Ian, Barbara	Bird
2	The Daleks Destroy the Zombites	-	Ian, Barbara	Daleks, Zomites
3	Dr Who and the Aqua Planet	1964	Ian, Barbara	Aquamonsters
4	Dr Who in the Spider's Web	1964	Ian, Barbara	Spider
5	Dr Who Meets the Watermen	1964	Ian, Barbara	-
6	The Defeat of the Daleks	1964	Ian	Daleks
7	The Secrets of the Tardis	1964	Ian, Barbara	-
8	The Daleks Are Foiled	1964	Ian, Barbara	Daleks, Earthmen Detector
9	Dr Who and the Nerve Machine	1964	Ian, Barbara	Daleks
10	The Ice-Age Monster	1964	Ian, Barbara	Monster
11	Rescued from the Daleks	1964	Ian	Daleks
12	Escaped from the Aquafien	1964	Ian, Barbara	Aquafein
13	Where Diamonds Are Worthless	1964	Ian, Barbara	-
14	The Prehistoric Monster	1964	Ian, Barbara	Creature
15	On the Planet Vortis	1965	Ian, Barbara	Zarbi
16	The Zarbi Are Destroyed	1965	Ian, Barbara	Zarbi, Animus

COMIC CREATOR ORIGINALS

NO.	TITLE	ARTIST	RELEASE DATE	COMPANION	FEATURING	MAIN ENEMY
1	A Stitch in Time	John Ross	18 March 2016	Clara	First Doctor, Second Doctor, Ninth Doctor, Tenth Doctor Eleventh Doctor, Susan, Victoria, Rose, Harriet Donna, River	Ethel

COMIC RELIEF COMIC

NO.	TITLE	ARTIST	RELEASE DATE	COMPANION	FEATURING	MAIN ENEMY
1	Comic Relief Comic	John Ridgway	16 February 1991	Ace	First Doctor, Susan, Second Doctor, Victoria, Third Doctor, Fourth Doctor, Leela, K9 Mark I, Fifth Doctor, Tegan, Sixth Doctor	The Mekon

DOCTOR WHO ADVENTURES

NO.	TITLE	ARTIST	RELEASE DATE	COMPANION	FEATURING	MAIN ENEMY
1	Time Trick	John Ross	6 November 2013	Clara	First Doctor, Susan	-

DOCTOR WHO ANNUAL

NO.	TITLE	ARTIST	RELEASE DATE	COMPANIONS	FEATURING	MAIN ENEMY
1	*Mission for Duh*	-	September 1966	-	-	-
2	*Where's the Doctor?*	-	1 November 2018	Graham, Yaz, Ryan	VARIOUS	Colby, Eva De Ville

DOCTOR WHO MAGAZINE

NO.	TITLE	ARTIST(s)	RELEASE DATE	COMPANIONS	FEATURING	MAIN ENEMY
1	*Timeslip*	Paul Neary	31 Jan – 7 Feb 1980	K9 Mark II	First Doctor, Second Doctor, Third Doctor	Space Amoeba
2	*Planet of the Dead*	Lee Sullivan	8 Sept-13 Oct 1988	-	First Doctor, Second Doctor, Third Doctor, Fourth Doctor, Fifth Doctor, Sixth Doctor	Gwanzulum
3	*Time & Time Again*	John Ridgway	25 November 1993	Ace, Benny	White Guardian, First Doctor, Second Doctor, Third Doctor, Fourth Doctor, Fifth Doctor, Sixth Doctor, Susan, Jamie, Zoe, Adric, Frobisher	The Black Guardian
4	*Food for Thought*	Colin Andrew	26 Sep-24 Nov 1994	Polly, Ben	-	Mollusi
5	*Operation Proteus*	Martin Geraghty	28 Sept-23 Nov 1995	Susan	-	Raldonn
6	*The World Shapers*	-	9 Jul-10 Sept 1987	Peri, Frobisher, Jamie	-	Voord. Cybermen
7	*The Final Chapter*	Martin Geraghty, Robin Smith	12 Feb-7 May 1998	Fey, Izzy	Shayde	Luther, the Elysians
8	*Happy Deathday*	Robin Langridge	19 Nov 1998	Izzy Sinclair	Seven Doctor, Sixth Doctor, Fifth Doctor, Fourth Doctor, Third Doctor, Second Doctor, First Doctor	The Beige Guardian
9	*Death to the Doctor!*	Roger Langridge	13 Dec 2007	Martha	First Doctor, Third Doctor, Fourth Doctor, Sixth Doctor, Eight Doctor, Ninth Doctor, Steven, Dodo, The Brigadier, Jo, K9 Mark II, Romana I, Frobisher Izzy, Rose	Valis, Kraarn of the Kraagaaron, Bolog, Zargath, The Mentor, Questor, Plink
10	*Blood and Ice*	-	2 Apr-25 Jun 2015	Clara	Winnie Clarence	Patricia Audley

DOCTOR WHO YEARBOOK

NO.	TITLE	ARTIST	RELEASE DATE	COMPANION	FEATURING
1	*A Religious Experience*	John Ridgway	September 1993	Ian	Barbara Seventh Doctor
2	*Untitled*	Dicky Howlett	September 1993	-	First Doctor, Second Doctor, Third Doctor Fourth Doctor, Fifth Doctor, Sixth Doctor Seventh Doctor, Peri Brow The Daleks

IDW PUBLISING

NO.	TITLE	ARTIST(s)	RELEASE DATE	COMPANION(s)	FEATURING	MAIN ENEMY
1	*The Forgotten*	Pia Guerra Stefano Martino Kelly Yates	20 Aug 2008 – 21 January 2009	"Martha"	First Doctor, Second Doctor Third Doctor, Fourth Doctor Fifth Doctor, Sixth Doctor Seventh Doctor, Eighth Doctor Ninth Doctor, Susan, Ian, Barbara Jamie Zoe, The Brigadier, Benton Yates, Jo, Romana II, Tegan, Turlough Peri, Ace, Chantir, Rose	Es'Cartrss
2	*To Sleep, Perchance to Scream*	Al Davison	14 July 2010	-	First Doctor, Second Doctor Third Doctor Eleventh Doctor	-
3	*Unnatural Selection*	Simon Fraser	29 January 2013	Ian, Barbara, Vicki	Zarbi, Cloaked figure	The Animus
4	*Endgame*	Kelly Yates	20 November 2013	-	Ninth Doctor, Tenth Doctor Eleventh Doctor Frobisher, Rose First Doctor, Second Doctor Third Doctor, Fourth Doctor Fifth Doctor, Sixth Doctor Seventh Doctor, Eighth Doctor	The Master
5	*Dead Man's Hand*	Charlie Kirchoff	18 September 2013 – 4 December 2013	Clara	Oscar Wilde	Es'Cartrss of the Tactires

SPECIALS

NO.	TITLE	ARTIST	RELEASE DATE	COMPANIONS	MAIN ENEMY
1	*Untitled TVC 696*	Neville Main	17 April 1965	-	Police Officer
2	*Untitled TVC 740*	Neville Main	17 February 1966	-	Police Officer
3	*Prisoners of Gritog*	Neville Main	1 July 1965	John, Gillian	Gritog
4	*Guests of King Neptune*	John Canning	1966	John, Gillian	-
5	*The Gaze of the Gorgon*	-	1966	John, Gillian	The Gorgon
6	*Prisoners of the Kleptons*	Neville Main	1 September 1965	John, Gillian	Klepton
7	*The Caterpillar Men*	Neville Main	1 September 1965	John, Gillian	Caterpillar Men
8	*Deadly Vessel*	John Canning	1 September 1966	John, Gillian	-
9	*Kingdom of the Animals*	-	1 September 1966	John, Gillian	Giant Birds

SPECIALS II

NO.	TITLE	ARTIST	RELEASE DATE	COMPANION(s)	MAIN ENEMY
1	*Flashback*	John Ridgway	November 1992	Benny	"Magnus"
2	*Are You Listening*	Colin Andrew	July 1994	Vicki, Steven	-

THE DOCTOR WHO FUN BOOK

NO.	TITLE	ARTIST	RELEASE DATE	COMPANIONS	FEATURING	MAIN ENEMY
1	*The Test of Time*	Tim Quinn, Dicky Howlett	21 May 1987	Susan, Barbara, Ian	Second Doctor Third Doctor Fourth Doctor Fifth Doctor Sixth Doctor	Father of Time

THE HISTORY TOUR

NO.	TITLE	ARTIST	RELEASE DATE	COMPANION
1	*The Doctor Who History Tour Number Nine*	Dicky Howett	12 November 1987	Peri

TITAN COMICS

NO.	TITLE	ARITST	RELEASE DATE	COMPANION(s)	FEATURING	MAIN ENEMY
1	*In-Between Times*	John Stokes	26 September 2018	Susan, Ian, Barbara	-	-
2	*Vortex Butterflies*	Giorgia Sposito	21 June - 18 Oct 2017	Gabby, Cindy, Noobis, Marcie	Twelfth Doctor Sarah	Vortex, Butterfly
3	*The Then and the Now*	Simon Fraser	7 Oct - 4 Nov 2015	Alice, The Squire, Daak	War Doctor	The Then and the Now
4	*Pull to Open*	Simon Fraser	9 Dec 2015	Alice, The Squire	-	-
5	*The One*	Simon Fraser Leandro Casco	2-23 March 2016	River, Alice The Squire, Daak	-	The Then and the Now
6	*Day of the Tune*	Neil Slorance	1 July 2015	Clara	First Doctor Second Doctor Third Doctor Fourth Doctor	-
7	*The Path of Skulls*	Mariano Laclaustra	26 September 2018	Susan, Ian, Barbara	-	-
8	*Prologue: The First Doctor*	Dan Boultwood	13 July 2016	Susan	Ian, Barbara	CyberMondans
9	*The Lost Dimension*	Rachael Scott Cris Bolson Pasquale Qualano Elton Thomasi Klebs Jr. JB Bastos and Iolanda Zanfardino	30 August - 1 November 2017	-	Rose, Vastra Jenny, Flint Rassilon Romana II Eighth Doctor Josie War Doctor Seventh Doctor Sixth Doctor Fifth Doctor Third Doctor Second Doctor First Doctor	Type 1 Tardis

TV COMICS

NO.	TITLE	ARTIST	RELEASE DATE	MAIN ENEMY	COMPANIONS
1	*The Klepton Parasites*	Neville Main	9 November 1964 – 11 January 1965	Klepton One	John, Gillian
2	*The Therovian Quest*	Neville Main	18 January – 22 February 1965	Ixa	John, Gillian
3	*The Hijackers of Thrax*	Neville Main	1-15 March 1965	Capt. Anastas Thrax	John, Gillian
4	*On the Web Planet*	Neville Main	22 March – 26 April 1965	Skirkons	John, Gillian
5	*The Gyros Injustice*	Neville Main	3 May – 7 June 1965	Gyros	John, Gillian
6	*Challenge of the Piper*	Neville Main	14 June – 12 July 1965	The Pied Piper	John, Gillian
7	*Moon Landing*	Neville Main	19 July – 2 August 1965	-	John, Gillian
8	*Time in Reverse*	Neville Main	9-23 August 1965	-	John, Gillian
9	*Lizardworld*	Neville Main	30 August-20 September 1965	Giant Lizards	John, Gillian
10	*The Ordeal of Demeter*	Bill Mevin	27 September-18 October 1965	Robert of Bellus	John, Gillian
11	*Enter: The Go-Ray*	Bill Mevin	25 October-15 November 1965	-	John, Gillian
12	*Shark Bait*	Bill Mevin	22 November-13 December 1965	-	John Gillian
13	*A Christmas Story*	Bill Mevin	20 December 1965 – 10 January 1966	Demon Magician	John, Gillian
14	*The Didus Expedition*	Bill Mevin	22 Januar-12 February 1966	-	John, Gillian
15	*Space Station Z-7*	Bill Mevin	19 February-12 March 1966	-	John, Gillian
16	*Plague of the Black Scorpi*	Bill Mevin	19 March-9 April 1966	Black Scorpi	John, Gillian
17	*The Trodos Tyranny*	John Canning	16 April-14 May 1966	Trods	John, Gillian
18	*The Secrets of Gemino*	John Canning	21 May-18 June 1966	-	John, Gillian
19	*The Haunted Planet*	John Canning	25 June-23 July 1966	Zentor	John, Gillian
20	*The Hunters of Zerox*	John Canning	30 July-27 August 1966	-	John, Gillian
21	*The Underwater Robot*	John Canning	3-24 September 1966	Underwater Robot, The Professor	John, Gillian
22	*Return of the Trods*	John Canning	1-22 October 1966	The Trods	John, Gillian
23	*The Galaxy Games*	John Canning	29 October-19 November 1966	A Klondite	John Gillian
24	*The Experiments*	John Canning	26 November-17 December 1966	The Master Race	John, Gillian

SHORT STORIES

ADVENTURES IN LOCKDOWN

NO.	TITLE	WRITER	RELEASE DATE	FEATURING	MAIN ENEMY
1	One Virtue, and a Thousand Crimes	Neil Gaiman	5 November 2020	First Doctor	Supreme Leader

BBC DOCTOR WHO WEBSITE

NO.	TITLE	WRITER	RELEASE DATE	FEATURING	MAIN ENEMY
1	Doctor Who and the Horror of Coal Hill	Gavin Collinson	21 December 2017	Third Doctor, Eleventh Doctor, Twelfth Doctor, Sarah, Missy	Space Wolves

BRIEF ENCOUNTER

NO.	TITLE	WRITER	RELEASE DATE	MAIN CHARACTER	FEATURING
1	The Meeting	John Lucarotti	1 November 1990	John Lucarotti	First Doctor
2	Echoes of Future Past	John Summerfield	28 November 1991	-	Seventh Doctor
3	Cambridge Previsited	Karen Dunn	September 1992	-	Chronotis
4	Roses	Robert Mammone	9 June 1994	-	-

DOCTOR WHO ANNUAL

NO.	TITLE	WRITER	RELEASE DATE	COMPANIONS	MAIN ENEMY
1	The Lair of Zarbi Supremo	David Whitaker	September 1965	-	Zarbi Supremo
2	Who is Doctor Who?	-	September 1965	-	-
3	The Sons of the Crab	-	September 1965	-	-
4	The Lost Ones	-	September 1965	-	Sons of the Sun
5	The Equations of Dr Who	-	September 1965	-	-
6	The Monsters from Earth	-	September 1965	Tony, Amy, Butch	Sensorites, Zilgan
7	Peril in Mechanistria	-	September 1965	-	-
8	The Fishmen of Kandalinga	-	September 1965	-	The Voord
9	The Cloud Exiles	-	September 1966	-	-
10	The Sons of Grekk	-	September 1966	-	Sons of Grekk, Deemon
11	Terror on Tiro	-	September 1966	-	Klarimo
12	The Devil-Birds of Corbo	-	September 1966	Jack, Dot Haroll	Ulla
13	The Playthings of Fo	-	September 1966	Jack, Dot, Haroll, Shelly, Chertzog, Hill	Fo
14	Justice of the Glacians	-	September 1966	-	Rraprro
15	Ten Fathom Pirates	-	September 1966	-	Pirates

DOCTOR WHO MAGAZINE

NO.	TITLE	WRITER	RELEASE DATE	COMPANIONS	FEATURING
1	Who Discovered America?	John Lucarotti	20 February 1992	Susan, Barbara, Ian	-
2	Rennigan's Record	David Whitaker	13 May 1993	-	First Doctor, Susan, Ian, Barbara
3	Gallifrey: A Rough Guide	Steve Lyons and Chris Howarth	19 October - 14 December 2000	-	Rassilon, Omega, the Pythia, The Doctor, The Enemy, Susan Foreman

DOCTOR WHO STORYBOOK

NO.	TITLE	WRITER	RELEASE DATE	COMPANIONS	MAIN ENEMY
1	*Urrozdinee*	Mark Gatiss	September 1994	Susan	Minister

NOW WE ARE SIX HUNDRED

NO.	TITLE	WRITER	RELEASE DATE	FEATURING	MAIN ENEMY
1	*Full Stop*	James Goss	26 September 2017	First Doctor, Second Doctor, Third Doctor, Fourth Doctor, Fifth Doctor, Sixth Doctor, Seventh Doctor, Eighth Doctor, Ninth Doctor, Tenth Doctor, Eleventh Doctor	-
2	*A Simple Truth*	James Goss	26 September 2017	-	-
3	*The Five Doctors*	James Goss	26 September 2017	First Doctor, Second Doctor, Third Doctor, Fourth Doctor, Flavia	Borusa
4	*Something Borrowed, Something Blue*	James Goss	26 September 2017	Fourth Doctor	-

OTHER

NO.	TITLE	WRITER	RELEASE DATE	MAIN ENEMY
1	*Doctor Who and the Daleks*	-	1964	Daleks, Voord
2	*Status Update*	Joseph Lidster	31 July 2014	Cybermen

PUFFIN ESHORT

NO.	TITLE	WRITER	RELEASE DATE	COMPANION	MAIN ENEMY
1	*A Big Hand for the Doctor*	Eoin Colfer	23 January 2013	Susan	Soul Pirates

SHORT TRIPS

NO.	TITLE	WRITER	RELEASE DATE	COMPANION (S) *Main Character*	FEATURING
1	*The Last Days*	Evan Pritchard	02/03/1998	Susan, Ian, Barbara	Eleazar
2	*There are Fairies at the Bottom of the Garden*	Sam Lester	02/03/1998	Dodo	-
3	*64 Carlysle Street*	Gary Russell	01/03/1999	Steven, Dodo	-
4	*Romans Cutaway*	David A. McIntee	01/03/1999	Barbara, Ian, Vicki	-
5	*The Longest Story in the World*	Paul Magrs	06/03/2000	Susan	-
6	*Nothing At the End of the Lane*	David O'Mahony	06/03/2000	**Barbara Wright**	First Doctor, Susan, Ian
7	*Planet of the Bunnoids*	Harriet Green	06/03/2000	Vicki, Steven	-
8	*The True and Indisputable Facts in the Matter of the Ram's Skull*	Mark Michalowski	31/12/2002	**Edgar All Poe**	First Doctor, Barbara, Ian
9	*Five Card Draw*	Todd Green	31/12/2002	Peri	First Doctor, Second Doctor, Third Doctor, Sixth Doctor
10	*The Little Drummer Boy*	Eddie Robson	02/04/2003	Steven, Sara	-
11	*A Long Night*	Alison Lawson	02/04/2003	Barbara	Joan Wright
12	*The Exiles*	Lance Parkin	16/06/2003	Susan	-
13	*Mire and Clay*	Gareth Wigmore	16/06/2003	**Ian Chesterton**	First Doctor, Susan, Barbara
14	*Ash*	Trevor Baxendale	16/06/2003	Susan	Steven
15	*The Glass Princess*	Justin Richards	Sep. 2003	-	Second Doctor, Third Doctor, Fourth Doctor, Fifth Doctor

NO.	TITLE	WRITER	RELEASE DATE	COMPANIONS	MAIN ENEMY
					Sixth Doctor, Seventh Doctor Eighth Doctor
16	Corridors of Power	Matthew Griffiths	Dec. 2003	Vicki, Steven	-
17	The Thief of Sherwood	Jonathan Morris	09/04/2004	Susan, Ian, Barbara	Robin Hood, Maid Marian
18	Bide-a-wee	Anthony Keetch	09/04/2004	Susan	-
19	White Man's Burden	John Binns	09/04/2004	Turlough	Barbara, Ian
20	Scribble in Chalk	Gareth Wigmore	26/06/2004	Steven, Katarina	-
21	The End	Alexander Leithes	26/06/2004	-	First Doctor
22	The Rag & Bone Man's Story	Colin Brake	Aug. 2004	Susan	-
23	The Schoolboy's Story	Trey Korte	Aug. 2004	Vicki, Steven	-
24	The Juror's Story	Eddie Robson	Aug. 2004	**Dr Harris**	First Doctor, Second Doctor Third Doctor, Fifth Doctor Eighth Doctor, Susan
25	From Eternity	Jim Mortimore	30/09/2004	-	-
26	Categorical Imperative	Simon Guerrier	30/09/2004	Sarah	First Doctor, Second Doctor Third Doctor, Fifth Doctor Sixth Doctor, Seventh Doctor Eighth Doctor, Susan, Jamie, Jo, Tegan, Peri, Ace, Charley
27	Every Day	Stephen Fewell	30/12/2004	Ian, Barbara, Vicki	-
28	The Duke's Folly	Gareth Wigmore	09/04/2005	Susan, Ian, Barbara	-
29	Waiting for Jeremy	Richard Salter	07/07/2005	Steven	-
30	Making History	Trevor Baxendale	07/07/2005	Steven	-
31	Mars	Trevor Baxendale	22/10/2005	Vicki, Steven	-
32	Set in Stone	Chris Auchterlonie and John Isles	26/11/2005	Barbara, Ian	-
33	The Gift	Robert Dick	26/11/2005	Susan	-
34	The Mother Road	Gareth Wigmore	04/05/2006	Susan, Ian, Barbara	-
35	The Three Paths	Ian Potter	04/05/2006	-	K'anpo Rimpoche
36	Childhood Living	Samantha Baker	18/09/2006	Susan	Edward, Linda
37	The Ruins of Time	Philip Purser-Hallard	Oct. 2006	Susan, Ian, Barbara	
38	Room for Improvement	James A. Moore	30/06/2007	Ian	-
39	Life from Lifelessness	Keith R.A. DeCandido	30/06/2007	K9 Mark II, Romana II	First Doctor, Susan
40	The Long Step Backward	Mike W. Barr	30/06/2007	Vicki, Steven	-
41	Indian Summer	James Goss	30/06/2007	*Suresh Parekh*	First Doctor, Susan
42	Tell Me You Love Me	Scott Matthewman	15/12/2007	Susan, Ian, Barbara	
43	Snowman in Manhattan	John Binns	15/12/2007	Vicki, Steven	-
44	Losing the Audience	Mat Coward	Mar. 2008	Susan	-
45	The Price of Conviction	Richard C. White	10/05/2008	Susan	-
46	iNtRUsioNs	Dave Hoskin	01/07/2008	-	-
47	Do You Smell Carrots?	Simon Guerrier	15/12/2008	*First Doctor, Steven Fifth Doctor*	-
48	White on White	Kate Orman	15/12/2008	Steven	-
49	The Power Supply	Eddie Robson	30/03/2009	Vicki, Steven	Fifth Doctor
50	The Reign Makers	Gareth Wigmore	30/03/2009	Susan, Ian, Barbara	Henry V

TALES OF TERROR

NO.	TITLE	WRITER	RELEASE DATE	COMPANIONS	MAIN ENEMY
1	Murder in the Dark	Jacqueline Rayner	7 September 2017	Steven, Dodo	The Celestial Toymaker

THE BLOGS OF DOOM

NO.	TITLE	WRITER	RELEASE DATE	MAIN CHARACTER
1	*Tlotoxl*	Jonathan Morris	28 May 2020	Tlotoxl

THE BRILLIANT BOOK 2011

NO.	TITLE	WRITER	RELEASE DATE	FEATURING
1	*The Lost Diaries of Winston Spencer Churchill*	Mark Gatiss	30 September 2010	First Doctor, Second Doctor, Third Doctor, Fourth Doctor, Fifth Doctor, Sixth Doctor, Seventh Doctor, Eighth Doctor, Ninth Doctor, Tenth Doctor

THE DOCTOR: HIS LIVES AND TIMES

NO.	TITLE	WRITER	RELEASE DATE	MAIN CHARACTER	FEATURING
1	*Report on Term's Work*	James Goss, Steve Tribe	26 September 2013	Borusa	First Doctor

THE SCIENTIFIC SECRETS OF DOCTOR WHO

NO.	TITLE	WRITER	RELEASE DATE	COMPANIONS
1	*The Arboreals*	Jacqueline Rayner	4 June 2015	Susan

THE SHAKESPEARE NOTEBOOKS

NO.	TITLE	WRITER	RELEASE DATE	FEATURING	MAIN ENEMY
1	*The Dream*	-	12 June 2014	Shakespeare	Rutan Host
2	*Troilus and Cressida*	-	12 June 2014	-	-

THE TARGET STORYBOOK

NO.	TITLE	WRITER	RELEASE DATE	COMPANIONS	FEATURING
1	*Journey out of Terror*	Simon Guerrier	24 October 2019	Ian, Barbara	-
2	*Punting*	Susie Day	24 October 2019	Romana II	-

TWELVE DOCTORS OF CHRISTMAS

NO.	TITLE	WRITER	RELEASE DATE	COMPANIONS
1	*All I Want for Christmas*	Jacqueline Rayner	6 October 2016	Barbara, Ian, Vicki

TWELVE ANGELS WEEPING

NO.	TITLE	WRITER	RELEASE DATE	FEATURING
1	*Celestial Intervention – A Gallifreyan Noir*	Dave Rudden	11 October 2018	The First Doctor' Tardis

VIRGIN DECALOG

NO.	TITLE	WRITER	RELEASE DATE	COMPANIONS	FEATURING
1	*The Book of Shadows*	Jim Mortimore	17 March 1994	Ian, Barbara	Ptolemy, Lagusn, Alexander the Great
2	*The Golden Door*	David Auger	17 March 1994	Steven, Dodo	Sixth Doctor
3	*The Nine-Day Queen*	Matthew Jones	20 July 1995	Ian, Barbara	Jane Gray
4	*Tarnished Image*	Guy Clapperton	18 July 1996	Dodo	-

VIDEO GAMES

NO.	TITLE	RELEASE DATE	FEATURING
1	*Destiny of the Doctors*	5 December 1997	First Doctor, Second Doctor, Third Doctor Fourth Doctor, Fifth Doctor Sixth Doctor Seventh Doctor
2	*LEGO Dimensions*	27 September 2015	Twelfth Doctor, Clara, K9, Missy, Osgood, Strax, Vastra, Rusty, Jack

DOCTOR WHO CONTRIBUTORS 1963-66

Adrienne Hill (1937-97): Born in Plymouth 1937, **Adrienne Hill** studied at the Bristol Old Vic before spending a brief spell with the Old Vic Company based in London. She spent eight years acting in repertory theatre where she spotted by *Doctor Who* production assistant **Viktor Ritelis** whilst understudying for **Maggie Smith** in *Mary, Mary*. Invited to audition for the role of Princess Joanna in *The Crusade*, the actress ultimately did not win the role. Less than a year later she was cast as Katarina in *The Myth Makers*, destined to become the new regular companion. However plans for Katarina's involvement in the show changed, and the character was killed off in the subsequent serial *The Daleks' Master Plan*. After leaving *Doctor Who*, Adrienne Hill found success as a radio actress with a regular role in BBC's *Waggoner's Walk*. In the late seventies, she returned to education to study for a degree, and become a drama teacher in the eighties. She found occasional acting work until her death in 1997.

Anneke Wills (1941-): Born in Buckinghamshire in 1941, **Anneke Wills** found success as a child actress appearing in various films and television series, most notably *The Railway Children* (1957) as Roberta, and *Gamble for a Throne* (1961) as Kaye Chance. During this time she studied at the Art Educational, a drama school for four years. Her studies took her to the Royal Academy of Dramatic Art, where she subsequently left before finishing her course. Becoming a house hold name after landing the part of Polly Wright in *The War Machines*, Anneke Wills remained with the show for just over a year. When approached to continue with *Doctor Who*, the actress opted to leave after learning that fellow actor **Michael Craze** would be leaving the series. She later appeared in *Strange Report* (1969), but fame was cut short when the cast turned down the opportunity to make a second series in America. After leaving the acting profession, Anneke ran a craft shop in Norfolk before staying in a religious retreat in India. She returned to stage acting in some Shakespeare productions before moving to Canada to work as an interior designer. During her time in Canada she directed a stage play of *Rashomon*, based on the Japanese film of the same name. In later life, Anneke moved back to the UK to settle down in Devon.

Brian Hayles (1931-78): Before finding success as a writer for television, **Brian Hyles** worked briefly as an artist and sculptor in Canada, before returning to work at Greenmore College in Birmingham. During his time in education, he began writing student plays before the writing bug pushed him to turn his passion into full-time employment.

His writing breakthrough came with a one-off BBC play *The Badger Game* (1962), with a second play, *Last Race, Ginger Gentleman* (1963). Hayles was soon writing for *Swizzlewick, Z Cars, Jury Room,* and *Crossroads*. Major success came with the twice-weekly soap opera *United!* with Hayles story lining most of the show's run, and writing over 50 episodes. During his time on *United!* Hayles became a *Doctor Who* writer with his fantasy narrative **The Celestial Toymaker**. Although heavily rewritten twice in space of a few months, he received a 'Based on a story' credit for all four episodes. Hayles later wrote **The Smugglers** a few months later before creating his popular *Doctor Who* monsters The Ice Warriors for *The Ice Warriors* (1967). Rewriting thrice more for *Doctor Who*; Hayles brought the Ice Warriors back for **The Seeds of Death**, **The Cruse of Peladon**, and **The Monster of Peladon**. Outside of *Doctor Who*, he wrote continuously for *Doomwatch* (1971), *The Iron Doctor* (1971), *Hair Trigger* (1972), *The Regiment* (1973), *Barlow* (1974), *The Mind Beyond* (1976) and *The Moon Stallion* (1978). A second major breakthrough came with radio series *The Archers* where Hayles wrote hundreds of plays between June 1968 and June 1978. Film screenplays came with *Nothing but the Night* (1973), *Warlords of the Deep* (1978) and *Arabian Adventure* (1979) – released posthumously. In later life Brian Hayles was as busy as ever, novelising his *Doctor Who* scripts and writing school plays in 1976, before dying suddenly at his home in Coventry in October 1978.

Carole Ann Ford (1940-): Born in Ilford Essex, **Carole Ann Ford**'s early acting work saw her work in commercials with the occasional 'walk-on work'. Her first proper role came with Women of the Street (1956) which led to television work, with one-off roles in *Emergency-Ward 10* (1957), *Z Cars* (1962), and *Moonstrike* (1963). Landing the role of Susan Foreman, Carole Ann Ford bonded with the show's leading star and quickly became a house-hold name. After spending 18 months on the show, the actress became disappointed with Susan's development as a character, and was tiring of screaming at monsters every week. Her departure was a heavy blow for **William Hartnell**. Later, acting work came predominantly in theatre, as scripts for television often entailed Carole Ann Ford auditing for teenagers, much to the actress' annoyance. An accident in 1977 put a hold on her acting career. In later life she became a successful voice coach to actors, politicians and industrialists. Although disappointed with the burden of being associated with *Doctor Who*, Carole Ann Ford returned to the show reprising Susan in a variety of audio dramas for Big Finish.

Christopher Barry (1925-2014): Born in Greenwich in 1925, **Christopher Barry**, after World War II ended, studied at the University of Cambridge before joining the RAF as a navigator. Determined to break into the film industry, he landed a script reader job at Ealing Studios. He later progressed to second assistant director on small feature length films. However, work proved to be scarce when the British film production began to dwindle in the 1950s, although a co-written play entitled 'Our Marie' made it to the screens in 1953. Advised to apply to the BBC for a production assistant job, Barry found work on *Jane Eyre* (1956). Directing stints came with *Private Investigator* (1958-59), *Compact* (1962), *Smuggler's Bay* (1964), *The Further Adventures of the Musketeers* (1967), *Z Cars* (1967-78), *Poldark* (1975), *Angels* (1976), *All Creatures Great and Small* (1978-80) and *The Tripods* (1984-85), and no less than 9½ serials for *Doctor Who*. *Doctor Who* highlights came with directing the voyeuristic cliffhanger for **The Daleks** where an unseen Dalek edges itself closer to Barbara, directing both **Patrick Troughton** and **Tom Baker**'s debut stories, and writing the mind-battle sequence for **The Brian of Morbius**. Disappointed that freelance directing work wasn't coming his way, Barry later worked on cooperate training videos made by **Peter Purves'** company. He later returned to the world of *Doctor Who* helming the direct-to-video adventure *Downtime* (1995) featuring the Yeti. Christopher Barry died on 7 February 2014.

David Anderson (1945-): Born in 1945, **David Anderson** has had a wide ranging career in film, TV, radio and theatre. During the **William Hartnell** era he appeared in no less than 6 serials, playing a different character each time. He served as a fight arranger for **The Aztecs**, **The Time**

Meddler, and *The Daleks' Master Plan*. Other well-known roles outside of *Doctor Who* include *Gregory's Girl* (1981) and a long-running role in *City Lights* (1984-1991). Besides acting David Anderson is a playwright and a jazz musician.

David Graham (1925-): Born in 1925, **David Graham** trained as an actor in New York City, following time in the Royal Air Force as a radar mechanic. The actor found himself in the world of voice acting early on in his career landing numerous roles in *Four Feather Falls*, *Supercar* (1961-62), *Fireball XL5* (1962-63), *Stingray* (1964-65), *Thunderbirds* (1965-66) whilst landing various on-screen roles in both TV and film. His voice-acting repertoire landed him the role to voice the Daleks in **The Daleks** along with fellow voice actor **Peter Hawkins**. Graham continued to voice the Daleks throughout 1965-66, making his last contribution with **The Daleks' Master Plan**. As well as voice-acting, David Graham landed two on-screen roles in the world of *Doctor Who*: Charlie the Barman in **The Gunfighters**, and Kerensky in **City of Death**. Throughout his later career, he continued voice-acting; delving into English dubs of popular anime cartoons and a new series of *Thunderbirds* - *Thunderbirds Are Go* (2015-20) as well popular children's shows *Peppa Pig* (2004-19), and *Ben & Holly's Little Kingdom* (2009-20).

David Whitaker (1928-80): Born in 1928, **David Whitaker** grew up as an avid reader of adventure stories written by **John Buchan** and science-fiction written by **Ray Bradbury**. After spending many years acting, directing, and producing for repertory theatre companies, Whitaker's main interest was writing. One of his early plays 'A Choice of Partner' was eventually adapted by the BBC for TV and aired on 4 June 1957. The play proved to be popular, landing Whitaker a three-month trial position in the scripting unit.

Assignments came with a variety of shows including *Crackerjack* (1958), *Showtime* (1959-61) and *Nina and Frederick* (1961). Permanent work came with *Garry Halliday* (1961-62) and *Compact* (1962) before the scripting unit was disbanded in 1962. Following this, David Whitaker landed the role as a script editor on the new Saturday TV drama *Doctor Who*. Roles included developing the dynamics of the main characters and hiring freelance writers to work on the series. After working just 12 months on the show, Whitaker left the series to avoid being 'associated' with *Doctor Who*. However he found himself writing two serials within months of leaving as script editor: **The Rescue** and **The Crusade**. Moving on from *Doctor Who* proved to be difficult for the writer with various commitments coming in the form of novelising the first Dalek story as *Dr Who in an exciting adventure with the Daleks*, scripting a majority of the comic strips published in *TV Century 21*; providing uncredited contributions to the movie *Dr Who and the Daleks*, and providing additional material for the stage play *The Curse of the Daleks*.

In 1966, the writer was appointed Chairman of the Writers' Guild of Great Britain, a position he kept until 1968. Writing assignments were on the decline due to numerous international congresses. During his time as the Chairman, he scripted four more *Doctor Who* serials: **The Power of the Daleks**, **The Evil of the Daleks**, **The Enemy of the World**, and **The Wheel in Space**. After leaving as chairman he found success as a screenwriter with *Subterfuge* (1968). Around 1970, the writer left the UK and moved to Australia where he found more success in Australian TV and film. Returning to the UK in 1979 to undergo treatment for cancer, Whitaker died on the February 4, 1980, whilst novelising **The Enemy of the World**.

Delia Derbyshire (1937-2001): Born in Coventry in 1937, **Delia** was a very bright young girl, teaching others to read and write by the time she was 4. Her parents purchased her a piano when she was eight years old, and the composer was educated at Barr's Hill Grammar School. Eventually being accepted to both Cambridge and Oxford, she won a scholarship to study Mathematics at Girton College, Cambridge but didn't quite succeed. She eventually switched her degree and studied Music, graduating in 1959 with a BA in Mathematics and Music. Upon graduating she approached the career office at her University to discuss career options, originally interested in deaf aids or depth sounding, she applied to work for Decca Records but was turned down. Instead she worked for the United Nations in Geneva where she taught children of the British Consul-General piano, and children of Canadian and South American diplomats Mathematics. After leaving the United Nations, she taught general subjects at a primary school in Coventry before moving to London where she found work as an assistant with music publishers Boosey & Hawkes.

Delia eventually landed a role as a trainee assistant studio manager within the BBC, and worked on *Record Review*, a magazine dedicated to reviewing classical music recordings. Upon hearing about the Radiophonic Workshop she expressed an interest in the department, and was assigned there in April 1962. Her first major piece of music work came with *Doctor* Who, where she provided an electronic realisation of **Ron Grainer**'s score. Never credited for work until **The Day of the Doctor** her arrangement lasted for seventeen years before the score was rearranged many times, much to the composer's horror.

Outside of *Doctor Who* the composer had a highly successful career across all aspects of film; collaborating with **Barry Bermange**, founding Unit Delta Plus in 1966 with **Brian Hodgson** and **Peter Zinovieff**, and set up Kaleidophon Studio with Brian Hodgson and **David Vorhaus** in Camden Town. The occasional work for TV and Film came Derbyshire's way as well as working as a radio operator for a British Gas pipelaying project. In later life she worked for the LYC Museum and Art Gallery in Cumbria and worked as an assistant to Li Yuan-chia. She briefly returned to the world of music in 2001 before dying in July 2001 aged 64 from renal failure.

Dennis Spooner (1932-86): Born in Tottenham 1932, **Dennis Spooner**'s first experience in writing came in the form of writing gags as a boy scout. A keen footballer in his youth, Spooner successfully became a professional with Third Division (South) side Leyton Orient until National Services interrupted his plans in 1950. During National Service, the writer collaborated with **Tony Williamson**, and together they toured in forces shows. After completing National Service it wasn't long until Spooner found himself in the world of stand-up comedy, forming a double act with **Leslie Darbon** and writing material with **Benny Davis**. An eventual meeting with **Harry Worth** lead to Spooner's first credits in professional writing.

Spooner was soon working for ATV and it didn't take long for him to break into TV drama writing for *The Avengers* (1961/68), the 87th episode of *Coronation Street* (1961), *No Hiding Place* (1962) and a numerous shows for BBC Radio. In 1962, Spooner formed a working relationship with husband and wife team **Gerry** and **Sylvia Anderson**, submitting scripts for their stop-motion puppet series *Supercar* which went unused. When *Supercar* ceased production, Spooner found himself as a regular writer on Anderson's subsequent series; *Fireball XL5* (1962-63), *Stingray* (1963-64) and *Thunderbirds* (1965-66). A CV full of science-fiction scripts, the writer was soon approached by **David Whitaker** to write for *Doctor Who*, the result being ***The Reign of Terror***. When David Whitaker left the series, Dennis Spooner was duly appointed as script editor remaining with the show until ***The Chase***. Duties during his time on *Doctor Who* included trimming down the overlong ***The Rescue*** and writing the preceding serial ***The Romans***. Following his departure from the show Spooner penned ***The Time Meddler***. After *Doctor Who* the writer was keen to continue writing for television, and soon joined **Terry Nation** with *The Baron* (1966-67), a television series destined to be disturbed worldwide. When *The Baron* finished production in November 1965, both Spooner and Terry Nation co-wrote the 12-part serial ***The Daleks' Master Plan*** (1965-66), and later returned to the show to perform uncredited rewrites to *The Power of the Daleks* (1966). Spooner later created *Man in a Suitcase* (1967-68), *The Champions* (1968), *Department S* (1969), *Randall and Hopkirk (Deceased)* (1969-70), and *Jason King* (1971-72), and wrote various stageplays with **Brian Clements** between 1979-82. In later life Dennis Spooner toured America looking for writing work, but found minimal success; a revival of *The Avengers* went unpurchased. Spooner's last writing credit came with *Dramarama* (1986), before suffering a fatal heart attack on 20 September 1986. A new TV series idea *Courier* ended following his death.

Derek Martinus (1931-2014): Born in 1931 in Ilford, Essex, **Martinus**, after completing National Service, studied directing and acting at the University of Oklahoma and Yale School of Drama. However, after running out of money, he returned to live in the UK where he found work acting in various repertory theatres including Library Theatre, Manchester, and the Royal Court. Further theatre work came with The Pembroke Theatre-in-the-round where he directed 20 plays before the theatre ultimately closed. Later acting work came with Monsewer in *The Hostage* and Malvolio in *Twelfth Night*. **Martinus** soon wished to pursue a career in television production as a presenter but was ultimately turned down for the job. He sent in a letter of complaint to **Sydney Newman**, which resulted in him completing the internal BBC directing course. The director was assigned to *Doctor Who* serial **Galaxy 4** after **Mervyn Pinfield** was taken ill. Unfamiliar with *Doctor Who*, he watched tapes to better understand the series, and was duly disappointed at what he saw; he wished to aim for higher standards. The director would later helm; **Mission to the Unknown**, **The Tenth Planet**, **The Evil of the Daleks**, **The Ice Warriors** and **Spearhead from Space**. Other director stints came with: *United!* (1965-66), *Z Cars* (1968-78), *Angels* (1975-78), *Blake's 7* (1979), and *Emmerdale* (1977-82). Derek Martinus died on 27 March 2014.

Derek Ware (1938-2015): Born in 1938, his family worked in the Entertainment Industry, so **Derek Ware** soon followed suit. Graduating from RADA in 1957 he found regular acting work with *An Age of Kings* (1960). A well-known stunt arranger, Ware founded HAVOC in 1966, a company dedicated in providing stuntmen and arrangers for TV and Film. Dominating stuntwork, the company was popular with both BBC and ITV, but ultimately dissolved in the 1970s, but the company was used many times by the *Doctor Who* production office in 1960s and 70s. A familiar face in the world of *Doctor Who*, Ware landed various credited roles over the years which included Tuthmos in **The Daleks' Master Plan**, Spaniard in **The Smugglers**, Private Wyatt in **Inferno**, and Pigbin Josh in **The Claws of Axos**. He also landed uncredited roles and was an occasional fight arranger between 1963 and 71. Derek Ware continued to do stunt work for TV and Film until an accident in 1990 forced him into retirement, he became a Fencing Coach in later life. Derek Ware died on 22 September 2015 aged 77.

Donald Tosh (1935-2019): Born in 1935, **Donald Tosh** was bit by the acting bug after being taken to theatre shows by an uncle. After completing his National Service, Donald Tosh won theatre parts in London, but soon developed stage fright and moved to behind-the-scenes. Initially he began to read and advise on scripts, where his critical reviews resulted in him being nicknamed 'Knocker Tosh'.

Joining Granada Television Story and Contract Department in 1957, his was responsible to find a new soap opera to revival the already popular *Emergency-Ward 10* in 1960, which ultimately became *Florizel Street* which eventually became *Coronation Street*. In 1963, he was made redundant, but was soon invited to join the BBC by **Donald Wilson** where he replaced the script editor of *Compact* who had taken ill. Initially Tosh was only meant to cover the position for a few weeks but this turned into 18 months. With very little interest for soap operas, Tosh was invited to either take up script editing duties on *199 Park Lane* or *Doctor Who*. He chose the latter. After joining as script editor on **The Time Meddler**, **The Myth Makers** was his first successful commission. His time on *Doctor Who* was not an easy one, he had different tastes about what type of serials should be produced compared to producer **John Wiles**, and he rewrote **Terry Nation**'s scripts for **The Daleks' Master Plan**, and extensively rewrote **The Massacre** due to **John Lucarotti**'s poor historical research. His biggest challenge came with **The Celestial Toymaker** where both he and John Wiles planned to replace **William Hartnell** with another actor, plans which were eventually blocked. His departure from the show soon followed, not before reworking **The Celestial Toymaker** which had been written by **Brian Hayles**. Departing for a delayed honeymoon, the script editor returned to discover that **The Celestial Toymaker** had been rewritten by new script editor **Gerry Davis**, and asked for his co-writer credit to be removed. He later submitted a storyline for the **Patrick Troughton** era which was rejected.

Donald Tosh was assigned to work on *The Regiment* and after five months of research he was moved to work on *Ryan International* (1970). However the pilot for the series, in his eyes was severely historically inaccurate and his subsequent departure from the TV industry followed. In later life, he worked in the legal profession, before becoming Chief Custodian of Sherborne Old Castle, Dorest, and then St Mawes in Cornwall. During his time he maintained the premises and spent time writing historical guidebooks. Tosh was later reunited with *Doctor Who* with a cameo appearance in the special TV movie *An Adventure in Time and Space* (2013). Tosh died on 3 December 2019 at the age of 84.

Douglas Camfield (1931-84): Born in India in 1931, **Douglas Camfield** was highly ambitious in early life, wishing to work for Walt Disney in his teenage years. National Services in 1951 saw his plans be put on hold, but Camfield soon found a flair for military life, but after injuring his ankle his military life came to an end. In 1955, he joined the BBC as a call-boy or runner in today's terms and quickly rose through the ranks working as an Assistant Floor Manager, Floor Manager and Production Assistant. He soon found himself contributing scripts to *Playbox* from 1961-62 and an episode of *Garry Halliday* (1962) and a TV Movie *An Adventure to Order* (1961).

Entering the world of *Doctor Who* right from the beginning Camfield worked as the Production Assistant on ***100,000BC***. Soon after he completed the BBC's internal directing course, and landed directing duties with *Swizzlewick* (1964). Invited to direct on *Doctor Who* by **Verity Lambert**, the director helmed the original fourth episode of ***Planet of Giants***. Verity Lambert was pleased with the results before the third and fourth episodes were merged into one. Camfield later returned to helm **The Crusade**, **The Time Meddler** and all 12 episodes of **The Daleks' Master Plan**. Outside of *Doctor Who*, the director found regular work om *Z Cars* (1967-69), *Public Eye* (1971-75) and *The Sweeney* (1975-78) plus many other TV shows. Returning to *Doctor Who*, the director oversaw **The Web of Fear**, **The Invasion**, **Inferno**, **Terror of the Zygons**, and **The Seeds of Doom**. It was during production of ***Inferno*** when the young director collapsed during studio rehearsals and many feared for his life. Producer **Barry Letts** took over directing duties, this was first time people learned about the director's heart condition. Besides from directing, Camfield submitted two story ideas which were rejected: 'Operation: Werewolf' for the 1967/68 series and 'The Lost Legion' in 1976. Invited to direct **The Five Doctors**, he declined, wishing to direct feature-length films and distancing himself from *Doctor Who*. Douglas Camfield continued to work continuously throughout his career including a TV Movie of *Ivanhoe* (1982). On 27 January 1984, Douglas Camfield died at his home due to a heart attack. His death came as a great shock to many working in the entertainment industry. He was survived by his wife Sheila Dunn.

Francis Chagrin (1905-72): Born in Bucharest, Romania in 1905, **Francis Chagrin** was born as Alexander Paucker, but changed his name after moving to Paris in 1928. Pressured to study for an engineering degree by his family, Chagrin secretly studied Music, much to his family's annoyance. He began playing in nightclubs and cafés, whilst writing songs on the side line. He successfully funded himself for two years, before settling in England in 1936. Speaking fluent French, English, Romanian and German, as well as a little bit of Russian, made Chagrin very employable all over the world. When World War II broke out, he was the music adviser and composer-in-chief to BBC's French Services. 1943 saw Chagrin found The Committee for the Promotion for New Music (or Society for the Promotion of New Music, in later years), with the intention of promoting young and unestablished composers to the world of music. He later founded his own group in 1951, the Francis Chagrin Ensemble and worked extensively for two decades. Francis Chagrin provided music for over 200 film, television and commercial works during his career which included *Castle in the Sky* (1952), *The Colditz Story* (1955), *The Snorkel* (1958), *The Four Just Men* (1959-60) and *Greyfriars Bobby* (1961). Chagrin won the 'Harriet Cohen Intentional Music Award' for best film composer of the year in 1963. A popular performer at concert halls and venues, Chagrin played at the 1947 proms with his 'Prelude and Fugue for Orchestra'. Upon his death in 1972, he left a third symphony unfinished and was due to write music for the SPNM's 30th anniversary concert at the Queen Elizabeth Hall. The event would have taken place on 5 February 1973.

Gerry Davis (1930-1991): Born in 1930, **Gerry Davis** developed a love of science fiction in youth, reading his father's collection of sci-fi works, and later ran an H.G.Wells fan club. He held a reporter job for a brief spell with Hasting Newspaper before leaving to serve four years in the Merchant Navy. During his time he developed a love for acting, and during shore leave he would appear in repertory theatres. Moving to Canada, Davis spent his free time writing his own radio scripts, one of which was eventually commissioned. He soon found himself working for Canada's National Film Board before working in television. Upon joining the Canadian Broadcasting Corporation in Toronto as a stagehand, he was promoted by **Sydney Newman** to join the scripting department. After a few years of working in Canada, Davis moved back to the UK and found work with Granada's script department. He helped develop new soap opera *Coronation Street* which debuted in 1960.

Upon the death of his wife, Davis trained as an opera singer and moved to Milan for 18 months where he worked in Italian Cinema mainly as a translator. Returning once again to the UK, he devised a scriptwriting correspondence course which was sent to BBC Head of Serials **Donald Wilson** for advice, Davis was soon hired to work as a script editor on *199 Park Lane* (1965). Moving on to work as a story liner for *United!* (1966), he joined the BBC after his second wife gave birth to a daughter. Requesting a transfer to London, he landed the job as script editor on *Doctor Who*. During his script editing duties, Davis co-created the Cybermen for **The Tenth Planet** and was formally invited by out-going producer **Innes Lloyd** to take over. Davis rejected this offer and suggested **Derrick Sherwin** for the job. During his time on *Doctor Who*, he heavily reworked **The Celestial Toymaker** and **The Moonbase** and heavily rewrote most of **The Highlanders**. Davis left his script editing post half-way through production of *The Evil of the Daleks* (1967) to take up script editing duties on *The First Lady* (1968-69). He later returned to *Doctor Who* to co-write **The Tomb of the Cybermen** and **Revenge of the Cybermen**. Davis went onto create *Doomwatch* (1970-72) and *Softly Softly: Task Force* (1971-72). He later moved back to Canada where he worked on *Sidestreet (*1975) before moving to Los Angeles to work on *The Bionic Woman* (1976) and *Vega$* (1979), before writing *The Final Countdown* (1980).

Over the years, Davis remained attached to *Doctor Who*, often novelising his own scripts featuring the Cybermen. He later submitted an unused storyline to the *Doctor Who* production office in 1980s entitled 'Genesis of the Cybermen' and was disappointed that he was never asked or invited to write future Cybermen stories. After *Doctor Who* was put on hiatus he attempted to make the show into an independent production and planned to revive *Doomwatch,* but his plans didn't come to pass. Davis died on 31 August 1991 from cancer, and his ashes were scattered on the Thames.

Ian Stuart Black (1915-97): Born in 1915, **Ian Stuart Black** attended Daniel Stewart's College in Edinburgh before studying Philosophy at Manchester University. Sending in a one-act play to the Donald Wolfit Theatre Company, the writer joined the theatre as an actor. During the early 1940s he served with RAF Intelligence, stationed in Egypt, and shortly after leaving, he landed a job at Pinewood within the script department.

He contributed material towards *Home to Danger* (1951), *The Limping Man* (1953), and *Soho Incident* (1956). The writer was also a successful novelist with *In the Wake a Stranger* (1953), *The Passionate City* (1958), *The Yellow Flag* (1959), *Love in Four Countries* (1961) and *The High Bright Sun* (1962). The writer broke into the world of television with his theatre comedy *We Must Kill Toni* (1951). Further writing credits came with *Fabian of the Yard* (1955-56) and *The Invisible Man* (1958-59). Script editing duties came on *Sir Francis Drake* (1961-62), *Man of the World* (1962-63), *The Sentimental Agent* (1963), and *The Man in Room 17* (1965). Helping to develop *Danger Man* with **Ralph Smart** saw the writer associate-produce the original half-hour episodes. Active in the film world whilst working in television, the writer adapted his novel *In the Wake of a*

Stranger for the big screen with other adaptions of his works coming with *We Must Kill Toni* released as *She'll Have to Go* (1962) and *The High Bright* (1965). Eventually writing for *Doctor Who*, the writer contacted the production office because he believed writing for the show would impress is family. The writer contributed three scripts for the show, and developed a fourth 'The Space War' which was ultimately never made.

Ian Stuart Black went onto to work on *Champion House* (1967), *The Revenue Men* (1967-68), and *The Champions* (1968). Associate producer credits came with *Elephant Man* (1972), *Castaway* (1974), and *The Outsiders* (1976-77), with writing assignments coming with *Star Maidens* (1976). International releases included with *Dossiers: Danger immédiat* (1977). Later life saw the writer publish more novels; *The Man on the Bridge* (1975), *Caribbean Strip* (1977), *Journey to a Safe Place* (1979), *Creatures in a Dream* (1985), and *Cry Wolf* (1990). He later novelised his *Doctor Who* scripts, and his final TV credit was the TV Movie *House of Glass* (1992). Residing in Devon, the writer died on 13 October 1997 aged 82.

Innes Lloyd (1925-1991): Born in 1925, **Innes Lloyd** originally trained as an actor at the Central School of Speech and Drama and later found acting work with the Malvern Festival (1948/49). Dreaming to write and direct in the world of drama, he joined the BBC in 1953 where he worked for a year within the radio's European Service at Bush House, before transferring to Television Outside Broadcast (OB) presentation. His time with OB saw him producing the coverage of the Queen's opening of Gatwick Airport, the Wimbledon Tennis Tournaments (1959-63), which included the 1963 final, the first series of *Match of the Day* (1964) and the 1960 Eurovision Song Contest.

Directing for drama came with two episodes apiece for *The Flying Swan*, *United!* and *The Newcomers* all in 1965. It wasn't long until he was asked by **Sydney Newman** to take over as producer of *Doctor Who* which Lloyd originally turned down; since he had no interest in science-fiction, but quickly changed his mind. With no interest in producing historical-based serials for *Doctor Who*, Lloyd changed the format of the show to incorporate more science-fiction driven narratives, and recruited **Kit Pedler** as a scientific adviser. Working generally well with **William Hartnell**, the producer was forced to change the leading star after Hartnell's health continued to decline. Overseeing the first changeover of leading actor, Lloyd, Sydney Newman and Head of Serials **Shaun Sutton** oversaw the first generation, and cast **Patrick Troughton** in the role. The producer stayed with the shows for just under 2 years and departed with *The Enemy of the World*, but took a short break during production of **The Tomb of the Cybermen** which was overseen by **Peter Bryant**.

Future producing credits came with *Thirty-Minute Theatre* (1968-72), *Dead of Night* (1972), *The Stone Tape* (1972), *Bedtime Stories* (1974), *Play for Today* (1975-82), *Brensham People* (1976), *BBC2 Play of the Week* (1976-78), *Screen Two* (1986-90), whilst producing extensively in TV Movies with *Across the Lake, Number 27* both in 1988 and *Bomber Harris* (1989). In 1991, Lloyd underwent surgery but quickly returned to work and saw a rough cut of *A Question of Attribution* before dying on 23 August 1991, with the film airing posthumously.

Jackie Lane (1941-2021): Born in 1941 in Manchester, **Jackie Lane** grew up in the world of theatre, since her dad Jack was a costumier and make-up artist. Jackie began acting at Whalley Range High School and amateur drama groups. A screen test for *A Taste of Honey* (1961) was unsuccessful, and the actress later joined Library Theatre, Manchester where she progressed to ASM (Assistant Stage Manager). Whilst with the theatre she starred in *The Same Sky* (1961), *Pinocchio* (1961/62), *Five Finger Exercise* (1962) and *Stop It, Whoever You Are* (1962). After leaving the theatre, she departed for London and starred in *The Caucasian Chalk Circle* (1962) later that year. Future work one-off roles came with *Coronation Street* (1964) and *The Protectors* (1964), but her big break came with *Compact* (1963), playing Rosemary Gray. Shortlisted to play Susan Foreman in the upcoming series *Doctor Who*, the actress met with **Verity Lambert** and **Waris Hussein**, but withdrew from consideration after learning the contract would last a year. When **John Wiles** took over *Doctor Who*, the actress was contracted for an initial 12 episodes to play Dodo. She filmed her first work on the show on 7 January 1966, however soon after arriving, producer **John Wiles** departed, and incoming producer **Innes Lloyd** decided to drop Dodo with the character leaving midway through **The War Machines**. Leaving the acting profession, Lane worked at the Australian Vice Consul in Paris as a secretary for over a year. Returning to England, she ran her own shop, Jackie Lane Antiques. She later became a theatrical agent where future *Doctor Who* stars **Tom Baker** and **Janet Fielding** were among her clients. Distancing herself from *Doctor Who* over the years, she made an appearance at a 1991 convention and participated in a 2006 signing. She made no other appearances in audio or DVD release commentaries. The actress died on June 23, 2021, aged 79.

Jacqueline Hill (1929-93): Born in 1929, **Jacquline Hill** was withdrawn from education at 14 years old to support her older brother. Working as a wage clerk at the local Cadbury chocolate factory in Bournville, she joined the firm's drama society. Eventually working backstage with Birmingham Rep, she won a scholarship to RADA at 16 years old, **Joan Collins** was among her classmates. Being 5'7" and very slender led to modelling work for a brief spell in Paris. Appearing on the talent show *Shop Window* (1953) brought her to public attention, and eventually she worked for **Sam Wanamaker** as Miss Cardell in *The Shrike* from February-March 1953. Film debut *The Blue Parrot* (1953) appeared later that year with her TV debut coming with *The Rose and the Ring* (1953).

Meeting Canadian-born director/producer **Alvin Rankoff** in 1953, the pair of them eventually married in 1958, but not before collaborating with each other many times over the years. One such collaboration put the actress into contact with BBC production assistant **Verity Lambert**. Their collaboration didn't come without its repercussions, with many directors refusing to cast the actress in fear that their work would be criticised by her husband, the actress managed to find regular work when not working with her husband, nonetheless. When **Verity Lambert** was made producer of *Doctor Who*, Lambert sought out Hill to play Barbara Wright; but doubted that she would accept the role. Whilst holidaying in Italy, the actress accepted the role and met her fellow cast members on 20 September 1963. Staying with the show for just under 2 years, she departed along with **William Russell**, the pair of them were reunited later that year to appear at the Grand Theatre, Leeds in *Separates Tables*. Appearing in an episode of *No Hiding Place* in 1966 she quit the acting business to raise a family. Returning to acting in the 70s, she found work with *Crown Court* (1978) and guest starred in *Doctor Who* as Lexa in **Meglos**. Other acting work came with *Angels* (1982), *Tales of the Unexpected* (1983/84), *Screenplay* (1986) and *Paradise Postponed* (1986). Hill was later diagnosed with cancer and withdrew from public life and died at her home on 18 February 1993 aged 63.

Jean Marsh (1934-): Born in 1934, **Jean Marsh** was introduced to the world of acting through dance and mime lesson, taken as a form of therapy to help a childhood illness. Early acting work came with the West End show *The Land of the Christmas Stocking* (1947/48). During his early career she landed dancing roles in various movies between 1951 and 52. Modelling swimsuits in the early 1950s, Marsh was entered, by her agent, as Miss West Hampstead in Britain's Miss Britain Contest of 1952. Whilst acting in Rep theatre at Huddersfield, and elsewhere, she took voice lessons at the Central School of Speech and Drama. Whilst appearing in *Will Any Gentlemen…* (1953), she met future *Doctor Who* star **Jon Pertwee**, with the pair of them marrying in 1955. However, the marriage soon broke up, and they divorced in 1960. Whilst in an American Restaurant, she was cast in the TV Movie *The Moon and Sixpence* (1959) and appeared in an episode apiece for *The Twilight Zone* and *The Third Man* (1959). Returning to the UK, she landed roles in *The Rebel* (1961), *Cleopatra* (1963) and *Unearthly Stranger* (1963), being uncredited on the latter two. Various one-off roles came between 1962 and 68 on many popular TV programmes of the time. Her first *Doctor Who* role come with **The Crusade**, her second being cast as Sara Kingdom, the new companion on the show, for **The Daleks' Master Plan**, only to be killed off at the end of the serial.

Landing the role of Sylvia Parrish in *The Informer* (1966-67) and Rose Buck, the maid for 54 episodes in *Upstairs Downstairs* (1971-75) brought her major success. The occasional film role came with *The Limbo Line* (1968), *Frenzy* (1972), *Dark Place* (1975), *The Changeling* (1980), with an array of Broadway appearances between 1975 and 79. Success in the states came with one-off roles in TV, *Nine to Five* (1982-83), and films *Return to Oz* (1985) and *Willow* (1988), ultimately the actresses was typecast for playing villainess roles. Landing the role as Morgaine in *Doctor Who*'s **Battlefield** – her third appearance on the show, and Morgana in *A Connecticut Yankee in King's Arthur Court* (1989) and *The Pale Horse* (1997) brought her more sorceress roles. Other varied roles kept the actress busy throughout the 1990s and she produced the popular series *The House of Eliott* (1991-94). Stage work followed in mid 2000s and a revival of *Upstairs Downstairs* (2010-12) saw her return at Mrs. Rose Buck. Reprising her role as Sara Kingdom for audio dramas, the actress reconnected with *Doctor Who* in later years. She was awarded an OBE in 2012 for her services to drama.

John Gorrie (1932-): Born in 1932, **John Gorrie** originally trained as an actor and landed roles in an episode of *BBC Sunday-Night Theatre* (1958), the TV Movie *Tom Barnardo* (1958), and an episode of *Sat'day While Sunday* (1967). He appeared regularly on stage in the 1950s and featured in a West End version of *Inherit the Wind*. Moving onto directing and writing for shows in London, he joined the BBC as an assistant floor manager and took the internal directing course in 1963. Directing his debut assignment for the *Suspense* anthology in 1963, he moved onto directing regularly on *Compact* (1963-64). Quickly recruited to direct **The Keys of Marinus** for *Doctor Who*, the director was not familiar with science fiction, and was not best pleased with the scripts. Whilst casting the serial, the director instantly thought of **George Coulouris** for the role of Arbitan after seeing him acting at the Bristol Old Vic, and was delighted when the actor agreed to take the part. It seems that the director came back to the show to handle 'A Change of Identity' for **The Reign of Terror** after director **Henrich Hirsh** took ill, but this remains unconfirmed. Later directing work came with 5 instalments of *The Wednesday Play* (1965-69), 7 instalment of *BBC Play of the Month* (1968-79), *Edward the Seventh* (1975), *Tales of the Unexpected* (1980-88), *Morgan's Boy* (1984), *Oasis* (1993) and *The Famous Five* (1995-97). The director reconnected with *Doctor Who*, providing a DVD commentary for the release of **The Keys of Marinus**.

John Lucarotti (1926-94): Born in 1926, **Lucarotti** fell in love with the air and sea from a young age and worked as a pilot in the Royal Navy during wartime and remained there for nine years. Eventually moving to Canada, he worked as a door-to-door encyclopaedia salesman, but quickly resigned after he could no longer bear it. Eventually writing for Canadian Broadcasting Corporation; 200 script contributions included a series of *Robin Hood* and an 18-part series *The Three Journeys of Marco Polo* (1955). Other work came with children's series *Tomahawk* (1957). During his time with CBS, **Sydney Newman** was Supervisor of Drama from 1954-58, and when the writer returned to the UK in 1960 he was recruited by Newman who was Head of Drama at ABC. Future writing assignments came with *Ghost Squad* (1962-63) and five episodes of *The Avengers* (1961-65) and *The Protectors* (1964).

When Newman helped create *Doctor Who* in 1963, Lucarotti was given his first BBC writing assignment with the show. Writing both **Marco Polo** and **The Aztecs** within months of each other, a third formal script was commissioned by **Dennis Spooner**. The script in question featuring Erik the Viking, was cancelled by **John Wiles** and **Donald Tosh**, and the storyline became **The Massacre of St. Bartholomew's Eve**. Outside of *Doctor Who*, the writer continuously worked throughout the 60s and 70s, predominantly with *The Troubleshooters* with 31 scripts written between 1965 and 71. Contributing a storyline to the *Doctor Who* production office in 1974 about a space ark was reworked by **Robert Holmes** and became the iconic cult classic **The Ark in Space**. Latter day writing credits came with an adaptation of *Treasure Island* (1977) and *Into the Labyrinth* (1981). Novelising his *Doctor Who* scripts in the 1980s, the writer wrote a short story for the *Doctor Who Magazine* in 1990 where he himself met The Doctor. In later life, he ran a restaurant with his second wife and a single radio play was written in 1990s. John Lucarotti died on 20 November 1994 from spinal cancer whilst living in Paris.

John Wiles (1925-99): Born in 1925 in South Africa, **John Wiles'** theatre career began at the age of just 14 years old when he became a stage manager and playwright with works including *Die Ehrenfels* (1948). Moving to the UK in 1949, he worked as a furniture remover, whilst spending time painting, sculpting, writing novels and scripts. Novels included *The Moon to Play With* (1954), *Scene of a Meeting* (1956), and *The Asphalt Playground* (1958). Eventually joining the BBC's script unit, he found work co-writing *The Dancing Bear* (1954), and an episode of *The Grove Family* (1957). The producer found success in the world of British Theatre with works being performed at Q Theatre, Brentford; Belgrade, Coventry; Theatre Royal, Stratford East, London; and the Edinburgh Festival. He also ran theatre workshops in borstals and approved schools, and later wrote about his experiences in future works. Story editor duties came with *The Midnight Men* (1964), *The Sleeper* (1964), *Compact* (1963-65), *Contract to*

Kill (1965), and *The Mind of the Enemy* (1965). Eventually asked to produce *Doctor Who*, Wiles was unsure, as he originally hoped to direct instead of produce. Trailing **Verity Lambert**, the producer wished to turn *Doctor Who* into something more adult; a factor greatly disliked by **William Hartnell**. The producer only stayed a matter of weeks before deciding to leave; *The Daleks' Master Plan* was a real strain on the Wiles, and the preceding serial *The Massacre of St. Bartholomew's Eve* was heavily rewritten due to historical inaccuracy. Having already commissioned *The Celestial Toymaker*, the producer had the intention of writing William Hartnell out, but was overruled by superiors. He left the series in late 1965, and was gone from the show by February 1966 whilst *The Ark* was in production. Returning to a scriptwriting career, he became a storyliner with *The Newcomers* (1966) and a script advisor/consultant with *Dixon of Dock Green* (1967-69). In his later career, he wrote continuously for a wide range of television series and occasionally directed in the theatre. John Wiles died on 5 April 1999 aged 73.

Julia Smith (1927-97): Born in 1927, **Julia Smith** began her directing career with an episode of *Suspense* (1963), although she remained uncredited. Regular directing work came with *Swizzlewick* (1964), *Alexander Graham Bell* (1965) and *Compact* (1965). Attached to direct *The Smugglers* for *Doctor Who*, she returned to helm *The Underwater Menace*. She continued finding constant directing work with *Dr. Finlay's Casebook* (1963-69), *Z Cars* (1971-74), *Spy Trap* (1973-75), and *Angels* (1975-76). It was during her time working on *Z Cars* when she met **Tony Holland** and together they had a successful working partnership in the world of television. Together they created successful television series with *The District Nurse* (1984-87) and more famously *EastEnders* (1985-present). Smith worked as an associate producer/producer on *Angels* (1978-83), a producer/executive producer on *The District Nurse* (1984-87) and a series producer on Tony Holland's ill-fated soap opera *Eldorado* (1993). After *Eldorado* failed to grip audiences and critics alike, Smith retired from television work. She died of cancer on 19 June 1997 aged 70.

Kit Pedler (1927-81): Born in 1927, **Kit Pedler** came from a long family line who worked within Medicine, although he obtained some artistic skills from his mother. Studying at London King's College Hospital, he eventually left general practice and moved into research. The writer eventually obtained a second doctorate in experimental pathology and lectured at the University of London, before heading the Department of Anatomy at its Institute of Ophthalmology in 1961. During his time there he studied eye disease and the biological processes of the retina. After providing scientific help on *Horizon* (c.1964) Pedler drew the attention of *Doctor Who* story editor **Gerry Davis** who by then was seeking out a scientific advisor for the show.

Eventually springing out an idea for *Doctor Who*, based on the new Post Office Tower, which obscured Pedler's view from his office, his idea eventually turned into *The War Machines*. It was during this time, when he was undergoing stomach operations, that he pondered the end effects of medial science. It was during a discussion with his wife about spare-part surgery that the Cybermen were born. Advising costume designer **Sandra Reid** on how the Cybermen should look, *The Tenth Planet* was largely written by Gerry Davis but the Snowcap setting was Pedler's idea. Over the years Kit Pedler continued to write story ideas which were largely written up by experienced scriptwriters; four future Cybermen serials followed, two of which were co-written with Gerry Davis, and the other two being written by **David Whitaker** and **Derrick Sherwin**. In 1969, Pedler left the medical profession, and moved on to create *Doomwatch* (1970-72) which grabbed the attention of up to 12 million viewers, but left the show before the third series after clashing with producer **Terence Dudley**.

A talented amateur engineer, he built racing carts in his spare time and drove powerful sports cars, but his passion was cut short after conflicting ecological beliefs which began in 1974. A standalone novel *The Quest of Gaia* explored how mankind can survive without destroying themselves. Another ecological wise show *Mind Over Matter* (1981) arose after a discussion in a pub. Pedler wrote and presented the show with **Tony Bastable**. Kit Pedler died on 27 May 1981 from a heart attack outside his home aged 53. The third episode of *Mind Over Matter* was shown the same day.

Louis Marks (1928-2010): Born in 1928, **Louis Marks** studied at Christ's College, Finchley. Reading History at Balliol College, Oxford he studied Italian Renaissance history in Florence, eventually gaining a PhD in the Financial History of the Florentine State. He moved on to become Head of History at a boarding school in England. His academic credentials earned him a position as the founding editor for *Books and Bookmen* between September 1955 and April 1956. It was through his work on *Bookmen* that he landed a job to assemble a promotion film for P&O Cruises, and working for a documentary film company, and then ITV.

Marrying in 1957, his wife was a production assistant on *The Adventures of Robin Hood* (1958-59) with Marks writing four episodes. Producer **Hannah Weinstein** moved onto *The Four Just Men* and made the writer script supervisor. He later found success writing for various TV shows throughout the 1960s and wrote his first *Doctor Who* scripts **Planet of Giants** in 1964. Landing a writing role on *No Hiding Place* (1966-67), he eventually became the script editor for the eighth and ninth series. Moving on to create *Honey Lane* (1967-69) brought him a fair amount of success and a great deal of money. Marks continued to write throughout the 1970s whilst contributing various *Doctor Who* scripts to the production office, with **Day of the Daleks**, **Planet of Evil**, and **The Masque of Mandragora**, all three scripts were written whilst performing script editing duties in the BBC's Plays department. More script editing positions came with *Trial* (1971), *No Exit* (1972), *Dead of Night* (1972), *BBC2 Playhouse* (1976) and *Brensham People* (1976). Eventually becoming a full fledge producer by 1977 he helmed various TV Films over the years including a production of *The Crucible* (1981). Continuing to produce in the 80s and 90s his final writing credit came with *Daniel Deronda* (2002). Retiring from the entertainment industry he ran a B&B with his wife, until her death in 2006. Louis Mark died on 17 September 2010 aged 82.

Maureen O'Brien (1943-): Born in 1943, **Maureen O'Brien** attended Notre Dame High School and later studied for a drama teaching diploma at London's Central School of Speech and Drama from 1961-64. Returning home after her studies she helped found the Liverpool Everyman Theatre, working as an assistant stage manager whilst taking small acting roles in various productions. When **Carole Ann Ford** left *Doctor Who* the production team set about looking for a replacement. Invited to try out for a screen test on 14 September 1964, another actress **Denise Upson** was also tested. She returned to the Everyman Theatre before winning the role of Vicki. During her time on the show she appreciated her debut story's resemblance to *The Tempest*, and enjoyed working with her fellow cast members. However she eventually became disappointed with what she saw as poor scripts and made her concerns known, and felt that Vicki was rather limited as a character. Her disappointment was noted by **Donald Tosh** and Vicki was written out of the series, but not before O'Brien returned from holiday to find out her contract had not been renewed. Moving on from *Doctor Who* she appeared very briefly in the theatre and 3 episodes of *Emergency-Ward 10* (1966), and appeared in a 2-part *Z Cars* narrative in 1969 but soon her agent was struggling to find work for her.

Taking up a supply teacher position at a girl's school in Kennington, she was eventually cast in a **Frank Hauser** stage play at the Oxford Playhouse which eventually transferred to the West End's Garrick Theatre. More theatre work soon followed between 1967 and 69 with the occasional one-off TV roles coming in a variety of TV shows. Moving to Canada in 1970 she directed and acted in theatre productions before returning to the UK where she found more theatre and radio work across the country. The 70s saw a steady stream of acting work with *The Poisoning of Charles Bravo* (1975), *The Squirrels* (1976), *The Lost Boys* (1978) and *The Legend of King Arthur* (1979). Appearing in the 1980-81 season at London Old Vic's saw her play Portia in *The Merchant of Venice*. The actress continued to land theatre roles throughout the 80s with the occasional TV role. Landing the part of Elizabeth Straker in *Casualty* for 15 episodes in 1987, and three separate episodes of *The Bill* (1993/95/97) and two separate episodes of *Heartbeat* (2000/03) kept the actress busy. More one-off roles came throughout the 90s and 2000s aswell as film work. As a novelist O'Brien wrote six crime novels between 1989 and 2004 starring her DI John Bright character. Over the years, the actress was keen to distance herself from *Doctor Who*, she did however appear in a companion line-up in 1985 for Children in Need, and later contributed to Big Finish Audio Dramas reprising her role as Vicki.

Mervyn Pinfield (1912-66): Born in 1912 **Mervyn Pinfield** began his career in the entertainment industry with the Morecombe Royalty Theatre where he spent four years as theatre manager. He spent time realising both comedies and classics at the theatre and directed a production of *Julius Caesar* in December 1952. He joined the BBC in the early 1950s displaying great technical skills whilst at Alexandra Palace. His first great success came with the invention of the Piniprompter (or autocue nowadays) after many viewers complained that newsreaders where always staring down at their scripts. Moving onto the Drama Experimental Unit in December 1958, Pinfield displayed more technical skills; developing camera tricks and the 'developing shot'. Directing stints came with *Starr and Company* (1958), an edition of *Saturday Playhouse* (1960), *The Franchise Affair* (1962) and *The Monsters* (1962). Because of his technical skills and knowledge he was duly appointed as associate producer on *Doctor Who*, acting mainly as a technical advisor. He was heavily involved with the interior design of the Tardis, the Daleks, and the opening credits sequence. During a filming session in August 1963 he described the opening credits as too graphic and suggested that title sequence designer **Bernard Lodge** study the works of **Norman Taylor** and **Ben Palmer** for inspiration. Occasionally directing for *Doctor Who* he helmed the first four episodes of **The Sensorites** and the first three of **Planet of Giants** and **The Space Museum**. As *Doctor Who* progressed, Pinfield's associate producer duties diminished. Drafted in to helm **Mission to the Unknown**, Pinfield was taken ill when filming inserts for *Galaxy 4* in June 1965. Retiring from television soon afterwards, Pinfield died 11 months later on 20 May 1966 aged 54.

Michael Craze (1942-98): Born on 29th November 1942, **Michael Craze** began acting in scout shows and gang groups and later discovered he had a unique soprano voice. The actor was unable to take up acting fulltime until he turned 12 where he appeared in *The King and I* at the Theatre Royal, Drury Lane. He later appeared in *Plain and Fancy* at the same venue and *Damn Yankee* (1957) at London's Coliseum. His family originally hoped he would study to be a solicitor, but the acting bug prevailed. Moving from Grammar School to Repertory Theatre, the actor spent time at Bradford, Richmond and Harrogate appearing as Jim in *Treasure Island* and the Genie in *Aladdin*. Continuing to act in the theatre, the actor dropped out of the profession for a while in mid 1960s and found work as a butcher's assistant. Whilst working at Harrogate, Craze was an avid watcher of *Doctor Who* often watching episodes between theatre performances.

His TV debut came in 1958 with a more regular role coming with *Target Luna* in 1960. Early film work often left him uncredited, but a credited role came with *Two Left Feet* (1965). TV work was steady throughout the 1960s with 4 episodes of *Dixon of Dock Green* (1962/64/65/66) and numerous one-off roles in popular programmes. When it was announced that **Peter Purves** and **Jackie Lane** were leaving *Doctor Who*, Craze was invited to audition for the role of Ben, and won the part after a third call back. Bonding with **Anneke Wills** the actor and actress found it hard to get along with **William Hartnell**. During his time on the show he met his future wife **Edwina Verner**, during filming for **The Tenth Planet**. When **Patrick Troughton** took over as Doctor Who, both Craze and Wills bonded with the leading actor. Staying with the show for just over a year, Craze left at the end of **The Faceless Ones** instead of episode 2 of **The Evil of the Daleks** as originally intended.

After leaving the show Craze found a steady stream of television work with a brief spell with radio drama *Waggoner's Walk* (1971). Films roles came with *Neither the Sea Nor the Sand* (1972), *Madhouse* (1974), *Satan's Slave* (1976), and *Terror* (1978). Outside of acting he ran a sixteenth-century Pub near Shepperton film Studios whilst taking the occasional acting role on the side-lines. He later became manager of the Otter Bar at The Phoenix Hotel, East Dereham. He later became vice-chairman of Dereham's Antiquarian Society. Originally director **Graeme Harper** wanted to cast the actor as Krepler for **The Caves of Androzani** but was overruled by **John Nathan-Turner**. Relocating to Beckenham, Kent, the actor appeared in RAF training films and worked for five years as a steward for NatWest sports club until 1992. Reconnecting with *Doctor Who* in later life, the actor was a familiar face at fan events and recorded material for the VHS releases of *The Tenth Planet* after the missing fourth episode had been found. This turned out to be a hoax. Craze died on 7 December 1998 aged 56 after suffering a heart attack after a fall. The *Doctor Who* theme tune was played at his funeral.

Michael Imison Smith (1935-): Born in 1935, **Michael Imison** attended Oxford University before becoming the president of the Edinburgh Festival Fringe Society. He later joined the BBC on an administrative course before moving to the drama department in 1961 where he briefly worked on *Storyboard* (1961). Moving onto become story editor on *Compact* (1963) and 2 episodes of *Out of the Unknown* (1966), he undertook the internal BBC directors course whilst directing onstage in the meantime. After completion of the course he handled 20 episodes of *Compact* (1963-65) and Glasgow serial *Mary Barton* (1964), and Birmingham's *Swizzlewick* (1964). Whilst working on *Buddenbrooks* (1965), one of the cast members Annette Carell, was the wife of **Gerald Savoy**, who in October 1965 had become head of drama serials, and Imison's new boss. The actress apparently did not like the director's approach to *Buddenbrooks* and he was duly removed from the series. Assigned to *Doctor Who*, the director was not impressed with his new assignment; but was happy to work with **John Wiles** again. After returning from a holiday, Imison Smith was determined to make the story look impressive (mixing up camera shots and angles), he worked closely with writer **Paul Erickson** and claims to have come up with the idea of calling the reptile aliens featured in *The Ark* as the Monoids. In later life, he became a literary agent representing Noël Coward, Terence Rattigan, David Edgar and Bernard Pomerance. Smith currently lives in Suffolk.

Norman Kay (1929-2001): Born in 1929 **Norman Kay** was born and educated in Bolton. Studying at the Royal Manchester College of Music and the Royal College of Music, Kay soon found regular work composing music for TV shows. Working as a composer on *The River Flows East* (1962), editions of *Armchair Theatre* (1960-63), and *BBC Sunday-Night Play* (1962-63), Kay soon began composing music for *Doctor Who*. Composing incidental music for **An Unearthly Child**, **The Keys of Marinus** and **The Sensorites** kept him busy with the new sci-fi show. Continuing to find work as a composer throughout his career he worked on *Contract to Kill* (1965), *Sir Arthur Conan Doyle* (1967), *Out of the Unknown* (1965-69) plus many one-off assignments on various TV shows and TV Movies. He also worked as a conductor on many shows where he composed music, and composed the theme music for *Special Branch* (1968) and *Out of the Unknown* (1965-69). He was a musical director for *Don Pasquale* (1973). Norman Kay died in 2001 from motor neuron disease aged 72.

Paddy Russell (1928-2017): Born in 1928, **Paddy Russell** originally trained as an actress at the Guildhall School of Music and Drama. During her studies she was spotted by BBC Producer **Michael Barry** who was looking for petite actors to play animals for *Wind in the Willow* (1949). Obtaining further small parts on Television productions, she quickly turned her hand at stage management since production personnel were paid more than actors. Starting off as a floor manager/production assistant she worked on *The Quatermass Experiment* (1953), *World Theatre* (1959), and *Studio 4* (1962). She later progressed to undertake the BBC's internal directing course, after producing for a while. When she failed to obtain assignments she stormed to **Sydney Newman** to resign. Her resignation letter at the ready, she quickly won a three-month contract to work on *Compact* (1963) directing 20 episodes. She then progressed onto *The Massingham Affair* (1964), *Reluctant Bandit* (1965), and *The Mind of the Enemy* (1965) to name a few. The director was originally going to be assigned to the *Doctor Who* serial **Inside the Spaceship** but ultimately directed **The Massacre of St. Bartholomew's Eve** over 2 years later.

The late 60s to mid-70s saw her helm 22 episodes of *The Newcomers* (1966-67) and 55 episodes of *Z Cars* (1967-76). Returning to *Doctor Who* to direct **Invasion of the Dinosaurs** came about after rejecting **Death to the Daleks** since the director didn't want to work with the title monsters. She returned to work on **Pyramids of Mars** and **Horror of Fang Rock**. The director never returned to the show, but didn't rule anything out, and admitted in a 1981 interview, she would return provided a good script was at hand. Continuing to direct throughout the late 70s and 80s, she handled 77 episodes of *Emmerdale* (1976-80). Paddy Russell ultimately retired from 40 years working in television in the 80s. In later life she was actively involved with charity work before her death in 2017 aged 89 years.

Peter Hawkins (1924-2006): Born in London in 1924, **Peter Hawkins** developed a love for acting and entertainment and wrote along with three friends a short sketch. Wartime services might have proved fatal had he not survived the sinking of H.M.S Limbourne in 1943 which had been torpedoed. Whilst recovering from the disaster he participated in plays which eventually led to him being taken in by Combined Operations Entertainment. Finding work at the East Riding Theatre, the actor undertook a two-year acting course at the Central School of Speech and Drama. The actor continued to act in the West End before moving onto TV work where he found great fame as a voice-actor.

Voice-acting work came with *Whirligig* (1950-56) and *Captain Pugwash* (1957-61) with plenty of TV work providing him with on-screen appearances. Providing voices for the Daleks in their debut story brought him fame, and he continued to voice the Daleks in subsequent serials. The introduction of The Cybermen in **The Tenth Planet** brought Hawkins into the spotlight again for *Doctor Who*. His biggest non-*Doctor Who* role came with *Rainbow* (1972) where he voiced the main puppet character Zippy for 50 episodes in 1972, before being replaced by Roy Skelton. The latter actor coincidentally replaced Hawkins as the regular Dalek voice actor aswell. Hawkins continued to provide his voice largely in a narrator role for children's TV over the years, whilst obtaining the odd on-screen TV and film role.

He worked on numerous foreign animated films when translated and released for English audiences, and was the original voice of Gromit for the *Wallace and Gromit* short *A Grand Day Out* (1989). Creator **Nick Park** eventually decided that Gromit worked well as a non-speaking character, where his facial expressions did all the work. The actor eventually voiced Gromit in various video games during the late 90s and mid-2000s. Having undergone surgery to remove a brain tumour in 1992, the actor soon retired from the professional after the operation left him with memory problems. Perter Hawkins died on 8 July 2006 the same day that the *Doctor Who* episode **Doomsday** broadcast, which starred both the Cybermen and Daleks.

Peter Purves (1939-): Born in New Longton in 1939, **Peter Purves** was educated at Blackpool's Arnold School from nine years old. During his time at School he began acting in school plays, landing title roles in *The Pied Piper* and *Robin Hood*. Purves later landed the part of the Sheriff in *The Rainmaker* at Her Majesty's Theatre, Barrow-in-Furness in 1957. Originally training to be English and Maths teacher, he studied for a DipEd at Alsager Teacher Training College, Stoke-on-Trent. During his time at Alsager he was the president of the dramatic society and later joined a rock band. After teaching two terms at the school he was offered more acting work back at Barrow. Between 1961 and 63 he performed a different play on a weekly basis in 96 productions. Moving to London, the actor toured with the Wimbledon Theatre Company, and sang in a chorus in *The Man in the Moon* (1963/64) at the London Palladium. His TV debut came with playing a bus conductor in *Z Cars* (1964) with more acting work coming with *Armchair Theatre* (1964), *Theatre 625* (1964) and *Dixon of Dock Green* (1965). Originally the actor auditioned to play a Menoptera character in **The**

Web Planet but director **Richard Martin** believed the actor would be done a disservice playing a monster character. Months later the director cast the actor in an episode of *The Chase* as an American Hillbilly Morton Dill. With both **Jacqueline Hill** and **William Russell** set to leave at the end of *The Chase*, **William Hartnell** and **Maureen O'Brien** suggested Peter Purves should take over as the new companion. Invited out for a drink by producer **Verity Lambert** and script editor **Dennis Spooner**, the actor was offered the job.

Filming his debut episode and the preceding serial *The Time Meddler*, Peter Purves landed a few more acting roles during *Doctor Who*'s summer break. During the actor's time on the show, no fewer than four female companions joined the Tardis crew, with three of them leaving before him. He took the lead role in *The Massacre of St. Bartholomew's Eve* and *The Celestial Toymaker*. The actor enjoyed the historical-based narratives, and got on fairly well with William Hartnell but not so much with producer **John Wiles**. When production personnel changed on *Doctor Who*, the actor quickly found out that his contract would not be renewed. Leaving at the end of *The Savages*, work became scarce.

Appearing in a 2-part *Z Cars* narrative in 1967, the actor also auditioned unsuccessfully to replace **Sean Connery** as James Bond. The actor was later dumped by his agent. Between acting jobs he worked a hire driver and a boom operator for a film company. After leaving *Doctor Who* he had taken home the Trilogic game prop from *The Celestial Toymaker*, and believing it was bringing him bad luck he threw it out. The next day however he received a job offer that he couldn't reject. Joining *Blue Peter* as a presenter he worked largely on the show with eight million viewers for an average episode. He quickly became a hero (again) to generations of children. He stayed with the show for 10 years leaving in 1978; but remained connected with the show until 1981. Moving onto present *We're Going Places* (1978-80) and *Bullseye* (1979-81) brought him more fame as TV presenter. Presenting *Kick Start* (1981-88) and *Junior Kick Start* (1981-92) kept him busy for the best part of 10 years. His constant work as a TV presenter brought him 3 episodes of *Eastenders* (1987) his first proper acting job largely since 1967. During the mid-80s he formed his own company Purves Wickes Video Projects Ltd providing cooperate videos for clients such as BT, Whitbread, and Castrol. He briefly spent time teaching on the BBC's Presenters Course at Elstree from 1993, and London Academy of Radio Film and Television. Moving onto direct pantomime productions, he directed **Colin Baker** and the **Chuckle Brothers** amongst 30 productions.

In later life he moved to a Suffolk Farmhouse not before surviving a fall from his Tudor rectory in 1999 in Northampton. Reconnecting with *Doctor Who* over the years he has attended conventions, contributed to Big Finish audio dramas and has narrated releases of missing episodes. An autobiography *Here's One I Wrote Earlier…* was released to mark his 70th birthday.

Rex Tucker (1913-96): Born in Cambridgeshire in 1913, **Rex Tucker** was educated in Cambridge before working as a schoolmaster. He joined BBC Birmingham in 1937 as a writer/producer and worked on the radio show *Children's Hour*. Moving onto produce in the 1940s he specialised in children's material. In 1950 he was appointed, along with six others as producer to children's television, working largely as a writer/director and producer for many years. Directing duties came with *The Three Musketeers* (1954), *St Ives* (1955) and *Jane Eyre* (1963) whilst producing assignments came with *The Man in Armour* (1951), *The Silver Swan* (1952-53) and *The Mulberry Accelerator* (1955) plus others. The late 50s saw him write numerous TV Movies and TV series including *Triton* (1961), *The Massingham Affair* (1964) and an adaption of *Vanity Fair* (1967). In early 1963, Tucker was assigned as a director of *Doctor Who*, and was for a while the producer of the show until the arrival of **Verity Lambert**. The director was eventually recruited to work on the show with *The Gunfighters*. Future work within the TV industry included writing scripts for *Pegasus* (1968) and three separate entries for *Jackanory Playhouse* (1975/76/79) and a TV Movie in 1972. Directing work included *The Paradise Makers* (1967), *Point Counter Point* (1968), *Sinister Street* (1969), and an episode a piece for *Paul Temple* (1970) and *Z Cars* (1972). Rex Tucker died 10 August 1996 aged 83.

Richard Martin (1935-): Born in 1935, **Richard Martin** was originally an actor landing one-off roles in *Ivanhoe* (1958), *ITV Playhouse* (1960), *ITV Play of the Week* (1960) and *Maigret* (1961). Eventually progressing into directing, he helmed episodes of *Suspense* (1963), *Viewpoint* (1963) and 12 episodes of *Compact* (1964-65). During the early stage of developing *Doctor Who*, the director was formally invited by new-producer **Rex Tucker** to work on the show. A keen fan of science-fiction and fantasy, the director quickly accepted. Assigned to helm 3 out of 7 episodes of *The Daleks* (1964-65), the preceding serial *The Edge of Destruction*, *The Dalek Invasion of Earth*, *The Web Planet*, and *The Chase* during which he cast **Peter Purves** as the new companion Steve Taylor. After leaving the show, the director went onto have a successful career helming episodes of *The Newcomers* (1966), *Sir Arthur Conan Doyle* (1967), *A Family at War* (1971), *Six Days of Justice* (1973-75), *Television Club* (1978) and four episodes of *All Creatures Great and Small* (1990). Other television production roles included being a researcher for 2 episodes of *World in Action* (1969-71) and producing three episodes of the show. In later life, he and his wife taught acting lessons at Mountview drama school. According to a *Doctor Who Magazine* the director was living in France by 2007.

Richard Rodney Bennett (1936-2012): Born in Kent in 1936, **Richard Rodney Bennett** came from a family working in the entertainment business. His mother was a pianist and this father was an author, poet and lyricist. Studying at the Royal Academy of Music, he was exposed to the serialism movement when taking Darmstadt summer courses in 1955. He later spent two years studying music in Paris and studied under Pierre Boulez. Returning to his former alma mater he was a teacher between 1963 and 65 at the Peabody Institute in Baltimore, Maryland from 1970-71. Developing a wide range of musical talents, his main strengths and interests were in electronic music, writing for many styles, but mainly jazz. By the late 50s he was writing musical scores for films which would lead to a very successful career, works include *Face in the Night* (1957), *Heavens Above!* (1963), *Billion Dollar Brain* (1967), *Nicholas and Alexandra* (1971), *Murder on the Orient Express* (1974) and *Four Weddings and a Funeral* (1994). During his time as a film composer, he wrote over 200 works for concerts halls and was actively involved in writing music for Operas and Ballet. As a keen jazz musician he performed with various artists in the same genre including Cleo Laine, Marion Montgomery, Mary Cleere Haran and Claire Martin. Richard Rodney Bennett died on Christmas Eve in 2012 aged 76.

Ron Grainer (1922-81): Born in 1922 in Australia, **Ron Grainer** was actively involved playing music from the age of 2 when he began playing the piano. Eventually playing concerts within his local community by the age of 6, Grainer previously displayed great musical integrity at 4 years old playing the violin. Consider a child genius; he was a proficient performer on both the violin and piano by his teenage years. A clever student whilst at school, Maths was his special subject, which proved invaluable in later life whenever he was writing orchestrations. Future studies led him to the University of Queensland in 1939 where he studied civil engineering and music. The musician had previously studied under Sir Eugene Goosens at the Sydney Conservatorium before the outbreak of World War II.

Eventually returning to the Sydney Conservatorium, the musician would end up giving up violin to concentrate on composition instead. During his time he met his future wife, and together the couple moved to England. Finding work almost instantly, he toured with the 'The Alien Brothers & June'. The musician would later play at the London Palladium and would help out at charity events. Moving on to work with Charlie McGhee and Patrick O'Hagan the musician became fascinated by antique instruments he had begun to collect. Experimenting with his collection he began writing musical works with one of his early works being a jazz-ballet score. Moving on to become a musical advisor for Associated Rediffusion TV, he became a much sought out person within the BBC TV rehearsals room, with many doors beginning to open up for him.

Ron Grainer soon became a regular composer and musician for TV working on *The Men from Room* (1961), *It's a Square World* (1961-63), *Benny Hill* (1962-63), *Shelley* (1982-84) to name a few. It was during his work on *Maigret* (1963) which put him into direct contact with Warner Bros. and proved to be a career changing assignment. A popular theme tune composer, he provided theme music for *Steptoe and Son* (1964-74), *The Prisoner* (1967-68), *Man in a Suitcase* (1967-68), *Paul Temple* (1970-71), *For the Love of Ada* (1970-71), *Kim and Co.* (1975), and *Tales of the Unexpected* (1979-88) to name a few. Recruited to compose the theme music for new sci-fi television series *Doctor Who* in 1963, the theme music went on to become iconic. During this time he lived in Portugal with second wife, Jenny in order to improve his health. Grainer also provided the occasional film score with *Hoffman* (1970) and *The Omega Man* (1971) plus other big-budget and small-budget films throughout his career. Some of his works earned him awards nominations with 3 wins over the course of his career. Working continuously up until his death in 1981 from cancer, the composer died in Cuckfield Hospital in Sussex. The composer left quite a legacy; his works have been continually 'rediscovered' with special CD releases appearing on a regular basis.

Stanley Myers (1930-93): Born in 1930 in Birmingham, **Myers** studied at King's Edward's School in Edgbaston, a school within a Birmingham suburb. Beginning his musical career in early 50s, Myers went to have a successful music career working as a composer, conductor and writer for a wide range of TV shows and films. Composing the incidental music for *Doctor Who*'s *The Reign of Terror* (1964) was an early piece of work. Composer assignments came with 6 instalments of *The Wednesday Play* (1965-66), the film *Ulysses* (1967), 31 episodes of *All Gas and Gaiters* (1967-71), *Frightmare* (1974), *Absolution* (1978), *The Chain* (1984), *Track 29* (1988), *Voyager* (1991). Whilst not composing music, Myers would occasionally writer a song especially for TV and Film assignments throughout his career. He was conductor on *Road to Saint Tropez* (1966), *Sitting Target* (1972), *Road Movie* (1973), *Incubus* (1981), *Black Arrow* (1985), *Dreamchild* (1985), and *The Boost* (1988) plus many others. The musician worked regularly throughout his life until his death on November 9, 1993, aged 60. He won a BAFTA Award for Best Original Television Music for *Middlemarch* (1994) posthumously.

Terry Nation (1930-97): Born in 1930 in Llandaff **Terry Nation** began his love for entertainment by visiting his local Odeon cinema, often truanting from school. During wartime he spent much of his time, listening to radio, reading comics, and writing his own stories, whilst sheltering in his family's bunker. Whilst working in his Dad's furniture business, he began writing material for *Welsh Rarebit*, a Welsh Radio series. With dreams of becoming a stand-up comic, he moved to London with writing partner, **Dick Barry**. Friends advised him that his material was better than his act. Advised to approach **Spike Milligan**, who during this time was also running Associate London Scripts (ALS) in Shepherd's Bush led to the writer writing a sample goons script, which went unmade; Nation was kept on ALS's books, nonetheless. His first radio credit, co-written with Barry was for *All My Eye and Kitty Bluett* (1955). Barry moved to Australia in 1956, and Nation began a writing partnership with **John Junkin** with writing assignments lasting from 1957-1961. During this time, Nation wrote for the BBC with *The Ted Ray Show* (1957), *Hi, Summer!* (1959), and *The Jimmy Logan Show* (1959). First screenplay *What a Whopper* appeared in 1961. With very little interest in science-fiction, Nation provided three scripts for *Out of This World* adapting works by **Philip K. Dick** and **Clifford Simak**, along with an original episode of his own. Finding himself in the world of comedy, Nation wrote material for **Tony Hancock**, after the comedian sacked his previous writer. The working relationship didn't last, and Nation fell out with Hancock, after the latter didn't use the material Nation had written for him. Remembering an invitation to write for a new children's science-fiction show, the writer phoned script editor **David Whitaker** to see if the invitation was still available. It was during this time that **Nation** would go onto create *Doctor Who*'s most iconic enemies to date, The Daleks! The metal pepper pots were an instant success with children and adults alike. Nation was soon writing for *The Saint* and would continue to do so until 1968, and provided more material for *Story Parade* (1964), before writing his second *Doctor Who* serial **The Keys of Marinus**.

Nation was soon a very wealthy man, earning roughly £4.5M in today's money just with Dalek merchandise alone. The writer agreed to a 50/50 spilt on all royalties on Dalek merchandise. More Dalek narratives came with **The Dalek Invasion of Earth**, **The Chase**, **Mission to the Unknown** and **The Daleks' Master Plan** co-written by **Dennis Spooner**. Moving on to become script editor on *The Baron* (1966-67) and *The Avengers* (1968-69) – Nation would provide scripts and teleplays for episodes during his time as script editor. With big American dreams behind him, the writer hoped to turn *The Baron* into an American series whilst also finding a buyer to do the same with The Daleks. The dream never came to fruition resulting in Nation withdrawing rights from the BBC to use The Daleks. **The Evil of the Daleks** would be the final Dalek serial for 5 years. Whilst finding a potential buyer for a Dalek spin-off series, Nation wrote for *The Champions* (1968), *Department S* (1969) and *The Persuaders!* (1971-72) for which he was also a story consultant. Collaborations with **Brian Clemens** followed in 1970 and 1974. A pilot for the TV show *The Incredible Robert Baldick* came in 1972, but was never turned into a series. Finally allowing the Daleks to return in **Day of the Daleks**, he himself would pen ***Planet of the Daleks*** and ***Death to the Daleks***, with a third script being rejected by **Terrance Dicks** and **Barry Letts**. Instead Nation wrote ***Genesis of the Daleks*** exploring the creation of the Daleks on Skaro, and would go onto write ***The Android Invasion***.

Creating *Survivors* (1975), the writer left after completion of the first season, due to creative differences with producer **Terence Dudley**, since producers outranked writers, Nation quit. Going onto to create *Blake's 7* (1978-81), the writer was not involved with the final series, by then the writer was living in the States. Before the leaving the UK, Nation provided ***Destiny of the Daleks*** for *Doctor Who*, his last writing credit in the UK. Living in the States, wasn't exactly the American Dream for the writer, finding menial work with *MacGyver* (1985) and many unrealised projects under his belt. Nation died on 9th March 1997 aged 66.

Tristram Cary (1925-2008): Born in 1925 in Oxford, he was educated at the Dragon School in Oxford and later Westminster School in London. Whilst working as a radar engineer for the Royal Navy, he developed his own creations of electronic and tape music, and after World War II ended he created one of the very first electronic music scores which led him to travel around Europe where he meet early pioneers of electronic music and composition. His interests eventually led him to study a whole range of subjects at the University of Oxford: composition, conducting, piano, viola and horn. Soon after finishing his studies he, along with Peter Zinovieff and David Cockerell, founded Electronic Music Studios (London) Ltd where they created the first portable synthesiser the EMS VCS 3, and was involved in later products such as the EMS Synthi 100. Eventually creating electronic music for the Royal College of Music in 1967, led to him being invited by the University of Melbourne to join a lecture tour in 1973. The invitation led to him becoming Visiting Composer at the University of Adelaide in 1974 where he remained until 1986.

Film compositions included *The Lady Killers* (1955), *The Boy Who Stole a Million* (1960), *Quatermass and the Pit* (1967), *Blood from the Mummy's Tomb* (1971), and *The Fourth Wish* (1976). Heavily involved with *Doctor Who* in the early years he provided musical scores for **The Daleks**, **Marco Polo**, **The Rescue**, **The Daleks' Master Plan**, **The Ark**, **The Gunfighters**, and **The Power of the Daleks** before returning in 1972 to helm **The Mutants**. Cary also wrote for radio between 1959 and 64 and was heavily involved in theatre production between 1961 and 84. Tristram Cary died on 24 April 2008 aged 82 years.

Verity Lambert (1935-2007): Born in 1935, **Verity Lambert** attended a noted girls' school, leaving at 16 with 6 O-Levels. Against her father's wishes to attended University, she ultimately completed a six-month programme gaining a diploma in French Language and Culture at the University of Paris, before taking a secretarial course at St James College. Working at the Kensington de Vere Hotel and then in a lawyer's office, she eventually landed a job at Granada Television through her father, working as a secretary. Her first television work came with *Armchair Theatre* when she worked as a production assistant. Beforehand she was secretary to series producer **Dennis Vance**. Verity soon founded herself working as a PA to director **Ted Kotcheff**, whom she had a relationship with, which ended after Lambert found work with TV Producer **David Susskind**. Hoping to direct in 1962, she resumed her PA job at ABC studios worked on shows such as *The Avengers* which was created by **Sydney Newman**, a mentor to the soon-to-be producer. When Newman left ABC to become Head of Drama for the BBC, Lambert decided that if she didn't progress in the world of TV soon, she would leave and find work elsewhere.

After *Doctor Who* was created a producer was hard to come by, with many possible candidates turning down the job. Newman telephoned Lambert to offer her the job. Arriving at the BBC at 27 years old, Lambert was the youngest and first female producer to work with the drama department. Her main duties included the casting of **William Hartnell** and friend **Jacqueline Hill**. She soon found some resistance however when Sydney Newman and Head of Serial **Donald Wilson** criticised the Daleks, seeing them as the typical bug-eyed monster villains, which they strived to avoid. Standing her ground, the producer believed in The Daleks, and they soon became a cultural icon, she was given free reign from then on. Remaining with the show for just under two years, Lambert bowed out with **Mission to the Unknown**. Her time on the show saw some incredible viewing figures, some of which reached into the 12 and 13 million mark.

Moving onto produce *199 Park Lane* (1965), she quickly left the project and moved onto *The Newcomers* (1965), *Adam Adamant Lives!* (1966-67) and *Detective* (1968). Producing for *W. Somerset Maugham* (1969-70) won her a proto-BAFTA Award. However, the BBC refused to renew her contract; she left and was soon sought out by ITV franchise LWT. The producer oversaw *Budgie* (1971-72), *Between the Wars* (1974), before returning to the BBC to handle *Shoulder to Shoulder* (1974).

July of 1974, saw her first major change of career, becoming Controller of Drama for Thames' Television where she greenlit many productions one of which was *Couples* (1975-76) acting as an executive producer on the show as well. She later became an executive producer for Euston Films in 1976, projects included *The Sweeney*. She left her Thames Television post in 1979 to become Euston Chief Executive. Her debut for Euston was *The Sailor's Return* made in 1977, which eventually aired in 1980. She worked on another big hit *Minder* (1979-84) again as an executive producer. A revival of *Quatermass and the Pit* appeared in 1979 with film releases including *The Knowledge* (1979). She later returned to Thames Television in 1982 as director of drama, before becoming director of production at Thames' Television Elstree Movie Studio. Finding the British Film Industry 'hard going' less than desirable projects included *Morons from Outer Space* (1985).

Eventually creating independent production company Cinema Verity in the mid-80s, releases included *A Cry in the Dark* (1988) which starred Oscar-nominated **Meryl Streep**. Her company produced TV shows in the early and mid-90s with *Coasting* (1990) and *So Haunt Me* (1992-94). Producing *GBH* (1991) lost a BAFTA award for Best Drama to *Prime Suspect*. Her company's first and MAJOR failure came with soap opera *Eldorado* (1992-93) which failed to grip audience and critics alike; shoddy camerawork, boring plotlines, pan-European casting were amongst the many factors which led to the show's endgame. Her company picked up however with other TV projects which included *A Perfect State* (1997) but her company closed shortly afterwards whilst developing another project. Going onto produce *Jonathan Creek* (1998-2004) and *Love Soup* (2005-08) were her last pieces of work before dying on November 22, 2007, hours before *Doctor Who*'s 44th birthday. Due to receive a Lifetime Achievement Award for Women in Television and Film by new *Doctor Who* executive producer/head writer **Russell T Davies,** her award was awarded in her name posthumously. A memorial message was added to the *Doctor Who* Christmas day special ***Voyage of the Damned*** which aired a little over a month later.

Waris Hussein (1938-): Born in 1938 in British India (or India now), Hussein moved to the UK with his family at the age of 7, where he eventually attended Clifton College before studying English Literature at Queen's College, Cambridge. During his time as a student he directed several plays. Upon graduating he joined the BBC with the intent of directing, it was during this time that the director changed his original surname Habibullah to Hussein. Directing single episodes of *Suspense, Moonstrike* and *BBC Sunday-Night Play* in 1963, the director handled 10 episodes of *Compact* between 1962 and 63. Hussein was quickly hired to oversee the first episodes of new Saturday Tea-Time Sci-Fi show *Doctor Who*. Directing the pilot episode in late 1963 was less than impressive in the eyes of **Sydney Newman** who requested a remount of the entire episode. The director completed *An Unearthly Child* (1963) before returning to oversee *Marco Polo* a few months later. The director never returned to work on the show; but was **John Nathan-Turner**'s first choice when looking for someone to helm **The Five Doctors**.

After his two stints on *Doctor Who* regular directing work came with *The Indian Tales of Rudyard Kipling* (1964), 6 editions of *BBC Play of the Month* (1965-75), and 9 episodes of *The Wednesday Play* (1966-68). Successfully breaking into movie directing Hussein handled *Melody* (1971) and *Henry VIII and His Six Wives* (1972). The mid-seventies saw the director working on episodes of *Notorious Woman* (1974), *The Glittering Prizes* (1976) and *Edward & Mrs. Simpson* (1978). Moving onto directing TV Movies, Hussein directed *Death Penalty* (1980), *Surviving* (1985), *Copacabana* (1985), *When the Bough Breaks* (1986), *The Shell Seekers* (1989), *Fall from Grace* (1994), and *A Fight for Justice* (1997) to name a few. During his directing career; Hussein has worked with Laurence Olivier, Bette Davis and Joan Plowright, with many collaborations with **Verity Lambert** over the years.

William Hartnell (1908-75): Born in 1908, various sources give conflicting information with regards to the actor's early life and childhood. The actor never knew his father and was brought up by another family, whilst his mother worked in Belgium. The actor fell into minor offences during his early years, and earned money performing various tasks, one of which saw him run errands for a crooked bookie. He spent his money on watching **Charlie Chaplin** movies. Eventually living with his mother, Hartnell found a father figure when his mother began going out with a policeman. At 13 he took up boxing under the mentorship of **Hugh Blaker** who also introduced him to Shakespeare and Poetry. A would be jockey for a while, Hartnell worked at a stable in Epsom, but was eventually too tall to race despite holding a jockey license.

Eventually going to the Italia Conti Stage School in 1924, the actor then went to Imperial Service College, a military school in Windsor, but soon left after finding it too strict. Eventually joining Sir Frank Benson's Shakespearean stage company, Hartnell worked as an assistant manager, moving on to walk-on roles, and then speaking roles. Finding work with other rep theatre companies, larger parts came the actor's way. Whilst touring in Canada for over year, he met his future wife **Heather McIntyre**. Finding work in West End Theatre, Hartnell also found work as an extra in movies, before landing non-speaking roles in *School for Scandal* (1930), *Man of Mayfair* (1931) and *Diamond Cut Diamond* (1932). Speaking roles came with *Say it With Music* (1932) and *The Night in London* (1933). Going onto to win leading roles in movies between 1933 and 35, movies included *The Perfect Flaw* (1934), and *Swinging the Lead* (1935). Moving on to work at the Richmond Theatre Rep, he and his wife Heather often played husband/wife roles in various productions between 1934 and 35. A musical assignment came with CB Cochran's London theatre in 1937, understudying Bud Flanagan. More movie roles came with *They Drive by Night* (1938) and *Murder Will Out* (1939).

With the outbreak of WW2, Hartnell joined the 22nd Dragoon in October 1940, but was discharged in July 1941 after a nervous breakdown. Ironically Hartnell would go on to land many strong military man roles in future assignments over the subsequent years. Film roles were common place between 1942 and 1943 appearing in *Sabotage at Sea* (1942), *The Bells Go Down* (1943), and *The Dark Place* (1943). The actor went on to be placed under contract by British National, with film roles in *Strawberry Roan* (1945), *Murder in Reverse* (1946), and *Appointment with Crime* (1946). A fan club *William Hartnell Bulletin* was established in 1947, and he was often referred to as 'the British Jimmy Cagney.' By 1950, the actor had grown tired of playing 'tough guys' after winning roles as a police superintendent in Escape (1948), an army sergeant in The Lost People (1949), a gangster in *Double Confession* (1950), plus others. Working at the Apollo Theatre between 1950-54, Hartnell appeared in *Seagulls Over Sorrento* playing another serviceman. Another police inspector role came with *Will Any Gentleman....?* (1953) which co-starred future Doctor Who actor **Jon Pertwee**. Constantly employed between 1955 and 57, the actor continued to play roles he had come to grow tired of with *Yangtse Incident* (1957), *Hell Drivers* (1957), *Jackpot* (1960). Comedy films during this time came with *Tons of Trouble* (1956), and *The Mouse That Roared!* (1959). Appearing in *The Army Game* between 1957 and 1961 as Sgt Major Bullimore boosted his fame even more with British Audiences and also landed him a role in *Carry on Sergeant* (1958).

In 1959, he and his wife moved to a seventeenth-century Old Mill Cottage, where Hartnell hoped to find other roles that did not have him playing a tough guy. With television growing into a big medium, the actor landed roles in various TV series, often one-off roles; his debut appearance saw him play a guide-dog trainer. More film roles came in 1963, on the cusp of his biggest role yet.

With *Doctor Who* now established at the BBC, producer **Verity Lambert** sought out an old actor to play the eccentric lead-role. Eventually coming to William Hartnell after the suggestions of **Leslie French** and **Cyril Cusack**, among others were dropped, the actor was phoned by his son-in-law and theatrical agent with the offered role. Reserved at first to take the part, the actor was persuaded by the producer and **Waris Hussein**. After a rough pilot episode, where Hartnell's performance was criticised by **Sydney Newman**, Hartnell was soon a hero for millions of children in the UK every Saturday evening. After a while the actor wished to insert more comedy into The Doctor and the show, his wishes were granted with **The Romans**, **The Myth Makers**, and **The Gunfighters**. Getting on remarkably well with Verity Lambert, the actor was never the same after her departure in 1965, and the departures of **Carole Ann Ford, William Russell,** and **Jacquline Hill** were also a big blow for the actor, and he didn't hit-it-off with her replacement **John Wiles**. The actor was growing displeased with the increasing levels of violence and horror within the show, and wished for the show to return to whimsical storytelling for young children. The actor eventually pitched his own idea for a serial, involving The Doctor meeting his evil-son, who would also be a doppelgänger to The Doctor. This element was eventually utilised for **The Massacre of St. Bartholomew Eve**. In December 1965, he told the press that he might be leaving the series, but later withdrew his statements, commenting he hoped the show could last five years with him as the star. *The Celestial Toymaker* was originally a device to replace Hartnell with another actor but these plans were cancelled. In 1966, the actor was growing tired of the series; he hated remembering long lines, and asked for a tone back from script editor **Donald Tosh**. When **Innes Lloyd** took over as producer, Lloyd quickly realised that a change of leading actor was paramount considering the actor's continued failing health. The casting of **Anneke Wills** and **Michael Craze** widen the age gap between The Doctor and his companions even further, the actor did not strike a chord with them, and on 16 July 1966, after being called into a meeting, Hartnell decided that his time on the show would be coming to an end. He apparently approved of **Patrick Troughton** as his successor, saying that's he the only man who can do the job. After a summer break he recorded his swansong **The Tenth Planet**, but fell ill during production, meaning The Doctor was written out of the action in episode three. A farewell party was held at Innes Lloyd's flat, which was an emotion affair for Hartnell.

Moving onto appear in *Puss in Boots* over Christmas 1966/67, the actor's final stage appearance came at The Bristol Old Vic in 1968. Hartnell found some minor parts in TV between 1968 and 70, but nothing major. Returning to *Doctor Who* for the 10th Anniversary Special **The Three Doctors**, the actor was forced to read his lines from hidden cue cards due to his failing memory loss, and didn't interact first hand with **Patrick Troughton** or **Jon Pertwee**. They did however pose for publicity shots to promote the anniversary special. By 1972, he and his wife Heather were forced to move in with his daughter in Kent after dwindling funds. Going into hospital in December 1974, the actor died on 23 April 1975 aged just 67. For **The Five Doctors**, the part of the First Doctor was filled in by **Richard Hurndall** and in recent years has been played by **David Bradley**, who also played Hartnell in *An Adventure in Space and Time* (2013) to mark the show's 50th Anniversary. His autobiography appeared in 1996 written by his granddaughter.

William Russell (1924-): Born on 19 November 1924, it was whilst listening to *Children's Hour* in his youth that encouraged Russell to pursue an interest in acting which he eventually did whilst attending Wolverhampton Grammar School. Wartime duties were completed in conjunction with studies at Fettes College, Edinburgh and Trinity College, Oxford University. For a while, Russell was a RAF Flight Lieutenant before completing his English Degree. During his time as a student he was involved with the Oxford University Amateur Dramatic Society and the Experimental Theatre Club. After graduating he worked as an assistant stage manager at Tunbridge Wells, Kent before moving on to gain small acting parts

Theatre work came with the Playhouse in Oxford, and Bristol Old Vic playing Mercutio in *Romeo and Juliet* and Antipholus in *The Comedy of Errors* respectively. Film roles came with *Glory at Sea* (1952), *They Who Dare* (1954), *Above Us the Waves* (1955), and *The Man Who Never Was* (1956). Eventually changing his name from William Enoch to William Russell, at the suggestion of producers whilst making *One Good Turn*, the actor was soon taking leading roles in TV. Lead parts came with *St. Ives* (1955), *The Adventures of Sir Lancelot* (1956-67) and *Nicolas Nickleby* (1957). In 1961, the actor was touring across Europe appearing in *St Joan, Macbeth* and *The Importance of Being Ernest*. A major film breakthrough came with *The Great Escape* (1963) appearing alongside **Steve McQueen**. TV work in 1963, was a busy year for the actor, with included a lead role in *The Patch Card*.

The actor was quickly cast as Ian Chesterton in a new sci-fi show *Doctor Who*. Interim producer **Rex Tucker** had been drawing up a list of possible candidates, and both he and Russell had a long-standing relationship, working on many productions before *Doctor Who*. Although the actor never envisioned the series to last as long as it did, he had a 'happy time' whilst on the show. After nearly two years working week after week on the show, the actor's enthusiasm for the show was waning, and commented he wished to return to the theatre. His decision to leave the show wasn't taken lightly by **William Hartnell** and together with **Jacqueline Hill**, left the show with **The Chase**.

After leaving *Doctor Who*, the actor appeared in *Separate Tables* at the Grand Theatre, Leeds which met with full houses. Landing one-off TV roles between 1966 and 69 kept the actor busy, as well as appearing with the Welsh Theatre Company with leading roles in *The Rose Affair, Rookery Nook, Rattle of a Simple Man,* and *The Prisoner*. The actor went on to appear with the Theatre Royal Windsor, Leicester Phoenix Theatre and Regent's Park. Appearing with RSC resulted in landing roles in *King John, Measure for Measure, Richard III* and *The Tempest*. A lengthy TV role came with *Harriet's Back in Town* and a small speaking role in *Superman: The Movie* (1978) as a Krypton elder.

Continuing to appear in the theatre over the 1980s resulted in the actor missing out on reprising his role as Ian Chesterton in two *Doctor Who* serials **Mawdryn Undead** and **The Five Doctors** a few months later. The mid-80s saw the actor take more TV parts and RSC touring productions. Landing the role as Ted Sullivan in *Coronation Street* (1992), the actor appeared in 46 episodes. More stage work came at London's Globe Theatre from 1996-98. TV work between the late 90s and 2000s, often one off roles in popular shows, kept the actor busy. William Russell has been reprising his role as Ian Chesterton since 2009 with Big Finish Productions. For the 50th anniversary special *An Adventure in Space and Time* (2013), Russell was played by actor Jamie Glover. The actor himself did appear in the special however, as a BBC commissionaire towards the beginning of the special.

Russell's son Alfred Enoch is also an actor, and is best known for playing Dean Thomas in the *Harry Potter* franchise.

TARDIS DATA LOGS: 1963-66

AN UNEARTHLY CHILD

- **Date:** late autumn-1963 (possibly a Tuesday in October); c.100,000BC
- **Location:** London inc. Coal Hill School and Foreman Junkyard; unknown location on Earth
- **Main Enemy:** Kal

THE DALEKS

- **Date:** an unknown date in either the past or future (possibly sometime in the 21st Century)
- **Location:** Skaro
- **Main Enemy:** Daleks
- **Other Enemy:** The Lake of Mutations Creature

THE EDGE OF DESTRUCTION

- **Date:** unknown (possibly somewhere where time and space do not exist)
- **Location:** Inside the Tardis
- **Main Enemy:** no enemy

MARCO POLO

- **Date:** 1289
- **Location:** Various locations across Asia, Earth
- **Main Enemy:** Tegana

THE KEYS OF MARINUS

- **Date:** an unknown date, possibly around c5000000BC
- **Location:** Marinus (various locations)
- **Main Enemy:** Yartek
- **Other Enemies:** Voords, Morpho, Vasor, Ice Soldiers, Kala, Aydan

THE AZTECS

- **Date:** c.1430 (sometime in the 15th Century), or 1507
- **Location:** Mexico
- **Main Enemy:** Tlotoxl

THE SENSORITES

- **Date:** 28th Century
- **Location:** Maitland's Ship in Orbit above Sense-Sphere; Sense-Sphere
- **Main Enemy:** City Administrator

THE REIGN OF TERROR

- **Date:** 24-27 July 1794
- **Location:** France, Earth (various location inc. Paris)
- **Main Enemy:** Maximilien Robespierre

PLANET OF GIANTS

- **Date:** 1964 (possibly 'Present Day' or 'Near Future'
- **Location:** England (somewhere along the South Coast)
- **Main Enemy:** Forester

THE DALEK INVASION OF EARTH

- **Date:** c.2167
- **Location:** London (surrounding area and Bedfordshire)
- **Main Enemy:** Daleks (inc. the Supreme Controller)
- **Other Enemies:** Robomen, Slyther, Woman in the Woods

THE RESCUE

- **Date:** c.2493
- **Location:** Dido
- **Main Enemy:** Bennett

THE ROMANS

- **Date:** Summer 64AD
- **Location:** Assisium (Villa, Marketplace, Walkways etc.); Rome
- **Main Enemy:** Emperor Nero

THE WEB PLANET

- **Date:** an unknown date in the distant future c.20,000AD (or roundabout)
- **Location:** Vortis
- **Main Enemy:** The Animus

THE CRUSADE

- **Date:** c.1191AD Autumn (sometime between Second and Third Crusade)
- **Location:** Palestine (Jaffa, Ramlah, Lydda)
- **Main Enemy:** El Akir

THE SPACE MUSEUM

- **Date:** unknown (far future)
- **Location:** Xeros
- **Main Enemy:** Lobos

THE CHASE

- **Date:** unknown date; 1966; 1872; 1996; future (c.22nd or 23rd Century); 1965
- **Location:** Aridius; New York, Earth; *Mary Celeste*; Ghana, Earth; Mechanus; London, Earth
- **Main Enemy:** Daleks
- **Other Enemies:** Mire Beasts, Fungoids, Mechonoids

THE TIME MEDDLER

- **Date:** Summer 1066
- **Location:** North of England (presumably Northumbria)
- **Main Enemy:** The Meddling Monk

GALAXY 4

- **Date:** unknown date
- **Location:** an unnamed planet in Galaxy 4
- **Main Enemy:** Maaga

MISSION TO THE UNKNOWN

- **Date:** 4000
- **Location:** Kembel
- **Main Enemy:** Daleks

- **Other Enemies:** Varga Plants, the Planetarians

THE MYTH MAKERS

- **Date:** c.1184BC
- **Location:** Ancient Greece (Troy and Surrounding Area)
- **Main Enemy:** Odysseus

THE DALEKS' MASTER PLAN

- **Date:** 4000AD; 1965-66; c.1927; c.2600BC (a time of the Great Pyramids)
- **Location:** Kembel; Earth (Hollywood and Ancient Egypt); Desperus; Mira; Tigus
- **Main Enemy:** Daleks (inc. Black Dalek Leader), Mavic Chen

THE MASSACRE OF ST BARTHOLOMEW'S EVE

- **Date:** 20-24 August 1572; c.1966
- **Location:** Paris, France; Earth (somewhere outside of London)
- **Main Enemy:** Catherine de Medici

THE ARK

- **Date:** Far Future (possibly c.10,000,000AD and c.10,000,700AD)
- **Location:** The Ark; Refusis II
- **Main Enemy:** Monoids

THE CELESTIAL TOYMAKER

- **Date:** No Time
- **Location:** The Domain of the Celestial Toymaker
- **Main Enemy:** The Celestial Toymaker
- **Other Enemies:** Everyone under The Celestial Toymaker's Control

THE GUNFIGHTERS

- **Date:** 24-26 October 1881
- **Location:** Tombstone, Arizona, Earth
- **Main Enemy:** The Clanton Brothers

THE SAVAGES

- **Date:** unknown date in the far, distant future
- **Location:** an unnamed planet of the Savages
- **Main Enemy:** Captain Edal

THE WAR MACHINES

- **Date:** 12-20 July 1966
- **Location:** London (various locations)
- **Main Enemy:** WOTAN

THE SMUGGLERS

- **Date:** c.1666AD (sometimes in the mid to latter half of the Seventeenth Century)
- **Location:** Cornwall, England, Earth
- **Main Enemy:** Samuel Pike

THE TENTH PLANET

- **Date:** December 1986
- **Location:** Snowcap Base in Antarctica (various locations around the Earth including Geneva)
- **Main Enemy:** Cybermen

THE COST OF DOCTOR WHO: 1963-66

	1	2	3	4	5	6	7	8	9	10	11	12
AN UNEARTHLY CHILD	2746	4307	2181	2316	-	-	-	-	-	-	-	-
THE DALEKS	2817	2796	2232	2641	2223	1919	2634	-	-	-	-	-
THE EDGE OF DESTRUCTION	1480	1506	-	-	-	-	-	-	-	-	-	-
MARCO POLO	2687	1618	1958	2317	2821	u/n	u/n	-	-	-	-	-
THE KEYS OF MARINUS	u/n	u/n	u/n	u/n	u/n	u/n	-	-	-	-	-	-
THE AZTECS	u/n	u/n	u/n	u/n	-	-	-	-	-	-	-	-
THE SENSORITES	u/n	u/n	u/n	u/n	u/n	u/n	-	-	-	-	-	-
THE REIGN OF TERROR	u/n	u/n	u/n	u/n	u/n	u/n	-	-	-	-	-	-
PLANET OF GIANTS	u/n	u/n	u/n	u/n	-	-	-	-	-	-	-	-
THE DALEK INVASION OF EARTH	u/n	u/n	u/n	u/n	u/n	u/n	-	-	-	-	-	-
THE RESCUE	u/n	u/n	-	-	-	-	-	-	-	-	-	-
THE ROMANS	u/n	u/n	2383	2221	-	-	-	-	-	-	-	-
THE WEB PLANET	3033	2428	2196	2850	2676	3342	-	-	-	-	-	-
THE CRUSADE	3515	2300	2150	2065	-	-	-	-	-	-	-	-
THE SPACE MUSEUM	2643	2394	2028	1636	-	-	-	-	-	-	-	-
THE CHASE	6083	2441	2614	2658	2529	2285	-	-	-	-	-	-
THE TIME MEDDLER	1949	1803	1677	1728	-	-	-	-	-	-	-	-
GALAXY 4	3100	2904	2293	2463	-	-	-	-	-	-	-	-
MISSION TO THE UNKNOWN	2440	-	-	-	-	-	-	-	-	-	-	-
THE MYTH MAKERS	3327	2566	2230	2091	-	-	-	-	-	-	-	-
THE DALEKS' MASTER PLAN	5318	4031	2268	2448	2194	1914	2562	2265	2398	2391	1919	1888
THE MASSACRE OF ST BARTHOLOMEW'S EVE	3576	2041	2632	2019	-	-	-	-	-	-	-	-
THE ARK	5678	1945	1939	1597	-	-	-	-	-	-	-	-
THE CELESTIAL TOYMAKER	3686	2535	1716	1449	-	-	-	-	-	-	-	-
THE GUNFIGHTERS	4065	2142	2196	2012	-	-	-	-	-	-	-	-
THE SAVAGES	4542	2806	2252	1931	-	-	-	-	-	-	-	-
THE WAR MACHINES	5098	2355	2069	2090	-	-	-	-	-	-	-	-
THE SMUGGLERS	4261	2299	1552	2369	-	-	-	-	-	-	-	-
THE TENTH PLANET	4835	2355	2171	2453	-	-	-	-	-	-	-	-

FURTHER DETAILS

- The pilot version of "An Unearthly Child" cost a total of £2143, the figure displayed was the cost of the remount recorded on Friday 18 October 1963. The actual cost of the first recording of "The Dead Planet" remains unknown, the figure displayed was the cost of the remount on Friday 6 December 1963.
- Any fees paid to writers who submitted storylines that were later rejected have not been included, since these details are hard to come by. Sometimes a writer was paid-off (seen as a 'sorry but thanks anyway') gesture for submitting a storyline that wasn't used. In these cases writers were actually paid for their time for writing the scripts that were unused. These fees were usually negotiated between producer and writer(s).
- The cost of the episodes excludes the use of the Tardis console room and any other Tardis room (corridor, living quarters etc.) has been excluded since the Tardis room only had to be constructed once. The ship itself cost roughly £4328 pounds.
- Details about actor's wages (regulars and guest actors) have not been included in a subsection since these are hard to come by and keep track of. Since regular actors often ask for pay rises after every season, they have not been included.

All figures displayed are a rough estimate and have been compiled from secondary sources. Exact break downs (location-shoots, model shots, pre-filming sequences etc) have not been complied due to a lack of information.

THE MISSING EPISODES: 1963-66

4) *Marco Polo* – all episodes missing from the BBC archives, sound recordings exist. A special LP release appeared in 2021, using off-air recordings to reconstruct the episodes.

8) *The Reign of Terror* – episodes four and five missing from the BBC Archives. Using off-air sound recordings, episodes four and five were entirely animated for the DVD release in 2013.

14) *The Crusade* – episodes two and four are missing from the BBC Archives. Episodes one and three were released on the DVD release *Lost in Time*. Episodes two and four were also released but as sound recordings. The scripts for the serial were released with additional background information about the production process in the 1990s.

17) *The Time Meddler* – 12 seconds from episode four no longer exist. The DVD release in 2008 included the surviving episodes, and came with a special feature which put the missing seconds into context.

18) *Galaxy 4* – for a while three of the four episodes were missing from the BBC Archives shortly after the original broadcast. Episode three was the only known surviving episode, some minor brief footage from episode one also survived. Episodes 1, 2, and 4 were all animated for the DVD release in 2021. Episode three was also animated, and the original remastered episode was included as well. A special LP release appeared before the DVD came out, using off-air recordings to reconstruct the missing episodes. The scripts for the serials were released during the 1990s with additional background information on the production process.

19) *Mission to the Unknown* – the single episode is entirely missing from the BBC archives. No known footage is known to exist. The serial was remade by students at the University of Central Lancashire in 2019 and premiered on the Doctor Who YouTube Channel at 5:45pm on October 9th. A special behind-the-scenes feature was released in conjunction with the remade episode.

20) *The Myth Makers* – All episodes no longer exist. An LP release of the serial was released in 2021 which included soundtracks of all four episodes. Off-air film clips from all 4 episodes were released on *Lost in Time*, surviving clips include model shots of the Wooden Horse being pushed by soldiers.

21) *The Daleks' Master Plan* – of the 12 episodes in this epic adventure, only three are known to survive in their entirety (episode 2, 5, and 10). The three surviving episodes were released on the *Lost in Time* DVD boxset, along with some brief footage from other episodes which is known to have survived. An LP release appeared in 2020, using off-air sound recordings, the missing 9 episodes were reconstructed for the release.

22) *The Massacre of St Bartholomew's Eve* – All episodes no longer exist, but the sound recordings are known to have survived. A special 2 LP release of the serial appeared in 2020 using off-air sound recordings to recreate the four-part historical serial. In a 2019 interview it transpired that an animated version of the serial was not likely due to the amount of money and resources it would take to replicate the characters and costumes.

24) *The Celestial Toymaker* – episodes 1-3 no longer exist. Episode 4 does in its entirety and was released as a part of the *Lost in Time* bookset. The surviving episode had previously been included in VHS release, although the quality of the episode was poor, the episode was enhanced for the DVD release.

26) *The Savages* – all episodes missing from the BBC archives. Some off-air film recordings were included on the *Lost in Time* DVD boxset that were apparently from episode 4 (actually material from episodes 3 and 4).

28) *The Smugglers* – all episodes are missing from the BBC archives. Some brief footage was released as part of the *Lost in Time* bookset.

29) *The Tenth Planet* – episode 4 no longer exists. Episodes 1-3 do exist and were released on the VHS release, with a complete reconstructed episode 4 put together from stills and the sound recordings. Episode four was believed to have been discovered sometime in the 1990s, but this turned out to be a hoax headline. Episode four was animated for the DVD release in 2013 with the surviving episodes. Some surviving footage from episode four was released on the *Lost in Time* DVD bookset.

THE UNMADE EPISODES: 1963-66

'American Civil War storyline': no scripts or story ideas were submitted for the proposal. **David Whitaker** drew up a possible timeline about how the second season of *Doctor Who* could be set up. The American Civil War was proposed for Serial G and six-parts long. No further advancements were taken forward for the storyline.

'Britain 408AD': a storyline written by **Malcolm Hulke**; the story would have centred round the departure of the Romans from Britain at the beginning of the Fifth Century. The story would have featured clashes with the Celts and the Saxons and ending with the time travellers fleeing to the safety of the Tardis. Ultimately it was felt that the story was too complicated, the ending mirrored that of *An Unearthly Child*, and another historical serial in the first season was not required. Hulke rewrote the story (presumably replacing Susan with Vicki) and resubmitted it for consideration. However with the production of *The Romans*, script editor **Dennis Spooner** also rejected the idea.

'Egyptian storyline': an idea suggested by **David Whitaker** for the second series of *Doctor Who*. Had the idea been taken forward it was envisioned the serial would be 4-parts long and appear third in the broadcast run.

'Farewell Great Macedon': written by **Moris Farhi**, the story was commissioned by script editor **David Whitaker** and was intended to feature sixth in the first season of the show. The time travellers would have encountered Alexander the Great in Babylon. Work on the serial was put on hold, and eventually abandoned when the writer felt script editor David Whitaker was asking for too many rewrites which would compromise the historical accuracies of the scripts.

'Future Setting storyline': a story idea suggested to appear in the second series of *Doctor Who*. The serial would have been written by **Tony Coburn** and last six episodes. The idea was merely a suggestion and nothing was taken forward.

'Future Setting storyline': a story idea suggested to appear in the second series. The serial would have been penned by **Malcolm Hulke** and last six episodes. The idea was merely a suggestion and nothing was taken forward.

'Future Setting storylines': ideas for serials D, H, and J to feature in the second series. Serials D and J would have been six episodes long, and Serial H would have been four episodes. No directors or writers were suggested to handle the serials, and they were subsequently suggestions for future adventures.

'Gunpowder Plot': a story which would have probably featured on the failed Gunpowder plot by Guy Fawkes to blow up parliament. The idea would no doubt have been a historical-based narrative to educate the children, keeping in line with **Sydney Newman**'s vision for the show. A detailed summary of the plot is unknown to this day.

'Livingston': a story idea under consideration, nothing much is known about it. It's possible the main character of the serial would have been David Livingston, and would have been a historical narrative.

'Nothing at the End of the Lane': a story which would have featured The Doctor and his companions being shrunk down in size in the Tardis. **Sydney Newman** liked the idea of the time travellers being reduced in size, left to face a world full of dangers. The idea was continually picked-up and dropped, and eventually cancelled.

'Salem Witch storyline': a story idea which would have probably centred on the Salem Witch trials in seventeenth- century Massachusetts. The idea probably would have been a historical based narrative keeping in line with **Sydney Newman**'s vision for the show that *Doctor Who* should also educate children. No documented paperwork can provide any more details as to who would have written and directed the adventure.

'Sideways storyline': a story idea suggested to appear in the second series of *Doctor Who*. The serial would have been four episodes long. No writers or directors were suggested to handle the serial, the idea was merely a suggestion and nothing further was taken forward.

'The Clock': a story written by **David Ellis** around January 1966. The story would have featured The First Doctor, Ben, and Polly battling a 'sinister mechanism' who had the ability to control and manipulate time with a clock. The idea was later rejected on 4 April 1966 by script editor **Gerry Davis**.

'The Dark Planet': a storyline submitted by **Brian Hayles.** The Tardis would have landed on a planet where the adult population turned into savage beasts during the night. The children living on the planet would be immune to effects. The Tardis crew would have allied with a group of young warriors to defend their village. The storyline wasn't used, as script editor **Dennis Spooner** felt the storyline would be a bad influence on children.

'The Evil Eye': a storyline submitted to the production office in 1966. Formerly rejected by script editor **Gerry Davis** on Monday 4 April 1966, the serial was proposed by **Geoffrey Orme**.

'The Face of God': an idea submitted by former producer **John Wiles** possibly after his departure from the show to pursue his director/writing career. No details are known about the serial.

'The Fragile Yellow Arc of Fragrance': written by **Moris Farhi**. The story was a single spec-script written by Farhi after receiving encouraging comments from **David Whitaker** who read Farhi's early work and encouraged him to continue to write. The storyline was rejected by the script editor on 24 January 1964.

'The Giants': The serial would have focused on the show's four main characters being shrunk down in size in Cliff's (Ian Chesterton's original name) laboratory. The serial in question would have appeared early in the show's run, possibly the first serial. However, late into the writing process, the serial was deemed unusable and was scrapped. **Sydney Newman** did like the 'monsters' that were to appear in the show (giant spiders) deeming them to be similar to the BEMs (bug-eyed monsters) he strived to avoid using in the show.

'The Great Gamble': a storyline written presumably by **Oliver Skene**. The Tardis would have landed on a Mississippi showboat only to be stolen by gamblers, believing the ship to be of value. The Doctor would gamble the lives of his companions to win the Tardis back. The storyline was rejected mainly due to the ethics (gun violence) of the storyline, although the setting of the serial was something admirable.

'The Hands of Aten': a storyline written by **Brian Hayles**. The episodes were commissioned to appear in the series run, but eventually rejected when **Innes Lloyd** and **Gerry Davis** deemed them unusable when they took over as producer and script editor of the series respectively.

'The Herdsmen of Aquarius': also known as 'The Herdsmen of Venus', nothing much is known about the story but it would have involved the use of the Loch Ness Monster. The story would have been written by **Donald Cotton** and was considered to appear in the show's run in autumn 1966.

'The Hearsay Machine': an idea written by **George F. Kerr** and under consideration around April 1966. The idea was eventually rejected by **Gerry Davis**. Little details are known about the plot.

'The Heavy Scent of Violence': an idea written by **George F. Kerr**. The idea was also submitted to the production office around April 1966, and rejected by **Gerry Davis** a few weeks later. Little details are known about the plot.

'The Hidden Planet': a story written by **Malcom Hulke** was considered to appear in the show's run twice; the fifth serial of season 1, and later the second in season 2. The story would have centred round a twin planet to Earth, dominated largely by women. The departure of Susan Foreman in *The Dalek Invasion of Earth* meant the serial had to be rewritten, and again when Ian and Barbara departed in *The Chase*. As such the serial was eventually abandoned.

'The Hounds of Time': a story written by **Brian Hayles**. The storyline was submitted to the production office around the time the writer had completed *The Smugglers*. It's possible that the story would have required The Second Doctor (a possible regeneration story?). The story was about a mad scientist who would be responsible for kidnapping humans from various time zones in Earth's history. The scientist would actually be working for an alien warlord who planned to invade Earth by determining when the planet would be at its weakest.

'The Jokers': an early storyline considered to feature in the show's run. Ian and Barbara would find themselves in 1943, but a different version of the year from what they know. Laughter has been outlawed, but the schoolteachers find themselves allying with a group of rebels to keep laughter alive.

'The Living World': an early story idea to feature in the show's run, but was eventually dropped.

'The Man from the Met': a third story idea submitted by **George Kerr** in April 1966. The story line was also rejected by **Gerry Davis**. Few details give any indication what the story would have been about.

'The Man in the Ice': written by **Brian Hayles** would have featured a Stone Age man encased in ice, and still alive. The antagonist of the serial would have been 'business moguls' who believe that the Stone Age man's genes would make them immortal. The story would have concluded with The Doctor returning the Stone Age Man to his own time.

'The Masters of Luxor': a story written by **Anthony Coburn** was an early storyline considered by the production office to follow *An Unearthly Child*. The reasons for the withdrawal of the serial are a little vague; however it is believed that the storyline had many religious overtones which were thought to be unsubtle. As such the story was abandoned, and *The Daleks* was commissioned instead. 'The Masters of Luxor' was later published in Titan Books Script Range in 1992, and as a Big Finish audio drama in the 'Lost Stories' range in 2012.

'The Nazis': an idea submitted by **Brian Hayles** who was commissioned to write a storyline in March 1966. Plans were put on hold when the writer was assigned to handle *The Smugglers*. The idea was subsequently cancelled in June, with the consensus being that the events of the plot were too close to the present-day.

'The New Armada': a story idea which would have possibly featured the Spanish Armada would have been possibly written by script editor **David Whitaker**. Not much is known about the proposed idea but it seem certain that **Gerald Blake** would have directed it. *The Reign of Terror* eventually took the serial's place.

'The Ocean Liner': a storyline submitted to the production office in 1966. Formerly rejected by script editor **Gerry Davis** on Monday 4 April 1966, the serial was proposed by **David Ellis**.

'The Outlaws': not much is known about the serial, possibly a historical narrative in the American West. As to who would have written and directed the serial had it come to be remains unknown.

'The People Who Couldn't Remember': a joint writing idea by **David Ellis** and **Malcolm Hulke**, although very few details are known about the plot. The idea was possibly a comedy, the scripts were rejected by **Gerry Davis** during June 1966, who wished to avoid airing comedy adventures in the wake of the critically panned *The Gunfighters*.

'The Red Fort': written by **Terry Nation**, the story would have focused on an Indian Mutiny or the 'British Raj' in India. With the Daleks growing in popularity, Nation was asked to submit and write another Dalek story instead.

'The Slide': an idea proposed by **Victor Pemberton**. Apparently the narrative would have featured sentient beings of mud trying to control the minds of British townsfolk. The idea was rejected by **David Whitaker** since the script editor believed it was too similar to *Quatermass and the Pit*. Victor Pemberton later rewrote his scripts and resubmitted them to the *Doctor Who* production as ***Fury from the Deep*** in 1968 which was commissioned to feature in the series.

'The Son of Doctor Who': a story idea suggested by **William Hartnell**. The story would have seen The Doctor battle against his evil son who resembles him in every detail. Whether or not Hartnell would have penned the serial remains unknown. The idea was never taken forward, although similarities where considered for *The Massacre of St Bartholomew's Eve* – The Doctor/Abbot of Amboise looking like each other.

'The Trap': submitted for season four, the storyline would have featured Robots which were deemed too similar to the Mechonoids. Writer **Robert Holmes** later rewrote his scripts and submitted them for consideration, eventually his scripts were produced as ***The Krotons*** featuring The Second Doctor, Jamie and Zoe.

'The White Witch': a storyline written by **Brian Hayles**. The episodes were commissioned to appear in the series run, but eventually rejected when **Innes Lloyd** and **Gerry Davis** deemed them unusable when they took over as producer and script editor of the series respectively.

'Untitled storyline': a potential serial featuring the Indian Mutiny of 1857. Director **Waris Hussein** had apparently put forth the suggestion of the Indian Mutiny for a potential serial. **Terry Nation** had submitted *The Red Fort* as a possible storyline but was rejected. **John Lucarotti** put forth an Indian Mutiny storyline that wasn't taken forward.

'Untitled storyline': a storyline written by **Alex Miller** during a time when *The Daleks' Master Plan* was in pre-production. Nothing much is known about the storyline, and went unused when *The Daleks' Master Plan* was extended to 12 episodes.

'Untitled storyline': a storyline written by **Alex Miller** during a time when *The Daleks' Master Plan* was in pre-production. Nothing much is known about the storyline, and went unused when *The Daleks' Master Plan* was extended to 12 episodes.

'Untitled storyline': a storyline written by **John Lucarotti**. In May of 1965, the writer met with new script editor **Donald Tosh** to submit a storyline featuring Vikings despite the fact that *The Time Meddler* was already commissioned. The story would have featured Erik(c) the Red discovering Newfoundland. The storyline was to feature Ian, Barbara, and Vicki before being scrapped.

'Untitled Storyline': an idea submitted by **Eric Laithwaite**. The production office received the idea in June 1966 but it was formerly rejected to appear in the run on 8 May 1967, sometime after **William Hartnell** had departed from the show.

'Untitled Storyline': writer **Margot Bennett** had apparently been in contact to write for the show possibly commissioned to write a historical narrative. No exact details are known as the writer instead concentrated writing for other shows at the time. Had her scripts been commissioned they would have replaced the miniscule narrative, which was in doubt at the time, the spot on the run was eventually taken up by *Planet of Giants*.

'Untitled storyline': written by **Robert Gould**, would have featured The Doctor and his companions being reduced down in size, another attempt by the production office to produce a miniscule narrative. Gould asked to submit another idea which would also eventually be dropped.

'Untitled storyline': an idea written by **Robert Gould**, instead of submitting a miniscule narrative was ultimately rejected because the storyline was felt to be too similar to *The Day of the Triffids*.

'Untitled storyline': written by **Terry Nation**, not much is known about the storyline, the writer was working on the possible serial, until other commitments put an idea to the idea. Not much is known about it.

BIBLIOGRAPHY

Atkinson, Richard, and Tucker, Mike, *Dalek Mark III Travel Machine: Combat Training Manual* (London: BBC Books, 2021).
Atkinson, Richard, and Tucker, Mike, *TARDIS Type 40 Instruction Manual* (London: BBC Books, 2018).
Campbell, Craig, *The Doctors Who's Who: The Story Behind Every Face of the Iconic Time Lord* (London: John Blake Publishing, 2010).
Campbell, Mark, *Doctor Who: The Episode Guide* (Herts: Pocket Essentials, 2010).
Cartmel, Andrew, *Through Time: An Unauthorised and Unofficial History of DOCTOR WHO* (London: International Publishing Group, 2005).
Clapham, Mark, Robson, Eddie, and Smith, Jim, *Who's Next: An Unofficial and Unauthorised Guide to Doctor Who* (London: Virgin Books, 2005).
Coburn, Anthony, *Doctor Who – The Scripts: The Tribe of Gum*, ed. by John McElroy (London: Titan Books, 1988).
Cornell, Paul, Day, Martin, and Topping, Keith, *The Discontinuity Guide*, 1st ed (London: Doctor Who Books, 1995).
Dicks, Terrance, and Hulke, Malcolm, *The Making of Doctor Who* (London: Target Books, 1976).
Doctor Who: The Complete History – Volume 1 (London: Hachette Partworks, 2015).
Doctor Who: The Complete History – Volume 2 (London: Hachette Partworks, 2016).
Doctor Who: The Complete History – Volume 3 (London: Hachette Partworks, 2016).
Doctor Who: The Complete History – Volume 4 (London: Hachette Partworks, 2017).
Doctor Who: The Complete History – Volume 5 (London: Hachette Partworks, 2016).
Doctor Who: The Complete History – Volume 6 (London: Hachette Partworks, 2017).
Doctor Who: The Complete History – Volume 7 (London: Hachette Partworks, 2018).
Doctor Who: The Complete History – Volume 8 (London: Hachette Partworks, 2016).
Doctor Who: The Complete History – Volume 9 (London: Hachette Partworks, 2016).
Doctor Who: The Complete History ¬Volume 10 (London: Hachette Partworks, 2017).
Doctor Who: The Complete History – Volume 11 (London: Hachette Partworks, 2016).
Doctor Who: The Complete History – Volume 17 (London: Hachette Partworks, 2016).
Emms, William, *Doctor Who – The Scripts: Galaxy 4*, ed. by John McElroy (London: Titan Books, 1994).
Goss, James, and Tribe, Steve, *A History of the Universe in 100 Objects* (London: BBC Books, 2012).
Guerrier, Simon, O'Brien, Steve, and Morris, Ben, *Whographica: An Infographic Guide to Space and Time* (London: BBC Books, 2016).
Hearn, Marcus, Doctor Who: *The Vault: Treasures from the First 50 Years* (London: BBC Books, 2013).
J. Howe, David, and Walker, Stephen James, *The Television Companion* (London: BBC Books, 1998).
J. Howe, David, Stammers, Mark, and Walker, Stephen James, *Doctor Who The Handbook: The First Doctor* (London: Doctor Who Books, 1994).
Parkin, Lance, *A History of the Universe* (London: Virgin Publishing, 1996).
Morris, Jonathan and CS Andrews, Penny, *Doctor Who: The Monsters Vault* (London: BBC Books, 2020).
Richards, Justin, *Doctor Who: Aliens and Enemies* (London: BBC Books, 2006).
Richards, Justin, *Doctor Who: Creatures and Demons* (London: BBC Books, 2007).
Richards, Justin, *Doctor Who: Monsters and Villains* (London: BBC Books, 2005).
Richards, Justin, *Doctor Who: The Secret Lives of Monsters* (London: BBC Books, 2014).
Richards, Justin, *The Legend Continues* (London: BBC Books, 2005).
Richards, Justin, and Martin, Andrew, *The Book of Lists* (London: BBC Books
Rigelsford, Adrian, *The Doctors – 30 Years of Time Travel* (London: Boxtree Limited, 1994).
Scoones, Paul, *The Comic Strip Companion* ((Denbighshire, Telos Publishing, 2012).
Scott, Cavan, and Wright, Mark, *Who-ology: The Official Miscellany* (London: BBC Books, 2013).
Tribe, Steve, and Goss, James, *The Dalek Handbook* (London: BBC Books, 2011).
Tribe, Steve, *The Tardis Handbook* (London: BBC Books, 2010).
Whitaker, David, *Doctor Who – The Scripts: The Crusade*, ed. by John McElroy (London: Titan Books, 1994).

Printed in Great Britain
by Amazon